First Workshop on Fact Extraction and VERification 2018

Brussels, Belgium
1 November 2018

ISBN: 978-1-5108-7422-0

EMNLP 2018

FEVER

Fact Extraction and VERification

Proceedings of the First Workshop

November 1, 2018
Brussels, Belgium

We thank our sponsor Amazon Research in Cambridge for their generous support.

research cambridge

Order copies of this and other ACL proceedings from:

Association for Computational Linguistics (ACL)
209 N. Eighth Street
Stroudsburg, PA 18360
USA
Tel: +1-570-476-8006
Fax: +1-570-476-0860
acl@aclweb.org

Introduction

With billions of individual pages on the web providing information on almost every conceivable topic, we should have the ability to collect facts that answer almost every conceivable question. However, only a small fraction of this information is contained in structured sources (Wikidata, Freebase, etc.) – we are therefore limited by our ability to transform free-form text to structured knowledge. There is, however, another problem that has become the focus of a lot of recent research and media coverage: false information coming from unreliable sources.

In an effort to jointly address both problems, herein we proposed this workshop to promote research in joint Fact Extraction and VERification (FEVER). We aim for FEVER to be a long-term venue for work in verifiable knowledge extraction.

To stimulate progress in this direction, we also hosted the FEVER Challenge, an information verification shared task on a purposely-constructed dataset. We received entries from 23 competing teams, 19 of which scored higher than the previously published baseline. We invited descriptions of the participating systems and we received 15 system descriptions, all of which are included in these proceedings. We offered the top 4 systems oral presentations.

For the main workshop, we received 23 submissions, out of which we accepted 14 (3 oral presentations and 11 posters).

Organizers:

James Thorne (University of Sheffield)
Andreas Vlachos (University of Sheffield)
Oana Cocarascu (Imperial College London)
Christos Christodoulopoulos (Amazon)
Arpit Mittal (Amazon)

Program Committee:

Nikolaos Aletras (University of Sheffield), Fernando Alva-Manchego (University of Sheffield), Isabelle Augenstein (University of Copenhagen), Esma Balkir (University of Edinburgh), Daniele Bonadiman (University of Trento), Matko Bošnjak (University College London), Kris Cao (University of Cambridge), Tuhin Chakrabarty (Columbia University), Weiwei Cheng (Amazon), Bich-Ngoc Do (Heidelberg University), Micha Elsner (The Ohio State University), Diego Esteves (Universität Bonn), Fréderic Godin (ELIS - IDLab, Ghent University), Ivan Habernal (UKP Lab, Technische Universität Darmstadt), Andreas Hanselowski (UKP lab, Technische Universität Darmstadt), Christopher Hidey (Columbia University), Julia Hockenmaier (University of Illinois Urbana-Champaign), Alexandre Klementiev (Amazon Development Center Germany), Jan Kowollik (University of Duisburg-Essen), Anjishnu Kumar (Amazon), Nayeon Lee (Hong Kong University of Science and Technology), Pranava Swaroop Madhyastha (University of Sheffield), Christopher Malon (NEC Laboratories America), Marie-Catherine de Marneffe (The Ohio State University), Stephen Mayhew (University of Pennsylvania), Marie-Francine Moens (KU Leuven), Jason Naradowsky (University College London), Yixin Nie (UNC), Farhad Nooralahzadeh (University of Oslo), Wolfgang Otto (GESIS – Leibniz-Institute for the Social Sciences in Cologne), Ankur Padia (University of Maryland, Baltimore County), Mithun Paul (University Of Arizona), Tamara Polajnar (University of Cambridge), Hoifung Poon (Microsoft Research), Preethi Raghavan (IBM Research TJ Watson), Marek Rei (University of Cambridge), Laura Rimell (DeepMind), Tim Rocktaschel (University College London and Facebook AI Research), Jodi Schneider (UIUC), Claudia Schulz (UKP Lab, Technische Universität Darmstadt), Diarmuid Ó Séaghdha (Apple), Sameer Singh (University of California, Irvine), Kevin Small (Amazon), Christian Stab (UKP Lab, Technische Universität Darmstadt), Motoki Taniguchi (Fuji Xerox), Paolo Torroni (Alma Mater - Università di Bologna), Serena Villata (Université Côte d'Azur, CNRS, Inria, I3S), Zeerak Waseem (University of Sheffield), Noah Weber (Stony Brook University), Johannes Welbl (University College London), Menglin Xia (University of Cambridge), Takuma Yoneda (Toyota Technological Institute)

Invited Speakers:

Luna Dong (Amazon)
Marie-Francine Moens (KU Leuven)
Delip Rao (Joostware AI Research, Johns Hopkins University)
Tim Rocktäschel (Facebook AI Research, University College London)

Table of Contents

Conference Program

Thursday, November 1, 2018

09:00–09:15   *Welcome Talk*
Organizers

09:15–10:00   *Invited Talk: Learning with Explanations*
Tim Rocktäschel

10:00–10:30   Research Talks 1

10:00–10:15   *The Data Challenge in Misinformation Detection: Source Reputation vs. Content Veracity*
Fatemeh Torabi Asr and Maite Taboada

10:15–10:30   *Towards Automated Factchecking: Developing an Annotation Schema and Benchmark for Consistent Automated Claim Detection*
Lev Konstantinovskiy, Oliver Price, Mevan Babakar and Arkaitz Zubiaga

10:30–11:30   Research Posters

Crowdsourcing Semantic Label Propagation in Relation Classification
Anca Dumitrache, Lora Aroyo and Chris Welty

Retrieve and Re-rank: A Simple and Effective IR Approach to Simple Question Answering over Knowledge Graphs
Vishal Gupta, Manoj Chinnakotla and Manish Shrivastava

Information Nutrition Labels: A Plugin for Online News Evaluation
Vincentius Kevin, Birte Högden, Claudia Schwenger, Ali Sahan, Neelu Madan, Piush Aggarwal, Anusha Bangaru, Farid Muradov and Ahmet Aker

Joint Modeling for Query Expansion and Information Extraction with Reinforcement Learning
Motoki Taniguchi, Yasuhide Miura and Tomoko Ohkuma

Towards Automatic Fake News Detection: Cross-Level Stance Detection in News Articles
Costanza Conforti, Mohammad Taher Pilehvar and Nigel Collier

Belittling the Source: Trustworthiness Indicators to Obfuscate Fake News on the Web
Diego Esteves, Aniketh Janardhan Reddy, Piyush Chawla and Jens Lehmann

14:45–15:30   Shared Task Flash Talks

14:45–14:50   *The Fact Extraction and VERification (FEVER) Shared Task*
Organizers

14:50–15:00   *Combining Fact Extraction and Claim Verification in an NLI Model*
Yixin Nie, Haonan Chen and Mohit Bansal

15:00–15:10   *UCL Machine Reading Group: Four Factor Framework For Fact Finding (HexaF)*
Takuma Yoneda, Jeff Mitchell, Johannes Welbl, Pontus Stenetorp and Sebastian Riedel

15:10–15:20   *Multi-Sentence Textual Entailment for Claim Verification*
Andreas Hanselowski, Hao Zhang, Zile Li, Daniil Sorokin, Benjamin Schiller, Claudia Schulz and Iryna Gurevych

15:20–15:30   *Team Papelo: Transformer Networks at FEVER*
Christopher Malon

15:30–16:30   Shared Task Posters

Uni-DUE Student Team: Tackling fact checking through decomposable attention neural network
Jan Kowollik and Ahmet Aker

SIRIUS-LTG: An Entity Linking Approach to Fact Extraction and Verification
Farhad Nooralahzadeh and Lilja Øvrelid

Integrating Entity Linking and Evidence Ranking for Fact Extraction and Verification
Motoki Taniguchi, Tomoki Taniguchi, Takumi Takahashi, Yasuhide Miura and Tomoko Ohkuma

Robust Document Retrieval and Individual Evidence Modeling for Fact Extraction and Verification.
Tuhin Chakrabarty, Tariq Alhindi and Smaranda Muresan

DeFactoNLP: Fact Verification using Entity Recognition, TFIDF Vector Comparison and Decomposable Attention
Aniketh Janardhan Reddy, Gil Rocha and Diego Esteves

The Fact Extraction and VERification (FEVER) Shared Task

James Thorne[1], Andreas Vlachos[1], Oana Cocarascu[2],
Christos Christodoulopoulos[3], and Arpit Mittal[3]

[1]Department of Computer Science, University of Sheffield
[2]Department of Computing, Imperial College London
[3]Amazon Research Cambridge
{j.thorne, a.vlachos}@sheffield.ac.uk
oana.cocarascu11@imperial.ac.uk
{chrchrs, mitarpit}@amazon.co.uk

Abstract

We present the results of the first Fact Extraction and VERification (FEVER) Shared Task. The task challenged participants to classify whether human-written factoid claims could be SUPPORTED or REFUTED using evidence retrieved from Wikipedia. We received entries from 23 competing teams, 19 of which scored higher than the previously published baseline. The best performing system achieved a FEVER score of 64.21%. In this paper, we present the results of the shared task and a summary of the systems, highlighting commonalities and innovations among participating systems.

1 Introduction

Information extraction is a well studied domain and the outputs of such systems enable many natural language technologies such as question answering and text summarization. However, since information sources can contain errors, there exists an additional need to verify whether the information is correct. For this purpose, we hosted the first Fact Extraction and VERification (FEVER) shared task to raise interest in and awareness of the task of automatic information verification - a research domain that is orthogonal to information extraction. This shared task required participants to develop systems to predict the veracity of human-generated textual claims against textual evidence to be retrieved from Wikipedia.

We constructed a purpose-built dataset for this task (Thorne et al., 2018) that contains 185,445 human-generated claims, manually verified against the introductory sections of Wikipedia pages and labeled as SUPPORTED, REFUTED or NOTENOUGHINFO. The claims were generated by paraphrasing facts from Wikipedia and mutating them in a variety of ways, some of which were meaning-altering. For each claim, and without the knowledge of where the claim was generated from, annotators selected evidence in the form of sentences from Wikipedia to justify the labeling of the claim.

The systems participating in the FEVER shared task were required to label claims with the correct class and also return the sentence(s) forming the necessary evidence for the assigned label. Performing well at this task requires both identifying relevant evidence and reasoning correctly with respect to the claim. A key difference between this task and other textual entailment and natural language inference tasks (Dagan et al., 2009; Bowman et al., 2015) is the need to identify the evidence from a large textual corpus. Furthermore, in comparison to large-scale question answering tasks (Chen et al., 2017), systems must reason about information that is not present in the claim. We hope that research in these fields will be stimulated by the challenges present in FEVER.

One of the limitations of using human annotators to identify correct evidence when constructing the dataset was the trade-off between annotation velocity and evidence recall (Thorne et al., 2018). Evidence selected by annotators was often incomplete. As part of the FEVER shared task, any evidence retrieved by participating systems that was not contained in the original dataset was annotated and used to augment the evidence in the test set.

In this paper, we present a short description of the task and dataset, present a summary of the submissions and the leader board, and highlight future research directions.

2 Task Description

Candidate systems for the FEVER shared task were given a sentence of unknown veracity called a claim. The systems must identify suitable evidence from Wikipedia at the sentence level and

Proceedings of the First Workshop on Fact Extraction and VERification (FEVER), pages 1–9
Brussels, Belgium, November 1, 2018. ©2018 Association for Computational Linguistics

> **Claim:** The Rodney King riots took place in the most populous county in the USA.
>
> **[wiki/Los_Angeles_Riots]**
> The 1992 Los Angeles riots, also known as the Rodney King riots were a series of riots, lootings, arsons, and civil disturbances that occurred in Los Angeles County, California in April and May 1992.
>
> **[wiki/Los_Angeles_County]**
> Los Angeles County, officially the County of Los Angeles, is the most populous county in the USA.
>
> **Verdict:** Supported

Figure 1: Example claim from the FEVER shared task: a manually verified claim that requires evidence from multiple Wikipedia pages.

assign a label whether, given the evidence, the claim is SUPPORTED, REFUTED or whether there is NOTENOUGHINFO in Wikipedia to reach a conclusion. In 16.82% of cases, claims required the combination of more than one sentence as supporting or refuting evidence. An example is provided in Figure 1.

2.1 Data

Training and development data was released through the FEVER website.[1] We used the reserved portion of the data presented in Thorne et al. (2018) as a blind test set. Disjoint training, development and test splits of the dataset were generated by splitting the dataset by the page used to generate the claim. The development and test datasets were balanced by randomly discarding claims from the more populous classes.

Split	SUPPORTED	REFUTED	NEI
Training	80,035	29,775	35,639
Dev	6,666	6,666	6,666
Test	6,666	6,666	6,666

Table 1: Dataset split sizes for SUPPORTED, REFUTED and NOTENOUGHINFO (NEI) classes

[1] http://fever.ai

2.2 Scoring Metric

We used the scoring metric described in Thorne et al. (2018) to evaluate the submissions. The FEVER shared task requires submission of evidence to justify the labeling of a claim. The training, development and test data splits contain multiple sets of evidence for each claim, each set being a minimal set of sentences that fully support or refute it. The primary scoring metric for the task is the label accuracy conditioned on providing at least one complete set of evidence, referred to as the FEVER score. Sentences labeled (correctly) as NOTENOUGHINFO do not require evidence. Correctly labeled claims with no or only partial evidence received no points for the FEVER score. Where multiple sets of evidence was annotated in the data, only one set was required for the claim to be considered correct for the FEVER score.

Since the development and evaluation data splits are balanced, random baseline label accuracy ignoring the requirement for evidence is 33.33%. This performance level can also be achieved for the FEVER score by predicting NOTENOUGHINFO for every claim. However, as the FEVER score requires evidence for SUPPORTED and REFUTED claims, a random baseline is expected to score lower on this metric.

We provide an open-source release of the scoring software.[2] Beyond the FEVER score, it computes precision, recall, F_1, and label accuracy to provide diagnostic information. The recall point is awarded, as is the case for the FEVER score, only by providing a complete set of evidence for the claim.

2.3 Submissions

The FEVER shared task was hosted as a competition on Codalab[3] which allowed submissions to be scored against the blind test set without the need to publish the correct labels. The scoring system was open from 24th to 27th July 2018. Participants were limited to 10 submissions (max. 2 per day).[4]

[2] The scorer, test cases and examples can be found in the following GitHub repository https://github.com/sheffieldnlp/fever-scorer

[3] https://competitions.codalab.org/competitions/18814

[4] An extra half-day was given as an artifact of the competition closing at midnight pacific time.

| Rank | Team Name | Evidence (%) | | | Label | FEVER |
		Precision	Recall	F1	Accuracy (%)	Score (%)
1	UNC-NLP	42.27	70.91	52.96	**68.21**	**64.21**
2	UCL Machine Reading Group	22.16	82.84	34.97	67.62	62.52
3	Athene UKP TU Darmstadt	23.61	**85.19**	36.97	65.46	61.58
4	Papelo	**92.18**	50.02	**64.85**	61.08	57.36
5	SWEEPer	18.48	75.39	29.69	59.72	49.94
6	Columbia NLP	23.02	75.89	35.33	57.45	49.06
7	Ohio State University	77.23	47.12	58.53	50.12	43.42
8	GESIS Cologne	12.09	51.69	19.60	54.15	40.77
9	FujiXerox	11.37	29.99	16.49	47.13	38.81
10	*withdrawn*	46.60	51.94	49.12	51.25	38.59
11	Uni-DuE Student Team	50.65	36.02	42.10	50.02	38.50
12	Directed Acyclic Graph	51.91	36.36	42.77	51.36	38.33
13	*withdrawn*	12.90	54.58	20.87	53.97	37.13
14	Py.ro	21.15	49.38	29.62	43.48	36.58
15	SIRIUS-LTG-UIO	19.19	70.82	30.19	48.87	36.55
16	*withdrawn*	0.00	0.01	0.00	33.45	30.20
17	BUPT-NLPer	45.18	35.45	39.73	45.37	29.22
18	*withdrawn*	23.75	86.07	37.22	33.33	28.67
19	*withdrawn*	7.69	32.11	12.41	50.80	28.40
20	FEVER Baseline	11.28	47.87	18.26	48.84	27.45
21	*withdrawn*	49.01	29.66	36.95	44.89	23.76
22	*withdrawn*	26.81	12.08	16.65	57.32	22.89
23	*withdrawn*	26.33	12.20	16.68	55.42	21.71
24	University of Arizona	11.28	47.87	18.26	36.94	19.00

Table 2: Results on the test dataset.

3 Participants and Results

86 submissions (excluding the baseline) were made to Codalab for scoring on the blind test set. There were 23 different teams which participated in the task (presented in Table 2). 19 of these teams scored higher than the baseline presented in Thorne et al. (2018). All participating teams were invited to submit a description of their systems. We received 15 descriptions at the time of writing and the remaining are considered as *withdrawn*. The system with the highest score was submitted by UNC-NLP (FEVER score: 64.21%).

Most participants followed a similar pipeline structure to the baseline model. This consisted of three stages: document selection, sentence selection and natural language inference. However, some teams constructed models to jointly select sentences and perform inference in a single pipeline step, while others added an additional step, discarding inconsistent evidence after performing inference.

Based on the team-submitted system description summaries (Appendix A), in the following section we present an overview of which models and techniques were applied to the task and their relative performance.

4 Analysis

4.1 Document Selection

A large number of teams report a multi-step approach to document selection. The majority of submissions report extracting some combination of Named Entities, Noun Phrases and Capitalized Expressions from the claim. These were used either as inputs to a search API (i.e. Wikipedia Search or Google Search), search server (e.g. Lucene[5] or Solr[6]) or as keywords for matching against Wikipedia page titles or article bodies. BUPT-NLPer report using S-MART for entity linking (Yang and Chang, 2015) and the highest scor-

[5] http://lucene.apache.org/
[6] http://lucene.apache.org/solr/

ing team, UNC-NLP, report using page viewership statistics to rank the candidate pages. This approach cleverly exploits a bias in the dataset construction, as the most visited pages were sampled for claim generation. GESIS Cologne report directly selecting sentences using the Solr search, bypassing the need to perform document retrieval as a separate step.

The team which scored highest on evidence precision and evidence F1 was Papelo (precision = 92.18% and F_1 = 64.85%) who report using a combination of TF-IDF for document retrieval and string matching using named entities and capitalized expressions.

The teams which scored highest on evidence recall were Athene UKP TU Darmstadt (recall = 85.19%) and UCL Machine Reading Group (recall = 82.84%) [7] [8] Athene report extracting noun-phrases from the claim and using these to query the Wikipedia search API. A similar approach was used by Columbia NLP who query the Wikipedia search API using named entities extracted from the claim as a query string, all the text before the first lowercase verb phrase as a query string and also combine this result with Wikipedia pages identified with Google search using the entire claim. UCL Machine Reading Group report a document retrieval approach that identifies Wikipedia article titles within the claim and ranks the results using features such as capitalization, sentence position and token match.

4.2 Sentence Selection

There were three common approaches to sentence selection: keyword matching, supervised classification and sentence similarity scoring. Ohio State and UCL Machine Reading Group report using keyword matching techniques: matching either named entities or tokens appearing in both the claim and article body. UNC-NLP, Athene UKP TU Darmstadt and Columbia NLP modeled the task as supervised binary classification, using architectures such as Enhanced LSTM (Chen et al., 2016), Decomposable Attention (Parikh et al., 2016) or similar to them. SWEEPer and BUPT-NLPer present jointly learned models for sentence

selection and natural language inference. Other teams report scoring based on sentence similarity using Word Mover's Distance (Kusner et al., 2015) or cosine similarity over smooth inverse frequency weightings (Arora et al., 2017), ELMo embeddings (Peters et al., 2018) and TF-IDF (Salton et al., 1983). UCL Machine Reading Group and Directed Acyclic Graph report an additional aggregation stage after the classification stage in the pipeline where evidence that is inconsistent is discarded.

4.3 Natural Language Inference

NLI was modeled as supervised classification in all reported submissions. We compare and discuss the approaches for combining the evidence sentences together with the claim, sentence representations and training schemes. While many different approaches were used for sentence pair classification, e.g. Enhanced LSTM (Chen et al., 2016), Decomposable Attention (Parikh et al., 2016), Transformer Model (Radford and Salimans, 2018), Random Forests (Svetnik et al., 2003) and ensembles thereof, these are not specific to the task and it is difficult to assess their impact due to the differences in the processing preceding this stage.

Evidence Combination: UNC-NLP (the highest scoring team) concatenate the evidence sentences into a single string for classification; UCL Machine Reading Group classify each evidence-claim pair individually and aggregate the results using a simple multilayer perceptron (MLP); Columbia NLP perform majority voting; and finally, Athene-UKP TU Darmstadt encode each evidence-claim pair individually using an Enhanced LSTM, pool the resulting vectors and use an MLP for classification.

Sentence Representation: University of Arizona explore using non-lexical features for predicting entailment, considering the proportion of negated verbs, presence of antonyms and noun overlap. Columbia NLP learn universal sentence representations (Conneau et al., 2017). UNC-NLP include an additional token-level feature the sentence similarity score from the sentence selection module. Both Ohio State and UNC-NLP report alternative token encodings: UNC-NLP report using ELMo (Peters et al., 2018) and WordNet (Miller, 1995) and Ohio State report using vector represen-

---

[7] The withdrawn team that ranked 18th on F_1 score had the highest recall: 86.07%. A system description was not submitted by this team preventing us from including it in our analysis.

[8] The scores for precision, recall and F_1 were computed independent of the label accuracy and FEVER Score.

tations of named entities. FujiXerox report representing sentences using DEISTE (Yin et al., 2018).

Training: BUPT-NLPer and SWEEPer model the evidence selection and claim verification using a multi-task learning model under the hypothesis that information from each task supplements the other. SWEEPer also report parameter tuning using reinforcement learning.

5   Additional Annotation

As mentioned in the introduction, to increase the evidence coverage in the test set, the evidence submitted by participating systems was annotated by shared task volunteers after the competition ended. There were 18,846 claims where at least one system returned an incorrect label, according to the FEVER score, i.e. taking evidence into account. These claims were sampled for annotation with a probability proportional to the number of systems which labeled each of them incorrectly.

The evidence sentences returned by each system for each claim was sampled further with a probability proportional to the system's FEVER score in an attempt to focus annotation efforts towards higher quality candidate evidence. These extra annotations were performed by volunteers from the teams participating in the shared task and three of the organizers. Annotators were asked to label whether the retrieved evidence sentences supported or refuted the claim at question, and to highlight which sentences (if any), either individually or as a group, can be used as evidence. We retained the annotation guidelines from Thorne et al. (2018) (see Sections A.7.1, A.7.3 and A.8 from that paper for more details).

At the time of writing, 1,003 annotations were collected for 618 claims. This identified 3 claims that were incorrectly labeled as SUPPORTED or REFUTED and 87 claims that were originally labeled as NOTENOUGHINFO that should be relabeled as SUPPORTED or REFUTED through the introduction of new evidence (44 and 43 claims respectively). 308 new evidence sets were identified for claims originally labeled as SUPPORTED or REFUTED, consisting of 280 single sentences and 28 sets of 2 or more sentences.

Further annotation is in progress and the data collected as well as the final results will be made public at the workshop.

6   Conclusions

The first Fact Extraction and VERification shared task attracted submissions from 86 submissions from 23 teams. 19 of these teams exceeded the score of the baseline presented in Thorne et al. (2018). For the teams which provided a system description, we highlighted the approaches, identifying commonalities and features that could be further explored.

Future work will address limitations in human-annotated evidence and explore other subtasks needed to predict the veracity of information extracted from untrusted sources.

Acknowledgements

The work reported was partly conducted while James Thorne was at Amazon Research Cambridge. Andreas Vlachos is supported by the EU H2020 SUMMA project (grant agreement number 688139).

References

Sanjeev Arora, Yingyu Liang, and Tengyu Ma. 2017. A simple but tough to beat baseline for sentence embeddings. In *Iclr*, pages 1–14.

Sean Baird, Doug Sibley, and Yuxi Pan. 2017. Cisco's Talos Intelligence Group Blog_ Talos Targets Disinformation with Fake News Challenge Victory.

Samuel R. Bowman, Gabor Angeli, Christopher Potts, and Christopher D. Manning. 2015. A large annotated corpus for learning natural language inference. In *Proceedings of the 2015 Conference on Empirical Methods in Natural Language Processing*.

Danqi Chen, Adam Fisch, Jason Weston, and Antoine Bordes. 2017. Reading Wikipedia to Answer Open-Domain Questions. *Proc. of ACL'17*.

Qian Chen, Xiaodan Zhu, Zhenhua Ling, Si Wei, Hui Jiang, and Diana Inkpen. 2016. Enhanced LSTM for Natural Language Inference. In *Proceedings of the 55th Annual Meeting of the Association for Computational Linguistics*, pages 1657–1668, Vancouver, Canada.

Alexis Conneau, Douwe Kiela, Holger Schwenk, Loic Barrault, and Antoine Bordes. 2017. Supervised Learning of Universal Sentence Representations from Natural Language Inference Data. In *Proceedings of the 2017 Conference on Empirical Methods in Natural Language Processing*, pages 670–680, Copenhagen, Denmark.

Ido Dagan, Bill Dolan, Bernardo Magnini, and Dan Roth. 2009. Recognizing textual entailment: Rational, evaluation and approaches. *Natural Language Engineering*, 15(4):i–xvii.

Tushar Khot, Ashish Sabharwal, and Peter Clark. 2018. SCITAIL: A Textual Entailment Dataset from Science Question Answering. *Aaai*.

Matt J Kusner, Yu Sun, Nicholas I Kolkin, and Kilian Q Weinberger. 2015. From Word Embeddings To Document Distances. *Proceedings of The 32nd International Conference on Machine Learning*, 37:957–966.

George a. Miller. 1995. WordNet: a lexical database for English. *Communications of the ACM*, 38(11):39–41.

Ankur P. Parikh, Oscar Täckström, Dipanjan Das, and Jakob Uszkoreit. 2016. A Decomposable Attention Model for Natural Language Inference. pages 2249–2255.

Matthew E Peters, Mark Neumann, Mohit Iyyer, Matt Gardner, Christopher Clark, Kenton Lee, and Luke Zettlemoyer. 2018. Deep contextualized word representations. In *Proceedings of NAACL-HLT*, pages 2227–2237, New Orleans, Louisiana.

Alec Radford and Tim Salimans. 2018. Improving Language Understanding by Generative Pre-Training. *arXiv*, pages 1–12.

Gerard Salton, Edward A. Fox, and Harry Wu. 1983. Extended boolean information retrieval. *Commun. ACM*, 26(11):1022–1036.

Vladimir Svetnik, Andy Liaw, Christopher Tong, J Christopher Culberson, Robert P Sheridan, and Bradley P Feuston. 2003. Random forest: a classification and regression tool for compound classification and qsar modeling. *Journal of chemical information and computer sciences*, 43(6):1947–1958.

James Thorne, Andreas Vlachos, Christos Christodoulopoulos, and Arpit Mittal. 2018. FEVER: a large-scale dataset for fact extraction and verification. In *NAACL-HLT*.

Yi Yang and Ming-Wei Chang. 2015. S-MART: Novel Tree-based Structured Learning Algorithms Applied to Tweet Entity Linking. In *Proceedings of the 53rd Annual Meeting of the Association for Computational Linguistics and the 7th International Joint Conference on Natural Language Processing*, pages 504–513, Beijing, China.

Wenpeng Yin, Hinrich Schütze, and Dan Roth. 2018. End-Task Oriented Textual Entailment via Deep Explorations of Inter-Sentence Interactions. In *Proceedings of the 56th Annual Meeting of the Association for Computational Linguistics (Short Papers)*, pages 540–545, Melbourne, Australia.

A Short System Descriptions Submitted by Participants

A.1 UNC-NLP

Our system is composed of three connected components namely, a document retriever, a sentence selector, and a claim verifier. The document retriever chooses candidate wiki-documents via matching of keywords between the claims and the wiki-document titles, also using external page-view frequency statistics for wiki-page ranking. The sentence selector is a sequence-matching neural network that conducts further fine-grained selection of evidential sentences by comparing the given claim with all the sentences in the candidate documents. This module is trained as a binary classifier given the ground truth evidence as positive examples and all the other sentences as negative examples with an annealing sampling strategy. Finally, the claim verifier is a state-of-the-art 3-way neural natural language inference (NLI) classifier (with WordNet and ELMo features) that takes the concatenation of all selected evidence as the premise and the claim as the hypothesis, and labels each such evidences-claim pair as one of 'support', 'refute', or 'not enough info'. To improve the claim verifier via better awareness of the selected evidence, we further combine the last two modules by feeding the sentence similarity score (produced by the sentence selector) as an additional token-level feature to the claim verifier.

A.2 UCL Machine Reading Group

The UCLMR system is a four stage model consisting of document retrieval, sentence retrieval, natural language inference and aggregation. Document retrieval attempts to find the name of a Wikipedia article in the claim, and then ranks each article based on capitalization, sentence position and token match features. A set of sentences are then retrieved from the top ranked articles, based on token matches with the claim and position in the article. A natural language inference model is then applied to each of these sentences paired with the claim, giving a prediction for each potential evidence. These predictions are then aggregated using a simple MLP, and the sentences are reranked to keep only the evidence consistent with the final prediction.

A.3 Athene UKP TU Darmstadt

Document retrieval We applied the constituency parser from AllenNLP to extract noun phrases in the claim and made use of Wikipedia API to search corresponding pages for each noun phrase. So as to remove noisy pages from the results, we have stemmed the words of their titles and the claim, and then discarded pages whose stemmed words of the title are not completely included in the set of stemmed words in the claim.

Sentence selection The hinge loss with negative sampling is applied to train the enhanced LSTM. For a given positive claim-evidence pair, negative samples are generated by randomly sampling sentences from the retrieved documents.

RTE We combine the 5 sentences from sentence selection and the claim to form 5 pairs and then apply enhanced LSTM for each pair. We combine the resulting representations using average and max pooling and feed the resulting vector through an MLP for classification.

A.4 Papelo

We develop a system for the FEVER fact extraction and verification challenge that uses a high precision entailment classifier based on transformer networks pretrained with language modeling (Radford and Salimans, 2018), to classify a broad set of potential evidence. The precision of the entailment classifier allows us to enhance recall by considering every statement from several articles to decide upon each claim. We include not only the articles best matching the claim text by TFIDF score, but read additional articles whose titles match named entities and capitalized expressions occurring in the claim text. The entailment module evaluates potential evidence one statement at a time, together with the title of the page the evidence came from (providing a hint about possible pronoun antecedents). In preliminary evaluation, the system achieved 57.36% FEVER score, 61.08% label accuracy, and 64.85% evidence F1 on the FEVER shared task test set.

A.5 SWEEPer

Our model for fact checking and verification consists of two stages: 1) identifying relevant documents using lexical and syntactic features from the claim and first two sentences in the Wikipedia article and 2) jointly modeling sentence extraction and verification. As the tasks of fact checking and finding evidence are dependent on each other, an ideal model would consider the veracity of the claim when finding evidence and also find only the evidence that supports/refutes the position of the claim. We thus jointly model the second stage by using a pointer network with the claim and evidence sentence represented using the ESIM module. For stage 2, we first train both components

using multi-task learning over a larger memory of extracted sentences, then tune parameters using reinforcement learning to first extract sentences and predict the relation over only the extracted sentences.

A.6 Columbia NLP

For document retrieval we use three components: 1) use google custom search API with the claim as a query and return the top 2 Wikipedia pages; 2) extract all name entities from the claims and use Wikipedia python API to return a page for each name entity and 3); use the prefix of the claim until the first lowercase verb phrase, and use Wikipedia API to return the top page.

For Sentence Selection we used the modified document retrieval component of DrQA to get the top 5 sentences and then further extracted the top 3 sentences using cosine similarity between vectors obtained from Elmo (Peters et al., 2018) sentence embeddings of the claim and the evidence.

For RTE we used the same model as outlined by (Conneau et al., 2017) in their work for recognizing textual entailment and learning universal sentence representations. If at least one out of the three evidences SUPPORTS/REFUTES the claim and the rest are NOT ENOUGH INFO , then we treat the label as SUPPORTS/REFUTES, else we return the majority among three classes as the predicted label.

A.7 Ohio State University

Our system was developed using a heuristics based approach for evidence extraction and a modified version of the inference model by Parikh et al. (2016) for classification into refute, support, or not enough info. Our process is broken down into three distinct phases. First, potentially relevant documents are gathered based on key words/phrases in the claim that appear in the wiki dump. Second, any possible evidence sentences inside those documents are extracted by breaking down the claim into named entities plus nouns and finding any sentences which match those entities, while allowing for various exceptions and additional potential criteria to increase recall. Finally, every sentences is classified into one of the three categories by the inference tool, after additional vectors are added based on named entity types. NEI sentences are discarded and the highest scored label of the remaining sentences is assigned to the claim.

A.8 GESIS Cologne

In our approach we used a sentence wise approach in all components. To find the sentences we set up a Solr database and indexed every sentence including information about the article where the sentence is from. We created queries based on the named entities and noun chunks of the claims. For the entailment task we used a Decomposable Attention Model similar to the one used in the baseline approach. But instead of comparing the claim with all top 5 sentences at once we treat every sentence separately. The results for the top 5 sentence where then joined with an ensemble learner incl. the rank of the sentence retriever of the wikipedia sentences.

A.9 FujiXerox

We prepared a pipeline system which composes of document selection, a sentence retrieval, and a recognizing textual entailment (RTE) components. A simple entity linking approach with text match is used as the document selection component, this component identifies relevant documents for a given claim by using mentioned entities as clues. The sentence retrieval component selects relevant sentences as candidate evidence from the documents based on TF-IDF. Finally, the RTE component selects evidence sentences by ranking the sentences and classifies the claim as SUPPORTED, REFUTED, or NOTENOUGH-INFO simultaneously. As the RTE component, we adopted DEISTE (Deep Explorations of Inter-Sentence interactions for Textual Entailment) (Yin et al., 2018) model that is the state-of-the-art in RTE task.

A.10 Uni-DuE Student Team

We generate a Lucene index from the provided Wikipedia dump. Then we use two neural networks, one for named entity recognition and the other for constituency parsing, and also the Stanford dependency parser to create the keywords used inside the Lucene queries. Depending on the amount of keywords found for each claim, we run multiple Lucene searches on the generated index to create a list of candidate sentences for each claim. The resulting list of claim-candidate pairs is processed in three ways:

1. We use the Standford POS-Tagger to generate POS-Tags for the claim and candidate sentences which are then used in a hand-crafted scoring script to assign a score on a 0 to 15 scale.

2. We run each pair through a modified version of the Decomposable Attention network.

3. We merge all candidate sentences per claim into one long piece of text and run the result paired with the claim through the same modified Decomposable Attention network as in (2.).

We then make the final prediction in a hand-crafted script combining the results of the three previous steps.

A.11 Directed Acyclic Graph

In this paper, we describe the system we designed for the FEVER 2018 Shared Task. The aim of this task was to conceive a system that can not only automatically assess the veracity of a claim but also retrieve evidence supporting this assessment from Wikipedia. In our approach, the Wikipedia documents whose Term Frequency - Inverse Document Frequency (TFIDF) vectors are most similar to the vector of the claim and those documents whose names are similar to the named entities (NEs) mentioned in the claim are identified as the documents which might contain evidence. The sentences in these documents are then supplied to a decomposable attention-based textual entailment recognition module. This module calculates the probability of each sentence supporting the claim, contradicting the claim or not providing any relevant information. Various features computed using these probabilities are finally used by a Random Forest classifier to determine the overall truthfulness of the claim. The sentences which support this classification are returned as evidence. Our approach achieved a 42.77% evidence F1-score, a 51.36% label accuracy and a 38.33% FEVER score.

A.12 Py.ro

We NER tagged the claim using SpaCy and used the Named Entities as candidate page IDs. We resolved redirects by following the Wikipedia URL if an item was not in the preprocessed dump. If a page could not be found, we fell back to the baseline document selection method. The rest of the system was identical to the baseline system, although we used our document retrieval system to generate alternative training data.

A.13 SIRIUS-LTG-UIO

This article presents the SIRIUS-LTG system for the Fact Extraction and VERification (FEVER) Shared Task. Our system consists of three components:

1. Wikipedia Page Retrieval: First we extract the entities in the claim, then we find potential Wikipedia URI candidates for each of the entities using the SPARQL query over DBpedia

2. Sentence selection: We investigate various techniques i.e. SIF embedding, Word Mover's Distance (WMD), Soft-Cosine Similarity, Cosine similarity with unigram TF-IDF to rank sentences by their similarity to the claim.

3. Textual Entailment: We compare three models for the claim classification. We apply a Decomposable Attention (DA) model (Parikh et al., 2016), a Decomposed Graph Entailment (DGE) model (Khot et al., 2018) and a Gradient-Boosted Decision Trees (TalosTree) model (Baird et al., 2017) for this task.

The experiments show that the pipeline with simple Cosine Similarity using TFIDF in sentence selection along with DA as labeling model achieves better results in development and test dataset.

A.14 BUPT-NLPer

We introduce an end-to-end multi-task learning model for fact extraction and verification with bi-direction attention. We propose a multi-task learning framework for the evidence extraction and claim verification because these two tasks can be accomplished at the same time. Each task provides supplementary information for the other and improves the results of another task.

For each claim, our system firstly uses the entity linking tool S-MART to retrieve relative pages from Wikipedia. Then, we use attention mechanisms in both directions, claim-to-page and page-to-claim, which provide complementary information to each other. Aimed at the different task, our system obtains claim-aware sentence representation for evidence extraction and page-aware claim representation for claim verification.

A.15 University of Arizona

Many approaches to automatically recognizing entailment relations have employed classifiers over hand engineered lexicalized features, or deep learning models that implicitly capture lexicalization through word embeddings. This reliance on lexicalization may complicate the adaptation of these tools between domains. For example, such a system trained in the news domain may learn that a sentence like "Palestinians recognize Texas as part of Mexico" tends to be unsupported, a fact which has no value in say a scientific domain. To mitigate this dependence on lexicalized information, in this paper we propose a model that reads two sentences, from any given domain, to determine entailment without using any lexicalized features. Instead our model relies on features like proportion of negated verbs, antonyms, noun overlap etc. In its current implementation, this model does not perform well on the FEVER dataset, due to two reasons. First, for the information retrieval part of the task we used the baseline system provided, since this was not the aim of our project. Second, this is work in progress and we still are in the process of identifying more features and gradually increasing the accuracy of our model. In the end, we hope to build a generic end-to-end classifier, which can be used in a domain outside the one in which it was trained, with no or minimal re-training.

The Data Challenge in Misinformation Detection:
Source Reputation vs. Content Veracity

Fatemeh Torabi Asr
Discourse Processing Lab
Simon Fraser University
Burnaby, BC, Canada
ftorabia@sfu.ca

Maite Taboada
Discourse Processing Lab
Simon Fraser University
Burnaby, BC, Canada
mtaboada@sfu.ca

Abstract

Misinformation detection at the level of full news articles is a text classification problem. Reliably labeled data in this domain is rare. Previous work relied on news articles collected from so-called "reputable" and "suspicious" websites and labeled accordingly. We leverage fact-checking websites to collect individually-labeled news articles with regard to the veracity of their content and use this data to test the cross-domain generalization of a classifier trained on bigger text collections but labeled according to source reputation. Our results suggest that reputation-based classification is not sufficient for predicting the veracity level of the majority of news articles, and that the system performance on different test datasets depends on topic distribution. Therefore collecting well-balanced and carefully-assessed training data is a priority for developing robust misinformation detection systems.

1 Introduction

Automatic detection of fake from legitimate news in different formats such as headlines, tweets and full news articles has been approached in recent Natural Language Processing literature (Vlachos and Riedel, 2014; Vosoughi, 2015; Jin et al., 2016; Rashkin et al., 2017; Volkova et al., 2017; Wang, 2017; Pomerleau and Rao, 2017; Thorne et al., 2018). The most important challenge in automatic misinformation detection using modern NLP techniques, especially at the level of full news articles, is data. Most previous systems built to identify fake news articles rely on training data labeled with respect to the general reputation of the sources, i.e., domains/user accounts (Fogg et al., 2001; Lazer et al., 2017; Rashkin et al., 2017). Even though some of these studies try to identify fake news based on linguistic cues, the question is whether they learn **publishers' general writing style** (e.g., common writing features of a few

clickbaity websites) or **deceptive style** (similarities among news articles that contain misinformation).

In this study, we collect two new datasets that include the full text of news articles and individually assigned veracity labels. We then address the above question, by conducting a set of cross-domain experiments: training a text classification system on data collected in a batch manner from suspicious and reputable websites and then testing the system on news articles that have been assessed in a one-by-one fashion. Our experiments reveal that the generalization power of a model trained on reputation-based labeled data is not impressive on individually assessed articles. Therefore, we propose to collect and verify larger collections of news articles with reliably assigned labels that would be useful for building more robust fake news detection systems.

2 Data Collection

Most studies on fake news detection have examined microblogs, headlines and claims in the form of short statements. A few recent studies have examined full articles (i.e., actual 'fake news') to extract discriminative linguistic features of misinformation (Yang et al., 2017; Rashkin et al., 2017; Horne and Adali, 2017). The issue with these studies is the data collection methodology. Texts are harvested from websites that are assumed to be fake news publishers (according to a list of suspicious websites), with no individual labeling of data. The so-called suspicious sources, however, sometimes do publish facts and valid information, and reputable websites sometimes publish inaccurate information (Mantzarlis, 2017). The key to collect more reliable data, then, is to not rely on the source but on the text of the article itself, and only after the text has been assessed by human

Proceedings of the First Workshop on Fact Extraction and VERification (FEVER), pages 10–15
Brussels, Belgium, November 1, 2018. ©2018 Association for Computational Linguistics

annotators and determined to contain false information. Currently, there exists only small collections of reliably-labeled news articles (Rubin et al., 2016; Allcott and Gentzkow, 2017; Zhang et al., 2018; Baly et al., 2018) because this type of annotation is laborious. The Liar dataset (Wang, 2017) is the first large dataset collected through reliable annotation, but it contains only short statements. Another recently published large dataset is FEVER (Thorne et al., 2018), which contains both claims and texts from Wikipedia pages that support or refute those claims. This dataset, however, has been built to serve the slightly different purpose of stance detection (Pomerleau and Rao, 2017; Mohtarami et al., 2018), the claims have been artificially generated, and texts are not news articles.

Our objective is to elaborate on the distinction between classifying **reputation-based** labeled news articles and **individually-assessed** news articles. We do so by collecting and using datasets of the second type in evaluation of a text classifier trained on the first type of data. In this section, we first introduce one large collection of news text from previous studies that has been labeled according to the list of suspicious websites, and one small collection that was labeled manually for each and every news article, but only contains satirical and legitimate instances. We then introduce two datasets that we have scraped from the web by leveraging links to news articles mentioned by fact-checking websites (Buzzfeed and Snopes). The distinguishing feature of these new collections is that they contain not only the full text of real news articles found online, but also individually assigned veracity labels indicative of their misinformative content.

Rashkin et al. dataset: Rashkin et al. (2017) published a collection of roughly 20k news articles from eight sources categorized into four classes: *propaganda* (The Natural News and Activist Report), *satire* (The Onion, The Borowitz Report, and Clickhole), *hoax* (American News and DC Gazette) and *trusted* (Gigaword News). This dataset is balanced across classes, and since the articles in their training and test splits come from different websites, the accuracy of the trained model on test data should be demonstrative of its understanding of the general writing style of each target class rather than author-specific cues. However, we suspect that the noisy strategy to label all articles of a publisher based on its reputation highly biases the classifier decisions and limits its power to distinguish individual misinformative from truthful news articles.

Rubin et al. dataset: As part of a study on satirical cues, Rubin et al. (2016) published a dataset of 360 news articles. This dataset contains balanced numbers of individually evaluated *satirical* and *legitimate* texts. Even though small, it is a clean data to test the generalization power of a system trained on noisy data such as the above explained dataset. We use this data to make our point about the need for careful annotation of news articles on a one-by-one fashion, rather than harvesting from websites generally knows as hoax, propaganda or satire publishers.

BuzzfeedUSE dataset: The first source of information that we used to harvest full news articles with veracity labels is from the Buzzfeed fact-checking company. Buzzfeed has published a collection of links to Facebook posts, originally compiled for a study around the 2016 US election (Silverman et al., 2016). Each URL in this dataset was given to human experts so they can rate the amount of false information contained in the linked article. The links were collected from nine Facebook pages (three right-wing, three left-wing and three mainstream publishers).[1] We had to follow the facebook URLs and then the link to the original news articles to obtain the news texts. We scraped the full text of each news article from its original source. The resulting dataset includes a total of 1,380 news articles on a focused topic (US election and candidates). Veracity labels come in a 4-way classification scheme including 1,090 *mostly true*, 170 *mixture of true and false*, 64 *mostly false* and 56 articles *containing no factual content*.

Snopes312 dataset: The second source of information that we used to harvest full news articles with veracity labels is Snopes, a well-known rumor debunking website run by a team of expert editors. We scraped the entire archive of fact-checking pages. On each page they talk about a claim, cite the sources (news articles, forums or social networks where the claim was distributed) and provide a veracity label for the claim. We automatically extracted all links mentioned on a Snopes page, followed the link to each original

---

[1] https://www.kaggle.com/mrisdal/fact-checking-facebook-politics-pages

Table 1: Results of the manual assessment of Snopes312 collection for items of each veracity label

Assessment / Veracity label	false	mixture	mostly false	mostly true	true	All
ambiguous	2	0	1	0	0	3
context	19	31	17	32	26	125
debunking	0	1	0	0	0	1
irrelevant	9	10	7	2	10	38
supporting	21	30	28	37	29	145
All	51	72	53	71	65	312

Table 2: Contingency table on disagreements between the first and second annotator in Snopes312 dataset

First annotator / Second annotator	ambiguous	context	debunking	irrelevant	supporting	All
ambiguous	0	0	0	0	0	0
context	1	0	1	8	71	81
debunking	0	0	0	0	1	1
irrelevant	0	36	0	0	16	52
supporting	0	11	1	0	0	12
All	1	47	2	8	88	146

news article, and extracted the text. The resulting datafile includes roughly 4,000 rows, each containing a claim discussed by Snopes annotators, the veracity label assigned to it, and the text of a news article related to the claim. The main challenge in using this data for training/testing a fake news detector is that some of the links on a Snopes page that we collect automatically do not actually point to the discussed news article, i.e., the source of the claim. Many links are to pages that provide contextual information for the fact-checking of the claim. Therefore, not all the texts in our automatically extracted dataset are reliable or simply the "supporting" source of the claim. To come up with a reliable set of veracity-labeled news articles, we randomly selected 312 items and assessed them manually. Two annotators performed independent assessments on the 312 items. A third annotator went through the entire list of items for a final check and resolving disagreements. Snopes has a fine-grained veracity labeling system. We selected *[fully] true, mostly true, mixture of true and false, mostly false,* and *[fully] false* stories. Table 1 shows the distribution of these labels in the manually assessed 312 items, and how many from each category of news articles were verified to be the "supporting" source (distributing the discussed claim), "context" (providing background or related information about the topic of the claim), "debunking" (against the claim), "irrelevant" (completely unrelated to the claim or distorted text) and ambiguous (not sure how it related

to the claim). Table 2 provides information on the confusing choices: About 50% of the items received different category labels from the two first annotators. The first annotator had a more conservative bias, trying to avoid mistakes in the "supporting" category, whereas the second annotator often assigned either "supporting" or "context", and rarely "irrelevant". For the disagreed items, the third annotator (who had access to all outputs) chose the final category. Results in Table 1 are based on this final assessment. We use the "supporting" portion of the data (145 items) in the following experiments.

3 Experiments

In text classification, Convolutional Neural Networks (CNNs) have been competing with the TF-IDF model, a simple but strong baseline using scored n-grams (Le and Mikolov, 2014; Zhang et al., 2015; Conneau et al., 2017; Medvedeva et al., 2017). These methods have been used for fake news detection in previous work (Rashkin et al., 2017; Wang, 2017). For our experiments, we trained and tuned different architectures of CNN and several classic classifiers (Naive Bayes and Support Vector Machines) with TF-IDF features on Rashkin et al.'s dataset. The best results on the development data were obtained from a Support Vector Machine (SVM) classifier using unigram TF-IDF features with L2 regularization.[2] There-

---

[2]We used the same train/dev/test split as in Rashkin's paper. However, the performance of our SVM classi-

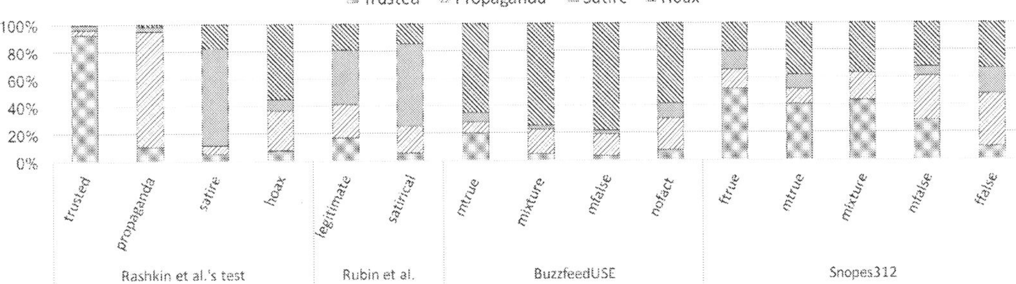

Figure 1: Classification of news articles from four test datasets by a model trained on Rashkin et al.'s training data. Labels assigned by the classifier are Capitalized (plot legend), actual labels of test items are in lowercase (x-axis).

fore, we use this model to demonstrate how a classifier trained on data labeled according to publisher's reputation would identify misinformative news articles.

It is evident in the first section of Figure 1, that the model performs well on similarly collected test items, i.e., *Hoax*, *Satire*, *Propaganda* and *Trusted* news articles within Rashkin et al.'s test dataset. However, when the model is applied to Rubin et al.'s data, which was carefully assessed for satirical cues in each and every article, the performance drops considerably (See the second section of the figure). Although the classifier detects more of the *satirical* texts in Rubin et al.'s data, the distribution of the given labels is not very different to that of *legitimate* texts. One important feature of Rubin et al.'s data is that topics of the legitimate instances were matched and balanced with topics of the satirical instances. The results here suggest that similarities captured by the classifier can be very dependent on the topics of the news articles.

Next we examine the same model on our collected datasets, BuzzfeedUSE and Snopes312, as test material. The BuzzfeedUSE data comes with 4 categories (Figure 1). The classifier does seem to have some sensitivity to true vs. false information in this dataset, as more of the *mostly true* articles were labeled as *Trusted*. The difference with *mostly false* articles, however, is negligible. The most frequent label assigned by the classifier was *Hoax* in all four categories, which suggests that most BuzzfeedUSE articles looked like *Hoax* in Rashkin's data. Finally, the last section of 1 shows the results on the Snopes312 plotted

along the 6-category distinction. A stronger correlation can be observed between the classifier decisions and the veracity labels in this data compared to BuzzfeedUSE. This suggests that distinguishing between news articles with true and false information is a more difficult task when topics are the same (BuzzfeedUSE data is all related to the US election). In Snopes312, news articles come from a variety of topics. The strong alignment between the classifier's *Propaganda* and *Hoax* labels with the *mostly false* and *[fully] false* categories in this dataset reveals that most misinformative news articles indeed discuss the topics or use the language of generally suspicious publishers. This is an encouraging result in the sense that, with surface features such as n-grams and approximate reputation-based training data, we already can detect some of the misinformative news articles. Observing classification errors across these experiments, however, indicates that the model performance varies a lot with the type of test material: In a focused topic situation, it fails to distinguish between categories (false vs. true, or satirical vs. legitimate articles). While a correlation is consistently observed between labels assigned by the classifier and the actual labels of target news articles,[3] reputation-based classification does not seem to be sufficient for predicting the veracity level of the majority of news articles.

4   Conclusion

We found that collecting reliable data for automatic misinformation detection at the level of full news articles is a challenging but necessary task for building robust models. If we want to benefit

---

fier was significantly better on both dev and test sets: 0.96 and 0.75 F1-score, respectively, compared to 0.91 and 0.65 reported in their paper. Source code will be made available at `https://github.com/sfu-discourse-lab/Misinformation_detection`

---

[3]A chi-square test indicates a significant correlation ($p < 0.001$) between assigned and actual labels in all four datasets.

from state-of-the-art text classification techniques, such as CNNs, we require larger datasets than what is currently available. We took the first steps, by scraping claims and veracity labels from fact-checking websites, extracting and cleaning of the original news articles' texts (resulting in roughly 4,000 items), and finally manual assessment of a subset of the data to provide reliable test material for misinformation detection. Our future plan is to crowd-source annotators for the remaining scraped texts and publish a large set of labeled news articles for training purposes.

Acknowledgement

This project was funded by a Discovery Grant from the Natural Sciences and Engineering Research Council of Canada. We gratefully acknowledge the support of NVIDIA Corporation with the donation of the Titan Xp GPU used for this research. We would like to thank members of the Discourse Processing Lab at SFU, especially Yajie Zhou and Jerry Sun for their help checking the datasets.

References

Hunt Allcott and Matthew Gentzkow. 2017. Social media and fake news in the 2016 election. *Journal of Economic Perspectives*, 31:211–236.

Ramy Baly, Mitra Mohtarami, James Glass, Lluís Màrquez, Alessandro Moschitti, and Preslav Nakov. 2018. Integrating stance detection and fact checking in a unified corpus. In *Proceedings of the 2018 Conference of the North American Chapter of the Association for Computational Linguistics: Human Language Technologies, Volume 2 (Short Papers)*, volume 2, pages 21–27.

Alexis Conneau, Holger Schwenk, Loc Barrault, and Yann LeCun. 2017. Very deep convolutional networks for text classification. In *Proceedings of the 15th Conference of the European Chapter of the Association for Computational Linguistics*, pages 1107–1116, Valencia.

B. J. Fogg, Jonathan Marshall, Othman Laraki, Alex Osipovich, Chris Varma, Nicholas Fang, Jyoti Paul, Akshay Rangnekar, John Shon, Preeti Swani, and Marissa Treinen. 2001. What makes web sites credible? A report on a large quantitative study. In *Proceedings of the SIGCHI Conference on Human Factors in Computing Systems*, CHI '01, pages 61–68, New York.

Benjamin D Horne and Sibel Adali. 2017. This just in: Fake news packs a lot in title, uses simpler, repetitive content in text body, more similar to satire than real news. *arXiv preprint arXiv:1703.09398*.

Zhiwei Jin, Juan Cao, Yongdong Zhang, and Jiebo Luo. 2016. News verification by exploiting conflicting social viewpoints in microblogs. In *Proceedings of the Thirtieth AAAI Conference on Artificial Intelligence*, pages 2972–2978, Phoenix.

David Lazer, Matthew Baum, Nir Grinberg, Lisa Friedland, Kenneth Joseph, Will Hobbs, and Carolina Mattsson. 2017. Combating fake news: An agenda for research and action. *Harvard Kennedy School, Shorenstein Center on Media, Politics and Public Policy*, 2.

Quoc Le and Tomas Mikolov. 2014. Distributed representations of sentences and documents. In *Proceedings of the 31st International Conference on Machine Learning*, pages II–1188–II–1196, Beijing.

Alexios Mantzarlis. 2017. Not fake news, just plain wrong: Top media corrections of 2017. *Poynter News*. Https://www.poynter.org/news/not-fake-news-just-plain-wrong-top-media-corrections-2017.

Maria Medvedeva, Martin Kroon, and Barbara Plank. 2017. When sparse traditional models outperform dense neural networks: The curious case of discriminating between similar languages. In *Proceedings of the 4th Workshop on NLP for Similar Languages, Varieties and Dialects (VarDial)*, pages 156–163, Valencia.

Mitra Mohtarami, Ramy Baly, James Glass, Preslav Nakov, Llus Mrquez, and Alessandro Moschitti. 2018. Automatic stance detection using end-to-end memory networks. In *Proceedings of the 2018 Conference of the North American Chapter of the Association for Computational Linguistics: Human Language Technologies, Volume 1 (Long Papers)*, pages 767–776, New Orleans, LA.

Dean Pomerleau and Delip Rao. 2017. Fake news challenge. Http://fakenewschallenge.org/.

Hannah Rashkin, Eunsol Choi, Jin Yea Jang, Svitlana Volkova, and Yejin Choi. 2017. Truth of varying shades: Analyzing language in fake news and political fact-checking. In *Proceedings of the 2017 Conference on Empirical Methods in Natural Language Processing*, pages 2921–2927, Copenhagen.

Victoria L Rubin, Niall J Conroy, Yimin Chen, and Sarah Cornwell. 2016. Fake news or truth? Using satirical cues to detect potentially misleading news. In *Proceedings of NAACL-HLT*, pages 7–17, San Diego.

Craig Silverman, Lauren Strapagiel, Hamza Shaban, Ellie Hall, and Jeremy Singer-Vine. 2016. Hyperpartisan Facebook pages are publishing false and misleading information at an alarming rate. *BuzzFeed News*. Https://www.buzzfeed.com/craigsilverman/partisan-fb-pages-analysis.

James Thorne, Andreas Vlachos, Christos Christodoulopoulos, and Arpit Mittal. 2018. FEVER: A large-scale dataset for Fact Extraction and VERification. In *Proceedings of the 2018 Conference of the North American Chapter of the Association for Computational Linguistics: Human Language Technologies, Volume 1 (Long Papers)*, pages 809–819, New Orleans, LA.

Andreas Vlachos and Sebastian Riedel. 2014. Fact checking: Task definition and dataset construction. In *Proceedings of the ACL 2014 Workshop on Language Technologies and Computational Social Science*, pages 18–22.

Svitlana Volkova, Kyle Shaffer, Jin Yea Jang, and Nathan Hodas. 2017. Separating facts from fiction: Linguistic models to classify suspicious and trusted news posts on Twitter. In *Proceedings of the 55th Annual Meeting of the Association for Computational Linguistics*, volume 2, pages 647–653, Vancouver.

Soroush Vosoughi. 2015. *Automatic detection and verification of rumors on Twitter*. Ph.D. thesis, Massachusetts Institute of Technology.

William Yang Wang. 2017. 'Liar, liar pants on fire': A new benchmark dataset for fake news detection. In *Proceedings of the 55th Annual Meeting of the Association for Computational Linguistics*, volume 2, pages 422–426, Vancouver.

Fan Yang, Arjun Mukherjee, and Eduard Dragut. 2017. Satirical news detection and analysis using attention mechanism and linguistic features. In *Proceedings of the 2017 Conference on Empirical Methods in Natural Language Processing*, pages 1979–1989.

Amy X Zhang, Aditya Ranganathan, Sarah Emlen Metz, Scott Appling, Connie Moon Sehat, Norman Gilmore, Nick B Adams, Emmanuel Vincent, Jennifer Lee, Martin Robbins, et al. 2018. A structured response to misinformation: Defining and annotating credibility indicators in news articles. In *Companion of the The Web Conference 2018 on The Web Conference 2018*, pages 603–612. International World Wide Web Conferences Steering Committee.

Xiang Zhang, Junbo Zhao, and Yann LeCun. 2015. Character-level convolutional networks for text classification. In *Proceedings of the 28th International Conference on Neural Information Processing Systems*, pages 649–657, Montréal.

Crowdsourcing Semantic Label Propagation in Relation Classification

Anca Dumitrache
Vrije Universiteit Amsterdam
IBM CAS Benelux
anca.dmtrch@gmail.com

Lora Aroyo
Vrije Universiteit Amsterdam
l.m.aroyo@gmail.com

Chris Welty
Google Research, New York
cawelty@gmail.com

Abstract

Distant supervision is a popular method for performing relation extraction from text that is known to produce noisy labels. Most progress in relation extraction and classification has been made with crowdsourced corrections to distant-supervised labels, and there is evidence that indicates still more would be better. In this paper, we explore the problem of propagating human annotation signals gathered for open-domain relation classification through the CrowdTruth methodology for crowdsourcing, that captures ambiguity in annotations by measuring inter-annotator disagreement. Our approach propagates annotations to sentences that are similar in a low dimensional embedding space, expanding the number of labels by two orders of magnitude. Our experiments show significant improvement in a sentence-level multi-class relation classifier.

1 Introduction

Distant supervision (DS) (Mintz et al., 2009) is a popular method for performing relation extraction from text. It is based on the assumption that, when a knowledge-base contains a relation between a pair of terms, then any sentence that contains that pair is likely to express the relation. This approach can generate false positives, as not every mention of a term pair in a sentence means a relation is also expressed (Feng et al., 2017).

Recent results (Angeli et al., 2014; Liu et al., 2016) have shown strong evidence that the community needs more annotated data to improve the quality of DS data. This work explores the possibility of automatically expanding smaller human-annotated datasets to DS scale. Sterckx et al. (2016) proposed a method to correct labels of sentence dependency paths by using expert annotators, and then propagating the corrected labels to a corpus of DS sentences by calculating the similar-

ity between the labeled and unlabeled sentences in the embedding space of their dependency paths.

In this paper, we adapt and simplify semantic label propagation to propagate labels without computing dependency paths, and using the crowd instead of experts, which is more scalable. Our simplified algorithm propagates crowdsourced annotations from a small sample of sentences to a large DS corpus. To evaluate our approach, we perform an experiment in open domain relation classification in the English-language, using a corpus of sentences (Dumitrache et al., 2017) whose labels have been collected using the CrowdTruth method (Aroyo and Welty, 2014).

2 Related Work

There exist several efforts to correct DS with the help of crowdsourcing. Angeli et al. (2014) present an active learning approach to select the most useful sentences that need human re-labeling using a query by committee. Zhang et al. (2012) show that labeled data has a statistically significant, but relatively low impact on improving the quality of DS training data, while increasing the size of the DS corpus has a more significant impact. In contrast, Liu et al. (2016) prove that a corpus of labeled sentences from a pool of highly qualified workers can significantly improve DS quality. All of these methods employ large annotated corpora of 10,000 to 20,000 sentences. In our experiment, we show that a comparatively smaller corpus of 2,050 sentences is enough to correct DS errors through semantic label propagation.

Levy et al. (2017) have shown that a small crowdsourced dataset of questions about relations can be exploited to perform zero-shot learning for relation extraction. Pershina et al. (2014) use a small dataset of hand-labeled data to generate relation-specific guidelines that are used as addi-

Proceedings of the First Workshop on Fact Extraction and VERification (FEVER), pages 16–21
Brussels, Belgium, November 1, 2018. ©2018 Association for Computational Linguistics

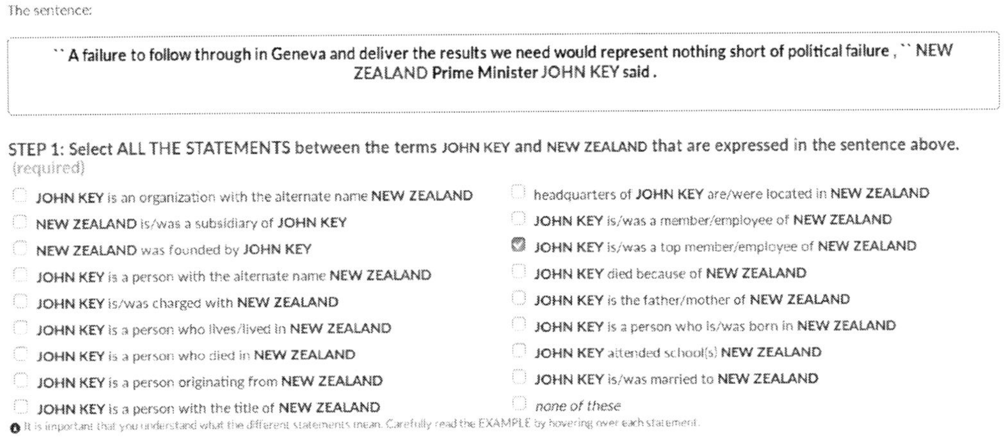

Figure 1: Fragment of the crowdsourcing task template.

tional features in the relation extraction. The label propagation method was introduced by Xiaojin and Zoubin (2002), while Chen et al. (2006) first applied it to correct DS, by calculating similarity between labeled and unlabeled examples an extensive list of features, including part-of-speech tags and target entity types. In contrast, our approach calculates similarity between examples in the word2vec (Mikolov et al., 2013) feature space, which it then uses to correct the labels of training sentences. This makes it easy to reuse by the state-of-the-art in both relation classification and relation extraction – convolutional (Ji et al., 2017) and recurrent neural network methods (Zhou et al., 2016) that do not use extensive feature sets. To evaluate our approach, we used a simple convolutional neural network to perform relation classification in sentences (Nguyen and Grishman, 2015).

3 Experimental Setup

3.1 Annotated Data

The labeled data used in our experiments consists of 4,100 sentences: 2,050 sentences from the CrowdTruth corpus (Dumitrache et al., 2017), which we have augmented by another 2,050 sentences picked at random from the corpus of Angeli et al. (2014). The resulting corpus contains sentences for 16 popular relations from the open domain, as shown in in Figure 1,[1] as well as candidate term pairs and DS seed relations for each sentence. As some relations

are more general than others, the relation frequency in the corpus is slightly unequal – e.g. $places\_of\_residence$ is more likely to be in a sentence when $place\_of\_birth$ and $place\_of\_death$ occur, but not the opposite.

The crowdsourcing task (Figure 1) was designed in our previous work (Dumitrache et al., 2017). We asked workers to read the given sentence where the candidate term pair is highlighted, and then pick between the 16 relations or *none of the above*, if none of the presented relations apply. The task was multiple choice and run on the Figure Eight[2] and Amazon Mechanical Turk[3] crowdsourcing platforms. Each sentence was judged by 15 workers, and each worker was paid $0.05 per sentence.

Crowdsourcing annotations are aggregated usually by measuring the consensus of the workers (e.g. using majority vote). This is based on the assumption that a single right annotation exists for each example. In the problem of relation classification, the notion of a single truth is reflected in the fact that a majority of proposed solutions treat relations as mutually exclusive, and the objective of the classification task is usually to find the best relation for a given sentence and term pair. In contrast, the CrowdTruth methodology proposes that crowd annotations are inherently diverse (Aroyo and Welty, 2015), due to a variety of factors such as the ambiguity that is inherent in natural language. We use a comparatively large number of workers per sentences (15) in order to collect inter-

---

[1]The *alternate_names* relation appears twice in the list, once referring to alternate names of persons, and the other referring to organizations.

[2]https://www.figure-eight.com/
[3]https://www.mturk.com/

annotator disagreement, which results in a more fine-grained ground truth that separates between clear and ambiguous expressions of relations. This is achieved by labeling examples with the inter-annotator agreement on a continuous scale, as opposed to using binary labels.

To aggregate the results of the crowd, we use CrowdTruth metrics[4] (Dumitrache et al., 2018) to capture and interpret inter-annotator disagreement as quality metrics for the workers, sentences, and relations in the corpus. The annotations of one worker over one sentence are encoded as a binary worker vector with 17 components, one for each relation and including *none*. The quality metrics for the workers, sentences and relations, are based on average cosine similarity over the worker vectors – e.g. the quality of a worker w is given by the average cosine similarity between the worker vector of w and the vectors of all other workers that annotated the same sentences. These metrics are mutually dependent (e.g. the sentence quality is weighted by the relation quality and worker quality), the intuition being that low quality workers should not count as much in determining sentence quality, and ambiguous sentences should have less of an impact in determining worker quality, etc.

We reused these scores in our experiment, focusing on the **sentence-relation score** (srs), representing the degree to which a relation is expressed in the sentence. It is the ratio of workers that picked the relation to all the workers that read the sentence, weighted by the worker and relation quality. A higher srs should indicate that the relation is more clearly expressed in a sentence.

3.2 Propagating Annotations

Inspired by the semantic label propagation method (Sterckx et al., 2016), we propagate the vectors of srs scores on each crowd annotated sentence to a much larger set of distant supervised (DS) sentences (see datasets description in Section 3.3), scaling the vectors linearly by the distance in low dimensional word2vec vector space (Mikolov et al., 2013). One of the reasons we chose the CrowdTruth set for this experiment is that the annotation vectors give us a score *for each relation* to propagate to the DS sentences, which have only one binary label.

Similarly to Sultan et al. (2015), we calcu-

late the vector representation of a sentence as the average over its word vectors, and like Sterckx et al. (2016) we get the similarity between sentences using cosine similarity. Additionally, we restrict the sentence representation to only contain the words between the term pair, in order to reduce the vector space to the one that is most likely to express the relations. For each sentence s in the DS dataset, we find the sentence l' from the crowd annotated set that is most similar to s: $l' = \underset{l \in Crowd}{\arg\max}\, cos\_sim(l, s)$. The score for relation r of sentence s is calculated as the weighted average between the $srs(l', r)$ and the original DS annotation, weighted by the cosine similarity to s ($cos\_sim(s, s) = 1$ for the DS term, and $cos\_sim(s, l')$ for the srs term):

$$DS^*(s, r) = \frac{DS(s, r) + cos\_sim(s, l') \cdot srs(l', r)}{1 + cos\_sim(s, l')} \quad (1)$$

where $DS(s, r) \in \{0, 1\}$ is the original DS annotation for the relation r on sentence s.

3.3 Training the Model

The crowdsourced data is split evenly into a dev and a test set of 2,050 sentences each chosen at random. In addition, we used a training set of 235,000 sentences annotated by DS from freebase relations, used in Riedel et al. (2013).

The relation classification model employed is based on Nguyen and Grishman (2015), who implement a convolutional neural network with four main layers: an embedding layer for the words in the sentence and the position of the candidate term pair in the sentence, a convolutional layer with a sliding window of variable length of 2 to 5 words that recognizes n-grams, a pooling layer that determines the most relevant features, and a softmax layer to perform classification.

We have adapted this model to be both multi-class and multi-label – we use a sigmoid cross-entropy loss function instead of softmax cross-entropy, and the final layer is normalized with the sigmoid function instead of softmax – in order to make it possible for more than one relation to hold between two terms in one sentence. The loss function is computed using continuous labels instead of binary positive/negative labels, in order to accommodate the use of the srs in training. The features of the model are the word2vec embeddings of the words in the sentences, together with the position embeddings of the two terms that ex-

---

[4]https://github.com/CrowdTruth/CrowdTruth-core

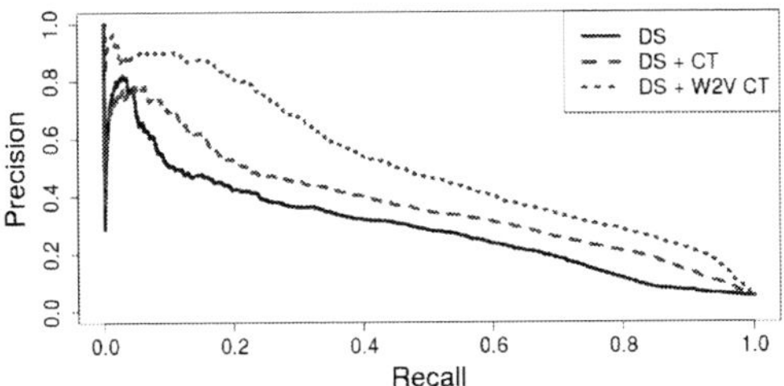

Figure 2: Precision / Recall curve, calculated for each sentence-relation pair.

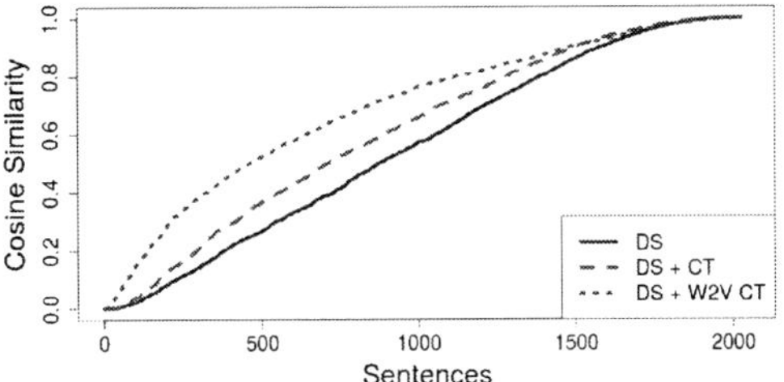

Figure 3: Distribution of sentence-level cosine similarity with test set values.

press the relation. The word embeddings are initialized with 300-dimensional word2vec vectors pre-trained on the Google News corpus[5]. Both the position and word embeddings are nonstatic and become optimized during training of the model. The model is trained for 25,000 iterations, after the point of stabilization for the train loss. The values of the other hyper-parameters are the same as those reported by Nguyen and Grishman (2015). The model was implemented in Tensorflow (Abadi et al., 2016), and trained in a distributed manner on the DAS-5 cluster (Bal et al., 2016).

For our experiment, we split the crowd data into a dev and a test set of equal size, and compared the performance of the model on the held-out test set when trained by the following datasets:

1. **DS:** The 235,000 sentences annotated by DS.

2. **DS + CT:** The 2,050 crowd dev annotated sentences added directly to the DS dataset.

3. **DS + W2V CT:** The DS^+ dataset (Eq. 1), with relation scores propagated over the 2,050 crowd dev sentences.

4   Results and Discussion

To evaluate the performance of the models, we calculate the micro precision and recall (Figure 2), as well as the cosine similarity per sentence with the test set (Figure 3). In order to calculate the precision and recall, a threshold of 0.5 was set in the srs, and each sentence-relation pair was labeled either as positive or negative. However, for calculating the cosine similarity, the srs was used without change, in order to better reflect the degree of

agreement the crowd had over annotating each example. We observe that **DS + W2V CT**, with a precision/recall $AUC = 0.512$, significantly outperforms **DS** (P/R $AUC = 0.294$). **DS + CT** (P/R $AUC = 0.372$) also does slightly better than **DS**, but not enough to compete with the semantic label propagation method. The cosine similarity result (Figure 3) shows that **DS + W2V CT** also produces model predictions that are closer to the different agreement levels of the crowd. Take advantage of the agreement scores in the CrowdTruth corpus, the cosine similarity evaluation allows us to assess relation confidence scores on a continuous scale. The crowdsourcing results and model predictions are available online.[6]

One reason for which the semantic label propagation method works better than simply adding the correctly labeled sentences to the train set is the high rate of incorrectly labeled examples in the DS training data. Figure 4 shows that some relations, such as *origin* and *places_of_residence*, have a ratio of over 0.8 false positive sentences, meaning that a vast majority of training examples are incorrectly labeled. The success of the **DS + W2V CT** comes in part because the method relabels all sentences in DS. Adding correctly labeled sentences to the train set would require a significantly larger corpus in order to correct the high false positive rate, but semantic label propagation only requires a small corpus (two orders of magnitude smaller than the train set) to achieve significant improvements.

5   Conclusion and Future Work

This paper explores the problem of propagating human annotation signals in distant supervision

[5] https://code.google.com/archive/p/word2vec/

[6] https://github.com/CrowdTruth/Open-Domain-Relation-Extraction

19

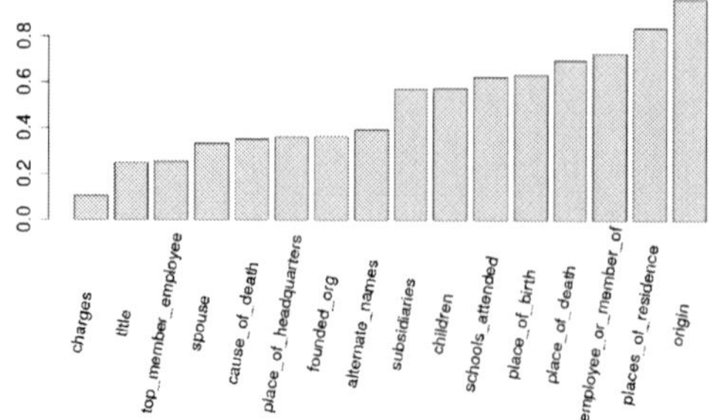

Figure 4: DS false positive ratio in combined crowd dev and test sets.

data for open-domain relation classification. Our approach propagates human annotations to sentences that are similar in a low dimensional embedding space, using a small crowdsourced dataset of 2,050 sentences to correct training data labeled with distant supervision. We present experimental results from training a relation classifier, where our method shows significant improvement over the DS baseline, as well as just adding the labeled examples to the train set.

Unlike Sterckx et al. (2016) who employ experts to label the dependency path representation of sentences, our method uses the general crowd to annotate the actual sentence text, and is thus easier to scale and not dependent on methods for extracting dependency paths, so it can be more easily adapted to other languages and domains. Also, since the semantic label propagation is applied to the data before training is completed, this method can easily be reused to correct train data for any model, regardless of the features used in learning. In our future work, we plan to use this method to correct training data for state-of-the-art models in relation classification, but also relation extraction and knowledge-base population.

We also plan to explore different ways of collecting and aggregating data from the crowd. CrowdTruth (Dumitrache et al., 2017) proposes capturing ambiguity through inter-annotator disagreement, which necessitates multiple annotators per sentence, while Liu et al. (2016) propose increasing the number of labeled examples added to the training set by using one high quality worker per sentence. We will compare the two methods to determine whether quality or quantity of data are more useful for semantic label propagation. To achieve this, we will investigate whether disagreement-based metrics such as sentence and

relation quality can also be propagated through the training data.

References

Martín Abadi, Paul Barham, Jianmin Chen, Zhifeng Chen, Andy Davis, Jeffrey Dean, Matthieu Devin, Sanjay Ghemawat, Geoffrey Irving, Michael Isard, et al. 2016. Tensorflow: A system for large-scale machine learning. In *OSDI*, volume 16, pages 265–283.

Gabor Angeli, Julie Tibshirani, Jean Wu, and Christopher D Manning. 2014. Combining distant and partial supervision for relation extraction. In *Proceedings of the 2014 conference on empirical methods in natural language processing (EMNLP)*, pages 1556–1567.

Lora Aroyo and Chris Welty. 2014. The Three Sides of CrowdTruth. *Journal of Human Computation*, 1:31–34.

Lora Aroyo and Chris Welty. 2015. Truth is a lie: Crowd truth and the seven myths of human annotation. *AI Magazine*, 36(1):15–24.

Henri Bal, Dick Epema, Cees de Laat, Rob van Nieuwpoort, John Romein, Frank Seinstra, Cees Snoek, and Harry Wijshoff. 2016. A medium-scale distributed system for computer science research: Infrastructure for the long term. *Computer*, 49(5):54–63.

Jinxiu Chen, Donghong Ji, Chew Lim Tan, and Zhengyu Niu. 2006. Relation extraction using label propagation based semi-supervised learning. In *Proceedings of the 21st International Conference on Computational Linguistics and the 44th Annual Meeting of the Association for Computational Linguistics*, ACL-44, pages 129–136, Stroudsburg, PA, USA. Association for Computational Linguistics.

Anca Dumitrache, Lora Aroyo, and Chris Welty. 2017. False positive and cross-relation signals in distant supervision data. In *Proceedings of the 6th Workshop on Automated Knowledge Base Construction*.

Anca Dumitrache, Oana Inel, Lora Aroyo, Benjamin Timmermans, and Chris Welty. 2018. CrowdTruth 2.0: Quality Metrics for Crowdsourcing with Disagreement. *arXiv preprint arXiv:1808.06080*.

Xiaocheng Feng, Jiang Guo, Bing Qin, Ting Liu, and Yongjie Liu. 2017. Effective deep memory networks for distant supervised relation extraction. In *Proceedings of the Twenty-Sixth International Joint Conference on Artificial Intelligence, IJCAI 2017, Melbourne, Australia, August 19-25, 2017*, pages 4002–4008. ijcai.org.

Guoliang Ji, Kang Liu, Shizhu He, Jun Zhao, et al. 2017. Distant supervision for relation extraction with sentence-level attention and entity descriptions. In *AAAI*, pages 3060–3066.

Omer Levy, Minjoon Seo, Eunsol Choi, and Luke Zettlemoyer. 2017. Zero-shot relation extraction via reading comprehension. *CoNLL 2017*, page 333.

Angli Liu, Stephen Soderland, Jonathan Bragg, Christopher H Lin, Xiao Ling, and Daniel S Weld. 2016. Effective crowd annotation for relation extraction. In *Proceedings of the 2016 Conference of the North American Chapter of the Association for Computational Linguistics: Human Language Technologies*, pages 897–906.

Tomas Mikolov, Ilya Sutskever, Kai Chen, Greg S Corrado, and Jeff Dean. 2013. Distributed representations of words and phrases and their compositionality. In *Advances in neural information processing systems*, pages 3111–3119.

Mike Mintz, Steven Bills, Rion Snow, and Dan Jurafsky. 2009. Distant supervision for relation extraction without labeled data. In *Proceedings of the Joint Conference of the 47th Annual Meeting of the ACL and the 4th International Joint Conference on Natural Language Processing of the AFNLP: Volume 2-Volume 2*, pages 1003–1011. Association for Computational Linguistics.

Thien Huu Nguyen and Ralph Grishman. 2015. Relation extraction: Perspective from convolutional neural networks. In *Proceedings of the 1st Workshop on Vector Space Modeling for Natural Language Processing*, pages 39–48.

Maria Pershina, Bonan Min, Wei Xu, and Ralph Grishman. 2014. Infusion of labeled data into distant supervision for relation extraction. In *Proceedings of the 52nd Annual Meeting of the Association for Computational Linguistics (Volume 2: Short Papers)*, volume 2, pages 732–738.

Sebastian Riedel, Limin Yao, Andrew McCallum, and Benjamin M Marlin. 2013. Relation extraction with matrix factorization and universal schemas. In *Proceedings of the 2013 Conference of the North American Chapter of the Association for Computational Linguistics: Human Language Technologies*, pages 74–84.

Lucas Sterckx, Thomas Demeester, Johannes Deleu, and Chris Develder. 2016. Knowledge base population using semantic label propagation. *Knowledge-Based Systems*, 108(C):79–91.

Md Arafat Sultan, Steven Bethard, and Tamara Sumner. 2015. DLS @ CU: Sentence Similarity from Word Alignment and Semantic Vector Composition. In *Proceedings of the 9th International Workshop on Semantic Evaluation (SemEval 2015)*, pages 148–153.

Zhu Xiaojin and Ghahramani Zoubin. 2002. Learning from labeled and unlabeled data with label propagation. *Technical Report CMU-CALD-02–107, Carnegie Mellon University*.

Ce Zhang, Feng Niu, Christopher Ré, and Jude Shavlik. 2012. Big data versus the crowd: Looking for relationships in all the right places. In *Proceedings of the 50th Annual Meeting of the Association for Computational Linguistics: Long Papers-Volume 1*, pages 825–834. Association for Computational Linguistics.

Peng Zhou, Wei Shi, Jun Tian, Zhenyu Qi, Bingchen Li, Hongwei Hao, and Bo Xu. 2016. Attention-based bidirectional long short-term memory networks for relation classification. In *Proceedings of the 54th Annual Meeting of the Association for Computational Linguistics (Volume 2: Short Papers)*, volume 2, pages 207–212.

Retrieve and Re-rank: A Simple and Effective IR Approach to Simple Question Answering over Knowledge Graphs

Vishal Gupta
IIIT Hyderabad, India
vishal.gupta@
research.iiit.ac.in

Manoj Chinnakotla
Microsoft, Bellevue, USA
manojc@
microsoft.com

Manish Shrivastava
IIIT Hyderabad, India
m.shrivastava@
iiit.ac.in

Abstract

SimpleQuestions is a commonly used benchmark for single-factoid question answering (QA) over Knowledge Graphs (KG). Existing QA systems rely on various components to solve different sub-tasks of the problem (such as entity detection, entity linking, relation prediction and evidence integration). In this work, we propose a different approach to the problem and present an information retrieval style solution for it. We adopt a two-phase approach: candidate generation and candidate re-ranking to answer questions. We propose a Triplet-Siamese-Hybrid CNN (TSHCNN) to re-rank candidate answers. Our approach achieves an accuracy of 80% which sets a new state-of-the-art on the SimpleQuestions dataset.

1 Introduction and Related Work

Knowledge Bases (KB) like Freebase (Google, 2017) and DBpedia[1] contain a vast wealth of information. A KB has information in the form of tuples, i.e. a combination of subject, predicate and object (s, p, o). SimpleQuestions (Bordes et al., 2015) is a common benchmark used for single factoid QA over KB.

Question answering (QA), both on KB (Lukovnikov et al., 2017; Yin et al., 2016; Fader et al., 2014) and in open domain (Chen et al., 2017; Hermann et al., 2015) is a well studied problem. Learning to rank approaches have also been applied successfully in QA (Agarwal et al., 2012; Bordes et al., 2014).

In this paper, we introduce an information retrieval (IR) style approach to the QA task and propose a Triplet-Siamese-Hybrid Convolutional Neural Network (TSHCNN) that jointly learns to rank candidate answers.

Many earlier works (Ture and Jojic, 2017; Yu et al., 2017; Yin et al., 2016) that tackle Simple-Questions divide the task into multiple sub-tasks (such as entity detection, entity linking, relation prediction and evidence integration), whereas our model tackles all sub-tasks jointly. Lukovnikov (2017) is more similar to our approach wherein they train a neural network in an end-to-end manner. However, we differ in the fact that we generate candidate answers jointly (matching both subject and predicate using a single query) as well as the fact that we combine both the subject and predicate as well as the question before obtaining the similarity score. At no stage in our approach, do we differentiate between the subject and the predicate. Thus our approach can also be applied in other QA scenarios with or without KBs.

Compared to existing approaches (Yin et al., 2016; Yu et al., 2017; Golub and He, 2016), our model does not employ Bi-LSTMs, attention mechanisms or separate segmentation models and achieves state-of-the-art results. We also introduce a custom negative sampling technique that improves results significantly. We conclude with an evaluation of our method and show an ablation study as well as qualitative analysis of our approach.

2 Our System: IRQA

Our system which consists of two components is as follows: (1) the candidate generation method for finding the set of relevant candidate answers and (2) a candidate re-ranking model, for getting the top answer from the list of candidate answers.

2.1 Candidate Generation

Any tuple in Freebase (specifically, the object in a tuple is the answer to the question) can be an answer to our question. Freebase contains millions of tuples and the FB2M subset provided with

---

[1] http://dbpedia.org/

Proceedings of the First Workshop on Fact Extraction and VERification (FEVER), pages 22–27
Brussels, Belgium, November 1, 2018. ©2018 Association for Computational Linguistics

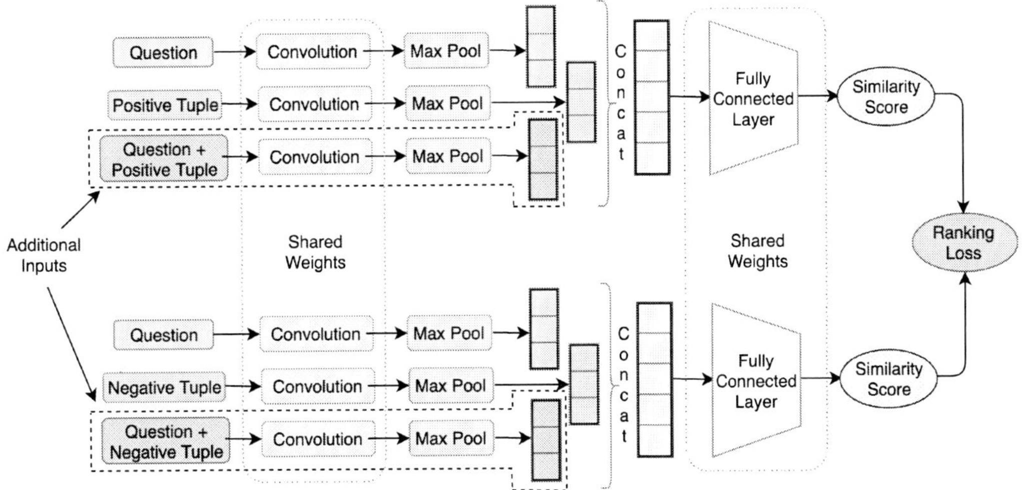

Figure 1: TSHCNN Architecture

SimpleQuestions contains 10.8 million tuples. As such, it is important to reduce the search space to make it feasible to apply semantic-based neural approaches. Thus, we propose a candidate retrieval system to narrow down our search space and focus on re-ranking only the most relevant candidates.

Solr[2] is an inverted index search system. We use Solr to index all our freebase tuples (FB2M) and query for the top-k relevant candidates providing a question as the input query. We adopt BM25 as the scoring metric to rank results. Our results demonstrate the effectiveness of the proposed method.

2.2 Candidate Re-ranking

We use Convolutional Neural Networks (CNN) to learn the semantic representation for input text (Kim, 2014; Hu et al., 2015; Zhang et al., 2015). CNNs learn globally word order invariant features and at the same time pick the order in short phrases. Thus, CNNs are ideal for a QA task since different users may paraphrase the same question in different ways. Siamese networks have shown promising results in distance-based learning methods (Bromley et al., 1993; Chopra et al., 2005; Das et al., 2016) and they possess the capability to learn a similarity metric between questions and answers.

Our candidate re-ranking module is motivated by the success of neural models in various image and text tasks (Vo and Hays, 2016; Das et al.,

2016). Our network as shown in figure 1, is a Triplet-Siamese Hybrid Convolutional neural network (TSHCNN). Vo and Hays (2016) show that classification-siamese hybrid and triplet networks work well on image similarity tasks. TSHCNN can jointly extract and exchange information from the question and tuple inputs. We attribute it to the fact that we concatenate the pooled outputs of the question and tuple before input to the fully connected network.

All convolution layers are siamese and share weights in TSHCNN. The fully connected layers also share weights. This weight sharing guarantees that the question and its relevant answer are nearer to each other in the semantics space and irrelevant answers to it are far away. It also reduces the required number of parameters to be learned.

We provide additional inputs to our network which is the concatenation of both the input question and tuple. This additional input is motivated by the need to learn features for both the question and tuple.

2.2.1 Loss Function

We use the distance based logistic triplet loss (Vo and Hays, 2016), which Vo and Hays (2016) report exhibits better performance in image similarity tasks. Considering $\mathcal{S}_{pos}$ / $\mathcal{S}_{neg}$ as the score obtained by the question+positive tuple / question+negative tuple, respectively and $\mathcal{L}$ as the logistic triplet loss, we have:

$$\mathcal{L} = \log_e(1 + e^{(\mathcal{S}_{neg} - \mathcal{S}_{pos})}) \qquad (1)$$

[2]http://lucene.apache.org/solr/

Table 1: Network Parameters

Parameter	Value
Batch Size	100
Non-linearity	Relu
CNN Filters & Width	90, 10 and 10 filters of width 1, 2 and 3 resp.
Pool Type	Global Max Pooling
Stride Length	1
FC Layer 1	100 units + 0.2 Dropout
FC Layer 2	100 units + 0.2 Dropout
FC Layer 3	1 unit + No Relu
Optimizer	Adam (default params)

Table 2: End-to-End Answer Accuracy for English Questions

Model	Acc.
Memory NN Bordes et al. (2015)	62.7
Attn. LSTM Golub and He (2016)	70.9
GRU Lukovnikov et al. (2017)	71.2
BiLSTM & BiGRU Mohammed et al. (2017)	74.9
CNN & Attn. CNN & BiLSTM-CRF Yin et al. (2016)	76.4
HR-BiLSTM & CNN & BiLSTM-CRF Yu et al. (2017)	77.0
BiLSTM-CRF & BiLSTM Petrochuk and Zettlemoyer (2018)	78.1
Candidate Generation (Ours)	68.4
Solr & TSHCNN (Ours)	80.0

Table 3: Candidate generation results: Recall of top-k answer candidates.

K	1	2	5	10	50	100	200
	68.4	75.7	82.3	85.6	91.4	92.9	94.3

Table 4: Candidate Re-ranking: Ablation Study. CQT: Additional inputs, concatenate question and tuple , SCNS: Solr Candidates as Negative Samples

CQT	SCNS	Accuracy
no	no	49.1
yes	no	68.2
no	yes	69.6
yes	yes	80.0

3 Experiments

We show experiments on the SimpleQuestions (Bordes et al., 2015) dataset which comprises 75.9k/10.8k/21.7k training/validation/test questions. Each question is associated with an answer, i.e. a tuple (subject, predicate, object) from a Freebase subset (FB2M or FB5M). The subject is given as a MID (a unique ID referring to entities in Freebase), and we obtain its corresponding entity name by processing the Freebase data dumps. We were unable to obtain entity name mappings for some MIDs, and removed these from our final set. Our resulting set contained 74,509/10,639/21,300 training/validation/test questions. As with previous work, we show results over the 2M-subset of Freebase (FB2M).

We use pre-trained word embeddings[3] provided by Fasttext (Bojanowski et al., 2016) and randomly initialized embeddings between [-0.25, 0.25] for words without embeddings.

3.1 Generating negative samples

In our experiments, we observe that the negative sample generation method has a significant influence on the results. We develop a custom negative sample generation method that generates negative samples similar to the actual answer and helps further increase the discriminatory ability of our network.

We generate 10 negative samples for each training sample. We use the approach in Bordes et al. (2014) to generate 5 of these 10 negative samples. These candidates are samples picked at random and then corrupted following Bordes et al. (2014). Essentially, Given $(q, t) \in D$, Bordes et al. (2014) create a corrupted triple $\acute{t}$ with the following method: pick another random triple $\acute{t}$ from K, and then, replace with 66% chance each member of t (left entity, predicate and right entity) by the corresponding element in $\acute{t}$.

Further, we obtain 5 more negative samples by querying the Solr index for top-5 candidates (excluding the answer candidate) providing each question in the training set as the input query. This second policy is unique as we generate negative samples closer to the actual answer thereby providing fine-grained negative samples to our network as compared to Bordes et al. (2014) who generate only randomly corrupted negative samples.

---

[3] https://fasttext.cc/

Examples
Example 1: CA (have wheels will travel, book written work subjects, family)
Question: what is the have wheels will travel book about?
Predicted Answer: (have wheels will travel, book written work subjects, adolescence)
Example 2: CA (traditional music, music genre artists, the henrys)
Question: which quartet is known for traditional music?
Predicted Answer: (traditional music, music genre albums, music and friends)

3.2 Evaluation

We report results using the standard evaluation criteria (Bordes et al., 2015), in terms of path-level accuracy, which is the percentage of questions for which the top-ranked candidate fact is correct. A prediction is correct if the system retrieves the correct subject and predicate. Network parameters and decisions are presented in Table 1. We use top-200 candidates as input to the re-ranking step.

4 Results

In Table 3, we report candidate generation results. As expected, recall increases as we increase k. This initial candidate generation step surpasses (Table 2) the original Bordes (2015) paper and comes close to other complex neural approaches (Golub and He, 2016; Lukovnikov et al., 2017). This is surprising since this initial step is an inverted-index based approach which retrieves the most relevant candidates based on term matching.

In Table 2, we present end-to-end results[4] of existing approaches as well as our model. There is a significant improvement of 17% in our accuracy after candidate re-ranking. We attribute it to our TSHCNN model. To obtain insights into these improvements, we do an ablation study (Table 4) of the various components in TSHCNN and describe them in more detail further.

SCNS: Using Solr Candidates as Negative Samples. The scores obtained using our custom negative sample generation method (described in section 3.1), were 17.3% and 41.8% higher as compared to using only 10 negative samples generated as per Bordes et al. (2014), with and without additional inputs respectively. This is a significant improvement in scores, and we attribute it to the reason that negative candidates similar to the actual answer increase the discriminatory ability of the network and lead to the robust training of our network.

CQT: Additional inputs, concatenate question and tuple. Compared to our model without additional inputs, we obtain an improvement of 14.9% and 38.9% in our scores when we provide additional inputs in the form of concatenated question and tuple, with and without our custom negative sampling approach respectively. One possible explanation for this increase is that this augmented network has 50% more features that help it in learning better intermediate representations. To verify this, we add more filters to our convolution layer such that the total features equalled that when additional input is provided. However, the improvement in results was only marginal. Another explanation for this improvement would be that the max pooling layer picks out the dominant features from this additional input, and these features improve the distinguishing ability of our network.

Combining both these techniques, we gain an impressive 62.9% in scores as compared to our model without neither of these techniques. Overall, we achieve an accuracy of 80%, a new state-of-the-art despite having a simple model.

In Table 5, some example outputs of our model are shown. Example 1 shows that the predicted answer is correct (subject and predicate match) but does not match the answer that comes with the question. Example 2 shows we can correctly predict the subject but cannot obtain the correct predicate owing to the high similarity between the correct answer predicate and the predicted answer predicate.

5 Conclusion

This paper proposes a simple and effective IR style approach for QA over a KB. Our TSHCNN model

---

[4](Ture and Jojic, 2017) reported a 86.8% accuracy but (Petrochuk and Zettlemoyer, 2018) and (Mohammed et al., 2017) have not been able to replicate their results.

shows impressive results on the SimpleQuestions benchmark. It outperforms many other approaches that use Bi-LSTMs, attention mechanisms or separate segmentation models. We also introduce a negative sample generation method which significantly improves results. Such negative samples obtained through Solr increase the discriminatory ability of our network. Our experiments highlight the effectiveness of using simple IR models for the SimpleQuestions benchmark.

References

Arvind Agarwal, Hema Raghavan, Karthik Subbian, Prem Melville, Richard D. Lawrence, David Gondek, and James Z Fan. 2012. Learning to rank for robust question answering. In *CIKM*.

Piotr Bojanowski, Edouard Grave, Armand Joulin, and Tomas Mikolov. 2016. Enriching word vectors with subword information. *arXiv preprint arXiv:1607.04606*.

Antoine Bordes, Nicolas Usunier, Sumit Chopra, and Jason Weston. 2015. Large-scale Simple Question Answering with Memory Networks.

Antoine Bordes, Jason Weston, and Nicolas Usunier. 2014. Open Question Answering with Weakly Supervised Embedding Models. In *Lecture Notes in Computer Science (including subseries Lecture Notes in Artificial Intelligence and Lecture Notes in Bioinformatics)*, volume 8724 LNAI, pages 165–180.

Jane Bromley, Isabelle Guyon, Yann LeCun, Eduard Säckinger, and Roopak Shah. 1993. Signature verification using a "siamese" time delay neural network. In *Proceedings of the 6th International Conference on Neural Information Processing Systems*, NIPS'93, pages 737–744, San Francisco, CA, USA. Morgan Kaufmann Publishers Inc.

Danqi Chen, Adam Fisch, Jason Weston, and Antoine Bordes. 2017. Reading wikipedia to answer open-domain questions. In *Proceedings of the 55th Annual Meeting of the Association for Computational Linguistics (Volume 1: Long Papers)*, pages 1870–1879. Association for Computational Linguistics.

Sumit Chopra, Raia Hadsell, and Yann LeCun. 2005. Learning a similarity metric discriminatively, with application to face verification. In *Proceedings of the 2005 IEEE Computer Society Conference on Computer Vision and Pattern Recognition (CVPR'05) - Volume 1 - Volume 01*, CVPR '05, pages 539–546, Washington, DC, USA. IEEE Computer Society.

Arpita Das, Harish Yenala, Manoj Kumar Chinnakotla, and Manish Shrivastava. 2016. Together we stand: Siamese networks for similar question retrieval. In *Proceedings of the 54th Annual Meeting of the Association for Computational Linguistics, ACL 2016, August 7-12, 2016, Berlin, Germany, Volume 1: Long Papers*.

Anthony Fader, Luke Zettlemoyer, and Oren Etzioni. 2014. Open question answering over curated and extracted knowledge bases. In *Proceedings of the 20th ACM SIGKDD International Conference on Knowledge Discovery and Data Mining*, KDD '14, pages 1156–1165, New York, NY, USA. ACM.

David Golub and Xiaodong He. 2016. Character-Level Question Answering with Attention.

Google. 2017. Freebase data dumps. `https://developers.google.com/freebase/data`.

Karl Moritz Hermann, Tomáš Kočiský, Edward Grefenstette, Lasse Espeholt, Will Kay, Mustafa Suleyman, and Phil Blunsom. 2015. Teaching machines to read and comprehend. In *Proceedings of the 28th International Conference on Neural Information Processing Systems - Volume 1*, NIPS'15, pages 1693–1701, Cambridge, MA, USA. MIT Press.

Baotian Hu, Zhengdong Lu, Hang Li, and Qingcai Chen. 2015. Convolutional Neural Network Architectures for Matching Natural Language Sentences. *NIPS*, page 2009.

Yoon Kim. 2014. Convolutional Neural Networks for Sentence Classification. pages 1746–1751.

Denis Lukovnikov, Asja Fischer, Jens Lehmann, and Sören Auer. 2017. Neural Network-based Question Answering over Knowledge Graphs on Word and Character Level. *Proceedings of the 26th International Conference on World Wide Web - WWW '17*, pages 1211–1220.

Salman Mohammed, Peng Shi, and Jimmy Lin. 2017. Strong Baselines for Simple Question Answering over Knowledge Graphs with and without Neural Networks.

Michael Petrochuk and Luke Zettlemoyer. 2018. SimpleQuestions Nearly Solved: A New Upperbound and Baseline Approach.

Ferhan Ture and Oliver Jojic. 2017. No Need to Pay Attention: Simple Recurrent Neural Networks Work! (for Answering "Simple" Questions). *Empirical Methods in Natural Language Processing (EMNLP)*, pages 2866–2872.

Nam N. Vo and James Hays. 2016. Localizing and orienting street views using overhead imagery. *Lecture Notes in Computer Science (including subseries Lecture Notes in Artificial Intelligence and Lecture Notes in Bioinformatics)*, 9905 LNCS:494–509.

Wenpeng Yin, Mo Yu, Bing Xiang, Bowen Zhou, and
Hinrich Schütze. 2016. Simple question answering
by attentive convolutional neural network. In *Proceedings of COLING 2016, the 26th International
Conference on Computational Linguistics: Technical Papers*, pages 1746–1756. The COLING 2016
Organizing Committee.

Mo Yu, Wenpeng Yin, Kazi Saidul Hasan, Cicero dos
Santos, Bing Xiang, and Bowen Zhou. 2017. Improved Neural Relation Detection for Knowledge
Base Question Answering. In *Proceedings of the
55th Annual Meeting of the Association for Computational Linguistics (Volume 1: Long Papers)*, pages
571–581, Stroudsburg, PA, USA. Association for
Computational Linguistics.

Xiang Zhang, Junbo Jake Zhao, and Yann LeCun.
2015. Character-level convolutional networks for
text classification. In *NIPS*.

Information Nutrition Labels: A Plugin for Online News Evaluation

Kevin Vincentius
Piyush Aggarwal
Ali Şahan

Birte Högden
Neelu Madan
Anusha Bangaru

Claudia Schwenger
Farid Muradov
Ahmet Aker

University of Duisburg-Essen
`a.aker@is.inf.uni-due.de`

Abstract

In this paper we present a browser plugin *NewsScan* that assists online news readers in evaluating the quality of online content they read by providing *information nutrition labels* for online news articles. In analogy to groceries, where nutrition labels help consumers make choices that they consider best for themselves, information nutrition labels tag online news articles with data that help readers judge the articles they engage with. This paper discusses the choice of the labels, their implementation and visualization.

1 Introduction

Nowadays, the amount of online news content is immense and its sources are very diverse. For the readers and other consumers of online news who value balanced, diverse and reliable information, it is necessary to have access to methods of evaluating the news articles available to them.

This is somewhat similar to food consumption where consumers are presented with a huge variety of alternatives and therefore face the challenge of deciding what is good for their health. This is why food packages come with nutrition labels that guide the consumers in their decision making. Taking this analogy, Fuhr and colleagues (2018) discuss the idea of implementing information nutrition labels for news articles. They propose to label every online news article with information nutrition labels that describe the ingredients of the article and give readers a chance to make an informed judgment about what they are reading. The authors discuss nine different information nutrition labels: factuality, readability, virality, emotion/sentiment, opinion/subjectivity/objectivity, controversy, authority/credibility/trust, technicality and topicality. Gollub and colleagues (2018) categorize these labels into fewer dimensions. Their aim is to establish group labels that are easily understood by readers. However, both studies do not go beyond discussing, proposing and grouping the labels.

In this work we actually implement information nutrition labels and deliver them as a browser plugin that we call *NewsScan*. Therefore we provide a basis for evaluating how well labels describe the online news content and for investigating how useful they are to real users for making decisions about whether to read the news and whether to trust its content. To avoid biasing the user in any way with respect to the consumption of an article, the information is solely presented but not interpreted. Judgments about news sources should be made by users themselves. Whether an article will be read or discarded depends on the user's own weighing of importance of the information nutrition labels.

The plugin supports the reader in these tasks through easy-to-understand visualizations of the labels. In this paper we discuss the methods behind the label computation (Section 2) and the design of the user interface (Section 3).

2 Information nutrition labels

NewsScan implements six information nutrition labels: *source popularity, article popularity, ease of reading, sentiment, objectivity and political bias. Ease of reading, sentiment* and *objectivity* have been proposed by Fuhr et al. (2018). We propose to add three more nutrition labels: Source as well as article popularity and political bias. Similar to food nutrition labels the information nutri-

Proceedings of the First Workshop on Fact Extraction and VERification (FEVER), pages 28–33
Brussels, Belgium, November 1, 2018. ©2018 Association for Computational Linguistics

tion labels aim to provide the reader some base to judge about the reliability of the article's content. The credibility nutrition label proposed by Fuhr et al. (2018), for instance, is able to give the reader the indication whether e.g. the source where the article come from is credible or not. However, the credibility label entails already a judgment. It already sums some pieces of information and makes conclusion based on them. We think instead of providing the reader such a judgment the user might be better informed when we provide information that are possible bases for computing e.g. the credibility label. The proposed three new labels aim this purpose, i.e. providing enough details to enable the user to make an informed judgment about an articles content.

In the following we describe the nutrition labels currently implemented within the plugin.

2.1 Source popularity

The label *source popularity* encompasses two dimensions: the reputation of the news source and its influence.

The reputation of a source is analyzed using the **Web of Trust Score**[1]. This score is computed by an Internet browser extension that helps people make informed decision about whether to trust a website or not. It is based on a unique crowd-sourcing approach that collects rating and reviews from global community of millions of users who rate and comment on websites based on their personal experiences.

The influence of a source is computed using Alexa Rank, Google PageRank[2] and popularity on Twitter.

Alexa Rank is a virtual ranking system set by Alexa.com (a subsidiary of Amazon) that audits and publishes the frequency of visits on various websites. The Alexa ranking is the geometric mean of reach and page views, averaged over a period of three months.

Google PageRank is a link analysis algorithm that assigns a numerical weight to each element of a hyperlinked set of documents, such as the World Wide Web, with the purpose of measuring its relative importance within the set.

Twitter Popularity is calculated as an average of the scores for the following two metrics:

- **Followers Count**: This gives the amount of users that are following a source.
- **Listed Count**: This indicates the number of memberships of the source to different topics. It is based on the user's activity to add/remove the source from their customized list. The higher it is, the more diverse the source is.

An overall *source popularity* score shown to the user is calculated by averaging these four metrics. However, when the icon card is flipped the user can also get detailed information about each of the above scores.

2.2 Article popularity

$$Popularity = alog(bx + 1) \qquad (1)$$

where x is the average amount of tweets per hour, so that the article popularity is *0* when x is *0*. The most popular article we found had around 23 tweets per hour in its peak 24 hours. This is used as a reference value, i.e. an article must have this many tweets to reach a score of 100. The logarithmic function is used because the output has to be scaled properly. For example, an article with five tweets per hour is still relatively popular, even though it is just a fraction of the reference score. Choosing a large value for b will make the function close to being linear, which will cause even the relatively popular articles to have low scores. A small b will make the function more curved. If b is too big however, any article with a decent amount of tweets will have a score very close to 100. b is chosen empirically to be *1* so that the scores are distributed well between 0 and 100 over a variety of typical news articles. a is determined to be *73* to give the reference article a score of 100.

2.3 Ease of reading

As described by Schwarm and Ostendorf (2005) the readability level is used to characterize the educational level a reader needs to understand a text. This topic has been in research since 1930 and several automatic solutions have been proposed to determine the readability level of an input text (Vajjala and Meurers, 2013; Xia et al., 2016; Schwarm and Ostendorf, 2005). The core concept in these studies is to use machine learning along with feature engineering covering lexical, structural, and heuristic based features. We followed this core concept and used Random Forest with features inspired by earlier studies. This approach achieved

---

[1]https://www.mywot.com/
[2]https://www.domcop.com/openpagerank/

73% accuracy on a data set of texts written by students in Cambridge English examinations (Xia et al., 2016). The classifier predicts five different levels of readability varying from A2 (easy) to C2 (difficult) (Xia et al., 2016). We map these values to percentages so that A2 becomes 100% (easy to read) and C2 becomes 20% (difficult to read) (see Table 1)

Table 1: Levels of readability

Text level	A2	B1	B2	C1	C2
Value	100%	80%	60%	40%	20%

2.4 Sentiment

A text containing sentiment is written in an emotional style. To determine the sentiment value of an article, our algorithm uses the pattern3.en library (Hayden and de Smet). In this library every word is assigned a sentiment value, which can be negative or positive [-1; 1]. If a word shows intense positive emotions (e.g. happy, amazing), it is given a high positive value. In line with that, a term indicating intense negative emotions (e.g. bad, disgusting) is assigned a high negative value. A word not containing any emotions (e.g. the, you, house), has a value of near to zero. First, the algorithm calculates the sentiment value for every sentence by averaging all absolute values of sentiment for the distinct words. After that, the overall sentiment value of the whole news article is calculated. For that, the average of the sentences is taken and multiplied by 100. [3]

2.5 Objectivity

Objectivity is given when a text is written from a neutral rather than a personal perspective. Phrases like *"in my opinion"* or *"I think"* are used by authors to reflect their individual thoughts, beliefs and attitudes. The process of determining the objectivity of a text is similar to the process of calculating the sentiment value. The aforementioned library pattern3.en (Hayden and de Smet) also includes a value of subjectivity for every word.[4] Therefore we use it to obtain an objectivity score for articles. Values range from 0 to 1, with a value near to 0 indicating objectivity and a value near to 1 indicating subjectivity. The overall score for subjectivity contained in an article is calculated as the average over all sentences. However, since we want to examine the objectivity and not the subjectivity of a text, the values need to be inverted:

$$Objectivity = 1 - Subjectivity \qquad (2)$$

This score is normalized by multiplying it by 100 to attain a consistent score range for all labels.

2.6 Political bias

Bias measures the degree to which an article is written from a one-sided perspective that enforces users to believe in a specific viewpoint without considering opposing arguments.

For calculating political bias we followed Fairbanks et al. (2018) and used two classes that represent different political orientations: conservatism (sources that are biased towards the right) and liberalism (sources that are biased towards the left). The authors also argue that the content of the article is a strong discriminant to distinguish between biased and non-biased articles. Following the authors we built a *content based model* for prediction of political bias in the news articles. To achieve that, a logistic regression classifier is trained on a dataset containing articles from The Global Database of Events Language and Tone Project (The GDELT Project). This database monitors the world's broadcast news in over 100 languages and provides a computing platform. However, it does not contain any information about the political bias. To retrieve the bias contained in an article, we crawled from the Media Bias Fact Check [5] the required bias information. The Media Bias Fack Check contains human annotated fact checks for various source domains. For our articles we have left-biased, right-biased and neutral labels. We use a simple bag-of-words approach as features to guide our logistic regression model. As the label values in our plugin are all shown in a range from 0-100%, the label's landing page shows 0% when the article has no political bias otherwise 100% – regardless whether the article is left or right biased. When the label's card is flipped the reader can see whether the article has left or right political bias.

---

[3] Since we use the absolute values of the sentiment scores we are interested in knowing how sentimental a news article is rather than focusing on the valence of emotions.

[4] Similar to sentiment the algorithm calculates the subjectivity score for every sentence by averaging all subjectivity scores of its words.

[5] https://mediabiasfactcheck.com

3 Visualization

3.1 Colors and icons

Our information nutrition labels are represented by simple, easy-to-identify and well-known icons, which have been shown to be easily understood by users (Antunez et al., 2013; Campos et al., 2011; Hersey et al., 2013; Roberto and Khandpur, 2014). Moreover, previous work reports that simple additional texts allow for a quicker processing of information represented by an icon (Campos et al., 2011). Therefore the information nutrition label is shown additionally as text.

To make nutrition labels more comprehensible, colors indicating amounts of nutrients are helpful (Aschemann-Witzel et al., 2013; Crosetto et al., 2016; Ducrot et al., 2016). Relevant research reports that both traffic light colors and monochromic colors work equally well (Aschemann-Witzel et al., 2013). Traffic light colors are most common with red indicating high (i.e. negative) and green indicating low (i.e. positive) levels of nutrients (Kim et al., 2018). Since we do not want to bias the users towards reading an article or not, but rather give information about its content, we chose to use different shades of blue in our plugin. A light blue indicates low and a dark blue indicates high levels of a certain label. Additionally, blue stands for trust, honesty and security (Venngage, 2018), which should indicate that the user is operating a reliable tool.

When deciding on what charts and figures to use, we again took into account that simple and commonly known visualizations are easiest to comprehend (Campos et al., 2011). Thus, we chose plain bar charts for representing overall nutrition label scores as well as scores of sub-labels. Additionally, we enriched it with percentages as well as coloring. Consequently, the amount of a label contained in a news article is visualized in an understandable and easy-to-process way.

For lettering, the font *Futura* is used. It is a modern, straightforward and clean typeface often used in state-of-the-art websites and fits the simple and genuine layout.

3.2 Positioning and information distribution

Following the so-called gestalt laws of grouping[6], objects that are closer to each other (*law of proximity*) are perceived as belonging together. More-

---

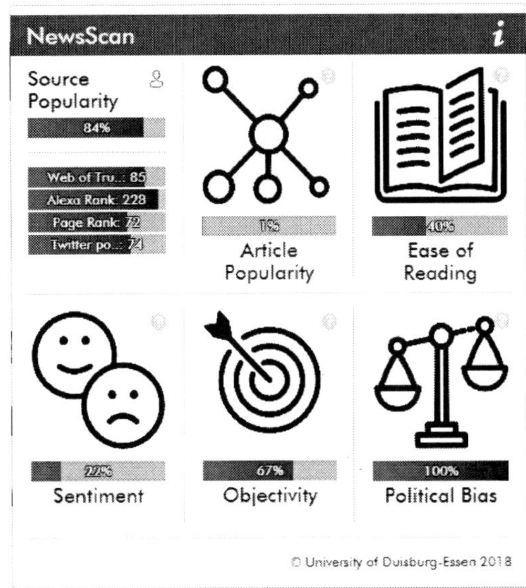

Figure 1: NewsScan plugin

over, to indicate the grouping of information, separations between those groups are useful (*law of continuity*). Therefore, the distinct labels are separated from each other by horizontal and vertical lines.

To obviate information overload (Eppler and Mengis, 2004) when using *NewsScan*, we reduced the information on the landing page to a minimum. Only the icons with their respective overall score are visible on the front side of the cards we used for visualization (as shown in Figure 1 for article popularity, ease of reading, sentiment, objectivity and political bias). Therefore, the users can get a first impression about different nutrition labels of the article. When time is scarce, a simple visualization where users can find the demanded information easily is most practicable (Crosetto et al., 2016). However, if users are interested in getting more detailed information, we created a backside for each card. The backside also shows the total score and, if available, relevant sub-labels that are used to calculate the overall scores (see Figure 1: source popularity). Additionally, on hovering over the names of the labels and sub-labels, the user gets a short explanation about what the wording and score mean. To further avoid possible confusion on the user side, all of the labels are represented in the same way. Overall and sub-label scores are mapped to a range from 0-100% and

---

[6]e-teaching.org

31

icons, texts and charts are arranged consistently.

4 Evaluation

To evaluate *NewsScan* in terms of wording, coloring and usability, we will conduct qualitative user studies. Participants will be interviewed and asked about their perception of the tool in general as well as concerning specific features. Since our aim is to not bias the user towards a consumption of one news article or another, we need to evaluate the plugin regarding that. Especially the wording of the features could affect the user in forming an opinion about an article. However, we want to help our users making an informed decision, so we need some kind of guiding, hence wording. To ensure that our tool only works as a guide and not a specific recommender, we do not interpret, for example, an easy-to-read article as being not worthwhile reading but just easy to understand. However, we believe some threshold label values about worthwhile and not worthwhile articles would indeed help readers in their decision making. In our evaluation we will aim to incorporate such information and draw conclusion between cases with threshold and without threshold values.

5 Conclusion and implications

In this paper we introduced *NewsScan*, a browser plugin to assist consumers of online news websites in their decision making about the content they engage with. Readers are guided to make an informed decision about editorials based on six labels: *source popularity, article popularity, ease of reading, sentiment, objectivity* and *political bias*. Label values are computed when a news article is retrieved. Through simple visualizations and an intuitive design, the user is confronted with the meta-information of the respective piece. To avoid biasing the user in any way with respect to the consumption of an article, the information is solely presented but not interpreted. Judgments about news sources should be made by users themselves. If an article is read or discarded relies on the user's opinion and individual weighing of the importance of the six labels.

In our immediate future work we plan to conduct user studies to analyse the validity of information nutrition labels and their usefulness for users. We also plan to investigate and integrate further information nutrition labels. Moreover it would be interesting to apply *NewsScan* to further media like videos or images accompanying news.

References

Lucia Antunez, Leticia Vidal, Alejandra Sapolinski, Ana Gimenez, Alejandro Maiche, and Gaston Ares. 2013. How do design features influence consumer attention when looking for nutritional information on food labels? results from an eye-tracking study on pan bread labels. *International Journal of Food Sciences and Nutrition*, 64(5):515–527.

Jessica Aschemann-Witzel, Klaus G. Grunert, Hans C.M. van Trijp, Svetlana Bialkova, Monique M. Raats, Charo Hodgkins, Grazyna Wasowicz-Kirylo, and Joerg Koenigstorfer. 2013. Effects of nutrition label format and product assortment on the healthfulness of food choice. *Appetite*, 71:63 – 74.

Sarah Campos, Juliana Doxey, and David Hammond. 2011. Nutrition labels on pre-packaged foods: a systematic review. *Public Health Nutrition*, 14(8):1496–1506.

Paolo Crosetto, Laurent Muller, and Bernard Ruffieux. 2016. Helping consumers with a front-of-pack label: Numbers or colors?: Experimental comparison between guideline daily amount and traffic light in a diet-building exercise. *Journal of Economic Psychology*, 55:30 – 50. Special issue on Food consumption behavior: Economic and psychological perspectives.

Pauline Ducrot, Chantal Julia, Caroline Mjean, Emmanuelle Kesse-Guyot, Mathilde Touvier, Lopold K. Fezeu, Serge Hercberg, and Sandrine Pneau. 2016. Impact of different front-of-pack nutrition labels on consumer purchasing intentions: A randomized controlled trial. *American Journal of Preventive Medicine*, 50(5):627 – 636.

Martin J. Eppler and Jeanne Mengis. 2004. The concept of information overload: A review of literature from organization science, accounting, marketing, mis, and related disciplines. *The Information Society*, 20(5):325–344.

James Fairbanks, Fitch, Knauf, and Briscoe. 2018. Credibility assessment in the news: Do we need to read? *ACM ISBN 123-4567-24-567/08/06*.

Norbert Fuhr, Anastasia Giachanou, Gregory Grefenstette, Iryna Gurevych, Andreas Hanselowski, Kalervo Jarvelin, Rosie Jones, YiquN Liu, Josiane Mothe, Wolfgang Nejdl, et al. 2018. An information nutritional label for online documents. In *ACM SIGIR Forum*, volume 51, pages 46–66. ACM.

Tim Gollub, Martin Potthast, and Benno Stein. 2018. Shaping the information nutrition label. *ECIR*.

Andy Hayden and Tom de Smet. Pattern 3. Retrieved July 27, 2018 from https://github.com/pattern3.

James C Hersey, Kelly C Wohlgenant, Joanne E Arsenault, Katherine M Kosa, and Mary K Muth. 2013. Effects of front-of-package and shelf nutrition labeling systems on consumers. *Nutrition Reviews*, 71(1):1–14.

Eojina Kim, Liang (Rebecca) Tang, Chase Meusel, and Manjul Gupta. 2018. Optimization of menu-labeling formats to drive healthy dining: An eye tracking study. *International Journal of Hospitality Management*, 70:37 – 48.

Christina A. Roberto and Neha Khandpur. 2014. Improving the design of nutrition labels to promote healthier food choices and reasonable portion sizes. *International Journal of Obesity*, 38(S1):S25.

Sarah E Schwarm and Mari Ostendorf. 2005. Reading level assessment using support vector machines and statistical language models. In *Proceedings of the 43rd Annual Meeting on Association for Computational Linguistics*, pages 523–530. Association for Computational Linguistics.

The GDELT Project. Watching our world unfold. Retrieved July 27, 2018 from `https://www.gdeltproject.org/`.

Sowmya Vajjala and Detmar Meurers. 2013. On the applicability of readability models to web texts. In *Proceedings of the Second Workshop on Predicting and Improving Text Readability for Target Reader Populations*, pages 59–68.

Venngage. 2018. What marketers should know about the psychology of visual content. Retrieved July 25, 2018 from `https://venngage.com/blog/marketing-psychology/`.

Menglin Xia, Ekaterina Kochmar, and Ted Briscoe. 2016. Text readability assessment for second language learners. In *Proceedings of the 11th Workshop on Innovative Use of NLP for Building Educational Applications*, pages 12–22.

Joint Modeling for Query Expansion and Information Extraction with Reinforcement Learning

Motoki Taniguchi, Yasuhide Miura and **Tomoko Ohkuma**
Fuji Xerox Co., Ltd.
{motoki.taniguchi, yasuhide.miura, ohkuma.tomoko}@fujixerox.co.jp

Abstract

Information extraction about an event can be improved by incorporating external evidence. In this study, we propose a joint model for pseudo-relevance feedback based query expansion and information extraction with reinforcement learning. Our model generates an event-specific query to effectively retrieve documents relevant to the event. We demonstrate that our model is comparable or has better performance than the previous model in two publicly available datasets. Furthermore, we analyzed the influences of the retrieval effectiveness in our model on the extraction performance.

1 Introduction

Information extraction about an event is gaining growing interest because of the increases in text data. The task of information extraction about an event from a text is defined to identify a set of values including entities, temporal expressions and numerical expressions that serve as a participant or attribute of the event. The extracted information is useful for various applications such as risk monitoring (Borsje et al., 2010) and decision making support (Wei and Lee, 2004).

Conventional information extraction systems provide higher performance if the amount of labeled data is larger. Labeled training data is expensive to produce and thus the data amount is limited. In this case, extraction accuracy can be improved using an alternative approach that incorporates evidence from external sources such as the Web (Kanani and McCallum, 2012; Narasimhan et al., 2016; Sharma et al., 2017). However, this approach faces the following challenges: issuing an effective query to the external source, identifying documents relevant to a target event from retrieval results and reconciling the values extracted from the relevant documents.

To overcome these problems, several attempts have been made to model the decisions as a Markov Decision Process (MDP) with deep reinforcement learning (RL) (Narasimhan et al., 2016; Sharma et al., 2017). The agent of these models is trained to maximize expected rewards (extraction accuracy) by performing actions to select an expanded query for external source and to reconcile values extracted from documents retrieved from the external source. The models use the title of source document as an original query and templates to expand this query. Expansion terms of the template are same in any event even though an optimal query depends on the event. Therefore, it is still a challenge to issue an effective query to an external source.

In this study, we extended the previous models by introducing a query expansion based on pseudo-relevance feedback (PRF) (Xu and Croft, 1996). The PRF based query expansion assumes that the top-ranked documents retrieved by an original query are relevant to the original query. An agent of our model selects a term from those documents and generates an expanded query by adding the term into the original query. The PRF based query expansion enables us to add an event-specific term into the query without additional resources. For instance, let us consider an information extraction about a shooting incident. The query "Shooting on Warren Ave. leaves one dead" retrieves the documents which may contain the term "New York". The addition of the event-specific term "New York" to the query leads to the filtering out of irrelevant documents, and thus to improves retrieval performance because "Warren Ave." is located in "New York". Therefore, we expect to improve extraction accuracy by introducing PRF based query expansion.

In contrast to the previous models, candidate terms for query expansion in our model vary de-

Proceedings of the First Workshop on Fact Extraction and VERification (FEVER), pages 34–39
Brussels, Belgium, November 1, 2018. ©2018 Association for Computational Linguistics

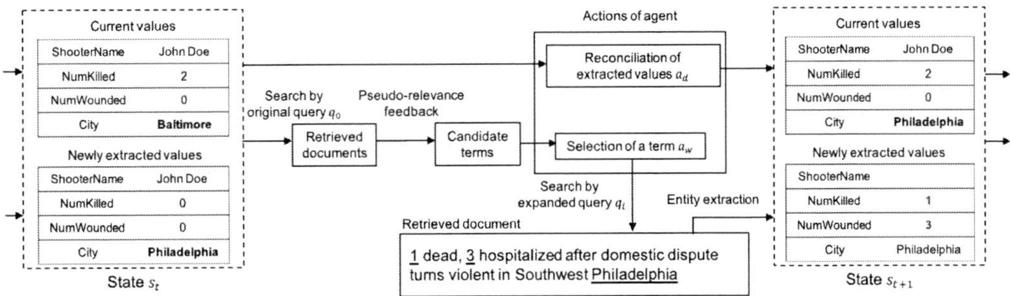

Figure 1: Illustration of states, actions and state transition in our framework. For simplicity, only the sets of current and newly extracted values are shown for the states.

pending on an event. Therefore, we exploit an original query and its candidate terms information as inputs of policy networks in addition to state information.

The contributions of this paper are follows:

- We propose a joint model for PRF based query expansion and information extraction with RL.

- We investigated the oracle extraction accuracy as an indicator of the model's retrieval performance to reveal that the PRF based query expansion outperforms the template query in two publicly available datasets.

- We demonstrate that our model is comparable or better extraction performance compared to the previous model in the datasets.

2 Related Work

Information extraction incorporating external sources: Information extraction incorporating external sources has been increasingly investigated in knowledge base population (Ji and Grishman, 2011; West et al., 2014) and multiple document extraction (Mann and Yarowsky, 2005). In contrast to the tasks of these studies, a challenge exists in our task to identify documents relevant to a target event, and this complicates extraction of information.

Narasimhan et al. (2016) and Sharma et al. (2017) modeled the information extraction tasks as an MDP with RL. They demonstrated that their models outperformed conventional extractors and meta-classifier models. There are two crucial differences between our model and aforementioned models. First, the proposed model is trained to select an optimal term of query expansion for each original query instead of a query template. Second, the proposed model also leverages an original query and its candidate terms as the input of policy networks, whereas the above-mentioned models use only state information.

Query expansion: Query expansion can be categorized into global and local methods (Manning et al., 2008). The global methods include query expansion using a manual thesaurus (Voorhees, 1994), and an automatically generated thesaurus based on word co-occurrence statistics over corpus (Qiu and Frei, 1993). The template query that is used in the previous RL based model belongs to the global methods.

There are several approaches of local methods that use query log (Cui et al., 2002), and are based on PRF (Xu and Croft, 1996). We employed a PRF based method because it does not require additional resources. Moreover, local methods have been evidenced to outperform global methods in information retrieval (Xu and Croft, 1996).

Nogueira and Cho (2017) proposed an RL based approach to model query reformulation in information retrieval. They also reformulated a query through PRF. In contrast, our proposed approach targets information extraction rather than document retrieval. The goal of our task is to extract multiple values of event attributes as well as to retrieve relevant documents. Moreover, the document collection in the RL-based approach (Nogueira and Cho, 2017) is limited to Wikipedia pages or academic papers, while we use the Web as an open document-collection platform.

3 Proposed Model

3.1 Framework

We model the information extraction task as an MDP in a similar manner to that by

Narasimhan et al. (2016) and Sharma et al. (2017); however, the query-selection strategy differs. An agent in our framework selects a term to add to an original query instead of selecting a query template. In this section, we mainly describe the difference between our framework and the previous framework.

At the beginning of each episode, an agent is given a source document to extract information about an event. Figure 1 illustrates an example of state transition. The state comprises the confidence score of current and newly extracted values, the match between current and new values, term frequency-inverse document frequency (TF-IDF) of context words, and TF-IDF similarity between source and current documents, similar to the method by Narasimhan et al. (2016). At each step, the agent performs two actions: a reconciliation decision a_d, which involves the accepting of extracted values for one or all attributes or rejecting all newly extracted values (or ending an episode), and a term selection for query expansion a_w. In the example, the agent takes a reconciliation decision a_d to update the value of *City* attribute from *Baltimore* to *Philadelphia* based on the state s_t in time step t. Simultaneously, the agent performs term selection a_w that is used to form the expanded query to retrieve the next document. The candidate terms $W = \{w_1, w_2, \cdots, w_N\}$ are collected from the documents retrieved by an original query q_0. Here, we use the title of the source document as q_0. The agent selects a term w_i from W and generates expanded query q_i by adding w_i into q_0. q_i is used to retrieve the next document and the new values are extracted from the document by base extractor. State s_{t+1} of the next step is determined according to the updated values of the event attributes and the newly extracted values. The agent receives a reward, which is defined as the difference between the accuracy in the current time step and the previous time step. We add a negative constant to the reward to avoid long episodes. In the subsequent time steps, the agent sequentially chooses the two actions a_d and a_w until a_d is a stop decision. For more details of state, reward and base extractor, refer to (Narasimhan et al., 2016).

The agent is trained to optimize the expected rewards by choosing actions to select an expansion term for query expansion and to reconcile values extracted from documents.

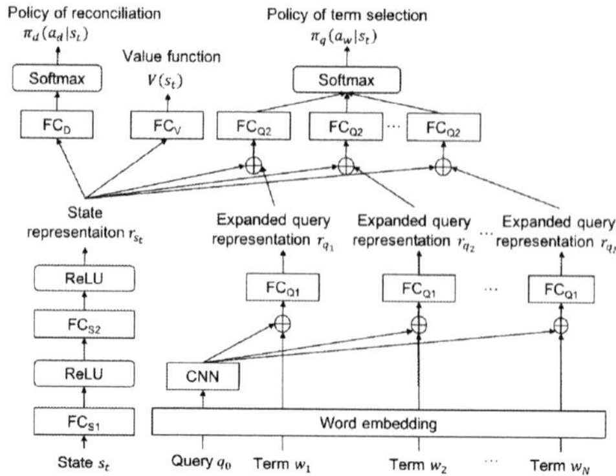

Figure 2: Overview of our model. FC: fully connected layer; $\oplus$: concatenation of vectors.

3.2 Network Architecture

We use neural networks to model decision policy $\pi_d(a_d|s_t)$ and term selection policy $\pi_q(a_w|s_t)$ as probability distributions over candidate actions a_d and a_w. Figure 2 represents an overview of our policy networks. Decision policy $\pi_d(a_d|s_t)$ and value function $V(s_t)$ is calculated using a state representation r_{s_t} that is obtained with two fully connected layers in the same manner as in Sharma et al. (2017).

In contrast to the previous framework, candidate terms in our framework depend on an event. Hence, we utilize a pairwise interaction function whose input is the state representation r_{s_t} and expanded query representation r_{q_i} to calculate term selection policy $\pi_q(a_w|s_t)$. The words of q_0 are embedded using a word embedding layer and process using a convolutional neural network (CNN) and a max pooling layer, similar to the method by Kim (2014). r_{q_i} for each term w_i is obtained by feeding the concatenation of the output of the max pooling layer and the word embedding of a candidate term w_i to a fully connected layer FC_{Q1}. We feed the concatenation of r_{s_t} and r_{q_i} for each term w_i to a fully connected layer FC_{Q2}. The parameters of the FC_{Q1} and FC_{Q2} are shared among the candidate terms. $\pi_q(a_w|s_t)$ is obtained by normalizing the outputs of the FC_{Q2} over the candidate terms.

We train the policy and value networks by using the Asynchronous Advantage Actor-Critic (A3C) (Mnih et al., 2016) as used in Sharma et al. (2017). A3C can speed up the learning process of the policy networks by training multiple agents asynchronously. Further details on the A3C can be found in Sharma et al. (2017).

Documents		Shooting			Adulteration		
		train	dev	test	train	dev	test
Source document		372	146	146	292	42	148
Template query	N=5/4	22,697	8,874	9,039	11,425	1,597	6,166
PRF based expanded query	N=5/4	20,243	8,877	8,128	10,994	1,383	5,460
	N=11	45,432	19,505	18,372	30,154	3,965	14,847
	N=21	90,006	37,256	36,013	57,636	7,785	27,963
	N=31	134,475	54,966	54,021	84,768	11,638	41,181

Table 1: The number of source documents and downloaded documents in each set.

4 Experiments

4.1 Experimental Setting

We evaluated our model on *Shooting* and *Adulteration* datasets that used in Narasimhan et al. (2016). For each an original query, we collected the candidate terms obtained from the first M words of the top-K documents retrieved through Bing Search API[1]. The vocabulary size of the candidate terms N is defined as $MK + 1$ because the null token, namely no query expansion, is also included in the candidate terms. We downloaded the top 20 documents from the Bing Search API as the external sources through an expanded query. Statistics of the original datasets and downloaded documents is described in Table 1.

Word embeddings are set to fixed vectors of 300 dimensions and is initialized with word2vec embedding trained on Google News Dataset[2]. We set the unit size of FC_{S1} and FC_{S2} to 20, FC_{Q1} to 300, FC_V and FC_{Q2} to 1. Further, we set the number of feature maps of CNN to 200 and the window size of CNN to 3. Discount factor and the constant of entropy regularization were set to 0.8 and 0.01, respectively. We utilize RMSprop (Hinton et al., 2012) as the optimizer and set the number of threads in A3C to 16.

We employed RLIE-A3C (Sharma et al., 2017) as a baseline model to compare with our model. We used their public implementation[3].

4.2 Results

We evaluated the average extraction accuracy for attributes as done in Sharma et al. (2017). Table 2 shows the results of *Shooting* and *Adulteration*.

[1] https://azure.microsoft.com/en-us/services/cognitive-services/bing-web-search-api/

[2] https://code.google.com/archive/p/word2vec/

[3] https://github.com/adi-sharma/RLIE_A3C

Our model achieved 1.9 pt increase of average accuracy in *Shooting* and 0.2 pt decrease in *Adulteration* against the RLIE-A3C model when the number of expanded queries N was 5 for *Shooting* and 4 for *Adulteration*; these correspond to $(M, K) = (4, 1)$ or $(3, 1)$ respectively. We varied (M, K) to $(10, 1)$, $(10, 2)$ and $(10, 3)$, which indicate $N = 11, 21$ and 31, to evaluate the effect of the number of expanded queries. The accuracy in our models rarely changes even though the number of expanded queries increases.

Model	External source		Shooting	Adulteration
	Query expansion	# query N	Average accuracy	
RLIE-A3C	Template	5(Shooter)/ 4(Adulteration)	0.646	0.612
Our model	PRF		0.665	0.610
		11	0.656	0.611
		21	0.666	0.607
		31	0.653	0.608

Table 2: Extraction accuracy of RLIE-A3C and our models on *Shooting* and *Adulteration* datasets. Underlined values represent the best values on each datasets.

4.3 Discussion

We evaluated oracle extraction accuracy to determine the effectiveness of PRF-based query expansion and to discover why our model does not perform well in *Adulteration*. The oracle extraction accuracy is calculated if an agent perfectly takes actions to select a term for query and reconcile the values from the documents. In other words, the oracle extraction accuracy can be regarded as an indicator of retrieval performance.

Table 3 presents the oracle extraction accuracies from only source documents, the documents retrieved by the original queries and the documents retrieved by the expanded queries by using templates and PRF. Compared with template queries, PRF based query expansion with the same number of queries performed better in *Shooting* and *Adulteration*. Oracle extraction accuracy further im-

Documents	# query N	Shooting	Adulteration
Source documents	-	0.612	0.580
Retrieved documents for original queries	1	0.747	0.560
Retrieved documents for template expanded queries	5(Shooting)/ 4(Adulteration)	0.768	0.592
Retrieved documents for PRF based expanded queries (ours)		0.807	0.608
	11	0.820	0.642
	21	0.823	0.663
	31	0.830	0.665

Table 3: Oracle extraction accuracy. "Documents" refers to documents to extract information.

Shooting	1 Dead, 3 Wounded In Shooting On Roxbury Street
	Police: 3 Dead, 1 In Surgery After Dallas Shooting CBS Dallas
	San Francisco police confirm 4 dead following shooting in Hayes Valley
Adulteration	Subway investigates china media reports of doctored expiry dates
	High level of seafood fraud found Denmark
	Fake honey worthing leads to trading standards prosecution

Table 4: Examples of titles of source documents in *Shooting* and *Adulteration* datasets

proved with the increases in the number of queries N. However, no difference was found in its extraction performance (see Table 2). This indicates that increasing the number of queries N complicates the selection of an optimal term for query expansion.

Compared to *Shooting*, the oracle accuracy of the original queries in *Adulteration* is relatively low. Therefore, the assumption that the top-ranked documents retrieved by the original query are relevant to the original query is not satisfied in *Adulteration*. We consider that this is why our model does not achieve an improvement in the extraction performance on *Adulteration*. Table 4 shows examples of the titles of source document used as original queries. We can observe that named entity and numerical expression appeared in more titles of the source documents in *Shooting* than those in *Adulteration*. Therefore, the original queries in *Adulteration* lack specifics and weaken the extraction performance.

5 Conclusions

We integrated the PRF based query expansion to the task of information extraction using RL. Our model can expand a query into an event-specific query without additional resources. To integrate the PRF based query expansion, we introduced a pairwise interaction function to calculate term selection policy $\pi_q(a_w|s)$. Experimental results showed that our model is comparable or better than the previous model in terms of extraction performance in two datasets. Furthermore, we analyzed the relationship between retrieval effectiveness and extraction performance.

In the future work, we plan to develop a model that can generate a complete term sequence of the expanded query rather than adding a term to a query.

References

Jethro Borsje, Frederik Hogenboom, and Flavius Frasincar. 2010. Semi-automatic financial events discovery based on lexico-semantic patterns. *Int. J. Web Eng. Technol.*, 6(2):115–140.

Hang Cui, Ji-Rong Wen, Jian-Yun Nie, and Wei-Ying Ma. 2002. Probabilistic query expansion using query logs. In *Proceedings of the 11th International Conference on World Wide Web*, WWW '02, pages 325–332, New York, NY, USA. ACM.

Geoffrey Hinton, Nitish Srivastava, and Kevin Swersky. 2012. Neural networks for machine learning lecture 6a overview of mini-batch gradient descent.

Heng Ji and Ralph Grishman. 2011. Knowledge base population: Successful approaches and challenges. In *Proceedings of the 49th Annual Meeting of the Association for Computational Linguistics: Human Language Technologies*, pages 1148–1158. Association for Computational Linguistics.

Pallika H. Kanani and Andrew K. McCallum. 2012. Selecting actions for resource-bounded information extraction using reinforcement learning. In *Proceedings of the Fifth ACM International Conference on Web Search and Data Mining*, WSDM '12, pages 253–262, New York, NY, USA. ACM.

Yoon Kim. 2014. Convolutional neural networks for sentence classification. In *Proceedings of the 2014 Conference on Empirical Methods in Natural Language Processing (EMNLP)*, pages 1746–1751. Association for Computational Linguistics.

Gideon Mann and David Yarowsky. 2005. Multi-field information extraction and cross-document fusion. In *Proceedings of the 43rd Annual Meeting of the Association for Computational Linguistics (ACL'05)*, pages 483–490. Association for Computational Linguistics.

Christopher D. Manning, Prabhakar Raghavan, and Hinrich Schütze. 2008. *Introduction to Information Retrieval*. Cambridge University Press, New York, NY, USA.

Volodymyr Mnih, Adria Puigdomenech Badia, Mehdi Mirza, Alex Graves, Timothy Lillicrap, Tim Harley, David Silver, and Koray Kavukcuoglu. 2016. Asynchronous methods for deep reinforcement learning. In *International Conference on Machine Learning*, pages 1928–1937.

Karthik Narasimhan, Adam Yala, and Regina Barzilay. 2016. Improving information extraction by acquiring external evidence with reinforcement learning. In *Proceedings of the 2016 Conference on Empirical Methods in Natural Language Processing*, pages

2355–2365. Association for Computational Linguistics.

Rodrigo Nogueira and Kyunghyun Cho. 2017. Task-oriented query reformulation with reinforcement learning. In *Proceedings of the 2017 Conference on Empirical Methods in Natural Language Processing*, pages 574–583. Association for Computational Linguistics.

Yonggang Qiu and Hans-Peter Frei. 1993. Concept based query expansion. In *Proceedings of the 16th Annual International ACM SIGIR Conference on Research and Development in Information Retrieval*, SIGIR '93, pages 160–169, New York, NY, USA. ACM.

Aditya Sharma, Zarana Parekh, and Partha Talukdar. 2017. Speeding up reinforcement learning-based information extraction training using asynchronous methods. In *Proceedings of the 2017 Conference on Empirical Methods in Natural Language Processing*, pages 2658–2663. Association for Computational Linguistics.

Ellen M. Voorhees. 1994. Query expansion using lexical-semantic relations. In *Proceedings of the 17th Annual International ACM SIGIR Conference on Research and Development in Information Retrieval*, SIGIR '94, pages 61–69, New York, NY, USA. Springer-Verlag New York, Inc.

Chih-Ping Wei and Yen-Hsien Lee. 2004. Event detection from online news documents for supporting environmental scanning. *Decis. Support Syst.*, 36(4):385–401.

Robert West, Evgeniy Gabrilovich, Kevin Murphy, Shaohua Sun, Rahul Gupta, and Dekang Lin. 2014. Knowledge base completion via search-based question answering. In *WWW*.

Jinxi Xu and W. Bruce Croft. 1996. Query expansion using local and global document analysis. In *Proceedings of the 19th Annual International ACM SIGIR Conference on Research and Development in Information Retrieval*, SIGIR '96, pages 4–11, New York, NY, USA. ACM.

Towards Automatic Fake News Detection:
Cross-Level Stance Detection in News Articles

Costanza Conforti   **Mohammad Taher Pilehvar**   **Nigel Collier**

`cc918@cam.ac.uk`   `mp792@cam.ac.uk`   `nhc30@cam.ac.uk`

Language Technology Lab, University of Cambridge

Abstract

In this paper, we propose to adapt the four-staged pipeline proposed by Zubiaga et al. (2018) for the Rumor Verification task to the problem of Fake News Detection. We show that the recently released FNC-1 corpus covers two of its steps, namely the *Tracking* and the *Stance Detection* task. We identify asymmetry in length in the input to be a key characteristic of the latter step, when adapted to the framework of Fake News Detection, and propose to handle it as a specific type of *Cross-Level Stance Detection*. Inspired by theories from the field of Journalism Studies, we implement and test two architectures to successfully model the internal structure of an article and its interactions with a claim.

1 Introduction

The rise of social media platforms, which allow for real-time posting of news with very little (or none at all) editorial review at the source, is responsible for an unprecedented growth in the amount of the information available to the public. While this constitutes an invaluable source of free information, it also facilitates the spread of misinformation. In particular, the literature distinguishes between *rumors*, i.e., pieces of information which are unverified at the time of posting and therefore can turn out to be true or false, and *fake news* (or *hoaxes*), i.e., false stories which are instrumentally made up with the intent to mislead the readers and spread disinformation (Zubiaga et al., 2018).

Both Rumor Verification (RV) and Fake News Detection (FND) constitute very difficult tasks even for trained professionals. Therefore, approaching them in an end-to-end fashion has generally been avoided. Both tasks, however, can be easily split into a number of sub-steps. For instance, Zubiaga et al. (2018) proposed a model

for RV which consists of four stages: a rumor *detection* stage, where potentially rumorous posts are identified, followed by a *tracking* stage, where posts concerning the identified rumor are collected; after determining the orientation expressed in each post with respect to the rumor (*stance detection*), the final truth value of the rumor is obtained by aggregating those single stance judgments (*veracity classification*). As shown in Figure 1, this pipeline can be naturally adapted to FND.

In recent years, several efforts have been made by the research community toward the automatization of some of these stages, in order to provide effective tools to enhance the performance of human journalists in rumor and fake news debunking (Thorne and Vlachos, 2018). Concerning FND, Pomerleau and Rao (2017) recently released a dataset for the Stance Detection step in the framework of the Fake News Challenge[1] (FNC-1). The core of the corpus is constituted by a collection of articles discussing 566 claims, 300 of which come from the EMERGENT dataset (Ferreira and Vlachos, 2016). Each article is summarized in a headline and labeled as *agreeing* (AGR), *disagreeing* (DSG) or *discussing* (DSC) the claim. Additionally, *unrelated* (UNR) samples were created by pairing headlines with random articles. The goal of the challenge was to classify the pairs constituted by a headline and an article as AGR, DSG, DSC or UNR.

Following the pipeline discussed above, it is clear that the FNC-1 actually covers two of the four steps, namely: (1) The *tracking* step, consisting in filtering out the irrelevant UNR samples; (2) The actual *stance detection* step, consisting in the classification of a related headline/article pair into AGR, DSC or DSC.

---

[1] `http://www.fakenewschallenge.org/`

40

Proceedings of the First Workshop on Fact Extraction and VERification (FEVER), pages 40–49
Brussels, Belgium, November 1, 2018. ©2018 Association for Computational Linguistics

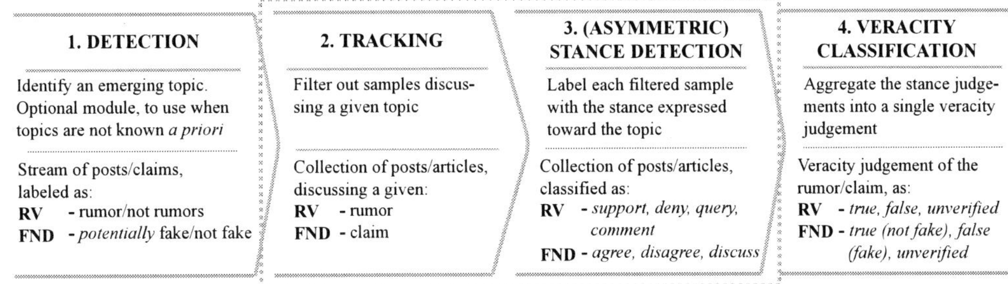

Figure 1: The rumor verification (RV) pipeline proposed by Zubiaga et al. (2018). The first row describes the corresponding step whereas the second row shows the outputs of each step for both the RV and the fake news detection (FND) tasks. The red rectangle indicates steps covered by the FNC-1 corpus. Figure adapted from Zubiaga et al. (2018).

Note that the amount of semantic understanding needed for the second task is much higher than for the first. In fact, even humans struggle in the related sample classification, as empirically demonstrated by Hanselowski et al. (2018): the inter-annotator agreement of five human judges drops from Fleiss' κ of .686 to .218, after filtering out the UNR samples. For this reason, we concentrate on the *stance detection* step, and we make the following contributions:

1. We identify asymmetry in length between headlines and articles as a key characteristic of the FNC-1 corpus: on average, an article contains more than 30 times the number of words contained in its associated headline. This is peculiar with respect to most of the commonly used datasets for stance detection (Mohammad et al., 2017) and require the development of architectures specifically tailored to this considerable asymmetry. Following on the terminology introduced by Jurgens et al. (2014) for Semantic Similarity, we propose to handle the problem as a *Cross-Level Stance Detection* task. To our knowledge, it is the first time that this task is investigated in isolation.

2. Inspired by theoretical principles in the field of Journalism Studies, we propose two simple neural architectures to model the argumentative structure of an article, and its complex interplay with a headline. We demonstrate that our systems can beat a strong feature-based baseline, based on one of the FNC-1 winning architectures, and that they can successfully model the internal structure of a news article and its relations with a claim, leveraging only word embeddings as input.

2 Related Work

2.1 Stance Detection

Stance Detection (SD) has been defined as the task of determining the attitude expressed in a *short piece of text* with respect to a target, usually expressed with one or few words (as *Feminism* or *Climate Change*, Mohammad et al. (2016)). In fact, most of the available corpora for SD consider very short samples, as Tweets. SD became very popular in recent years, resulting in a large number of publications (Mohammad et al., 2017).

To our knowledge, however, no one explicitly considered the problem of stance detection giving as input two items which are considerably asymmetric in length, that is, a long and structured document and a target expressed in the form of a complete sentence and not as a concept. For this reason, we propose to call the task introduced in the FNC-1 challenge *Cross-Level Stance Detection*. This is in line with the definition of Cross-Level Semantic Similarity, which measures the degree to which the meaning of a larger (in terms of length) linguistic item is captured by a smaller item (Jurgens et al., 2014).

After reporting on the systems participating to the FNC-1, which released the first SD dataset collecting long documents, we briefly mention some of the most relevant works on SD using Twitter data.

Fake News Challenge. With more than 50 participating groups, the FNC-1 drew high interest from both the research community and in-

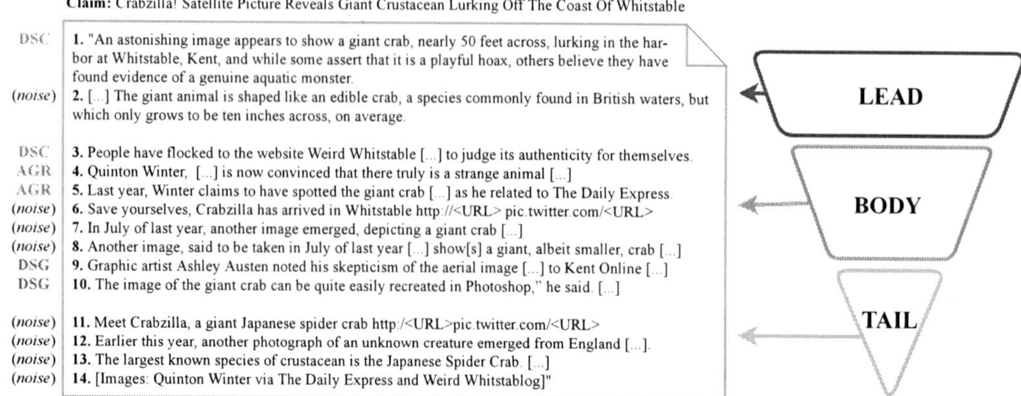

Figure 2: Article from the FNC-1 test set (sample no. 998), analyzed following the *inversed pyramid* principles (Scanlan, 1999). Notice that single sentences may express a different stance with respect to a claim, while others can be irrelevant, as shown in the leftmost column.

dustry. Due to the high number of UNR samples, which constituted almost three quarters of the training set, most of the groups proposed architectures which could perform well in this specific class - that is, in the *tracking* step of the FND pipeline. The second (Hanselowski et al., 2017) and third (Riedel et al., 2017) classified teams proposed multi-layer perceptrons (MLPs)-based systems. The best performing system (Baird et al., 2017) is an ensemble of a convolutional neural network (CNN) and a gradient-boosted decision tree. All models, with the exception of the CNN, take as input a number of hand-engineered features. Recently, Hanselowski et al. (2018) enriched the feature set used in Hanselowski et al. (2017) and added a stacked BiLSTM layer to their model, resulting in a modest gain in performance.

All models described above performed very well in the UNR classification (with F_1 usually above .98 for this class), achieving considerably worse results on the related samples (Hanselowski et al., 2018).

Rumor Stance Detection on Tweets. The most commonly used datasets for rumor stance detection, the RumorEval (Derczynski et al., 2017) and the PHEME (Zubiaga et al., 2016b) corpora, collect Tweets. State-of-the-art results on the PHEME corpus has been obtained by Aker et al. (2017), who used a very rich set of problem-specific features. Their model beat the previous state-of-the-art system by Zubiaga et al. (2016a), who modeled the tree-structured Twitter conversations using a LSTM, taking as input a conversation's branch at time.

2.2 Journalism Studies: News-writing Prose

Each genre develops its peculiar narrative forms, which allow for the most effective transmission of a message. In modern news-writing prose, especially in the Anglo-Saxon journalism, the *inverted pyramid* style is widely adopted (Scanlan, 1999).

Key element of this well standardized template consists in the fact that the most newsworthy facts (the so-called *5W*), are presented at the very beginning of the article - the *lead* - with the remaining information following, in order of importance, in the *body* of the article: in this section, we can find less essential element as quotes, interviews and background or explanatory information; any additional input, as related stories, images and credits, are put in the very last paragraphs, the *tail* (Scanlan, 1999). Usually, no more than one or two ideas are expressed in the same paragraph (Sun Technical Publications, 2003). Those characteristic elements are clearly visible in Figure 2. This style is particularly suited for rapidly evolving breaking news event, where a journalist can update an article by attaching a new paragraph with the last updates at the beginning of it. Moreover, putting most newsworthy facts at the beginning of an article allows the impatient readers to quickly decide on their level of interest in the report.

After manual analysis of excerpts of the FNC-1 corpus, we concluded that most articles were actu-

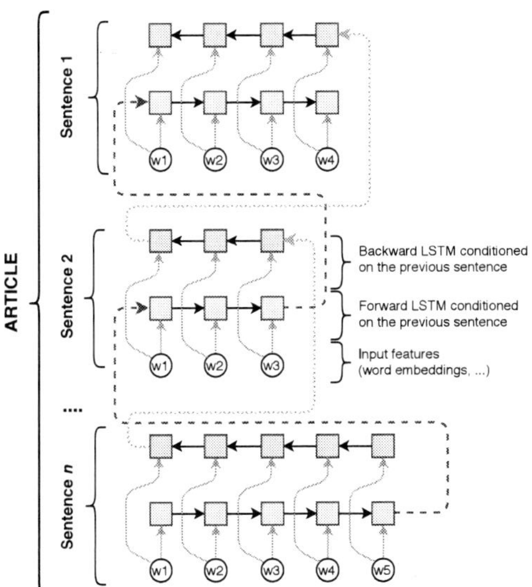

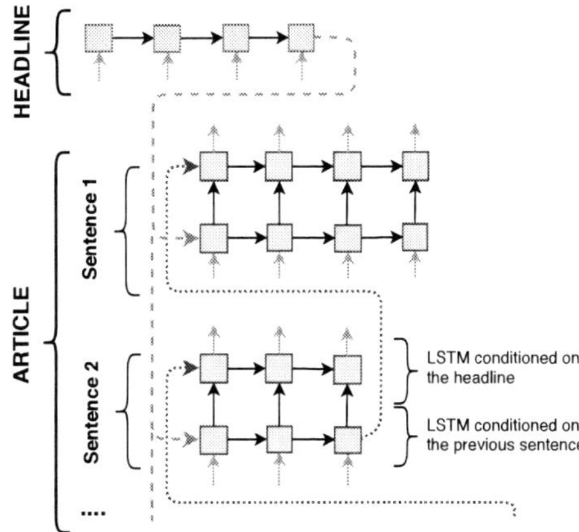

Figure 4: Detail of the forward component of the double-conditional encoding architecture (best seen in color). Dotted arrows represent conditional encoding and networks with the same color share the weights. The system reads an article from the last sentence to the first, processing each sentence twice: first conditioning on the headline, then conditioning on the previous sentence. Due to lack of space, only the first two sentences of the article are represented.

Figure 3: The architecture of our article encoder, which is based on that of Augenstein (2016). Dotted arrows represent conditional encoding and networks with the same color share the weights.

ally written following the *inverted pyramid* principles.

3 Modeling

3.1 Encoding the article

Based on the elements of Journalism Studies discussed above, we propose a simple architecture based on bidirectional conditional encoding (Augenstein et al., 2016) to encode an article split into n sentences.

Each sentence S_i is first converted into its embedding representation $E_{S_i} \in \mathbb{R}^{e \times s_i}$, where e is the embedding size and s_i is the length of the i_{th} tokenized sentence. Then, we encode the article using BiLSTM$_A$, a Bidirectional LSTM which reads the article sentence by sentence in backward order, initializing the first states of its forward and backward components with the last states it has produced after processing the previous sentence (Figure 3).

Notice that we process the article from the bottom to the top, as we assume the most salient information to be concentrate in the *lead*. By considering an article as an ensemble of sentences which are separately encoded conditioned to their preceding ones, we can model the relationship of each sentence with respect to the others and, at the same time, reduce the number of parameters.

3.2 Encoding the relationship between the headline and the article

After having encoded the article, we model its relationship with the headline. As shown in Figure 2, we expect single sentences to express a potentially different stance with respect to the headline, while some sentences - especially in the *body* and the *tail* - can be irrelevant. For this reason, we separately evaluate the relationship of each sentence, conditioned on the previous sentence(s), with the headline. In this paper, we consider two approaches:

Double-conditional Encoding. As a first method, we modeled the relationship between the headline and the article using conditional encoding.

First, the headline is encoded using a bidirectional LSTM. Then, we separately process each sentence of the article with BiLSTM$_H$, a BiLSTM conditioned on the last states of the BiLSTM which processed the headline. We finally stack BiLSTM$_A$ on top of BiLSTM$_H$. In this way, we obtain a matrix $\overline{H}_{S_i} \in \mathbb{R}^{l \times s_i}$ for each sentence S_i.

Following Wang et al. (2018), we notate this as:

$$H_{S_i} = \text{Bi-LSTM}_H(E_{S_i}) \quad \forall i \in \{1, ..., n\} \quad (1)$$

$$\overline{H}_{S_i} = \text{Bi-LSTM}_A(H_{S_i}) \quad \forall i \in \{1, ..., n\} \quad (2)$$

This process is shown in Figure 4. In this way, we read each sentence S_i, which is encoded in a headline-specific manner, conditioning on the previous sentence(s). Clearly, it could have been possible to obtain a hidden representation for each sentence by first conditioning on the previous sentence(s), and then on the headline. Results of preliminary experiments, however, showed worse results for this variant, suggesting that having the conditioning on the previous sentence(s) nearer to the decoder is beneficial for the cross-level stance detection task.

Co-matching Attention. We also explored the use of attention in order to connect the headline $H_H \in \mathbb{R}^{l \times c}$, encoded using a BiLSTM layer, with the article's sentences $H_{S_1}...H_{S_n}$, embedded as explained in Subsection 3.1. Inspired by the architecture proposed by Wang et al. (2018) for multi-choice reading comprehension, we obtain a matrix $\overline{H}_{S_i}$, attentively read with respect to the headline, for each sentence at position $i \in \{1, ..., n\}$ as follows: we first obtain an aggregated representation of the headline and the i_{th} sentence $\overline{H}_{S_i} \in \mathbb{R}^{l \times S_i}$ (Eq 4), obtained by dot product of H_H with the attention weights $A_i \in \mathbb{R}^{c \times s_i}$ (Eq 3); then, we obtain co-matching states of each sentence with $\overline{H}_{H_i}$ using Eq 5:

$$A_i = \text{softmax}((W_h H_H + b_h))^{\top} H_{S_i} \quad (3)$$

$$\overline{H}_{H_i} = H_H A_i \quad (4)$$

$$\overline{H}_{S_i} = \text{ReLU}(W_s \begin{bmatrix} \overline{H}_{Hi} \ominus H_{S_i} \\ \overline{H}_{Hi} \otimes H_{S_i} \end{bmatrix} + b_s) \quad (5)$$

where $W_h \in \mathbb{R}^{l \times l}$, $W_s \in \mathbb{R}^{l \times 2l}$, $b_h \in \mathbb{R}^l$ and $b_s \in \mathbb{R}^{2l}$ are the parameters to learn. As in Wang et al. (2018), we use the element-wise subtraction $\ominus$ and multiplication $\otimes$ to build matching representations of the headline.

Self-attention. After encoding of the relationship between the headline and the article, we employ a similar self-attention mechanism as in Yang et al. (2016) in order to soft-select the most relevant elements of the encoded sentence. Given the sequence of vectors $\{h_1, ..., h_S\}$ in $\overline{H}_{S_i}$, obtained with the double-conditional encoding or the co-matching attention approaches described above,

the final vector representation of the i_{th} sentence S_i is obtained as follows:

$$u_{it} = \tanh(W_s h_{it} + b_s) \quad (6)$$

$$\alpha_{it} = \exp \frac{u_{it}^{\top} u_s}{\sum_t u_{it}^{\top} u_s} \quad (7)$$

$$s_i = \sum_t \alpha_t h_{it} \quad (8)$$

where the hidden representation of the word at position t, u_{it}, is obtained though a one-layer MLP (Eq 6). The normalized attention matrix α_t is then obtained though a softmax operation (Eq 7). Finally, s_i is computed by a weighted sum of all hidden states h_t with the weight matrix α_t (Eq 8).

3.3 Decoding

Following the *inverted pyramid* principles, according to which the most relevant information is concentrated at the beginning of the article, we aggregate the sentence vector representations $\{s_1, ..., s_n\}$ using a backward LSTM. The final prediction $\hat{y}$ is finally obtained with a softmax operation over the tagset.

4 Experimental Setup

4.1 Data and Preprocessing

We downloaded the FNC-1 corpus from the challenge website[2]. As we wanted to concentrate on the cross-level stance detection sub-task, we only considered *related* (AGR, DSC and DSC) samples, discarding the noisy UNR samples, which would constitute the output of the *tracking* step. The distribution of related samples is also very unbalanced, with the DSC class constituting more than a half of the subset and the DSG samples accounting for only 7.5% of the related samples, as shown in Table 1.

	samples	AGR	DSG	DSC	UNR
all	75,385	7.4%	2.0%	17.7%	72.8%
REL	20,491	27.2%	7.5%	65.2%	-

Table 1: Label distribution for the FNC-1 dataset, considering all classes, or only the related samples.

As discussed in the Introduction, the cross-level stance detection task is characterized by an asymmetry in length in the input: on average, headlines are 12.40 tokens long, while articles span from 4 up to 4788 tokens, with an average length

[2]https://github.com/FakeNewsChallenge/

	headline	entire article	sentence
avg no. tokens	12.40	417.69	30.88

Table 2: Asymmetry in length between headlines and articles in the FNC-1 corpus.

of 417.69 tokens. An article, however, presents a compositional internal structure, as it can be divided into smaller elements. We used the NLTK sentence tokenizer[3] to split articles into sentences, obtaining an average number of 11.97 sentences per article. On average, sentences are 30.88 tokens long, as reported in Table 2.

4.2 Baseline

As a baseline, we implemented the *Athena* model proposed by Hanselowski et al. (2017), which scored second in the FNC-1. We did not use the first-ranked system, as it is an ensemble model, nor the modification to *Athena* proposed in Hanselowski et al. (2018), as the new feature set and the BiLSTM layer did not significantly improve the performance of the original model. The model consists in a 7-layers deep MLP, with varying number of units, followed by a softmax. Input is presented as a large matrix of concatenated features, some of which separately encode the headline or the body:

- Presence of *refuting* and *polarity* words
- Tf-idf-weighted BoW unigram features, considering a vocabulary of 5000 entries.

while others jointly consider the headline/body:

- Word overlap between headline and article.
- Count of headline's token and ngrams which appear in the article.
- Cosine similarity of the embeddings of nouns and verbs of the headline and the article.

Moreover, they use topic models based on non-negative matrix factorization, latent Dirichlet allocation, and latent semantic indexing. This results in a final set of 10 features. In this way, the asymmetry in length between is solved by compressing both the headline and the article into two fixed-sized vectors of the same size.

The same hyperparameters as in Hanselowski et al. (2017) have been used for the implementation

Max headline length (in tokens)	15
Max sentence length (in tokens)	35
Max number of sentences for article	7
Word embedding size	300
BiLSTM cell size	2×128
Embedding dropout	0.1
BiLSTM dropout	0.3
Dense layer dropout	0.2
Epochs	70
Batch size	32
Optimizer	Adam
Learning rate	0.001
Experiments using additional input channels	
Max word length (in characters)	35
Character embedding size	30
Character BiLSTM cell size	2×64
Character BiLSTM dropout	0.2
NE embedding size	30

Table 3: Hyperparameters configuration

of the model. For training, we downloaded the feature matrices which had been used in *Athena* best submission [4], taking only the indices corresponding to the related samples.

4.3 (Hyper-)Parameters

The high-level structure of the models has been implemented with Keras, while single layers have been written in Tensorflow. (Hyper-)parameters used for training, useful for experiments replication, are reported in Table 3. Concerning vocabulary creation, we included only words occurring more than 7 times. The embedding matrix has been initialized with *word2vec* embeddings[5], which performed better than other set of pre-trained embeddings according to some preliminary experiments. This can be partially explained as *word2vec* embeddings are trained on part of the Google News corpus, thus on the same domain as the FNC-1 dataset. OOV words have been zero-initialized. In order to avoid overfitting, we did not update word vectors during training.

4.4 Evaluation Metrics

As we are not considering the UNR samples, the FNC-1 score would not constitute a good metric, as it distinguishes between related and unrelated samples for scoring[6]. Following Zubiaga et

---

[3]https://www.nltk.org/_modules/nltk/tokenize.html

[4]https://drive.google.com/open?id=0B0-muIdcdTp7UWVyU0duSDRUd3c

[5]https://code.google.com/archive/p/word2vec/

[6]https://github.com/FakeNewsChallenge/fnc-1-baseline/blob/master/utils/score.py

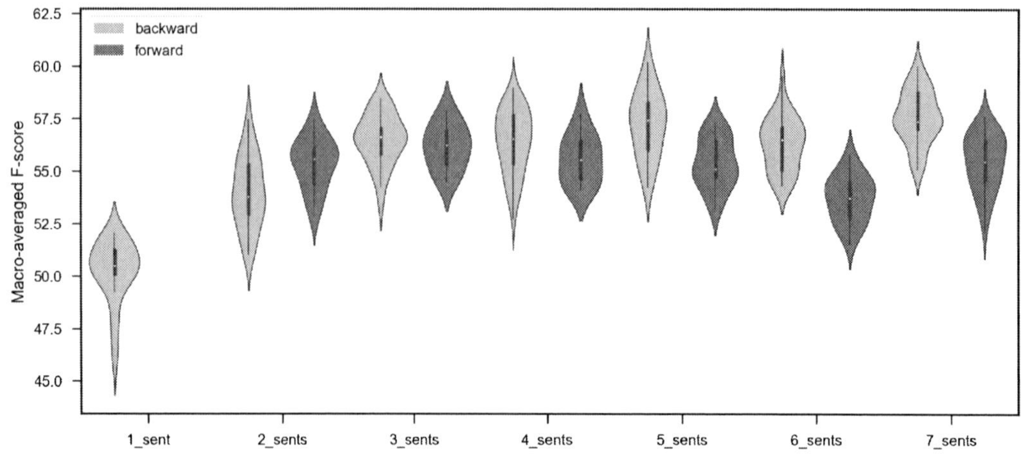

Figure 5: Performance of the co-matching encoder in term of macro-averaged F_1 score on the test set, considering the first n sentences of an article. Blue and red violins represent respectively backward and forward encoding of the considered sentences.

al. (2018) and Hanselowski et al. (2018), we use macro-average precision, recall and F_1 measure, which is less affected by the high class unbalance (Table 1). We also consider the accuracy with respect to the single AGR, DSG and DSC classes.

5 Results and Discussion

As shown in Table 4, both encoders described in Section 3 outperformed the baseline (line 1), despite having a considerably minor number of parameters. In particular, the feature-based model obtained a relatively good performance in classifying the very infrequent DSG labels, probably thanks to its large number of hand-engineered features. However, it shows some difficulties in discriminating between AGR and DSC samples. This is probably a consequence of the system flattening the entire article into a fixed-size vector: this inevitably causes the system to loose the subtle nuances in the argumentative structure of the news story, which allows for distinguishing between AGR and DSC samples, and to favor the most common DSC class. On the contrary, our architectures approach the asymmetry in length in the input by carefully encoding the articles as a hierarchical sequence of sentences, and by separately modeling their relative positions with respect to the headline. In this way, they are able to successfully discriminate between AGR and DSC samples.

In general, the encoder based on co-matching attention performed clearly better than the architecture based on double-conditional encoding (line

2 and 10), reaching a higher performance in all metrics but the classification of the DSC samples.

5.1 Modeling the *Inverted Pyramid*

In order to test our assumption that the great majority of the FNC-1 corpus were written following the *inverted pyramid* style, we took the co-matching attention model, which performed better than the double-conditionally encoded architecture, and progressively reducing the number of considered sentences. Moreover, we modified the article encoder (Subsection 3.1) in order to process the input sequence in forward and not in backward order. For each of these 13 settings[7], we run 10 simulations.

As the violin plots in Figure 5 show (blue violins), considering a reduced number sentences does not correlate with an overly big drop in performance, until a number of less than four sentences is taken. Below this threshold, the ability of the system to correctly classify the stance of the article is compromised. This can be explained with the inverted pyramid theory: until we consider a number of sentences sufficient in order to include the *lead* and part of the *body* of the article, the system can rely on a sufficient number of elements in order to discriminate its stance. On the contrary, if we consider only the very first sentences, the system can get confused, being exposed to only

---

[7]Specifically: 7 backward-encoded co-matching architectures (considering a number of sentences from 1 up to 7) and 6 forward-encoded co-matching architectures (considering a number of sentences from 2 up to 7).

	Model		anonymized input	accuracy			macro-averaged		
				AGR	DSG	DSC	P	R	F_1
1	Baseline		–	26.69	11.76	74.77	39.39	37.74	38.00
2	Double-conditional Encoding	–	no	68.84	9.61	**77.42**	52.50	51.25	49.81
3		–	yes	63.11	9.76	76.03	52.31	49.63	**51.77**
4		+ char	no	51.45	**23.96**	76.32	50.12	50.57	50.32
5		+ char	yes	59.64	16.93	77.64	53.27	**51.40**	51.38
6		+ ner	no	69.57	5.02	76.97	52.14	51.22	48.86
7		+ ner	yes	75.78	9.33	69.96	54.41	51.31	51.17
8		+ char + ner	no	62.11	13.20	77.11	52.83	50.80	50.42
9		+ char + ner	yes	**76.77***	12.34	67.47	**53.45**	49.85	50.56
10	Co-matching attention	–	no	69.57	**33.0***	74.91	**64.14***	**58.53***	**59.01***
11		–	yes	64.37	29.27	**78.94***	59.64	55.20	57.12
12		+ char	no	**74.46**	24.82	71.95	61.77	56.46	58.55
13		+ char	yes	70.52	15.06	76.39	63.88	55.23	56.01
14		+ ner	no	66.05	18.79	72.38	58.51	51.48	52.52
15		+ ner	yes	69.42	31.85	72.38	58.59	54.67	57.32
16		+ char + ner	no	63.95	20.95	77.76	57.32	53.10	53.90
17		+ char + ner	yes	67.26	11.05	76.99	57.19	51.84	54.85

Table 4: Results of experiments using double-conditional encoding or co-matching attention. Best results for each encoding type are shown in bold. Best results overall are indicated with an asterisk.

a portion of the (sometimes opposing) opinions expressed in the article. Interestingly, our system seems to be pretty robust to the noisy sentences which could be included when considering a higher number of sentences.

The assumption that most of the articles in the FNC-1 corpus are written following the *inverted pyramid* principles is further confirmed by the fact that, after the threshold of 4 considered sentences, simulations using forward encoding perform always consistently worse than using backwards encoding (the red violins in Figure 5). Reasonably, below this threshold, we do not observe a considerable difference in performance between backward and forward models.

5.2 Additional Experiments

5.2.1 Using additional Input Channels

To investigate the impact of features other than word embeddings, we consider two further input channels:

- **Named Entities (NE)** - NEs were obtained using the Stanford NE Recognizer (Finkel et al., 2005), resulting in a tagset of 13 labels.
- **Characters** - Each input word was split into characters. Only characters occurring more than 100 times in the training set were considered, obtaining a final vocabulary of 149 characters. As in Lample et al. (2016), in we concatenate the output of a BiLSTM run over the character sequence.

The output of each input channel is concatenated with the word embedding, and passed to the article encoder described in Section 3.1. Hyperparameters used for experiments are reported in Table 3.

5.2.2 Anonymizing the input

After manual analysis of the predictions, we suspected that some models could have spotted some correlations between certain Named Entities and a specific stance in the training set. Some of those correlations are well known and can be useful in veracity detection (Wang, 2017). In this paper, however, we wanted to train a model for stance detection only based on its language understanding, without counting on such possibly accidental correlations.

In order to avoid the systems to rely on chance correlations, which would not generalize on the test set, we modified the input sequences by substituting all input tokens labeled as <PERSON>, <ORGANIZATION> and <LOCATION> by the Stanford Named Entity Recognizer with the corresponding NE tags.

5.2.3 Results

Results of experiments concatenating the previously mentioned features to the word embedding input to both architectures are reported in Table 4 (even lines). In general, using NE embeddings alone with word embeddings was not beneficial for both models. Considering the architecture based on double-conditional encoding, using both characters and NE features actually lead to (sometimes small) improvements in almost all considered evaluation metrics. Moving to the architecture using co-matching attention, adding characters or NE embeddings, even in combination, caused a considerable drop in all evaluation metrics, apart on some single label classification (as the AGR class).

As shown in Table 4 (odd lines), anonymizing the input was always useful for the architecture using double-conditional encoding, resulting in a consistently higher macro-averaged F_1 score. Considering the architecture based on co-matching attention, however, anonymizing the input was beneficial only for architectures leveraging NE tags (only with word embeddings, or in combination with character embeddings), which were also the ones showing the highest drop in performance with respect to the model using only word embeddings.

The best performance according to macro-averaged precision, recall and F_1 score is obtained using the co-matching attention model leveraging only word embeddings. The high performance of this model is mainly due to its ability to discriminate the very unfrequent DSG class.

6 Conclusions

We proposed two simple architectures for Cross-Level Stance Detection, which were carefully designed to model the internal structure of a news article and its relations with a claim. Results show that our "journalistically"-motivated approach can beat a strong feature-based baseline, without relying on any language-specific resources other than word embeddings. This indicates that an interdisciplinary dialogue between Natural Language Processing and Journalism Studies can be very fruitful for fighting Fake News.

In future work, we aim to put together the different stages of the FND pipeline. Following the work of Kochkina et al. (2018) for RV, it could be interesting to compare a sequential approach to separately solve each step of the pipeline in isolation, with a joint multi-task system. The generalizability of the models trained on the FND pipeline to other domains could be tested with the recently released ARC corpus (Hanselowski et al., 2018), which has similar statistical characteristics as the FNC-1 corpus.

Acknowledgments

Special thanks to Chiara Severgnini, journalist at 7 (the weekly magazine supplement of *Corriere della Sera*) for her comments on Section 2.2. The first author (CC) would like to thank the Siemens Machine Intelligence Group (CT RDA BAM MIC-DE, Munich) and the NERC DREAM CDT (grant no. 1945246) for partially funding this work. The third author (NC) is grateful for support from the UK EPSRC (grant no. EP/MOO5089/1). We thank the anonymous reviewers of this paper for their efforts and for the constructive comments and suggestions.

References

Ahmet Aker, Leon Derczynski, and Kalina Bontcheva. 2017. Simple open stance classification for rumour analysis. In *Proceedings of the International Conference Recent Advances in Natural Language Processing, RANLP 2017, Varna, Bulgaria, September 2 - 8, 2017*, pages 31–39.

Isabelle Augenstein, Tim Rocktäschel, Andreas Vlachos, and Kalina Bontcheva. 2016. Stance detection with bidirectional conditional encoding. In *Proceedings of the 2016 Conference on Empirical Methods in Natural Language Processing, EMNLP 2016, Austin, Texas, USA, November 1-4, 2016*, pages 876–885.

Sean Baird, Doug Sibley, and Yuxi Pan. 2017. Talos targets disinformation with fake news challenge victory. https://blog.talosintelligence.com/2017/06/.

Leon Derczynski, Kalina Bontcheva, Maria Liakata, Rob Procter, Geraldine Wong Sak Hoi, and Arkaitz Zubiaga. 2017. Semeval-2017 task 8: Rumoureval: Determining rumour veracity and support for rumours. In *Proceedings of the 11th International Workshop on Semantic Evaluation, SemEval@ACL 2017, Vancouver, Canada, August 3-4, 2017*, pages 69–76.

William Ferreira and Andreas Vlachos. 2016. Emergent: a novel data-set for stance classification. In *Proceedings of the 2016 conference of the North American chapter of the association for computational linguistics: Human language technologies*, pages 1163–1168.

Jenny Rose Finkel, Trond Grenager, and Christopher Manning. 2005. Incorporating non-local information into information extraction systems by gibbs sampling. In *Proceedings of the 43rd annual meeting on association for computational linguistics*, pages 363–370. Association for Computational Linguistics.

Andreas Hanselowski, PVS Avinesh, Benjamin Schiller, and Felix Caspelherr. 2017. Description of the system developed by team athene in the fnc-1. Technical report, Technical report.

Andreas Hanselowski, Avinesh P. V. S., Benjamin Schiller, Felix Caspelherr, Debanjan Chaudhuri, Christian M. Meyer, and Iryna Gurevych. 2018. A retrospective analysis of the fake news challenge stance-detection task. In *Proceedings of the 27th International Conference on Computational Linguistics, COLING 2018, Santa Fe, New Mexico, USA, August 20-26, 2018*, pages 1859–1874.

David Jurgens, Mohammad Taher Pilehvar, and Roberto Navigli. 2014. Semeval-2014 task 3: Cross-level semantic similarity. In *Proceedings of the 8th international workshop on semantic evaluation (SemEval 2014)*, pages 17–26.

Elena Kochkina, Maria Liakata, and Arkaitz Zubiaga. 2018. All-in-one: Multi-task learning for rumour verification. In *Proceedings of the 27th International Conference on Computational Linguistics, COLING 2018, Santa Fe, New Mexico, USA, August 20-26, 2018*, pages 3402–3413.

Guillaume Lample, Miguel Ballesteros, Sandeep Subramanian, Kazuya Kawakami, and Chris Dyer. 2016. Neural architectures for named entity recognition. In *NAACL HLT 2016, The 2016 Conference of the North American Chapter of the Association for Computational Linguistics: Human Language Technologies, San Diego California, USA, June 12-17, 2016*, pages 260–270.

Saif Mohammad, Svetlana Kiritchenko, Parinaz Sobhani, Xiaodan Zhu, and Colin Cherry. 2016. Semeval-2016 task 6: Detecting stance in tweets. In *Proceedings of the 10th International Workshop on Semantic Evaluation (SemEval-2016)*, pages 31–41.

Saif M Mohammad, Parinaz Sobhani, and Svetlana Kiritchenko. 2017. Stance and sentiment in tweets. *ACM Transactions on Internet Technology (TOIT)*, 17(3):26.

Dean Pomerleau and Delip Rao. 2017. Fake news challenge. `http://www.fakenewschallenge.org/`.

Benjamin Riedel, Isabelle Augenstein, Georgios P Spithourakis, and Sebastian Riedel. 2017. A simple but tough-to-beat baseline for the fake news challenge stance detection task. *arXiv preprint arXiv:1707.03264*.

Christopher Scanlan. 1999. *Reporting and writing: Basics for the 21st century*. Oxford University Press.

Sun Technical Publications. 2003. *Read Me First!: A Style Guide for the Computer Industry*. Prentice Hall Professional.

James Thorne and Andreas Vlachos. 2018. Automated fact checking: Task formulations, methods and future directions. In *Proceedings of the 27th International Conference on Computational Linguistics, COLING 2018, Santa Fe, New Mexico, USA, August 20-26, 2018*, pages 3346–3359.

Shuohang Wang, Mo Yu, Jing Jiang, and Shiyu Chang. 2018. A co-matching model for multi-choice reading comprehension. In *Proceedings of the 56th Annual Meeting of the Association for Computational Linguistics, ACL 2018, Melbourne, Australia, July 15-20, 2018, Volume 2: Short Papers*, pages 746–751.

William Yang Wang. 2017. "liar, liar pants on fire": A new benchmark dataset for fake news detection. In *Proceedings of the 55th Annual Meeting of the Association for Computational Linguistics, ACL 2017, Vancouver, Canada, July 30 - August 4, Volume 2: Short Papers*, pages 422–426.

Zichao Yang, Diyi Yang, Chris Dyer, Xiaodong He, Alex Smola, and Eduard Hovy. 2016. Hierarchical attention networks for document classification. In *Proceedings of the 2016 Conference of the North American Chapter of the Association for Computational Linguistics: Human Language Technologies*, pages 1480–1489.

Arkaitz Zubiaga, Ahmet Aker, Kalina Bontcheva, Maria Liakata, and Rob Procter. 2018. Detection and resolution of rumours in social media: A survey. *ACM Computing Surveys (CSUR)*, 51(2):32.

Arkaitz Zubiaga, Elena Kochkina, Maria Liakata, Rob Procter, and Michal Lukasik. 2016a. Stance classification in rumours as a sequential task exploiting the tree structure of social media conversations. In *COLING 2016, 26th International Conference on Computational Linguistics, Proceedings of the Conference: Technical Papers, December 11-16, 2016, Osaka, Japan*, pages 2438–2448.

Arkaitz Zubiaga, Maria Liakata, Rob Procter, Geraldine Wong Sak Hoi, and Peter Tolmie. 2016b. Analysing how people orient to and spread rumours in social media by looking at conversational threads. *PloS one*, 11(3):e0150989.

Belittling the Source:
Trustworthiness Indicators to Obfuscate Fake News on the Web

Diego Esteves
SDA Research
University of Bonn, Germany
`esteves@cs.uni-bonn.de`

Aniketh Janardhan Reddy[+,*]
Carnegie Mellon University
Pittsburgh, USA
`ajreddy@cs.cmu.edu`

Piyush Chawla[*]
The Ohio State University
Ohio, USA
`chawla.81@osu.edu`

Jens Lehmann
SDA Research / Fraunhofer IAIS
University of Bonn, Germany
`jens.lehmann@cs.uni-bonn.de`

Abstract

With the growth of the internet, the number of *fake-news* online has been proliferating every year. The consequences of such phenomena are manifold, ranging from lousy decision-making process to bullying and violence episodes. Therefore, fact-checking algorithms became a valuable asset. To this aim, an important step to detect fake-news is to have access to a credibility score for a given information source. However, most of the widely used Web indicators have either been shutdown to the public (e.g., Google PageRank) or are not free for use (Alexa Rank). Further existing databases are short-manually curated lists of online sources, which do not scale. Finally, most of the research on the topic is theoretical-based or explore confidential data in a restricted simulation environment. In this paper we explore current research, highlight the challenges and propose solutions to tackle the problem of classifying websites into a credibility scale. The proposed model automatically extracts source reputation cues and computes a credibility factor, providing valuable insights which can help in belittling dubious and confirming trustful unknown websites. Experimental results outperform state of the art in the 2-classes and 5-classes setting.

1 Introduction

With the enormous daily growth of the Web, the number of *fake-news* sources have also been increasing considerably (Li et al., 2012). This social network era has provoked a communication revolution that boosted the spread of misinformation, hoaxes, lies and questionable claims. The proliferation of unregulated sources of information allows any person to become an opinion provider with no restrictions. For instance, websites spreading manipulative political content or hoaxes can be persuasive. To tackle this problem, different *fact-checking* tools and frameworks have been proposed (Zubiaga et al., 2017), mainly divided into two categories: *fact-checking* over natural language claims (Thorne and Vlachos, 2018) and *fact-checking* over knowledge bases, i.e., triple-based approaches (Esteves et al., 2018). Overall, *fact-checking* algorithms aim at determining the veracity of claims, which is considered a very challenging task due to the nature of underlying steps, from natural language understanding (e.g. *argumentation mining*) to common-sense verification (i.e., humans have prior knowledge that makes far easier to judge which arguments are plausible and which are not). Yet an important underlying fact-checking step relies upon computing the credibility of sources of information, i.e. indicators that allow answering the question: *"How reliable is a given provider of information?"*. Due to the obvious importance of the Web and the negative impact that misinformation can cause, methods to demote the importance of websites also become a valuable asset. In this sense the high number of new websites appearing at everyday (Netcraft, 2016), make straightforward approaches - such as *blacklists* and *whitelists* - impractical. Moreover, such approaches are not designed to compute credibility scores for a given website but rather to binary label them. Thus, they aim at detecting mostly "fake" (threatening) websites; e.g., *phishing detection*, which is out of scope of this work. Thus, open credibility models have a great importance, especially due to the increase of fake news being propagated. There is much research into credibility factors. However, they are mostly grouped as follows: (1) theoretical research on psychological aspects of credibility and (2) experiments performed over private

---

[+]Work was completed while the author was a student at the Birla Institute of Technology and Science, India and was interning at SDA Research.

[*]These two authors contributed equally to this work.

Proceedings of the First Workshop on Fact Extraction and VERification (FEVER), pages 50–59
Brussels, Belgium, November 1, 2018. ©2018 Association for Computational Linguistics

and confidential users information, mostly from web browser activities (strongly supported by private companies). Therefore, while (1) lacks practical results (2) report *findings* which are not much appealing to the broad open-source community, given the non-open characteristic of the conducted experiments and data privacy. Finally, recent research on credibility has also pointed out important drawbacks, as follows:

1. Manual (human) annotation of credibility indicators for a set of websites is costly (Haas and Unkel, 2017).

2. Search engine results page (SERP) do not provide more than few information cues (URL, title and snippet) and the dominant heuristic happens to be the search engine (SE) rank itself (Haas and Unkel, 2017).

3. Only around 42.67% of the websites are covered by the credibility evaluation knowledge base, where most domains have a low credibility confidence (Liu et al., 2015)

Therefore, automated credibility models play an important role in the community - although not broadly explored yet, in practice. In this paper, we focus on designing computational models to predict the credibility of a given website rather than performing sociological experiments or experiments with end users (simulations). In this scenario, we expect that a website from a domain such as `bbc.com` gets a higher trustworthiness score compared to one from `wordpress.com`, for instance.

2 Related Work

Credibility is an important research subject in several different communities and has been the subject of study over the past decades. Most of the research, however, focuses on theoretical aspects of credibility and its persuasive effect on different fundamental problems, such as economic theories (Sobel, 1985).

2.1 Fundamental Research

A thorough examination of psychological aspects in evaluating documents credibility has been studied (Fogg and Tseng, 1999; Fogg et al., 2001, 2003), which reports numerous challenges. Apart from sociological experiments, *Web Credibility* -
in a more practical perspective - has a different focus of research, described as follows:

Rating Systems, Simulations are mostly platform-based solutions to conduct experiments (mostly using private data) in order to detect credibility factors. Nakamura et al. (2007) surveyed internet users from all age groups to understand how they identified trustworthy websites. Based on the results of this survey, they built a graph-based ranking method which helped users in gauging the trustworthiness of search results retrieved by a search engine when issued a query Q. A study by Stanford University revealed important factors that people notice when assessing website credibility (Fogg et al., 2003), mostly visual aspects (*web site design*, *look* and *information design*). The *writing style* and *bias of information* play a small role as defining the level of credibility (selected by approximately 10% of the comments). However, this process of evaluating the credibility of web pages by users is impacted only by the number of heuristics they are aware of (Fogg, 2003), biasing the human evaluation w.r.t. a limited and specific set features. An important factor considered by humans to judge credibility relies on the search engine results page (SERP). The higher ranked a website is when compared to other retrieved websites the more credible people judge a website to be (Schwarz and Morris, 2011). Popularity is yet another major credibility factor (Giudice, 2010). Liu et al. (2015) proposed to integrate recommendation functionality into a Web Credibility Evaluation System (WCES), focusing on the user's feedback. Shah et al. (2015) propose a full list of important features for credibility aspects, such as 1) the quality of the design of the website and 2) how well the information is structured. In particular, the perceived accuracy of the information was ranked only in 6th place. Thus, superficial website characteristics as heuristics play a key role in credibility evaluation. Dong et al (2015) propose a different method (KBT) to estimate the trustworthiness of a web source based on the information given by the source (i.e., applies fact-checking to infer credibility). This information is represented in the form of triples extracted from the web source. The trustworthiness of the source is determined by the correctness of the triples extracted. Thus, the score is computed based on *endogenous* (e.g., correctness of facts) signals rather then *exogenous* signals (e.g., links).

Unfortunately, this research from Google does not provide open data. It is worth mentioning that - surprisingly - their hypothesis (content is more important than visual) contradicts previous research findings (Fogg et al., 2003; Shah et al., 2015). While this might be due to the dynamic characteristic of the Web, this contradiction highlights the need for more research into the real use of web credibility factors w.r.t. automated web credibility models. Similar to (Nakamura et al., 2007), Singal and Kohli (2016) proposes a tool (dubbed TNM) to re-rank URLs extracted from Google search engine according to the trust maintained by the actual users). Apart from the search engine API, their tool uses several other APIs to collect website usage information (e.g., traffic and engagement info). (Kakol et al., 2017) perform extensive crowdsourcing experiments that contain credibility evaluations, textual comments, and labels for these comments.

SPAM/phishing detection: Abbasi et al. (2010) propose a set of design guidelines which advocated the development of SLT-based classification systems for fraudulent website detection, i.e., despite seeming credible - websites that try to obtain private information and defraud visitors. PhishZoo (Afroz and Greenstadt, 2011) is a phishing detection system which helps users in identifying phishing websites which look similar to a given set of protected websites through the creation of profiles.

2.2 Automated Web Credibility

Automated Web Credibility models for website classification are not broadly explored, in practice. The aim is to produce a predictive model given training data (annotated website ranks) regardless of an input query Q. Existing gold standard data is generated from surveys and simulations (see *Rating Systems, Simulations* related work). Currently, state of the art (SOTA) experiments rely on the Microsoft Credibility dataset[1] (Schwarz and Morris, 2011). Recent research use the website label (Likert scale) released in the Microsoft dataset as a gold standard to train automated web credibility models, as follows:

Olteanu et al. (2013) proposes a number of properties (37 linguistic and textual features) and

---

[1]It is worth mentioning that this survey is mostly based on confidential data and it is not available to the open community (e.g., overall popularity, popularity among domain experts, geo-location of users and number of awards)

applies machine learning methods to recognize trust levels, obtaining 22 relevant features for the task. Wawer et al. (2014) improve this work using psychosocial and psycholinguistic features (through The General Inquirer (GI) Lexical Database (Stone and Hunt, 1963)) achieving state of the art results.

Finally, another resource is the Content Credibility Corpus (C3) (Kakol et al., 2017), the largest Web credibility Corpus publicity available so far. However, in this work authors did not perform experiments w.r.t. *automated credibility models* using a standard measure (i.e., Likert scale), such as in (Olteanu et al., 2013; Wawer et al., 2014). Instead, they rather focused on evaluating the theories of web credibility in order to produce a much larger and richer corpus.

3 Experimental Setup

3.1 State-of-the-art (SOTA) Features

Recent research on credibility factors for web sites (Olteanu et al., 2013) have initially divided the features into the following logical groups:

1. **Content-based** (25 features): number of special characters in the text, spelling errors, web site category and etc..

    (a) **Text** (20 features)
    (b) **Appearance** (4 features)
    (c) **Meta-information** (1 feature)

2. **Social-based** (12 features): Social Media Metadata (e.g., Facebook shares, Tweets pointing to a certain URL, etc.), Page Rank, Alexa Rank and similar.

    (a) **Social Popularity** (9 features)
    (b) **General Popularity** (1 feature)
    (c) **Link structure** (2 features)

According to (Olteanu et al., 2013), a resultant number of 22 features (out of 37) were selected as most significant (10 for **content-based** and all **social-based** features). Surprisingly (but also following (Dong et al., 2015)), none from the subgroup **Appearance**, although studies have systematically shown the opposite, i.e., that visual aspects are one of the most important features (Fogg et al., 2003; Shah et al., 2015; Haas and Unkel, 2017).

In this picture, we claim the most negative aspect is the reliance on **Social-based** features. This dependency not only affects the final performance of the credibility model, but also implies in financial costs as well as presenting high discriminative capacity, adding a strong bias to the performance of the model[2]. The computation of these features relies heavily on external (e.g., Facebook API[3] and AdBlock[4]) and commercial libraries (Alchemy[5], PageRank[6], Alexa Rank[7]. Thus, engineering and financial costs are a must. Furthermore, popularity on Facebook or Twitter can be measured only by data owners. Additionally, vendors may change the underlying algorithms without further explanation. Therefore, also following Wawer et al. (2014), in this paper we have excluded **Social-based** features from our experimental setup.

On top of that, (Wawer et al., 2014) incremented the model, adding features extracted from the General Inquirer (GI) Lexical Database, resulting in a vector of 183 extra categories, apart from the selected 22 base features, i.e. total of 205 features (However, this is subject to contradictions. Please see Section 4.1 for more information).

3.2 Datasets

3.2.1 Website credibility evaluation

Microsoft Dataset (Schwarz and Morris, 2011) consists of thousands of URLs and their credibility ratings (five-point Likert Scale[8]), ranging from 1 ("very non-credible") to 5 ("very credible"). In this study, participants were asked to rate the websites as credible following the definition: *"A credible webpage is one whose information one can accept as the truth without needing to look elsewhere"*. Studies by (Olteanu et al., 2013; Wawer et al., 2014) use this dataset for evaluation. **Content Credibility Corpus (C3)**[9] is the most recent and the largest credibility dataset currently publicly available for research (Kakol et al., 2017). It contains 15.750 evaluations of 5.543 URLs from 2.041 participants with some additional information about website characteristics and basic demographic features of users. Among many metadata information existing in the dataset, in this work we are only interested in the URLs and their re-

spective five-point Likert scale, so that we obtain the same information available in the Microsoft dataset.

3.2.2 Fact-checking influence

In order to verify the impact of our web credibility model in a real use-case scenario, we ran a fact-checking framework to verify a set of input claims. Then we collected the sources (URLs) containing proofs to support a given claim. We used this as a dataset to evaluate our web credibility model.

The primary objective is to verify whether our model is able, on average, to assign *lower* scores to the websites that contain *proofs* supporting *claims* which are labeled as *false* in the FactBench dataset (i.e., the source is providing false information, thus should have a lower credibility score). Similarly, we expect that websites that support *positive* claims are assigned with higher scores (i.e., the source is supporting an accurate claim, thus should have a higher credibility score).

The (gold standard) input claims were obtained from the **FactBench** dataset[10], a multilingual benchmark for the evaluation of fact validation algorithms. It contains a set of RDF[11] models (10 different relations), where each model contains a singular fact expressed as a *subject-predicate-object* triple. The data was automatically extracted from DBpedia and Freebase KBs, and manually curated in order to generate true and false examples.

The website list extraction was carried out by DeFacto (Gerber et al., 2015), a fact-checking framework designed for RDF KBs. DeFacto returns a set of websites as pieces of evidence to support its prediction (true or false) for a given input claim.

3.3 Final Features

We implemented a set of **Content-based** features (Section 3.1) adding more lexical and textual based features. **Social-based** features were not considered due to financial costs associated with paid APIs. The final set of features for each website w is defined as follows:

1. *Web Archive*: the temporal information w.r.t. cache and freshness. Δ_b and Δ_e correspond to the temporal differences of the first and last 2 updates, respectively. Δ_a represents the age of w and finally Δ_u represents the temporal difference for

---

the last update to today. γ is a penalization factor when the information is obtained from the *domain* of w (w_d) instead w.

$$f_{arc}(w) = \left(\left[\frac{1}{\log(\Delta_b \times \Delta_e)} + \log(\Delta_a) + \frac{1}{\Delta_u}\right]\right) \times \gamma$$

2. *Domain*: refers to the (encoded) domain w (e.g. org)

3. *Authority*: searches for authoritative keywords within the page HTML content w_c (e.g., contact email, business address, etc..)

4. *Outbound Links*: searches the number of different outbound links in $w \wedge w_d \in d$, i.e., $\sum_{n=1}^{P} \phi(w_c)$ where P is the number of web-based protocols.

5. *Text Category*: returns a vector containing the probabilities P for each pre-trained category c of w w.r.t. the sentences of the website w_s and page title w_t: $\sum_{s=1}^{w_s} \gamma(s)^\frown \gamma(w_t)$. We trained a set of binary multinomial Naive Bayes (NB) classifiers, one per class, as follows: *business, entertainment, politics, religion, sports* and *tech*.

6. *Text Category - LexRank*: reduces the noisy of w_b by classifying only top N sentences generated by applying LexRank (Erkan and Radev, 2004) over w_b ($Sl = \Gamma(w_b, N)$), which is a graph-based text summarizing technique: $\sum_{sl=1}^{Sl} \gamma(sl)^\frown \gamma(w_t)$.

7. *Text Category - LSA*: similarly, we apply Latent Semantic Analysis (LSA) (Steinberger and Jeek, 2004) to detect semantically important sentences in w_b ($Sl = \Omega(w_b, N)$): $\sum_{sl=1}^{Sl} \gamma(sl)^\frown \gamma(w_t)$.

8. *Readability Metrics*: returns a vector resulting of the concatenation of several R readability metrics (Si and Callan, 2001)

9. *SPAM*: detects whether the w_b or w_t are classified as spam: $\psi(w_b)^\frown \psi(w_t)$

10. *Social Tags*: returns the frequency of social tags in w_b: $\bigcup_{i=1}^{R} \varphi(i, w_b)$

11. *OpenSources*: returns the open-source classification (x) for a given website:

$$x = \begin{cases} 1, & \text{if } w \in \mathcal{O} \\ 0, & \text{if } w \notin \mathcal{O} \end{cases}$$

12. *PageRankCC*: PageRank information computed through the CommonCrawl[12] Corpus

13. *General Inquirer* (Stone and Hunt, 1963): a 182-lenght vector containing several lexicons

14. *Vader Lexicon*: lexicon and rule-based sentiment analysis tool that is specifically attuned to sentiments

15. *HTML2Seq*: we introduce the concept of *bag-of-tags*, where similarly to *bag-of-words*[13] we group the HTML tag occurrences in each web site. We additionally explore this concept along with a sequence problem, i.e. we encode the tags and evaluate this considering a window size (offset) from the header of the page.

4 Experiments

Previous research proposes two **application settings** w.r.t. the classification itself, as follows: (A.1) casting the credibility problem as a classification problem and (A.2) evaluating the credibility on a five-point Likert scale (regression). In the classification scenario, the models are evaluated both w.r.t. the 2-classes as well as 3-classes. In the 2-classes scenario, websites ranging from 1 to 3 are labeled as "low" whereas 4 and 5 are labeled as "high" (credibility). Analogously, in the 3-classes scenario, websites labeled as 1 and 2 are converted to "low", 3 remains as "medium" while 4 and 5 are grouped into the "high" class.

We first explore the impact of the *bag-of-tags* strategy. We encode and convert the tags into a sequence of tags, similar to a sequence of sentences (looking for opening and closing tags, e.g., <a>and </a>). Therefore, we perform document classification over the resulting vectors. Figures 1a to 1d show results of this strategy for both 2 and 3-classes scenarios. The x-axis is the log scale of the paddings (i.e., the offset of HTML tags we retrieved from w, ranging from 25 to 10.000). The charts reveal an interesting pattern in both gold-standard datasets (Microsoft Dataset and C3 Corpus): the first tags are the most relevant to predict the credibility class. Although this strategy does not achieve state of the art performance[14], it presents reasonable performance by just inspecting website metadata: F1-measures = 0.690 and 0.571 for the 2-classes and 3-classes settings, respectively. However, it is worth mentioning that the main advantage of this approach lies in the fact that it is language agnostic (while current research

---

[12]http://commoncrawl.org/

[13]https://en.wikipedia.org/wiki/Bag-of-words_model

[14]F1 measures = 0.745 (2-classes) and 0.652 (3-classes).

Microsoft Dataset
(Gradient Boosting, $K = 25$)

Class	Precision	Recall	F1
low	0.851	0.588	0.695
high	0.752	0.924	0.829
weighted	0.794	0.781	0.772
micro	0.781	0.781	0.781
macro	0.801	0.756	0.762

C3 Corpus
(AdaBoost, $K = 75$)

Class	Precision	Recall	F1
low	0.558	0.355	0.434
high	0.732	0.862	0.792
weighted	0.675	0.695	0.674
micro	0.695	0.695	0.695
macro	0.645	0.609	0.613

Table 1: Text+HTML2Seq features (2-class): best classifier performance

Microsoft Dataset
(Gradient Boosting, $K = 75$)

Class	Precision	Recall	F1
low	0.567	0.447	0.500
medium	0.467	0.237	0.315
high	0.714	0.916	0.803
weighted	0.626	0.662	0.626
micro	0.662	0.662	0.662
macro	0.583	0.534	0.539

C3 Corpus
(AdaBoost, $K = 100$)

Class	Precision	Recall	F1
low	0.143	0.031	0.051
medium	0.410	0.177	0.247
high	0.701	0.916	0.794
weighted	0.583	0.660	0.598
micro	0.660	0.660	0.660
macro	0.418	0.375	0.364

Table 2: Text+HTML2Seq features (3-class): best classifier performance

focuses on English) as well as less susceptible to overfitting.

We then evaluate the performance of the textual features (Section 3.3) isolated. Results for the 2-classes scenario are presented as follows: Figure 2a highlights the best models performance using textual features only. While this as a single feature does not outperform the lexical features, when we combine the *bag-of-tags* approach (predictions of probabilities for each class) we boost the performance (F1 from 0.738 to 0.772) and outperform state of the art (0.745), as shown in Figure 2b. Tables 1 to 3 shows detailed results for both datasets (2-classes, 3-classes and 5-classes configurations, respectively). For 5-class regression, we found that the *best pad = 100* for the Microsoft dataset and *best pad = 175* for the C3 Corpus. We preceded the computing of both classification and regression models with feature selection according to a percentile of the highest scoring features (*SelectKBest*). We tested the choice of 3, 5, 10, 25, 50 75 and K=100 percentiles (thus, no selection) of features and did not find a unique K value for every case. It is worth noticing that in general it is easy to detect high credible sources (F1 for "high" class around 0.80 in all experiments and both datasets) but recall of "low" credible sources is still an issue.

Table 4 shows statistics on the data generated by the fact-checking algorithm. For 1500 claims, it collected pieces of evidence for over 27.000 websites. Table 5 depicts the impact of the credibility model in the fact-checking context. We collected a small subset of 186 URLs from the FactBench dataset and manually annotated[15] the credibility for each URL (following the Likert scale). The model corrected labeled around 80% of the URLs associated with a positive claim and, more importantly, 70% of non-credible websites linked to false claims were correctly identified. This helps to minimize the number of non-credible information providers that contain information that supports a *false* claim.

4.1 Discussion

Reproducibility is still one of the cornerstones of science and scientific projects (Baker, 2016). In the following, we list some relevant issues encountered while performing our experiments:

Experimental results: this gap is also observed w.r.t. results reported by (Olteanu et al., 2013), which is acknowledged by (Wawer et al., 2014), despite numerous attempts to replicate experiments. Authors (Wawer et al., 2014) believe this is

---

[15]By four human annotators. In the event of a tie we exclude the URL from the final dataset.

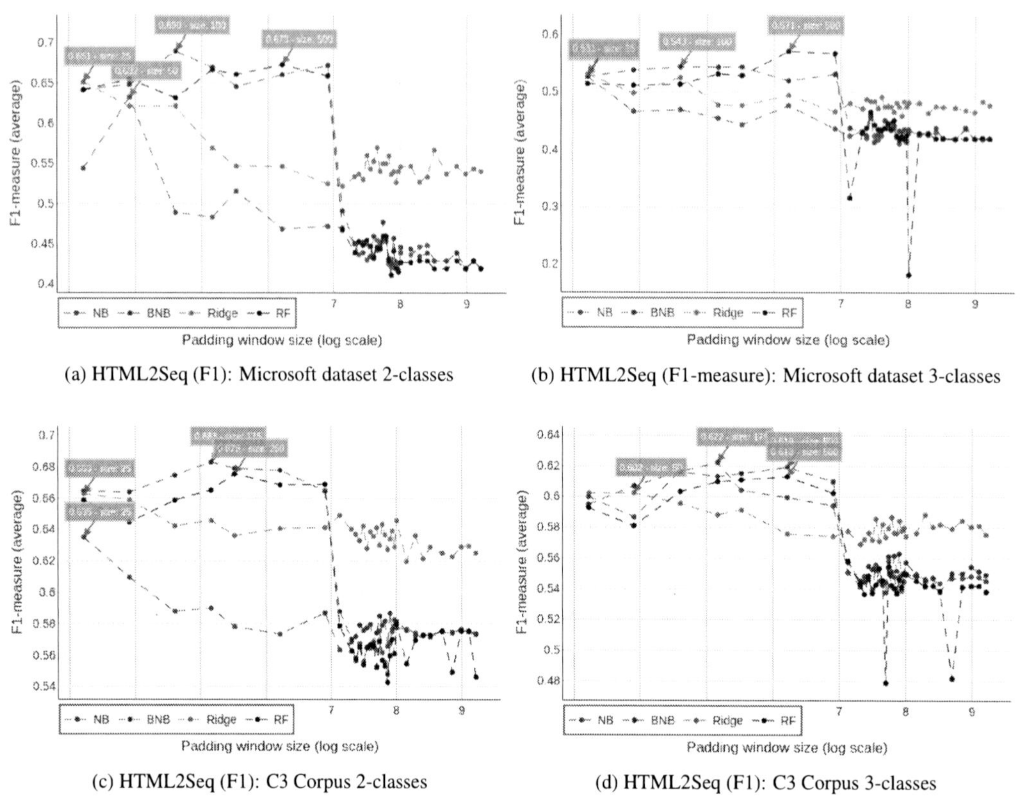

(a) HTML2Seq (F1): Microsoft dataset 2-classes

(b) HTML2Seq (F1-measure): Microsoft dataset 3-classes

(c) HTML2Seq (F1): C3 Corpus 2-classes

(d) HTML2Seq (F1): C3 Corpus 3-classes

Figure 1: HTML2Seq (F1-measure) over different padding sizes.

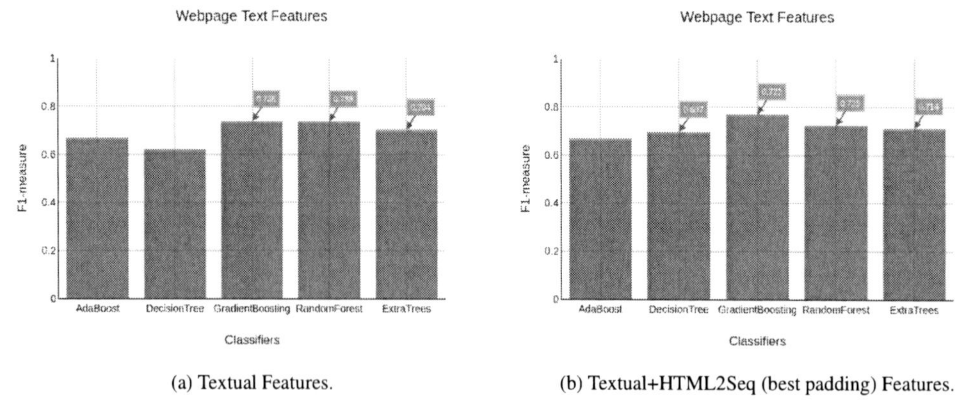

(a) Textual Features.

(b) Textual+HTML2Seq (best padding) Features.

Figure 2: Evaluating distinct classifiers in the 2-classes setting (Microsoft dataset): increasing almost +3% (from 0.745 to 0.772) on average F1 (Gradient Boosting). Feature selection performed with ANOVA *SelectKBest* method, K=0.25.

Microsoft Dataset					
model	K	R^2	RMSE	MAE	EVar
SVR	3	0.232	0.861	0.691	0.238
Ridge	3	0.268	0.841	0.683	0.269
C3 Corpus					
model	K	R^2	RMSE	MAE	EVar
SVR	25	0.096	0.939	0.739	0.102
Ridge	25	0.133	0.920	0.750	0.134

Table 3: Text+HTML2Seq: regression measures (5-class). Selecting top K lexical features.

FactBench (Credibility Model)		
label	**claims**	**sites**
true	750	14.638
false	750	13.186
-	1500	27.824

Table 4: FactBench: Web sites collected from claims.

FactBench (Sample - Human Annotation)				
label	**claims**	**sites**	**non-cred**	**cred**
true	5	96	57	39
false	5	80	48	32
-	10	186	105	71

FactBench (Sample - Credibility Model)				
label	**non-cred**	**%**	**cred**	**%**
true	40	0.81	31	0.79
false	34	0.70	24	0.75

Table 5: FactBench Dataset: analyzing the performance of the credibility model in the fact-checking task.

due to the lack of parameters and hyperparameters explicitly cited in the previous research (Olteanu et al., 2013).

Microsoft dataset: presents inconsistencies. Although all the web pages are cached (in theory) in order to guarantee a deterministic environment, the dataset - in its original form[16] - has a number of problems, as follows: (a) web pages not physically cached (b) URL not matching (dataset links *versus* cached files) (c) Invalid file format (e.g., PDF). Even though these issues have also been previously identified by related research (Olteanu et al., 2013) it is not clear what the URLs for the final dataset (i.e., the support) are nor where this new version is available.

Contradictions: w.r.t. the divergence of the importance of visual features have drawn our attention (Dong et al., 2015) and (Fogg, 2003; Shah et al., 2015) which corroborate to the need of more methods to solve the web credibility problem, in practice. The main hypothesis that supports this contradiction relies on the fact that feature-based credibility evaluation eventually ignites cat-and-mouse play between scientists and people inter-

ested in manipulating the models. In this case, *reinforcement learning* methods pose as a good alternative for adaptation.

Proposed features: The acknowledgement made by authors in (Wawer et al., 2014) that "*solutions based purely on external APIs are difficult to use beyond scientific application and are prone for manipulation*" confirming the need to exclude **social features** from research of (Olteanu et al., 2013) contradicts itself. In the course of experiments, authors mention the usage of all features proposed by (Olteanu et al., 2013): "*Table 1 presents regression results for the dataset described in [13] in its original version (37 features) and extended with 183 variables from the General Inquirer (to 221 features)*".

Therefore, due to the number of relevant issues presented w.r.t. reproducibility and contradiction of arguments, the comparison to recent research becomes more difficult. In this work, we solved the technical issues in the Microsoft dataset and released a new fixed version[17]. Also, since we need to perform evaluations in a deterministic environment, we cached and released the websites for the C3 corpus. After scraping, 2.977 URLs were used (out of 5.543). Others were left due to processing errors (e.g., 404). The algorithms and its hyperparameters and further relevant metadata are available through the MEX Interchange Format (Esteves et al., 2015). By doing this, we provide a computational environment to perform safer comparisons, being engaged in recent discussions about mechanisms to measure and enhance

---

[16]The original dataset can be downloaded from `http://research.microsoft.com/en-us/projects/credibility/`

[17]more information at the project website: `https://github.com/DeFacto/WebCredibility`

the reproducibility of scientific projects (Wilkinson et al., 2016).

5 Conclusion

In this work, we discuss existing alternatives, gaps and current challenges to tackle the problem of web credibility. More specifically, we focused on automated models to compute a credibility factor for a given website. This research follows the former studies presented by (Olteanu et al., 2013; Wawer et al., 2014) and presents several contributions. First, we propose different features to avoid the financial cost imposed by external APIs in order to access website credibility indicators. This issue has become even more relevant in the light of the challenges that have emerged after the shutdown of Google PageRank, for instance. To bridge this gap, we have proposed the concept of bag-of-tags. Similar to (Wawer et al., 2014), we conduct experiments in a highly-dimensional feature space, but also considering web page metadata, which outperforms state of the art results in the 2-classes and 5-classes settings. Second, we identified and fixed several problems on a gold standard dataset for web credibility (Microsoft), as well as indexed several web pages for the C3 Corpus. Finally, we evaluate the impact of the model in a real fact-checking use-case. We show that the proposed model can help in belittling and supporting different websites that contain evidence of true and false claims, which helps the very challenging fact verification task. As future work, we plan to explore deep learning methods over the HTML2Seq module.

Acknowledgments

This research was partially supported by an EU H2020 grant provided for the WDAqua project (GA no. 642795) and by DAAD under the project "International promovieren in Deutschland für alle" (IPID4all).

References

Ahmed Abbasi, Zhu Zhang, David Zimbra, Hsinchun Chen, and Jay F Nunamaker Jr. 2010. Detecting fake websites: the contribution of statistical learning theory. *Mis Quarterly*, pages 435–461.

Sadia Afroz and Rachel Greenstadt. 2011. Phishzoo: Detecting phishing websites by looking at them. *2012 IEEE Sixth International Conference on Semantic Computing*, 00:368–375.

Monya Baker. 2016. 1,500 scientists lift the lid on reproducibility. *Nature News*, 533(7604):452.

Xin Luna Dong, Evgeniy Gabrilovich, Kevin Murphy, Van Dang, Wilko Horn, Camillo Lugaresi, Shaohua Sun, and Wei Zhang. 2015. Knowledge-based trust: Estimating the trustworthiness of web sources. *Proc. VLDB Endow.*, 8(9):938–949.

Günes Erkan and Dragomir R. Radev. 2004. Lexrank: Graph-based lexical centrality as salience in text summarization. *J. Artif. Int. Res.*, 22(1):457–479.

Diego Esteves, Diego Moussallem, Ciro Baron Neto, Tommaso Soru, Ricardo Usbeck, Markus Ackermann, and Jens Lehmann. 2015. Mex vocabulary: A lightweight interchange format for machine learning experiments. In *Proceedings of the 11th International Conference on Semantic Systems*, SEMANTICS '15, pages 169–176, New York, NY, USA. ACM.

Diego Esteves, Anisa Rula, Aniketh Janardhan Reddy, and Jens Lehmann. 2018. Toward veracity assessment in rdf knowledge bases: An exploratory analysis. *Journal of Data and Information Quality (JDIQ)*, 9(3):16.

BJ Fogg, Jonathan Marshall, Othman Laraki, Alex Osipovich, Chris Varma, Nicholas Fang, Jyoti Paul, Akshay Rangnekar, John Shon, Preeti Swani, et al. 2001. What makes web sites credible?: a report on a large quantitative study. In *Proceedings of the SIGCHI conference on Human factors in computing systems*, pages 61–68. ACM.

BJ Fogg and Hsiang Tseng. 1999. The elements of computer credibility. In *Proceedings of the SIGCHI conference on Human Factors in Computing Systems*, pages 80–87. ACM.

Brian J Fogg. 2003. Prominence-interpretation theory: Explaining how people assess credibility online. In *CHI'03 extended abstracts on human factors in computing systems*, pages 722–723. ACM.

Brian J Fogg, Cathy Soohoo, David R Danielson, Leslie Marable, Julianne Stanford, and Ellen R Tauber. 2003. How do users evaluate the credibility of web sites?: a study with over 2,500 participants. In *Proceedings of the 2003 conference on Designing for user experiences*, pages 1–15. ACM.

Daniel Gerber, Diego Esteves, Jens Lehmann, Lorenz Bühmann, Ricardo Usbeck, Axel-Cyrille Ngonga Ngomo, and René Speck. 2015. Defacto - temporal and multilingual deep fact validation. *Web Semantics: Science, Services and Agents on the World Wide Web*.

Katherine Del Giudice. 2010. Crowdsourcing credibility: The impact of audience feedback on web page credibility. In *Proceedings of the 73rd ASIS&T Annual Meeting on Navigating Streams in an Information Ecosystem-Volume 47*, page 59. American Society for Information Science.

Alexander Haas and Julian Unkel. 2017. Ranking versus reputation: perception and effects of search result credibility. *Behaviour & Information Technology*, 36(12):1285–1298.

Michal Kakol, Radoslaw Nielek, and Adam Wierzbicki. 2017. Understanding and predicting web content credibility using the content credibility corpus. *Information Processing & Management*, 53(5):1043–1061.

Xian Li, Xin Luna Dong, Kenneth Lyons, Weiyi Meng, and Divesh Srivastava. 2012. Truth finding on the deep web: Is the problem solved? *Proc. VLDB Endow.*, 6(2):97–108.

Xin Liu, Radoslaw Nielek, Paulina Adamska, Adam Wierzbicki, and Karl Aberer. 2015. Towards a highly effective and robust web credibility evaluation system. *Decision Support Systems*, 79:99–108.

Satoshi Nakamura, Shinji Konishi, Adam Jatowt, Hiroaki Ohshima, Hiroyuki Kondo, Taro Tezuka, Satoshi Oyama, and Katsumi Tanaka. 2007. *Trustworthiness Analysis of Web Search Results*. Springer Berlin Heidelberg, Berlin, Heidelberg.

Netcraft. 2016. Netcraft survey (2016). `http://www.webcitation.org/6lhJlHtez`. Accessed: 2017-10-01.

Alexandra Olteanu, Stanislav Peshterliev, Xin Liu, and Karl Aberer. 2013. Web credibility: features exploration and credibility prediction. In *European conference on information retrieval*, pages 557–568. Springer.

Julia Schwarz and Meredith Morris. 2011. Augmenting web pages and search results to support credibility assessment. In *Proceedings of the SIGCHI Conference on Human Factors in Computing Systems*, pages 1245–1254. ACM.

Asad Ali Shah, Sri Devi Ravana, Suraya Hamid, and Maizatul Akmar Ismail. 2015. Web credibility assessment: affecting factors and assessment techniques. *Information Research*, 20(1):20–1.

Luo Si and Jamie Callan. 2001. A statistical model for scientific readability. In *Proceedings of the Tenth International Conference on Information and Knowledge Management*, CIKM '01, pages 574–576, New York, NY, USA. ACM.

Himani Singal and Shruti Kohli. 2016. Trust necessitated through metrics: Estimating the trustworthiness of websites. *Procedia Computer Science*, 85:133–140.

Joel Sobel. 1985. A theory of credibility. *The Review of Economic Studies*, 52(4):557–573.

Josef Steinberger and Karel Jeek. 2004. Using latent semantic analysis in text summarization and summary evaluation. In *In Proc. ISIM 04*, pages 93–100.

Philip J. Stone and Earl B. Hunt. 1963. A computer approach to content analysis: Studies using the general inquirer system. In *Proceedings of the May 21-23, 1963, Spring Joint Computer Conference*, AFIPS '63 (Spring), pages 241–256, New York, NY, USA. ACM.

James Thorne and Andreas Vlachos. 2018. Automated fact checking: Task formulations, methods and future directions. *CoRR*, abs/1806.07687.

Aleksander Wawer, Radoslaw Nielek, and Adam Wierzbicki. 2014. Predicting webpage credibility using linguistic features. In *Proceedings of the 23rd international conference on world wide web*, pages 1135–1140. ACM.

Mark D Wilkinson, Michel Dumontier, IJsbrand Jan Aalbersberg, Gabrielle Appleton, Myles Axton, Arie Baak, Niklas Blomberg, Jan-Willem Boiten, Luiz Bonino da Silva Santos, Philip E Bourne, et al. 2016. The fair guiding principles for scientific data management and stewardship. *Scientific data*, 3.

Arkaitz Zubiaga, Ahmet Aker, Kalina Bontcheva, Maria Liakata, and Rob Procter. 2017. Detection and resolution of rumours in social media: A survey. *CoRR*, abs/1704.00656.

Automated Fact-Checking of Claims
in Argumentative Parliamentary Debates

Nona Naderi
Department of Computer Science
University of Toronto
Toronto, Ontario, Canada
nona@cs.toronto.edu

Graeme Hirst
Department of Computer Science
University of Toronto
Toronto, Ontario, Canada
gh@cs.toronto.edu

Abstract

We present an automated approach to distinguish true, false, stretch, and dodge statements in questions and answers in the Canadian Parliament. We leverage the truthfulness annotations of a U.S. fact-checking corpus by training a neural net model and incorporating the prediction probabilities into our models. We find that in concert with other linguistic features, these probabilities can improve the multi-class classification results. We further show that dodge statements can be detected with an F_1 measure as high as 82.57% in binary classification settings.

1 Introduction

Governments and parliaments that are selected and chosen by citizens' votes have *ipso facto* attracted a certain level of trust. However, governments and parliamentarians use combinations of true statements, false statements, and exaggerations in strategic ways to question other parties' trustworthiness and to thereby create distrust towards them while gaining credibility for themselves. Creating distrust and alienation may be achieved by using ad hominem arguments or by raising questions about someone's character and honesty (Walton, 2005). For example, consider the claims made within the following question that was asked in the Canadian Parliament:

Example 1.1 [Dominic LeBlanc, 2013-10-21]
The RCMP and Mike Duffy's lawyer have shown us that the Prime Minister has not been honest about this scandal. When will he come clean and stop hiding his own role in this scandal?

These claims, including the presupposition of the second sentence that the Prime Minister has a role in the scandal that he is hiding, may be true, false, or simply exaggerations. In order to be able to analyze how these claims serve their presenter's purpose or intention, we need to determine their truth.

Here, we will examine the linguistic characteristics of true statements, false statements, dodges, and stretches in argumentative parliamentary statements. We examine whether falsehoods told by members of parliament can be identified with previously proposed approaches and we find that while some of these approaches improve the classification, identifying falsehoods by members of parliament remains challenging.

2 Related work

Vlachos and Riedel (2014) proposed to use data from fact-checking websites, such as PolitiFact for the fact-checking task and suggested that one way to approach this task would be using the semantic similarity between statements. Hassan et al. (2015) used presidential debates and proposed three labels — *Non-Factual, Unimportant Factual*, and *Check-worthy Factual* sentence — for the fact-checking task. They used a traditional feature-based method and trained their models using sentiment scores using AlchemyAPI, word counts of a sentence, bag of words, part-of-speech tags, and entity types to classify the debates into these three labels. They found that the part-of-speech tag of cardinal numbers was the most informative feature and word counts was the second most informative feature. They also found that check-worthy actual claims were more likely to contain numeric values and non-factual sentences were less likely to contain numeric values.

Patwari et al. (2017) used primary debates and presidential debates for analyzing check-worthy statements. They used topics extracted using LDA, entity history and type counts, part-of-speech tuples, counts of part-of-speech tags, unigrams, sentiment, and token counts for their classi-

Proceedings of the First Workshop on Fact Extraction and VERification (FEVER), pages 60–65
Brussels, Belgium, November 1, 2018. ©2018 Association for Computational Linguistics

Label	True	False	Dodge	Stretch	Total
#	255	60	70	93	478

Table 1: Distribution of labels in the *Toronto Star* dataset

Label	#
True	1,780
Mostly true	2,003
Half true	2,152
Mostly false	1,717
False	1,964
Pants-on-fire false	867
Total	10,483

Table 2: Distribution of labels in the PolitiFact dataset

fication task. Ma et al. (2017) used a kernel-based model to detect rumors in tweets. Wang (2017) used the statements from PolitiFact and the 6-point scale of truthfulness; he compared the performance of multiple classifiers and reported some improvement by using metadata related to the person making the statements.

Rashkin et al. (2017) examined the effectiveness of LIWC (Linguistic Inquiry and Word Count) and stylistic lexicon features in determining the reliability of the news corpus and truthfulness of the PolitiFact dataset. The only reliability measurement reported on the PolitiFact dataset is by Wang (2017), who manually analyzed 200 statements from PolitiFact and reached an agreement of 0.82 using Cohen's kappa measurement with the journalists' labels. Jaradat et al. (2018) used a set of linguistic features to rank check-worthy claims. Throne et al. (2018) created a dataset for claim verification. This dataset consists of 185,445 claims verified against Wikipedia pages. Here, we do not consider any external resources and we focus only on the text of claims to determine whether we can classify claims as true, false, dodge, or stretch.

3   Data

For our analysis, we extracted our data from a project by the *Toronto Star* newspaper.[1] The *Star* reporters[2] fact-checked and annotated questions and answers from the Oral Question Period of the Canadian Parliament (over five days in April and May 2018). Oral Question Period is a session of 45 minutes in which the Opposition and Government backbenchers ask questions of ministers of the government, and the ministers must respond. The reporters annotated all assertions within both the questions and the answers as either *true, false, stretch,* (half true), or *dodge* (not actually answering the question). Further, they provided a narrative justification for the assignment of each label (we do not use that data here). Here is an example of the annotated data (not including the justifications):

Example 3.1 *Q.* [Michelle Rempel] *Mr. Speaker, [social programs across Canada are under severe strain due to tens of thousands of unplanned immigrants illegally crossing into Canada from the United States.]*False *[Forty per cent in Toronto's homeless shelters are recent asylum claimants.]*True *[This, food bank usage, and unemployment rates show that many new asylum claimants are not having successful integration experiences.]*False

A. [Ahmed Hussen (Minister of Immigration, Refugees and Citizenship)] *Mr. Speaker, we commend the City of Toronto, as well as the Province of Ontario, the Province of Quebec, and all Canadians, on their generosity toward newcomers. That is something this country is proud of, and we will always be proud of our tradition. [In terms of asylum processing, making sure that there are minimal impacts on provincial social services, we have provided $74 million to make sure that the Immigration and Refugee Board does its work so that legitimate claimants can move on with their lives and those who do not have legitimate claims can be removed from Canada.]*True

Here is an example of dodge annotation:

Example 3.2 *Q.* [Jacques Gourde] *... How much money does that represent for the families that will be affected by the sexist carbon tax over a one-year period?*

A. [Catherine McKenna (Minister of Environment and Climate Change)] *[Mr. Speaker, I am quite surprised to hear them say they are concerned about sexism. That is the party that closed 12 out of 16 Status of Women Canada offices.]*Dodge *We know that we must take action

---

[1] http://projects.thestar.com/ question-period/index.html. All the data is publicly available.

[2] Bruce Campion-Smith, Brendan Kennedy, Marco Chown Oved, Alex Ballingall, Alex Boutilier, and Tonda MacCharles.

Features	F_1	Accuracy	Dodge	True	False	Stretch
Majority class (True)	–	53.35				
BOW (tf-idf)	49.20	53.14	55.20	67.00	4.60	24.80
+ POS	52.92	58.15	62.40	71.00	4.80	27.40
+ NUM	53.40	58.58	**63.80**	70.80	4.80	28.80
+ Superlatives (Rashkin et al., 2017)	54.24	59.42	**63.80**	71.60	9.20	30.00
+ PolitiFact predictions	**55.10**	**59.63**	63.60	**71.60**	12.80	**30.80**
BOW + NE	50.66	53.33	57.40	66.40	**17.20**	24.40

Table 3: Five-fold cross-validation results (F_1 and % accuracy) of four-way classification of fact-checking for the overall dataset and F_1 for each class.

on climate change. Canadians know that we have a plan, but they are not so sure if the Conservatives do.

For our analysis, we extracted the annotated span of the text with its associated label. The distribution of the labels in this dataset is shown in Table 1. This is a skewed dataset with more than half of the statements annotated as *true*.

We also use a publicly available dataset from PolitiFact, a website at which statements by American politicians and officials are annotated with a 6-point scale of truthfulness.[3] The distribution of labels in this data is shown in Table 2. We examine PolitiFact data to determine whether these annotations can help the classification of the *Toronto Star* annotations.

4 Method

We formulate the analysis as a multi-class classification task; given a statement, we identify whether the statement is true, false, stretch, or a dodge.

We first examine the effective features used for identifying deceptive texts in the prior literature.

- Tuples of words and their part-of-speech tags (unigrams and bigrams weighted by *tf-idf*, represented by POS in the result tables).

- Number of words in the statement (Hassan et al., 2015; Patwari et al., 2017).

- Named entity type counts, including organizations and locations (Patwari et al., 2017) (represented by NE in the result tables).

- Total number of numbers in the text, e.g., *six organizations heard the assistant deputy*

minister (Hassan et al., 2015) (represented by NUM in the result tables).

- LIWC (Tausczik and Pennebaker, 2010) features (Rashkin et al., 2017).

- Five lexicons of intensifying words from Wiktionary: superlatives, comparatives, action adverbs, manner adverbs, modal adverbs (Rashkin et al., 2017).

In addition, we leverage the American PolitiFact data to fact-check the Canadian Parliamentary questions and answers by training a Gated Recurrent Unit classifier (GRU) (Cho et al., 2014) on this data. We will use the truthfulness predictions of this classifier — the probabilities of the 6-point-scale labels — as additional features for our SVM classifier (using the scikit-learn package (Pedregosa et al., 2011)). For training the GRU classifier, we initialized the word representations using the publicly available GloVe pretrained 100-dimension word embeddings (Pennington et al., 2014)[4], and restricted the vocabulary to the 5,000 most-frequent words and a sequence length of 300. We added a dropout of 0.6 after the embedding layer and a dropout layer of 0.8 before the final sigmoid unit layer. The model was trained with categorical cross-entropy with the Adam optimizer (Kingma and Ba, 2014) for 10 epochs and batch size of 64. We used 10% of the data for validation, with the model achieving an average F_1 measure of 31.44% on this data.

5 Results and discussion

We approach the fact-checking of the statements as a multi-class classification task. Our baselines

---

[3]The dataset has been made available by Hannah Rashkin at `https://homes.cs.washington.edu/~hrashkin/factcheck.html`.

[4]`https://nlp.stanford.edu/projects/glove/`

Features	Dodge	Stretch	False
True			
Majority class	54.84	52.25	58.62
BOW	76.09	54.21	58.20
BOW + NE	75.65	52.99	61.67
BOW + LIWC	52.38	49.11	53.41
BOW + PolitiFact	**77.96**	**55.73**	58.11
BOW + NE + Politifact	76.25	53.76	**63.69**
BOW + POS + NUM + Superlative + PolitiFact	77.51	54.96	55.24
False			
Majority class	53.85	**60.00**	
BOW	81.36	55.89	
BOW + NE	**82.57**	56.91	
BOW + LIWC	52.02	53.31	
BOW + PolitiFact	80.69	52.97	
BOW + NE + Politifact	82.52	55.08	
BOW + POS + NUM + Superlative + PolitiFact	78.29	54.82	
Stretch			
Majority class	57.06		
BOW	75.15		
BOW + NE	76.93		
BOW + LIWC	45.37		
BOW + PolitiFact	79.39		
BOW + NE + Politifact	77.73		
BOW + POS + NUM + Superlative + PolitiFact	**80.59**		

Table 4: Average F_1 of different models for two-way classification of fact-checking (five-fold cross-validation).

are the majority class (truths) and an SVM classifier trained with unigrams extracted from the annotated spans of texts (weighted by *tf-idf*). We performed five-fold cross-validation. Table 3 reports the results on the multi-class classification task with these baselines and with the additional features described in section 4, including the truthfulness predictions of the GRU classifier trained on PolitiFact data. The best result is achieved using unigrams, POS tags, total number of numbers (NUM), superlatives, and the GRU's truthfulness predictions (PolitiFact predictions). We examined all five lexicons from Wiktionary provided by Rashkin et al. (2017); however, only superlatives affected the performance of the classifier, so we report only the results using superlatives.

We also report in Table 3 the average F_1 measure for classification of four labels in multi-class classification using five-fold cross-validation. The truthfulness predictions did not improve the classification of the *dodge* and *true* labels in multi-class classification setting. Superlatives slightly improved the classification of all labels except *dodge*.

We further perform pairwise classification (one-versus-one) for all possible pairs of labels to get better insight into the impact of the features and

characteristics of labels.

Therefore, we created three rather balanced datasets of truths and falsehoods by randomly resampling the *true* statements without replacement (85 *true* statements in each dataset). The same method was used for comparing *true* labels with *dodge* and *stretch* labels, i.e., we created three relatively balanced datasets for analyzing *true* and *dodge* labels and three datasets for analyzing *true* and *stretch* labels. This allows us to compare the prior work on the 6-point scale truthfulness labels on the U.S. data with the Canadian 4-point scale.

Table 4 presents the classification results using five-fold cross-validation with an SVM classifier. The reported F_1 measure is the average of the results on all three datasets for each pairwise setting. *Dodge* statements were classified more accurately than the other statements with an F_1 measure as high as 82.57%. This shows that the answers that do not provide a response to the question can be detected with relatively high confidence. The most effective features for classifying *false* against *true* and *dodge* statements were named entities.

The predictions obtained from training the GRU model on the PolitiFact annotations, on their own, were not able to distinguish *false* from *true* and *stretch* statements. However, the predictions did help in distinguishing *true* against *stretch* and *dodge* statements. None of the models were able to improve the classification of *false* against *stretch* statements over the majority baseline.

Overall, *stretch* statements were the most difficult statements to identify in the binary classification setting. This could also be due to some inconsistency in the annotation process, with *stretch* and *false* not always clearly separated. Here is an example of *stretch* in the data:

Example 5.1 [Catherine McKenna] *Carbon pricing works and it can be done while growing the economy. ... Once again, I ask the member opposite, "What are you going to do?" [Under 10 years of the [Conservative] Harper government, you did nothing.]Stretch*

Elsewhere in the data, essentially the same claim is labelled *false*:

Example 5.2 [Justin Trudeau] *The Conservatives promised that they would also tackle environmental challenges and that they would do so by means other than carbon pricing. ... They have no proposals, [they did nothing for 10 years.]False*

We further performed the analysis using the two predictions of *more true* and *more false* from the PolitiFact dataset; however, we didn't observe any improvements. Using the total number of words in the statements also did not improve the results.

While Rashkin et al. (2017), found that LIWC features were effective for predicting the truthfulness of the statements in PolitiFact, we did not observe any improvements in the performance of the classifier in our classification task on Canadian Parliamentary data. Furthermore, we did not observe any improvements in the classification tasks using sentiment and subjectivity features extracted using OpinionFinder (Wilson et al., 2005; Riloff et al., 2003; Riloff and Wiebe, 2003).

6   Comparison with PolitiFact dataset

In this section, we perform a direct analysis with the PolitiFact dataset. We first train a GRU model (used a sequence length of 200, other hyperparameters the same as those of the experiment described above) using 3-point scale annotations of PolitiFact (used 10% of the data for validation). We treat the top two truthful ratings (true and mostly true) as true; half true and mostly false as stretch; and the last two ratings (false and pants-on-fire false) as false. We then test the model on three annotations of true, stretch, and false from the *Toronto Star* project. The results are presented in Table 5. As the results show, none of the false statements are detected as *false* and the overall F_1 score is lower than the majority baseline.

We further train a GRU model (trained with binary cross-entropy and sequence length of 200, other hyperparameters the same as above) using 2-point scale where we treat the top three truthful ratings as true and the last three false ratings as false. We then test the model on two annotations of true and false from the *Toronto Star* project. The results are presented in Table 6; the F_1 score remains below baseline.

The Politifact dataset provided by Rashkin et al. includes a subset of direct quotes by original speakers. We further performed the 3-point scale and 2-point scale analysis using only the direct quotes. Using only the direct quotes, also shown in Tables 5 and 6, did not improve the classification performance.

	F_1	True	Stretch	False
Majority	63			
GRU (All)	40	53	29	0
GRU (DQ)	50	75	13	8

Table 5: 3-point scale comparison of the PolitiFact data and *Toronto Star* annotations. **All**: GRU model is trained with all PolitiFact data and tested on *Toronto Star* annotations. **DQ**: GRU model is trained with only direct quotes from the PolitiFact data and tested on *Toronto Star* annotations.

	F_1	True	False
Majority	81		
GRU (All)	73	84	29
GRU (DQ)	72	88	8

Table 6: 2-point scale comparison of the PolitiFact data and *Toronto Star* annotations. **All**: GRU model is trained with all PolitiFact data and tested on *Toronto Star* annotations. **DQ**: GRU model is trained with only direct quotes from the PolitiFact data and tested on *Toronto Star* annotations.

7   Conclusion

We have analyzed classification of *truths, falsehoods, dodges,* and *stretches* in the Canadian Parliament and compared it with the truthfulness classification of statements in the PolitiFact dataset. We studied whether the effective features in the prior research can help us characterize the truthfulness in Canadian Parliamentary debates and found out that while some of these features help us identify *dodge* statements with an F_1 measure as high as 82.57%, they were not very effective in identifying *false* and *stretch* statements. The truthfulness predictions obtained from training a model on annotations of American politicians' statements, when used with other features, helped slightly in distinguishing truths from other statements. In future work, we will take advantage of journalists' justifications in determining the truthfulness of the statements as relying on only linguistic features is not enough for determining falsehoods in parliament.

Acknowledgements

This research is financially supported by an Ontario Graduate Scholarship, the Natural Sciences and Engineering Research Council of Canada, and the University of Toronto. We thank the anonymous reviewers for their thoughtful comments and suggestions.

References

KyungHyun Cho, Bart van Merrienboer, Dzmitry Bahdanau, and Yoshua Bengio. 2014. On the properties of neural machine translation: Encoder-decoder approaches. *arXiv preprint arXiv:1409.1259,*.

Naeemul Hassan, Chengkai Li, and Mark Tremayne. 2015. Detecting check-worthy factual claims in presidential debates. In *Proceedings of the 24th ACM International on Conference on Information and Knowledge Management*, pages 1835–1838. ACM.

Israa Jaradat, Pepa Gencheva, Alberto Barrón-Cedeño, Lluís Màrquez, and Preslav Nakov. 2018. Claimrank: Detecting check-worthy claims in arabic and english. In *Proceedings of the 2018 Conference of the North American Chapter of the Association for Computational Linguistics: Demonstrations*, pages 26–30. Association for Computational Linguistics.

Diederik Kingma and Jimmy Ba. 2014. Adam: A method for stochastic optimization. *arXiv preprint arXiv:1412.6980.*

Jing Ma, Wei Gao, and Kam-Fai Wong. 2017. Detect rumors in microblog posts using propagation structure via kernel learning. In *Proceedings of the 55th Annual Meeting of the Association for Computational Linguistics (Volume 1: Long Papers)*, pages 708–717, Vancouver, Canada. Association for Computational Linguistics.

Ayush Patwari, Dan Goldwasser, and Saurabh Bagchi. 2017. TATHYA: A multi-classifier system for detecting check-worthy statements in political debates. In *Proceedings of the 2017 ACM on Conference on Information and Knowledge Management*, pages 2259–2262. ACM.

F. Pedregosa, G. Varoquaux, A. Gramfort, V. Michel, B. Thirion, O. Grisel, M. Blondel, P. Prettenhofer, R. Weiss, V. Dubourg, J. Vanderplas, A. Passos, D. Cournapeau, M. Brucher, M. Perrot, and E. Duchesnay. 2011. Scikit-learn: Machine learning in Python. *Journal of Machine Learning Research*, 12:2825–2830.

Jeffrey Pennington, Richard Socher, and Christopher D. Manning. 2014. GloVe: Global vectors for word representation. In *Proceedings of the 2014 Conference on Empirical Methods in Natural Language Processing (EMNLP)*, pages 1532–1543.

Hannah Rashkin, Eunsol Choi, Jin Yea Jang, Svitlana Volkova, and Yejin Choi. 2017. Truth of varying shades: Analyzing language in fake news and political fact-checking. In *Proceedings of the 2017 Conference on Empirical Methods in Natural Language Processing*, pages 2931–2937, Copenhagen, Denmark. Association for Computational Linguistics.

Ellen Riloff and Janyce Wiebe. 2003. Learning extraction patterns for subjective expressions. In *Proceedings of the 2003 Conference on Empirical Methods in Natural Language Processing*, EMNLP '03, pages 105–112, Stroudsburg, PA, USA. Association for Computational Linguistics.

Ellen Riloff, Janyce Wiebe, and Theresa Wilson. 2003. Learning subjective nouns using extraction pattern bootstrapping. In *Proceedings of the Seventh Conference on Natural Language Learning at HLT-NAACL 2003 - Volume 4*, CONLL '03, pages 25–32, Stroudsburg, PA, USA. Association for Computational Linguistics.

Yla R. Tausczik and James W. Pennebaker. 2010. The psychological meaning of words: LIWC and computerized text analysis methods. *Journal of Language and Social Psychology*, 29(1):24–54.

James Thorne, Andreas Vlachos, Christos Christodoulopoulos, and Arpit Mittal. 2018. FEVER: a large-scale dataset for fact extraction and verification. In *NAACL-HLT*.

Andreas Vlachos and Sebastian Riedel. 2014. Fact checking: Task definition and dataset construction. In *Proceedings of the ACL 2014 Workshop on Language Technologies and Computational Social Science*, pages 18–22, Baltimore, MD, USA. Association for Computational Linguistics.

Douglas Walton. 2005. *Fundamentals of critical argumentation.* Cambridge University Press.

William Yang Wang. 2017. "Liar, liar pants on fire": A new benchmark dataset for fake news detection. *arXiv preprint arXiv:1705.00648.*

Theresa Wilson, Janyce Wiebe, and Paul Hoffmann. 2005. Recognizing contextual polarity in phrase-level sentiment analysis. In *Proceedings of the Conference on Human Language Technology and Empirical Methods in Natural Language Processing*, HLT '05, pages 347–354, Stroudsburg, PA, USA. Association for Computational Linguistics.

Stance Detection in Fake News: A Combined Feature Representation

Bilal Ghanem
PRHLT Research Center,
Universitat Politècnica de València,
Spain
bigha@doctor.upv.es

Paolo Rosso
PRHLT Research Center,
Universitat Politècnica de València,
Spain
prosso@dsic.upv.es

Francisco Rangel
PRHLT Research Center,
Universitat Politècnica de València,
Autoritas Consulting,
Spain
francisco.rangel@autoritas.es

Abstract

With the uncontrolled increasing of fake news and rumors over the Web, different approaches have been proposed to address the problem. In this paper, we present an approach that combines lexical, word embeddings and n-gram features to detect the stance in fake news. Our approach has been tested on the Fake News Challenge (FNC-1) dataset. Given a news title-article pair, the FNC-1 task aims at determining the relevance of the article and the title. Our proposed approach has achieved an accurate result (59.6 % Macro F1) that is close to the state-of-the-art result with 0.013 difference using a simple feature representation. Furthermore, we have investigated the importance of different lexicons in the detection of the classification labels.

1 Introduction

Recently, many phenomena appeared and spread in the Internet, especially with the huge propagation of information and the growth of social networks. Some of these phenomena are fake news, rumors and misinformation. In general, the detection of these phenomena is crucial since in many situations they expose the people to danger[1]. Journalism made several efforts in addressing these problems by presenting a validity proof to the audience. Unfortunately, these manual attempts take much time and effort from the journalists and, at the same time, they cannot cover the rapid spread of these fake news. Hence, there is the need for addressing the problem from an automatic perspective. Fake news gained large attention recently from the natural language processing (NLP) research community and many approaches have been proposed. These approaches investigated fake news from network and textual perspectives (Shu et al., 2017). Some of the textual approaches handled the phenomenon from a validity aspect, where they labeled a claim as "False", "True", or "Half-True". Others tried to tackle it from a stance perspective, similar to stance detection works on Twitter (Mohammad et al., 2016; Taulé et al., 2017; Lai et al., 2018) that tried to determine whether a tweet is in favor, against, or neither to a given target entity (person, organization, etc.). Where in fake news, they replaced the tuple of the tweet and the target entity with a claim and an article; also a different stances' set is used (agree, disagree, discuss, and unrelated).

Several shared tasks have been proposed: Fake News Challenge (FNC-1) (Rao and Pomerleau, 2017), RumorEval (Derczynski et al., 2017), CheckThat (Barrón-Cedeño et al., 2018), and Fact Extraction and Verification (FEVER)[2]. In FNC-1, the organizers proposed the task to be approached from a stance perspective; the goal is to predict how other articles orient to a specific fact, similarly than in RumorEval (task-A). While in both RumorEval (task-B) and CheckThat (task-B) a rumor/claim has been submitted and the task objective is to validate the truthfulness of this sentence (true, half-true, or false). In the first task of CheckThat (task-A) participants were asked to detect claims that are worthy for checking (may have facts), as preliminary step to task B. Finally, the purpose of FEVER shared task is to evaluate the ability of a system to verify a factual claim using evidences from Wikipedia, where each re-

---

[1] https://www.theguardian.com/media/2016/dec/18/what-is-fake-news-pizzagate

[2] http://fever.ai/task.html

Proceedings of the First Workshop on Fact Extraction and VERification (FEVER), pages 66–71
Brussels, Belgium, November 1, 2018. ©2018 Association for Computational Linguistics

trieved evidence (in case there are many) should be labeled as "Supported", "Refuted" or "NotEnoughInfo" (if there isn't sufficient evidence to either support or refute it). The given attention to fake news and rumors detection in the literature is more than the one gained by detecting worthy claims. The orientation in these works was towards inferring these worthy claims using linguistic and stylistic aspects (Ghanem et al., 2018c; Hassan et al., 2015).

2   Related Work

From an NLP perspective, many approaches proposed to employ statistical (Magdy and Wanas, 2010), linguistic (Markowitz and Hancock, 2014; Volkova et al., 2017), and stylistic (Potthast et al., 2017) features. Other approaches incorporated different combination of features, such as word or character n-grams overlapping score, bag-of-words (BOW), word embeddings, and latent semantic analysis features (Riedel et al., 2017; Hanselowski et al., 2017; Karadzhov et al., 2018). In some cases, authors used external features and retrieved evidences from the Web. For example, in (Ghanem et al., 2018b) the authors utilized both Google and Bing search engines to investigate the factuality of political claims. In (Mihaylov et al., 2015), a similar work has also retrieved evidences from Google and online blogs to validate sentences in question answering forums. In other attempts, some approaches utilized deep learning architectures to validate fake news. In (Baird et al., 2017), an approach combined a Convolutional Neural Network with a Gradient Boost classifier to predict the stance on FNC. As a result, their approach achieved the highest accuracy in the task results. Using a different deep learning architecture, the authors in (Hanselowski et al., 2018) used a Long Short-Term Memory (LSTM) network combined with other features such as bag-of-characters (BOC), BOW and topic model features based on non-negative matrix factorization, Latent Dirichlet Allocation, and Latent Semantic Indexing. They achieved state-of-the-art results (60.9% Macro F1) on the FNC-1 dataset.

The approaches that were proposed in both fake news and rumors detection are slightly different, since both phenomena were studied in different environment. Fake news datasets generally were collected from formal sources (political debates or Web news articles). On the other hand, Twitter was the source for rumors datasets. Therefore, the proposed approaches for rumors focused more on the propagation of tweets (ex. retweet ratio (Enayet and El-Beltagy, 2017)) and the writing style of the tweets (Kochkina et al., 2017).

3   Stance Detection in FNC-1

3.1   Task

Given a pair of text fragments (title and article) obtained from news, the task goal is to estimate the relative perspective (stance) of these two fragments with respect to a specific topic. In other words, the stance prediction of an article towards the title of this article. For each input pair, there are 4 stance labels: Agree, Disagree, Discuss, and Unrelated. "Agree" if the article supports the title; "disagree" if refuses it; "discuss" whether the article discusses the title but without showing an in favor or against stance; and "unrelated" when the article describes a different topic than the one of the title. The task's dataset is imbalanced in a high ratio (see next section). Therefore, the organizers introduced a weighted accuracy score for the evaluation. Their proposed score gave 25% of the final score for predicting the unrelated class, while 75% for the other classes. Later, the authors in (Hanselowski et al., 2018) proposed an in-depth analysis to discuss FNC-1 experimental setup. They showed that this accuracy metric is not appropriate and fails to take into account the imbalanced class distribution, where models performing well on the majority class and poorly on the minority classes are favored. Therefore, they proposed Macro F1 metric to be used in this task. Accordingly, in this paper we show the experimental results using the Macro F1 measure.

3.2   Corpus

The presented dataset was built using 300 different topics. The training part consists of 49,972 tuples in a form of title, article, and label, while the test part consists of 25,413 tuples. The ratio of each label (class) in the dataset is: 73.13% Unrelated, 17.82% Discuss, 7.36% Agree, and 1.68% Disagree. Clearly the dataset is heavily biased towards the unrelated label. Titles length ranges between 8 and 40 words, whereas for the articles ranges between 600 and 7000 words (Bhatt et al., 2018). These numbers show a real challenge to predict the stance between these two fragments that are totally different in lengths.

3.3 Tough-to-beat Baseline

The organizers presented a tough baseline using Gradient Boost decision tree classifier. In contrast to other shared tasks, their baseline employed more sophisticated features. As features, they employed n-gram co-occurrence between the titles and articles using both character and word grams (using a combination of multiple lengths) along with other hand-crafted features such as: word overlapping between the title and the article and the existence of highly polarized words from a lexicon (ex. fake, hoax). Their baseline achieved an FNC-1 score value of 75% and 45.4% value of Macro F1.

4 Approach and Results

The literature work on the FNC dataset showed that the best results are not obtained with a pure deep learning architecture, and simple BOW representations showed a good performance. In our approach, we combine n-grams, word embeddings and cue words to detect the stance of the title with respect to its article.

4.1 Preprocessing

Before building the feature representation, we perform a set of text preprocessing steps. In some articles we found links, hashtags, and user mentions (ex. @USER), so we remove them to make the text less biased. Similarly, we remove non-English and special characters.

4.2 Features

In our approach we combine simple feature representation to model the title-article tuples:

- **Cue words**: We employ a set of cue words categories that were used previously in (Bahuleyan and Vechtomova, 2017) to identify the stance of Twitter users towards rumor tweets. As Table 1 shows, the cue words categories are *Belief, Denial, Doubt, Report, Knowledge, Negation and Fake*. The Fake cue list is a combination of some words from FNC-1 baseline polarized words list and words from the original list. The provided set of cue words is quite small, therefore, we use Google News word2vec to expand it. For each word, we retrieve the most 5 similar words. As an example, for the word "misinform", we retrieved "mislead ","misinform-

Feature	Example Words
Belief	assume, believe, think, consider
Denial	refuse, reject, rebuff, oppose
Doubt	wonder, unsure, guess, doubt
Report	evidence, assert, told, claim
Knowledge	confirm, definitely, support
Negation	no, not, never, don't, can't
Fake	liar, false, rumor, hoax, debunk

Table 1: The cue words categories and examples.

ing","disinform","misinformation", and "demonize" as the most similar words.

- **Google News word2vec embedding**: For each title-article tuple, we measure the cosine similarity of the embedding of each sentence. Also, we use the full 300 length embedding vector for both the title and the article. The sentence embeddings is obtained by averaging its words embeddings. Previously in (Ghanem et al., 2018a), the authors showed that using the main sentence components (verbs, nouns, and adjectives) improved the detection accuracy of a plagiarism detection approach[3] rather than using the full sentence components. Therefore, we build these embeddings vectors using the main sentence components. Furthermore, we maintain the set of cue words that showed in the previous point.

- **FNC-1 features**: we use the same baseline feature set (see Section 3.3).

4.3 Experiments

In our experiments, we tested Support Vector Machines (SVM) (using each Linear and RBF kernels), Gradient Boost, Random Forest and Naive Bayes classifiers but the Neural Network (NN) showed better results[6]. Our NN architecture consists of two hidden layers with rectified linear unit (ReLU) activation function as non-linearity for the hidden layers, and Softmax activation function for the output layer. Also, we employed the

---

[3]For extracting the main sentence components, we used NLTK POS tagger: https://www.nltk.org/book/ch05.html.

[5]The stackLSTM is not one of the FNC-1 participated approaches, but it achieved state-of-the-art result.

[6]The Scikit-learn python package was used in our implementation

Systems	Macro-F1
Majority vote	0.210
FNC-1 baseline	0.454
Talos (Baird et al., 2017)	0.582
UCLMR (Riedel et al., 2017)	0.583
Athene (Hanselowski et al., 2017)	0.604
stackLSTM (Hanselowski et al., 2018)	0.609
Our approach	0.596
Cue words	0.250
Word2vec embeddings	0.488

Table 2: The Macro F1 score results of the participants in the FNC-1 challenge.[5]

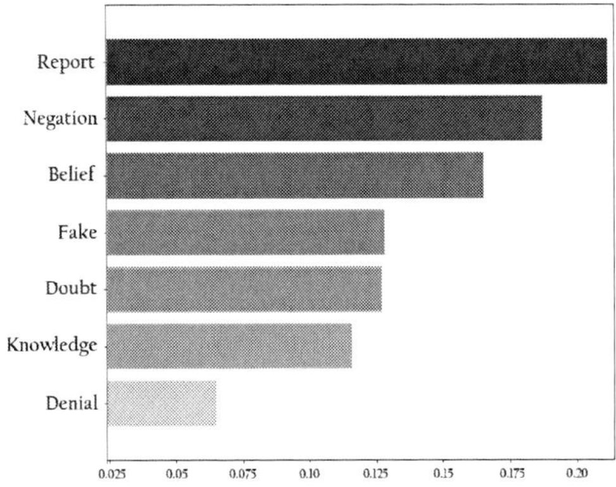

Figure 1: The importance of each cue words category using Information Gain.

Adam weight optimizer. The used batch size is 200. Table 2 shows the results of our approach and those of the FNC-1 participants. We investigated the score of each of our features independently. The word2vec embeddings feature set has achieved 0.488 Macro F1 value, while the cue words achieved 0.25. The extension of the cue words has improved the final result by 2.5%.

The tuples of the "Unrelated" class had been created artificially by assigning articles from different documents. This abnormal distribution can affect the result of the cue words feature when we test it independently; since we extract the cue words feature from the articles part (without the titles) and some articles could be found with different class labels, this can bias the classification process. As we mentioned previously, the state-of-the-art result was obtained by an approach that combined LSTM with other features (see Section 2). Our approach achieved 0.596 value of Macro F1 score which is very close to the best result.

The combination of the cue words categories with the other features has improved the overall result. Each of them had impact in the classification process. In Figure 1, we show the importance of each category using the Information Gain. We extract it using Gradient Boost classifier as it achieves the highest result comparing to the other decision tree-based classifiers. The figure clarifies that *Report* is the category that has the highest importance in the classification process, where *Negation* and *Belief* categories have lower importance, whereas both of the *Denial* and *Knowledge* categories have the lowest importance. Surprisingly, both of the *Fake* and *Doubt* categories have a lower importance than the other three. Our intuition was

that the *Fake* category will have the highest importance in discriminating the classes, where this category contains words that: may not appear in the "Agree" class records, appear profusely in the "Disagree" class (where the title is fake and the article proving that), and a medium appearance amount in the "Discuss" class. Similarly, for the *Doubt* category, it seems that it may appear frequently in both "Discuss" and "Disagree" classes where its words normally mentioned when an article discusses a specific idea or when refuse it. To understand deeper our Information Gain results, we conducted another experiment to infer the importance of each category with respect to each classification class.

To do so, we use SVM classifier coefficients (linear kernel) to extract the most important category to each classification class. In our initial experiments, the SVM produced a result that is similar to the NN (58% Macro F1), so based on the good performance we used it in this experiment, where we couldn't extract the feature importance using the NN. Once the SVM fits the data and creates a hyperplane that uses support vectors to maximize the distance between the classes, the importance of the features can be extracted based on the absolute size of the coefficients (vector coordinates). In Table 3 we show the importance of each category by their order. We can notice that for the "Agree" class, generally, the categories that are used when there is a disagreement (Denial, Fake, Negation) tend to be less important than the other categories. On the contrary, for the "Disagree", disagreement categories appear in general in higher order comparing to the "Agree" class.

#	Unrelated	Discuss	Disagree	Agree
1	Belief	Fake	Report	Belief
2	Negat.	Negat.	Fake	Report
3	Report	Belief	Denial	Doubt
4	Knowl.	Knowl.	Belief	Knowl.
5	Doubt	Denial	Negat.	Denial
6	Fake	Doubt	Knowl.	Fake
7	Denial	Report	Doubt	Negat.

Table 3: Importance order of the cue words categories for each class.

For the "Discuss" class, due to the unclear stance towards the title where articles did not show a clear in favor or against stance, we can notice an overlapping in the highest order between the categories that are important for both "Disagree" and "Agree" classes. Finally, as we mentioned previously that the articles in the "Unrelated" class are created artificially by assigning articles from different titles, the order of the categories is not meaningful.

5   Conclusion and Future Work

Fake news is still an open research topic. Further contributions are required, especially to deal automatically with the massive growth of information over the Web. Our work attempted to approach the stance detection of fake news using a simple model based on a combination of n-grams, word embeddings and lexical representation of cue words. These lexical cue words have been employed previously in the literature in rumors stance detection approaches. Although we used a simple feature set, we achieved similar results than the state of the art. This work is an initial step towards a further investigation of features to improve stance detection in fake news. As a future work, we plan to focus on summarizing the articles in the dataset. As we mentioned in Section 3.2, the length ratio difference between the titles and the articles is large. Therefore, summarizing the articles may be a worthy attempt to improve the comparison between the two text fragments.

Acknowledgement

This research work was done in the framework of the SomEMBED TIN2015-71147-C2-1-P MINECO research project.

References

Hareesh Bahuleyan and Olga Vechtomova. 2017. Uwaterloo at semeval-2017 task 8: Detecting stance towards rumours with topic independent features. In *Proceedings of the 11th International Workshop on Semantic Evaluation (SemEval-2017)*, pages 461–464.

Sean Baird, Doug Sibley, and Yuxi Pan. 2017. *Talos Targets Disinformation with Fake News Challenge Victory.* http://blog.talosintelligence.com/2017/06/talos-fake-news-challenge.

Alberto Barrón-Cedeño, Tamer Elsayed, Reem Suwaileh, Lluís Màrquez, Pepa Atanasova, Wajdi Zaghouani, Spas Kyuchukov, Giovanni Da San Martino, and Preslav Nakov. 2018. Overview of the clef-2018 checkthat! lab on automatic identification and verification of political claims, task 2: Factuality. In *CLEF 2018 Working Notes. Working Notes of CLEF 2018 - Conference and Labs of the Evaluation Forum*, CEUR Workshop Proceedings, Avignon, France. CEUR-WS.org.

Gaurav Bhatt, Aman Sharma, Shivam Sharma, Ankush Nagpal, Balasubramanian Raman, and Ankush Mittal. 2018. Combining neural, statistical and external features for fake news stance identification. In *Companion of the The Web Conference 2018 on The Web Conference 2018*, pages 1353–1357. International World Wide Web Conferences Steering Committee.

Leon Derczynski, Kalina Bontcheva, Maria Liakata, Rob Procter, Geraldine Wong Sak Hoi, and Arkaitz Zubiaga. 2017. Semeval-2017 task 8: Rumoureval: Determining rumour veracity and support for rumours. *arXiv preprint arXiv:1704.05972*.

Omar Enayet and Samhaa R El-Beltagy. 2017. Niletmrg at semeval-2017 task 8: Determining rumour and veracity support for rumours on twitter. In *Proceedings of the 11th International Workshop on Semantic Evaluation (SemEval-2017)*, pages 470–474.

Bilal Ghanem, Labib Arafeh, Paolo Rosso, and Fernando Sánchez-Vega. 2018a. Hyplag: Hybrid arabic text plagiarism detection system. In *International Conference on Applications of Natural Language to Information Systems*, pages 315–323. Springer.

Bilal Ghanem, Manuel Montes-y Gòmez, Francisco Rangel, and Paolo Rosso. 2018b. Upv-inaoe-autoritas - check that: An approach based on external sources to detect claims credibility. In *CLEF 2018 Working Notes. Working Notes of CLEF 2018 - Conference and Labs of the Evaluation Forum*, CEUR Workshop Proceedings, Avignon, France. CEUR-WS.org.

Bilal Ghanem, Manuel Montes-y Gòmez, Francisco Rangel, and Paolo Rosso. 2018c. Upv-inaoe-autoritas - check that: Preliminary approach for checking worthiness of claims. In *CLEF 2018 Working Notes. Working Notes of CLEF 2018 - Conference and Labs of the Evaluation Forum*, CEUR Workshop Proceedings, Avignon, France. CEUR-WS.org.

Andreas Hanselowski, Avinesh PVS, Benjamin Schiller, and Felix Caspelherr. 2017. *Team Athene on the Fake News Challenge.* `https://medium.com/@andre134679/team-athene-on-the-fake-news-/challenge-28a5cf5e017b`.

Andreas Hanselowski, Avinesh PVS, Benjamin Schiller, Felix Caspelherr, Debanjan Chaudhuri, Christian M Meyer, and Iryna Gurevych. 2018. A retrospective analysis of the fake news challenge stance detection task. *arXiv preprint arXiv:1806.05180*.

Naeemul Hassan, Chengkai Li, and Mark Tremayne. 2015. Detecting check-worthy factual claims in presidential debates. In *Proceedings of the 24th ACM International on Conference on Information and Knowledge Management*, pages 1835–1838. ACM.

Georgi Karadzhov, Pepa Gencheva, Preslav Nakov, and Ivan Koychev. 2018. We built a fake news & clickbait filter: What happened next will blow your mind! *arXiv preprint arXiv:1803.03786*.

Elena Kochkina, Maria Liakata, and Isabelle Augenstein. 2017. Turing at semeval-2017 task 8: Sequential approach to rumour stance classification with branch-lstm. *arXiv preprint arXiv:1704.07221*.

Mirko Lai, Viviana Patti, Giancarlo Ruffo, and Paolo Rosso. 2018. Stance evolution and twitter interactions in an italian political debate. In *23rd International Conference on Applications of Natural Language to Information Systems*, pages 15–27. Springer.

Amr Magdy and Nayer Wanas. 2010. Web-based statistical fact checking of textual documents. In *Proceedings of the 2nd international workshop on Search and mining user-generated contents*, pages 103–110. ACM.

David M Markowitz and Jeffrey T Hancock. 2014. Linguistic traces of a scientific fraud: The case of diederik stapel. *PloS one*, 9(8):e105937.

Todor Mihaylov, Georgi Georgiev, and Preslav Nakov. 2015. Finding opinion manipulation trolls in news community forums. In *Proceedings of the Nineteenth Conference on Computational Natural Language Learning*, pages 310–314.

Saif Mohammad, Svetlana Kiritchenko, Parinaz Sobhani, Xiaodan Zhu, and Colin Cherry. 2016. Semeval-2016 task 6: Detecting stance in tweets. In *Proceedings of the 10th International Workshop on Semantic Evaluation (SemEval-2016)*, pages 31–41, San Diego, California.

Martin Potthast, Johannes Kiesel, Kevin Reinartz, Janek Bevendorff, and Benno Stein. 2017. A stylometric inquiry into hyperpartisan and fake news. *arXiv preprint arXiv:1702.05638*.

Delip Rao and Dean Pomerleau. 2017. *Fake News Challenge.* `http://www.fakenewschallenge.org`.

Benjamin Riedel, Isabelle Augenstein, Georgios P Spithourakis, and Sebastian Riedel. 2017. A simple but tough-to-beat baseline for the fake news challenge stance detection task. *arXiv preprint arXiv:1707.03264*.

Kai Shu, Amy Sliva, Suhang Wang, Jiliang Tang, and Huan Liu. 2017. Fake news detection on social media: A data mining perspective. *ACM SIGKDD Explorations Newsletter*, 19(1):22–36.

Mariona Taulé, M Antonia Martí, Francisco M Rangel, Paolo Rosso, Cristina Bosco, Viviana Patti, et al. 2017. Overview of the task on stance and gender detection in tweets on catalan independence at ibereval 2017. In *2nd Workshop on Evaluation of Human Language Technologies for Iberian Languages, IberEval 2017*, volume 1881, pages 157–177. CEUR-WS.

Svitlana Volkova, Kyle Shaffer, Jin Yea Jang, and Nathan Hodas. 2017. Separating facts from fiction: Linguistic models to classify suspicious and trusted news posts on twitter. In *Proceedings of the 55th Annual Meeting of the Association for Computational Linguistics (Volume 2: Short Papers)*, volume 2, pages 647–653.

Zero-shot Relation Classification as Textual Entailment

Abiola Obamuyide
Department of Computer Science
University of Sheffield
avobamuyide1@sheffield.ac.uk

Andreas Vlachos
Department of Computer Science
University of Sheffield
a.vlachos@sheffield.ac.uk

Abstract

We consider the task of relation classification, and pose this task as one of textual entailment. We show that this formulation leads to several advantages, including the ability to (i) perform zero-shot relation classification by exploiting relation descriptions, (ii) utilize existing textual entailment models, and (iii) leverage readily available textual entailment datasets, to enhance the performance of relation classification systems. Our experiments show that the proposed approach achieves 20.16% and 61.32% in F1 zero-shot classification performance on two datasets, which further improved to 22.80% and 64.78% respectively with the use of conditional encoding.

1 Introduction

The task of determining the relation between various entities from text is an important one for many natural language understanding systems, including question answering, knowledge base construction and web search. Relation classification is an essential part of many high-performing relation extraction systems in the NIST-organised TAC Knowledge Base Population (TAC-KBP) track (Ji and Grishman, 2011; Adel et al., 2016). As a result of its wide application, many approaches and systems have been proposed for this task (Zelenko et al., 2003; Surdeanu et al., 2012; Riedel et al., 2013; Zhang et al., 2017).

A shortcoming common to previous proposed approaches, however, is that they identify only relations observed at training time, and are unable to generalize to new (unobserved) relations at test time. To address this challenge, we propose to formulate relation classification as follows: Given a unit of text T which mentions a subject X and a candidate object Y of a knowledge base relation $R(X, Y)$, and a natural language description d of R, we wish to evaluate whether T expresses $R(X, Y)$. We formulate this task as a textual entailment problem in which the unit of text and the relation description can be considered as the premise P and hypothesis H respectively. The challenge then becomes that of determining the truthfulness of the hypothesis given the premise. Table 1 gives examples of knowledge base relations and their natural language descriptions.

This formulation brings a number of advantages. First, we are able to perform zero-shot classification of new relations by generalizing from the descriptions of seen training relations to those of unseen relations at test time. Given a collection of relations, for instance, *spouse(X,Y)* and *city_of_birth(X,Y)* together with their natural language descriptions and training examples, we can learn a model that can classify other instances of these relations, as well as instances of other relations that were not observed at training time, for instance *child(X,Y)*, given their descriptions. In addition to being able to utilize existing state-of-the-art textual entailment models for relation classification, our approach can use distant supervision data together with data from textual entailment as additional supervision for relation classification.

In experiments on two datasets, we assess the performance of our approach in two supervision settings: in a *zero-shot* setting, where no supervision examples are available for new relations, and in a *few-shot* setting, where our models have access to limited supervision examples of new relations. In the former setting our approach achieves 20.16% and 61.32% in F1 classification performance in the two datasets considered, which further improved to 22.80% and 64.78% respectively with the use of conditional encoding. Similar improvements hold in the latter setting as well.

Proceedings of the First Workshop on Fact Extraction and VERification (FEVER), pages 72–78
Brussels, Belgium, November 1, 2018. ©2018 Association for Computational Linguistics

Relation	Subject (**X**)	Object (**Y**)	Text (Premise)	Description (Hypothesis)
religious_order	Lorenzo Ricci	Society of Jesus	**X** (August 1, 1703 – November 24, 1775) was an Italian Jesuit, elected the 18th Superior General of the **Y**.	*X was a member of the group Y*
director	Kispus	Erik Balling	**X** is a 1956 Danish romantic comedy written and directed by **Y**.	*The director of X is Y*
designer	Red Baron II	Dynamix	**X** is a computer game for the PC, developed by **Y** and published by Sierra Entertainment.	*Y is the designer of X*

Table 1: Examples of relations, entities, sample text instances, and relation descriptions.

2 Related Work

Most recent work, including Adel et al. (2016) and Zhang et al. (2017), proposed models that assume the availability of supervised data for the task of relation classification. Rocktäschel et al. (2015) and Demeester et al. (2016) inject prior knowledge in the form of propositional logic rules to improve relation extraction for new relations with zero and few training labels, in the context of the *universal schema* approach (Riedel et al., 2013). They considered the use of propositional logic rules, which for instance, can be mined from external knowledge bases (such as Freebase (Bollacker et al., 2008)) or obtained from ontologies such as Word-Net (Miller, 1995). However, the use of propositional logic rules assumes prior knowledge of the possible relations between entities, and is thus of limited application in extracting new relations.

Levy et al. (2017) showed that a related and complementary task, that of entity/attribute relation extraction, can be reduced to a question answering problem. The task we address in this work is that of zero-shot *relation classification*, which determines if a given relation exists between two given entities in text. As a result the output of our approach is a binary classification decision indicating whether a given relation exists between two given entities in text. The task performed by Levy et al. (2017) is that of zero-shot entity/attribute *relation extraction*, since their approach returns the span corresponding to the relation arguments ("answers") from the text.[1] In addition, our approach for zero-shot relation classification utilizes relation descriptions, which is typically available in relation ontologies, and is thus not reliant on crowd-sourcing.

Our approach also takes inspiration from var-

ious approaches for leveraging knowledge from a set of source tasks to target tasks, such as recent transfer learning methods in natural language processing (Peters et al., 2018; McCann et al., 2017). Closest to our work is that of Conneau et al. (2017), who showed that representations learned from natural language inference data can enhance performance when transferred to a number of other natural language tasks. In this work, we consider the task of zero-shot relation classification by utilizing relation descriptions.

3 Model

Our approach takes as input two pieces of text, a sentence containing the subject and object entities of a candidate relation, and the relation's description, and returns as output a binary response indicating whether the meaning of the description can be inferred between the two entities in the sentence. See Table 1 for some examples. The problem of determining whether the meaning of a text fragment can be inferred from another is that of natural language inference/textual entailment (Dagan et al., 2005; Bowman et al., 2015).

We take as our base model the Enhanced Sequential Inference Model (*ESIM*) introduced by Chen et al. (2017), one of the commonly used models for text pair tasks (**?**). *ESIM* utilizes Bidirectional Long Short-Term Memory (Hochreiter and Schmidhuber, 1997; Graves and Schmidhuber, 2005) (BiLSTM) units as a building block and accepts two sequences of text as input. It then passes the two sequences through three model stages - input encoding, local inference modelling and inference composition, and returns the class c with the highest classification score, where c in textual entailment is one of *entailment, contradiction* or *neutral*. In our experiments, for each (sentence, relation description) pair we return a 2-way classification prediction instead.

In this section we briefly describe the input en-

---

[1] Note that for this reason, a direct comparison between the two approaches is not straightforward, as this would be akin to comparing a text classification model and a question answering model.

coding and inference composition stages, which we adapt using conditional encoding as described in the following subsection. The *input encoding* and *inference composition* stages operate analogously, and each receives as input two sequences of vectors, $\{p_i\}$ and $\{h_j\}$, or more compactly two matrices $P \in \mathbb{R}^{I \times d}$ for the premise and $H \in \mathbb{R}^{J \times d}$ for the hypothesis, where I and J are respectively the number of words in the premise and hypothesis, and d is the dimensionality of each vector representation. In the case of the *input encoding* layer, P and H are word embeddings of words in the premise and hypothesis respectively, while in the case of *inference composition*, P and H are internal model representations derived from the preceding local inference modelling stage. Then the input sequences are processed with BiLSTM units to yield new sequences $\bar{P} \in \mathbb{R}^{I \times 2d}$ for the premise and $\bar{H} \in \mathbb{R}^{J \times 2d}$ for the hypothesis:

$$\bar{P}, \overrightarrow{c}_p, \overleftarrow{c}_p = BiLSTM(P) \qquad (1)$$
$$\bar{H}, \overrightarrow{c}_h, \overleftarrow{c}_h = BiLSTM(H) \qquad (2)$$

where $\overrightarrow{c}_p, \overleftarrow{c}_p \in \mathbb{R}^d$ are respectively the last cell states in the forward and reverse directions of the BiLSTM that reads the premise. $\overrightarrow{c}_h, \overleftarrow{c}_h \in \mathbb{R}^d$ are similarly defined for the hypothesis.

3.1 Conditional encoding for ESIM

When used for zero-shot relation classification, *ESIM* encodes the sentence independently of the relation description. Given a new target relation's description, it is desirable for representations computed for the sentence to take into account the representations for the target relation description. Therefore we explicitly condition the representations of the sentence on that of the relation description using a conditional BiLSTM (cBiLSTM) (Rocktäschel et al., 2016) unit. Thus, Equation 1 is replaced with:

$$\bar{P} = cBiLSTM(P, \overrightarrow{c}_h, \overleftarrow{c}_h) \qquad (3)$$

where $\overrightarrow{c}_h$ and $\overleftarrow{c}_h$ respectively denote the last memory cell states in the forward and reverse directions of the BiLSTM that reads the relation description. This adaptation is made to both input encoding and inference composition stages. We refer to the adapted *ESIM* as the Conditioned Inference Model (*CIM*) in subsequent sections.

4 Datasets

We evaluate our approach using the datasets of Adel et al. (2016) and (Levy et al., 2017). The dataset of Adel et al. (2016) (*LMU-RC*) is split into training, development and evaluation sets. The training set was generated by distant supervision, and the development and test data were obtained from manually annotated TAC-KBP system outputs. We obtained the descriptions for the relations from the TAC-KBP relation ontology guidelines.[2] This resulted in a dataset of about 6 million positive and negative instances, each consisting of a relation, its subject and object entities, a sentence containing both entities and a relation description.

We applied a similar process to the relation extraction dataset of (Levy et al., 2017) (*UW-RE*). It consists of 120 relations and a set of question templates for each relation, containing both positive and negative relation instances, with each instance consisting of a subject entity, a knowledge base relation, a question template for the relation, and a sentence retrieved from the subject entity's Wikipedia page. We wrote descriptions for each of the 120 relations in the dataset, with each relation's question templates serving as a guide. Thus all instances in the dataset (30 million positive and 2 million negative ones) now include the corresponding relation description, making them suitable for relation classification using our approach.

In addition to the two datasets, we also utilize the *MultiNLI* natural language inference corpus (Williams et al., 2018) in our experiments as a source of supervision. We map its *entailment* and *contradiction* class instances to positive and negative relation instances respectively.

5 Experiments and Results

We conduct two sets of experiments. The first set of experiments tests the performance of our approach in the zero-shot setting, where no supervision instances are available for new relations (Section 5.1). The second set of experiments measures the performance of our approach in the limited supervision regime, where varying levels of supervision is available (Section 5.2).

Implementation Details Our model is implemented in Tensorflow (Abadi et al., 2016).

---

[2]`https://tac.nist.gov/2015/KBP/ColdStart/guidelines/TAC_KBP_2015_Slot_Descriptions_V1.0.pdf`

Dataset	Model	F1 (%)
LMU-RC	ESIM	20.16
	CIM	**22.80**
UW-RE	ESIM	61.32
	CIM	**64.78**

Table 2: Zero-shot relation learning results for *ESIM* and *CIM*.

Dataset	Supervision	F1 (%)
LMU-RC	TE	25.54
	TE+DS	**26.28**
UW-RE	TE	44.38
	TE+DS	**62.33**

Table 3: Zero-shot relation learning results for model CIM pre-trained on two sources of data: Textual Entailment (TE), or both Distant Supervision and Textual Entailment (TE+DS). The results in Table 2 correspond to DS only supervision.

We initialize word embeddings with 300D Glove (Pennington et al., 2014) vectors. We found a few epochs of training (generally less than 5) to be sufficient for convergence. We apply Dropout with a keep probability of 0.9 to all layers. The result reported for each experiment is the average taken over five runs with independent random initializations. In order to prevent overfitting to specific entities, we mask out the subject and object entities with the tokens *SUBJECT_ENTITY* and *OBJECT_ENTITY* respectively.

5.1 Zero-shot Relation Learning

For this experiment we created ten folds of each dataset, with each fold partitioned into train/dev/test splits along relations. In each fold, a relation belongs exclusively to either the train, dev or test split.

Table 2 shows averaged F1 across the folds for the models on the *LMU-RC* and *UW-RE* datasets. We observe that using only distant supervision for the training relations and without supervision for the test relations, the models were still able to make predictions for them, though at different performance levels. *CIM* obtained better performance compared to *ESIM*, as a result of its use of conditional encoding.

Table 3 shows F1 scores of model *CIM* pretrained on only MultiNLI (referred to as TE) or a combination of MultiNLI and distant supervision (referred to as TE+DS) data in the zero-shot set-

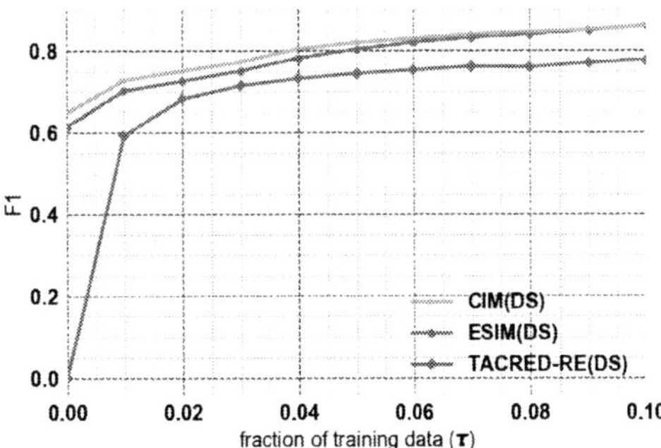

Figure 1: Limited supervision results: F1 scores on *UW-RE* as fraction of training data (τ) is varied. When $\tau=0$, we get the zero-shot results in Table 2

ting. We find that *CIM* pre-trained on only textual entailment data is already able to make predictions for unseen test relations, while using a combination of distant supervision and textual entailment data achieved improved F1 scores across both datasets, demonstrating the validity of our approach in this setting. We also note that using TE+DS data performs worse than DS data alone in the case of the *UW-RE* dataset, unlike in the case of *LMU-RC*. We hypothesize that this is because DS data performs much better for the former.

5.2 Few-shot Relation Learning

For the experiments in the limited-supervision setting, we randomly partition the dataset along relations into a train/dev/test split. Similar to the zero-shot setting, a relation belongs to each split exclusively. Then for each experiment, we make available to each model a fraction τ of example instances of the relations in the test set as supervision. Note that the particular example instances we use are a disjoint set of instances which are not present in the development and evaluation sets. In addition to ESIM and our proposed model CIM, we also report results for the TACRED Relation Extractor (*TACRED-RE*), the position-aware RNN model that was found to achieve state-of-the-art results on the TACRED (Zhang et al., 2017) dataset. *TACRED-RE* is a supervised model that expects labelled data for all relations during training, and thus not applicable in the zero-shot setup.

Results for this set of experiments are shown in Figure 1 for the *UW-RE* dataset. We find that only about 5% of the training data is required for both *ESIM* and *CIM* to reach around 80% in F1

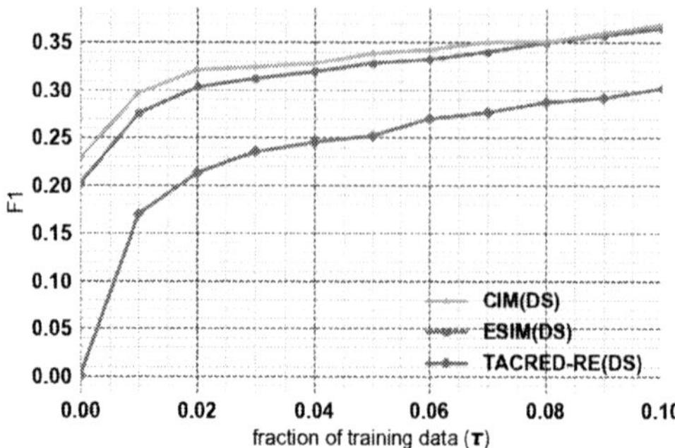

Figure 2: F1 scores on *LMU-RC* as fraction of training data (τ) is varied.

performance, with *CIM* outperforming *ESIM* in the 0-6% interval. However, beyond this interval, we do not observe any major difference in performance between ESIM and *CIM*, demonstrating that CIM performs well in both the zero-shot and limited supervision settings. For context, when given full supervision on the *UW-RE* dataset, *CIM* and *TACRED-RE* obtain F1 scores of 94.82% and 87.73% respectively. A similar trend is observed for the *LMU-RC* dataset, whose plot can be found in Figure 2.

In general, all models obtain better results on *UW-RE* than on *LMU-RC*. We hypothesize that the performance difference is due to *UW-RE* being derived from Wikipedia documents (which typically have well-written text), while LMU-RC was obtained from different genres and sources (such as discussion forum posts and web documents), which tend to be noisier.

5.3 Qualitative Results

Figure 3 depicts a visualization of the normalized attention weights assigned by model *CIM* on instances drawn from the development set. We observe that it is able to attend to words that are semantically coherent with the premise ("novel" and "author", Figure 3a), ("studied" and "university", Figure 3b).

6 Conclusions

We show that the task of relation classification can be achieved through the use of relation descriptions, by formulating the task as one of textual entailment between the relation description and the piece of text. This leads to several advantages, including the ability to perform zero-shot relation

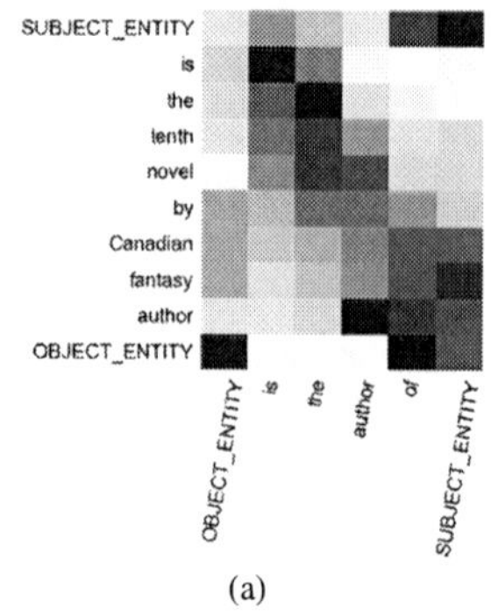

(a)

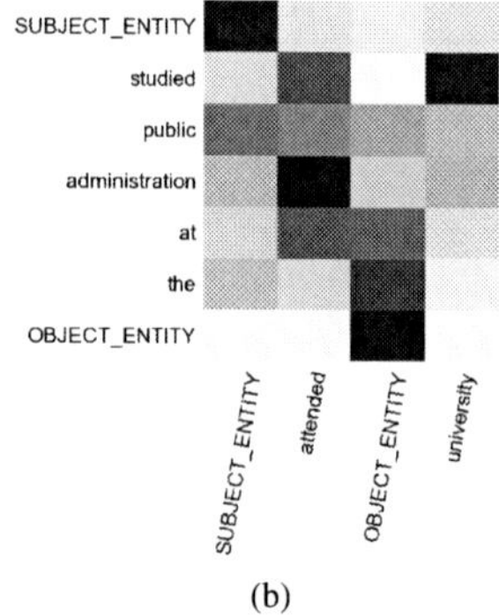

(b)

Figure 3: Attention visualization

classification and use textual entailment models and datasets to improve performance.

Acknowledgments

We are grateful to Pasquale Minervini and Jeff Mitchell for helpful conversations and suggestions, and the Sheffield NLP group and anonymous reviewers for valuable feedback. This research is supported by the EU H2020 SUMMA project (grant agreement number 688139).

References

Martin Abadi, Paul Barham, Jianmin Chen, Zhifeng Chen, Andy Davis, Jeffrey Dean, Matthieu Devin, Sanjay Ghemawat, Geoffrey Irving, Michael Isard, and Others. 2016. TensorFlow: A System for Large-Scale Machine Learning. In *OSDI*, volume 16, pages 265–283.

Heike Adel, Benjamin Roth, and Hinrich Schütze. 2016. Comparing convolutional neural networks to traditional models for slot filling. In *Proceedings of the 2016 Conference of the North American Chapter of the Association for Computational Linguistics: Human Language Technologies*, pages 828–838, San Diego, California. Association for Computational Linguistics.

Kurt Bollacker, Colin Evans, Praveen Paritosh, Tim Sturge, and Jamie Taylor. 2008. Freebase: a collaboratively created graph database for structuring human knowledge. *SIGMOD 08 Proceedings of the 2008 ACM SIGMOD international conference on Management of data*, pages 1247–1250.

Samuel R. Bowman, Gabor Angeli, Christopher Potts, and Christopher D. Manning. 2015. A large annotated corpus for learning natural language inference. In *EMNLP*.

Qian Chen, Xiaodan Zhu, Zhen-Hua Ling, Si Wei, Hui Jiang, and Diana Inkpen. 2017. Enhanced lstm for natural language inference. In *Proceedings of the 55th Annual Meeting of the Association for Computational Linguistics (Volume 1: Long Papers)*, pages 1657–1668. Association for Computational Linguistics.

Alexis Conneau, Douwe Kiela, Holger Schwenk, Loïc Barrault, and Antoine Bordes. 2017. Supervised Learning of Universal Sentence Representations from Natural Language Inference Data. In *Proceedings of the 2017 Conference on Empirical Methods in Natural Language Processing*, pages 670–680. Association for Computational Linguistics.

Ido Dagan, Oren Glickman, and Bernardo Magnini. 2005. The PASCAL Recognising Textual Entailment Challenge. In *Machine Learning Challenges, Evaluating Predictive Uncertainty, Visual Object Classification and Recognizing Textual Entailment, First PASCAL Machine Learning Challenges Workshop, MLCW 2005, Southampton, UK, April 11-13, 2005, Revised Selected Papers*, pages 177–190.

Thomas Demeester, Tim Rocktäschel, and Sebastian Riedel. 2016. Lifted Rule Injection for Relation Embeddings. *Proceedings of the 2016 Conference on Empirical Methods in Natural Language Processing (EMNLP-16)*, pages 1389–1399.

Alex Graves and Jürgen Schmidhuber. 2005. Framewise phoneme classification with bidirectional LSTM networks. In *Proceedings of the International Joint Conference on Neural Networks*, volume 4, pages 2047–2052.

Sepp Hochreiter and Jürgen Schmidhuber. 1997. Long Short-Term Memory. *Neural Computation*, 9(8):1735–1780.

Heng Ji and Ralph Grishman. 2011. Knowledge base population: Successful approaches and challenges. In *Proceedings of the 49th Annual Meeting of the Association for Computational Linguistics: Human Language Technologies*, pages 1148–1158. Association for Computational Linguistics.

Omer Levy, Minjoon Seo, Eunsol Choi, and Luke Zettlemoyer. 2017. Zero-Shot Relation Extraction via Reading Comprehension.

Bryan McCann, James Bradbury, Caiming Xiong, and Richard Socher. 2017. Learned in translation: Contextualized word vectors. In *Advances in Neural Information Processing Systems*, pages 6297–6308.

George A. Miller. 1995. WordNet: a lexical database for English. *Communications of the ACM*, 38(11):39–41.

Jeffrey Pennington, Richard Socher, and Christopher D Manning. 2014. GloVe: Global Vectors for Word Representation. In *Empirical Methods in Natural Language Processing (EMNLP)*, pages 1532–1543.

Matthew E Peters, Mark Neumann, Mohit Iyyer, Matt Gardner, Christopher Clark, Kenton Lee, and Luke Zettlemoyer. 2018. Deep contextualized word representations. In *Proc. of NAACL*.

Sebastian Riedel, Limin Yao, Andrew McCallum, and Benjamin M. Marlin. 2013. Relation Extraction with Matrix Factorization and Universal Schemas. *Proceedings of the 2013 Conference of the North American Chapter of the Association for Computational Linguistics: Human Language Technologies*, (June):74–84.

Tim Rocktäschel, Edward Grefenstette, Karl Moritz Hermann, Tomas Kocisky, and Phil Blunsom. 2016. Reasoning about entailment with neural attention. In *International Conference on Learning Representations (ICLR)*.

Tim Rocktäschel, Sameer Singh, and Sebastian Riedel. 2015. Injecting logical background knowledge into embeddings for relation extraction. In *NAACL HLT 2015, The 2015 Conference of the North American Chapter of the Association for Computational Linguistics: Human Language Technologies, Denver, Colorado, USA, May 31 - June 5, 2015*, pages 1119–1129.

Mihai Surdeanu, Julie Tibshirani, Ramesh Nallapati, and Christopher D Manning. 2012. Multi-instance Multi-label Learning for Relation Extraction. *Proceedings of the 2012 Joint Conference on Empirical Methods in Natural Language Processing and Computational Natural Language Learning, EMNLP '12*, (July):455–465.

Adina Williams, Nikita Nangia, and Samuel Bowman. 2018. A broad-coverage challenge corpus for sentence understanding through inference. In *Proceedings of the 2018 Conference of the North American Chapter of the Association for Computational Linguistics: Human Language Technologies, Volume 1 (Long Papers)*, pages 1112–1122, New Orleans, Louisiana. Association for Computational Linguistics.

Dmitry Zelenko, Chinatsu Aone, and Anthony Richardella. 2003. Kernel methods for relation extraction. *The Journal of Machine Learning Research*, 3:1083–1106.

Yuhao Zhang, Victor Zhong, Danqi Chen, Gabor Angeli, and Christopher D. Manning. 2017. Position-aware attention and supervised data improve slot filling. In *Proceedings of the 2017 Conference on Empirical Methods in Natural Language Processing*, pages 35–45. Association for Computational Linguistics.

Teaching Syntax by Adversarial Distraction

Juho Kim
University of Illinois
Urbana, IL
juhokim2@illinois.edu

Christopher Malon
NEC Laboratories America
Princeton, NJ
malon@nec-labs.com

Asim Kadav
NEC Laboratories America
Princeton, NJ
asim@nec-labs.com

Abstract

Existing entailment datasets mainly pose problems which can be answered without attention to grammar or word order. Learning syntax requires comparing examples where different grammar and word order change the desired classification. We introduce several datasets based on synthetic transformations of natural entailment examples in SNLI or FEVER, to teach aspects of grammar and word order. We show that without retraining, popular entailment models are unaware that these syntactic differences change meaning. With retraining, some but not all popular entailment models can learn to compare the syntax properly.

1 Introduction

Natural language inference (NLI) is a task to identify the entailment relationship between a premise sentence and a hypothesis sentence. Given the premise, a hypothesis may be true (entailment), false (contradiction), or not clearly determined (neutral). NLI is an essential aspect of natural language understanding. The release of datasets with hundreds of thousands of example pairs, such as SNLI (Bowman et al., 2015) and MultiNLI (Williams et al., 2018), has enabled the development of models based on deep neural networks that have achieved near human level performance.

However, high accuracies on these datasets do not mean that the NLI problem is solved. Annotation artifacts make it possible to correctly guess the label for many hypotheses without even considering the premise (Gururangan et al., 2018; Poliak et al., 2018; Tsuchiya, 2018). Successful trained systems can be disturbed by small changes to the input (Glockner et al., 2018; Naik et al., 2018).

In this paper, we show that existing trained NLI systems are mostly unaware of the relation between syntax and semantics, particularly of how word order affects meaning. We develop a technique, "adversarial distraction," to teach networks to properly use this information. The adversarial distraction technique consists of creating pairs of examples where information matching the premise is present in the hypothesis in both cases, but differing syntactic structure leads to different entailment labels. We generate adversarial distractions automatically from SNLI and an NLI dataset derived from FEVER (Thorne et al., 2018), thus augmenting the datasets. We observe the behavior of several existing NLI models on the added examples, finding that they are mostly unaware that the syntactic changes have affected the meaning. We then retrain the models with the added examples, and find whether these weaknesses are limitations of the models or simply due to the lack of appropriate training data.

2 Related work

Datasets for NLI: SNLI and MultiNLI are both based on crowdsourced annotation. In SNLI all the premises came from image captions (Young et al., 2014), whereas MultiNLI collected premises from several genres including fiction, letters, telephone speech, and a government report. SciTail (Khot et al., 2018) constructed more complicated hypotheses based on multiple-choice science exams, whose premises were taken from web text. More recently, FEVER introduced a fact verification task, where claims are to be verified using all of Wikipedia. As FEVER established ground truth evidence for or against each claim, premises can be collected with a retrieval module and labeled as supporting, contradictory, or neutral for an NLI dataset.

Neural network based NLI systems: Dozens of neural network based models have been submitted to the SNLI leaderboard. Some systems have

79

Proceedings of the First Workshop on Fact Extraction and VERification (FEVER), pages 79–84
Brussels, Belgium, November 1, 2018. ©2018 Association for Computational Linguistics

been developed based on sentence representations (Conneau et al., 2017; Nie and Bansal, 2017), but most common models apply attention between tokens in the premise and hypothesis. We focus on three influential models of this kind: Decomposable Attention (Parikh et al., 2016), ESIM (Chen et al., 2017), and a pre-trained transformer network (Radford et al., 2018) which obtains state-of-the-art results for various NLI datasets including SNLI and SciTail.

Adversarial examples for NLI systems: Jia and Liang (2017) introduced the notion of distraction for reading comprehension systems by trying to fool systems for SQuAD (Rajpurkar et al., 2016) with information nearly matching the question, added to the end of a supporting passage. Glockner et al. (2018) showed that many NLI systems were confused by hypotheses that were identical to the premise except for the replacement of a word by a synonym, hypernym, co-hyponym, or antonym. Naik et al. (2018) found that adding the same strings of words to NLI examples without changing the logical relation could significantly change results, because of word overlap, negation, or length mismatches.

Other work (Kang et al., 2018; Zhao et al., 2018) aimed to improve model robustness in the framework of generative adversarial networks (Goodfellow et al., 2014). Ribeiro et al. (2018) generated semantically equivalent examples using a set of paraphrase rules derived from a machine translation model. In contrast to these kinds of adversarial examples, we focus on the model not being sensitive enough to small changes that do change meaning.

3 Teaching Syntax

Our adversarial examples attack NLI systems from a new direction: not in their failure to capture the relations between words as in Glockner et al. (2018), but their failure to consider the syntax and word order in premises and hypotheses to decide upon the entailment relation. As position-agnostic approaches such as Decomposable Attention and SWEM (Shen et al., 2018) provide competitive baselines to existing datasets, the power of models to interpret token position information has not been rigorously tested.

3.1 Passive voice

We first evaluate and teach the use of the passive voice. By changing a hypothesis to passive, we can obtain a semantically equivalent hypothesis with identical tokens except for a different conjugation of the verb, the insertion of the word "by," and a different word order.

To perform the conversion, we use semantic role labeling results of SENNA (Collobert et al., 2011) to identify verbs and their ARG0 and ARG1 relations. We change the form of the verb and move the ARG0 and ARG1 phrases to opposite sides of the verb to form the passive. Here, we use head words identified in dependency parsing results and the part-of-speech tagging information of the verb from spaCy (Honnibal and Johnson, 2015) to change the verb form correctly according to the plurality of these nouns and the tense of the verb. The transformation is applied only at the root verb identified in dependency parsing output.

If the addition of the passive were the only augmentation, models would not be learning that word order matters. Thus, in the cases where the original pair is an entailment, we add an adversarial distraction where the label is contradiction, by reversing the subject and object in the hypothesis after transformation to passive. We call this the *passive reversal*. We filter out cases where the root verb in the hypothesis is a reciprocal verb, such as "meet" or "kiss," or a verb appearing with the preposition "with," so that the resulting sentence is surely not implied by the premise if the original is. For example, the hypothesis, "A woman is using a large umbrella" (entailment), generates the passive example, "A large umbrella is being used by a woman" (entailment), and the passive reversal, "A woman is being used by a large umbrella" (contradiction).

3.2 Person reversal

One weakness of adversarial distraction by passive reversal is that many hypotheses become ridiculous. A model leveraging language model information can guess that a hypothesis such as "A man is being worn by a hat" is a contradiction without considering the premise. Indeed, when we train a hypothesis only baseline (Poliak et al., 2018) with default parameters using the SNLI dataset augmented with passive and passive reversal examples, 95.98% of passive reversals are classified correctly from the hypothesis alone, while only

	SNLI			FEVER		
	original	passive	passive rev	original	person rev	birthday
# train	549,367	129,832	39,482	602,240	3,154	143,053
# validation	9,842	2,371	724	42,541	95	9,764
# test	9,824	2,325	722	42,970	69	8,880

Table 1: The number of examples in the original SNLI and FEVER data, and the number of examples generated for each adversarial distraction.

67.89% of the original and 64.69% of the passive examples are guessed correctly.

To generate more plausible adversarial distractions, we try reversing named entities referring to people. Most person names should be equally likely with or without reversal, with respect to a language model, so the generated examples should rely on understanding the syntax of the premise correctly.

SNLI generally lacks named entities, because it is sourced from image captions, so we consider FEVER data instead. The baseline FEVER system (Thorne et al., 2018) retrieves up to five sentences of potential evidence from Wikipedia for each claim, by comparing TFIDF scores. We label each of these evidence/claim pairs as entailment or contradiction, according to the claim label, if the evidence appears in the ground truth evidence set, and as neutral otherwise. Because the potential evidence is pulled from the middle of an article, it may be taken out of context with coreference relations unresolved. To provide a bit of context, we prefix each premise with the title of the Wikipedia page it comes from, punctuated by brackets.

Our *person reversal* dataset generates contradictions from entailment pairs, by considering person named entities identified by SENNA in the hypothesis, and reversing them if they appear within the ARG0 and ARG1 phrases of the root verb. Again, we filter examples with reciprocal verbs and the preposition "with." For example, the FEVER claim, "Lois Lane's name was taken from Lola Lane's name" (entailment), leads to a person reversal of "Lola Lane's name was taken from Lois Lane's name" (contradiction).

To compare the plausibility of the examples, we train the same hypothesis only baseline on the FEVER dataset augmented with the person reversals. It achieves 15.94% accuracy on the added examples, showing that the person reversals are more plausible than the passive reversals.

3.3 Life spans

Our third adversarial distraction (*birthday*) involves distinguishing birth and death date information. It randomly inserts birth and death dates into a premise following a person named entity, in parentheses, using one of two date formats. If it chooses a future death date, no death date is inserted. A newly generated hypothesis randomly gives a statement about either birth or death, and either the year or the month, with a label equally balanced among entailment, contradiction, and neutral. For half of the contradictions it simply reverses the birth and death dates; otherwise it randomly chooses another date. For the neutral examples it asks about a different named entity, taken from the same sentence if possible.

For example, a birthday and death date are randomly generated to yield the premise, "[Daenerys Targaryen] Daenerys Targaryen is a fictional character in George R. R. Martin's A Song of Ice and Fire series of novels, as well as the television adaptation, Game of Thrones, where she is portrayed by Emilia Clarke (April 25, 860 November 9, 920)," and hypothesis, "Emilia Clarke died in April" (contradiction).

4 Evaluation

4.1 Experiments

We consider three NLI systems based on deep neural networks: Decomposable Attention (DA) (Parikh et al., 2016), ESIM (Chen et al., 2017), and a Finetuned Transformer Language Model (FTLM) (Radford et al., 2018). For Decomposable Attention we take the AllenNLP implementation (Gardner et al., 2017) without ELMo features (Peters et al., 2018); for the others, we take the releases from the authors. We modify the code released for FTLM to support entailment classification, following the description in the paper.

For the FEVER-based datasets, for DA and ESIM, we reweight each class in the training data

	SNLI			FEVER		
	Original	Passive	Passive rev.	Original	Person rev.	Birthday
DA	.8456	.8301	.0111	.8416 (.1503)	.0435	.2909
ESIM	.8786	.8077	.0139	.8445 (.3905)	.0290	.3134
FTLM	.8980	.8430	.0540	.9585 (.6656)	.0000	.2953

Table 2: Accuracy and (Cohen's Kappa) when training on original SNLI or FEVER data and testing on original or added examples.

	SNLI			Person rev.		Birthday	
	Original	Passive	Passive rev.	Original	Added	Original	Added
DA	.8517	.7333	.5042	.8552 (.1478)	.1449	.8925 (.1550)	.4700
ESIM	.8781	.8667	.9833	.8406 (.3809)	.6232	.8721 (.4404)	.9684
FTLM	.8953	.8920	.9917	.9581 (.6610)	.7536	.9605 (.6809)	.9926

Table 3: Accuracy and (Cohen's Kappa) when training on augmented SNLI (SNLI + passive + passive reversal) or augmented FEVER (FEVER + person reversal or FEVER + birthday) and testing on original or added examples.

in inverse proportion to its number of examples. This reweighting is necessary to produce nontrivial (most frequent class) results; the NLI training set we derive from FEVER has 92% neutral, 6% entailment, and 2% contradiction examples. FTLM requires no such reweighting. When evaluating on the original FEVER examples, we report Cohen's Kappa between predicted and ground truth classifications, in addition to accuracy, because the imbalance pushes DA and ESIM below the accuracy of a trivial classifier.

Whereas FTLM uses a byte-pair encoding vocabulary (Sennrich et al., 2016) that can represent any word as a combination of subword tokens, DA and ESIM rely on word embeddings from GloVe (Pennington et al., 2014), with a single out-of-vocabulary (OOV) token shared for all unknown words. Therefore it is unreasonable to expect DA and ESIM not to confuse named entities in FEVER tasks. We extend each of these models by allocating 10,000 random vectors for out-of-vocabulary words, and taking a hash of each OOV word to select one of the vectors. The vectors are initialized from a normal distribution with mean 0 and standard deviation 1.

4.2 Results

When we train the three models using original SNLI without augmentation, the models have slightly lower performance on the passive examples than the original data. However, all three models fail to properly classify the passive reversal data: without training, it looks too similar to the original hypothesis. The augmented data succeeds in training two out of three of the models about the passive voice: ESIM and FTLM can classify the passive examples with approximately the accuracy of the original examples, and with even higher accuracy, they can pick out the passive reversals as preposterous. However, DA cannot do better than guess whether a passive sentence is reversed or not. This is because its model is defined so that its output is invariant to changes in word order. Because it must consider the possibility of a passive reversal, its performance on the passive examples actually goes down after training with augmentations.

Person reversal also stumps all three models before retraining. Of course DA can get a person reversal right only when it gets an original example wrong, because of its insensitivity to word order. ESIM and FTLM find person reversals to be more difficult than the original examples. Compared to passive reversal, the lack of language hints seems to make the problem more challenging. However, the multitude of conditions necessary to perform a person reversal makes the added examples less than 1% of the overall training data.

No model trained on FEVER initially does better than random guessing on the birthday problem. By training with augmented examples, ESIM and FTLM learn to use the structure of the premise properly to solve this problem. DA learns some hints after retraining, but essentially the problem depends on word order, which it is blind to. It is noteworthy that the performance of all three models on the original data improves after the birthday examples are added, unlike the other two augmentations, where performance remains the same. Four percent of the original FEVER claims use the word "born" or "died," and extra practice with these concepts proves beneficial.

5   Discussion

We have taken two basic aspects of syntax, the equivalence of passive and active forms of the same sentence, and the distinction between subject and direct object, and shown that they are not naturally learned through existing NLI training sets. Two of the models we evaluated could master these concepts with added training data, but the Decomposable Attention model could not even after retraining.

We automatically generated training data to teach these syntactic concepts, but doing so required rather complicated programs to manipulate sentences based on parsing and SRL results. Generating large numbers of examples for more complicated or rarer aspects of syntax will be challenging. An obvious difficulty in extending our approach is the need to make a distraction template that affects the meaning in a known way. The other difficulty lies in making transformed examples plausible enough not to be rejected by language model likelihood.

References

Samuel Bowman, Gabor Angeli, Christopher Potts, and Christopher Manning. 2015. A large annotated corpus for learning natural language inference. In *Proceedings of the Conference on Empirical Methods in Natural Language processing (EMNLP)*.

Qian Chen, Xiaodan Zhu, Zhen-Hua Ling, Si Wei, Hui Jiang, and Diana Inkpen. 2017. Enhanced LSTM for natural language inference. In *Proceedings of the 55th Annual Meeting of the Association for Computational Linguistics (ACL) Volume 1*, pages 1657–1668.

Ronan Collobert, Jason Weston, Léon Bottou, Michael Karlen, Koray Kavukcuoglu, and Pavel Kuksa. 2011. Natural language processing (almost) from scratch. *Journal of Machine Learning Research (JMLR)*, 12:2493–2537.

Alexis Conneau, Douwe Kiela, Holger Schwenk, Loïc Barrault, and Antoine Bordes. 2017. Supervised learning of universal sentence representations from natural language inference data. In *Proceedings of the Conference on Empirical Methods in Natural Language Processing (EMNLP)*, pages 670–680.

Matt Gardner, Joel Grus, Mark Neumann, Oyvind Tafjord, Pradeep Dasigi, Nelson F. Liu, Matthew Peters, Michael Schmitz, and Luke S. Zettlemoyer. 2017. AllenNLP: A deep semantic natural language processing platform. *CoRR*, abs/1803.07640.

Max Glockner, Vered Shwartz, and Yoav Goldberg. 2018. Breaking NLI systems with sentences that require simple lexical inferences. In *Proceedings of the 56th Annual Meeting of the Association for Computational Linguistics (ACL) Volume 2*, pages 650–655.

Ian Goodfellow, Jean Pouget-Abadie, Mehdi Mirza, Bing Xu, David Warde-Farley, Sherjil Ozair, Aaron Courville, and Yoshua Bengio. 2014. Generative adversarial nets. In *Advances in Neural Information Processing Systems (NIPS) 27*, pages 2672–2680.

Suchin Gururangan, Swabha Swayamdipta, Omer Levy, Roy Schwartz, Samuel Bowman, and Noah A. Smith. 2018. Annotation artifacts in natural language inference data. In *Proceedings of the 2018 Conference of the North American Chapter of the Association for Computational Linguistics: Human Language Technologies (NAACL-HLT) Volume 2*, pages 107–112.

Matthew Honnibal and Mark Johnson. 2015. An improved non-monotonic transition system for dependency parsing. In *Proceedings of the Conference on Empirical Methods in Natural Language Processing (EMNLP)*, pages 1373–1378.

Robin Jia and Percy Liang. 2017. Adversarial examples for evaluating reading comprehension systems. In *Proceedings of the Conference on Empirical Methods in Natural Language Processing (EMNLP)*, pages 2021–2031.

Dongyeop Kang, Tushar Khot, Ashish Sabharwal, and Eduard Hovy. 2018. Adversarial training for textual entailment with knowledge-guided examples. In *Proceedings of the 56th Annual Meeting of the Association for Computational Linguistics (ACL)*.

Tushar Khot, Ashish Sabharwal, and Peter Clark. 2018. SciTail: A textual entailment dataset from science question answering. In *Proceedings of the Thirty-Second AAAI Conference on Artificial Intelligence*.

Aakanksha Naik, Abhilasha Ravichander, Norman Sadeh, Carolyn Rose, and Graham Neubig. 2018. Stress test evaluation for natural language inference. In *Proceedings of the 27th International Conference on Computational Linguistics (COLING)*, Santa Fe, New Mexico, USA.

Yixin Nie and Mohit Bansal. 2017. Shortcut-stacked sentence encoders for multi-domain inference. In *Proceedings of the 2nd Workshop on Evaluating Vector Space Representations for NLP, RepEval@EMNLP*, pages 41–45.

Ankur Parikh, Oscar Täckström, Dipanjan Das, and Jakob Uszkoreit. 2016. A decomposable attention model for natural language inference. In *Proceedings of the Conference on Empirical Methods in Natural Language Processing (EMNLP)*, pages 2249–2255.

Jeffrey Pennington, Richard Socher, and Christopher D. Manning. 2014. GloVe: Global vectors for word representation. In *Proceedings of the Conference on Empirical Methods in Natural Language Processing (EMNLP)*, pages 1532–1543.

Matthew E. Peters, Mark Neumann, Mohit Iyyer, Matt Gardner, Christopher Clark, Kenton Lee, and Luke Zettlemoyer. 2018. Deep contextualized word representations. In *Proceedings of the Conference of the North American Chapter of the Association for Computational Linguistics: Human Language Technologies (NAACL-HLT) Volume 1*, pages 2227–2237.

Adam Poliak, Jason Naradowsky, Aparajita Haldar, Rachel Rudinger, and Benjamin Van Durme. 2018. Hypothesis only baselines in natural language inference. In *Proceedings of the Joint Conference on Lexical and Computational Semantics (*Sem)*.

Alec Radford, Karthik Narasimhan, Tim Salimans, and Ilya Sutskever. 2018. Improving language understanding by generative pre-training. In *OpenAI Blog*.

Pranav Rajpurkar, Jian Zhang, Konstantin Lopyrev, and Percy Liang. 2016. SQuAD: 100, 000+ questions for machine comprehension of text. In *Proceedings of the Conference on Empirical Methods in Natural Language Processing (EMNLP)*, pages 2383–2392.

Marco Tulio Ribeiro, Sameer Singh, and Carlos Guestrin. 2018. Semantically equivalent adversarial rules for debugging NLP models. In *Proceedings of the 56th Annual Meeting of the Association for Computational Linguistics (ACL) Volume 1*, pages 856–865.

Rico Sennrich, Barry Haddow, and Alexandra Birch. 2016. Neural machine translation of rare words with subword units. In *Proceedings of the 54th Annual Meeting of the Association for Computational Linguistics (ACL) Volume 1*, pages 1715–1725.

Dinghan Shen, Guoyin Wang, Wenlin Wang, Martin Renqiang Min, Qinliang Su, Yizhe Zhang, Chunyuan Li, Ricardo Henao, and Lawrence Carin. 2018. Baseline needs more love: On simple word-embedding-based models and associated pooling mechanisms. In *Proceedings of the 56th Annual Meeting of the Association for Computational Linguistics (ACL) Volume 1*, pages 440–450.

James Thorne, Andreas Vlachos, Christos Christodoulopoulos, and Arpit Mittal. 2018. FEVER: a large-scale dataset for fact extraction and verification. In *Proceedings of the Conference of the North American Chapter of the Association for Computational Linguistics: Human Language Technologies (NAACL-HLT) Volume 1*.

Masatoshi Tsuchiya. 2018. Performance impact caused by hidden bias of training data for recognizing textual entailment. In *Proceedings of the Eleventh International Conference on Language Resources and Evaluation (LREC)*.

Adina Williams, Nikita Nangia, and Samuel Bowman. 2018. A broad-coverage challenge corpus for sentence understanding through inference. In *Proceedings of the Conference of the North American Chapter of the Association for Computational Linguistics: Human Language Technologies (NAACL-HLT) Volume 1*, pages 1112–1122.

Peter Young, Alice Lai, Micah Hodosh, and Julia Hockenmaier. 2014. From image descriptions to visual denotations: New similarity metrics for semantic inference over event descriptions. In *Transactions of the Association for Computational Linguistics (TACL)*, volume 2, pages 67–78.

Zhengli Zhao, Dheeru Dua, and Sameer Singh. 2018. Generating natural adversarial examples. In *Proceedings of the International Conference on Learning Representations (ICLR)*.

Where is your Evidence: Improving Fact-checking by Justification Modeling

Tariq Alhindi and **Savvas Petridis**
Department of Computer Science
Columbia University
tariq@cs.columbia.edu
sdp2137@columbia.edu

Smaranda Muresan
Department of Computer Science
Data Science Institute
Columbia University
smara@columbia.edu

Abstract

Fact-checking is a journalistic practice that compares a claim made publicly against trusted sources of facts. Wang (2017) introduced a large dataset of validated claims from the POLITIFACT.com website (LIAR dataset), enabling the development of machine learning approaches for fact-checking. However, approaches based on this dataset have focused primarily on modeling the claim and speaker-related metadata, without considering the evidence used by humans in labeling the claims. We extend the LIAR dataset by automatically extracting the justification from the fact-checking article used by humans to label a given claim. We show that modeling the extracted justification in conjunction with the claim (and metadata) provides a significant improvement regardless of the machine learning model used (feature-based or deep learning) both in a binary classification task (true, false) and in a six-way classification task (pants on fire, false, mostly false, half true, mostly true, true).

1 Introduction

Fact-checking is the process of assessing the veracity of claims. It requires identifying evidence from trusted sources, understanding the context, and reasoning about what can be inferred from the evidence. Several organizations such as FACTCHECK.org, POLITIFACT.com and FULLFACT.org are devoted to such activities, and the final verdict can reflect varying degrees of truth (e.g., POLITIFACT labels claims as true, mostly true, half true, mostly false, false and pants on fire).

Until recently, the bottleneck for developing automatic methods for fact-checking has been the lack of large datasets for building machine learning models. Thorne and Vlachos (2018) provide a survey of current datasets and models for fact-checking (e.g., (Wang, 2017; Rashkin et al., 2017; Vlachos and Riedel, 2014; Thorne et al., 2018; Long et al., 2017; Potthast et al., 2018; Wang et al., 2018)). Wang (2017) has introduced a large dataset (LIAR) of claims from POLITIFACT, the associated metadata for each claim and the verdict (6 class labels). Most work on the LIAR dataset has focused on modeling the content of the claim (including hedging, sentiment and emotion analysis) and the speaker-related metadata (Wang, 2017; Rashkin et al., 2017; Long et al., 2017).

However, these approaches do not use the evidence and the justification provided by humans to predict the label. Extracting evidence from (trusted) sources for fact-checking or for argument mining is a difficult task (Rinott et al., 2015; Thorne et al., 2018; Baly et al., 2018). For the purpose of our paper, we rely on the fact-checking article associated with the claim. We extend the original LIAR dataset by automatically extracting the justification given by humans for labeling the claim, from the fact-checking article (Section 2). We release the extended LIAR dataset (LIAR-PLUS) to the community[1].

The main contribution of this paper is to show that modeling the extracted justification in conjunction with the claim (and metadata) provides a significant improvement regardless of the machine learning model used (feature-based or deep learning) both in a binary classification task (true, false) and in a six-way classification task (pants on fire, false, mostly false, half-true, mostly true, true) (Section 4). We provide a detailed error analysis and per-class results.

Our work complements the recent work on providing datasets and models that enable the development of an end-to-end pipeline for fact-

---

[1] https://github.com/Tariq60/LIAR-PLUS

85

Proceedings of the First Workshop on Fact Extraction and VERification (FEVER), pages 85–90
Brussels, Belgium, November 1, 2018. ©2018 Association for Computational Linguistics

checking ((Thorne et al., 2018) for English and (Baly et al., 2018) for Arabic). We are primarily concerned on showing the impact of modeling the human-provided justification for predicting the veracity of a claim. In addition, our task aims to capture the varying degrees of truth that some claims might have and that are usually labeled as such by professionals (rather than binary true vs. false labels).

2 Dataset

The LIAR dataset introduced by (Wang, 2017) consists of 12,836 short statements taken from POLITIFACT and labeled by humans for truthfulness, subject, context/venue, speaker, state, party, and prior history. For truthfulness, the LIAR dataset has six labels: pants-fire, false, mostly-false, half-true, mostly-true, and true. These six label sets are relatively balanced in size. The statements were collected from a variety of broadcasting mediums, like TV interviews, speeches, tweets, debates, and they cover a broad range of topics such as the economy, health care, taxes and election.

We extend the LIAR dataset to the LIAR-PLUS dataset by automatically extracting for each claim the justification that humans have provided in the fact-checking article associated with the claim. Most of the articles end with a summary that has a headline "our ruling" or "summing up". This summary usually has several justification sentences that are related to the statement. We extract all sentences in these summary sections, or the last five sentences in the fact-checking article when no summary exists. We filter out the sentence that has the verdict and related words. These extracted sentences can support or contradict the statement, which is expected to enhance the accuracy of the classification approaches. Excerpt from the LIAR-PLUS dataset is shown in Table 1.

3 Methods

The main goal of our paper is to show that modeling the human-provided justification — which can be seen as a summary evidence — improves the assessment of a claim's truth when compared to modeling the claim (and metadata) alone, regardless of the machine learning models (feature based vs. deep learning models). All our models

Statement: "Says Rick Scott cut education to pay for even more tax breaks for big, powerful, well-connected corporations."   **Speaker:** Florida Democratic Party   **Context:** TV Ad   **Label:** half-true   **Extracted Justification:** A TV ad by the Florida Democratic Party says Scott "cut education to pay for even more tax breaks for big, powerful, well-connected corporations." However, the ad exaggerates when it focuses attention on tax breaks for "big, powerful, well-connected corporations." Some such companies benefited, but so did many other types of businesses. And the question of whether the tax cuts and the education cuts had any causal relationship is murkier than the ad lets on.

Table 1: Excerpt from the LIAR-PLUS dataset

use 4 different conditions: *basic claim/statement[2] representation* using just word representations (**S condition**), *enhanced claim/statement representation* that captures additional information shown to be useful such as hedging, sentiment strength and emotion (Rashkin et al., 2017) as well as *metadata information* (**S^+M condition**), *basic claim/statement* and the associated *extracted justification* (**SJ condition**) and finally *enhanced claim/statement representation, metadata and justification* (**S^+MJ condition**).

Feature-based Machine Learning. We experiment with both Logistic Regression (LR) and Support Vector Machines (SVM) with linear kernel. For the basic representation of the claim/statement (S condition) we experimented with unigram features, tf-idf weighted unigram features and Glove word embeddings (Pennington et al., 2014). The best representation proved to be unigrams. For the enhanced statement representation (S^+) we modeled: sentiment strength using SentiStrength, which measures the negativity and positivity of a statement on a scale of 1-to-5 (Thelwall et al., 2010); emotion using the NRC Emotion Lexicon (EmoLex), which associates each word with eight basic emotions (Mohammad and Turney, 2010), and the Linguistic Inquiry and Word Count (LIWC) lexicon (Pennebaker et al., 2001). In addition, we include metadata information such as the number of claims each speaker makes for every truth-label (history) (Wang, 2017; Long et al., 2017). Finally for representing the justification in the SJ and S^+MJ conditions, we just use unigram features.

---

[2]In the rest of the paper we will refer to the claim as statement.

Cond.	Model	Binary		Six-way	
		valid	test	valid	test
S	LR	0.58	0.61	0.23	0.25
	SVM	0.56	0.59	0.25	0.23
	BiLSTM	0.59	0.60	0.26	0.23
SJ	LR	0.68	0.67	0.37	0.37
	SVM	0.65	0.66	0.34	0.34
	BiLSTM	0.70	0.68	0.34	0.31
	P-BiLSTM	0.69	0.67	0.36	0.35
S^+M	LR	0.61	0.61	0.26	0.25
	SVM	0.57	0.60	0.26	0.25
	BiLSTM	0.62	0.62	0.27	0.25
S^+MJ	LR	0.69	0.67	0.38	0.37
	SVM	0.66	0.66	0.35	0.35
	BiLSTM	0.71	0.68	0.34	0.32
	P-BiLSTM	0.70	0.70	0.37	0.36

Table 2: Classification Results

Class	class size	S		SJ		
		LR	BiLSTM	LR	BiLSTM	P-BiLSTM
pants-fire	116	0.18	0.19	0.37	0.34	0.37
false	263	0.28	0.34	0.33	0.3	0.33
mostly-false	237	0.21	0.13	0.35	0.31	0.32
half-true	248	0.22	0.28	0.39	0.31	0.37
mostly-true	251	0.23	0.33	0.40	0.39	0.39
true	169	0.22	0.18	0.37	0.42	0.39
total/avg	1284	0.23	0.26	0.37	0.34	0.36

Table 3: F1 Score Per Class on Validation Set

Class	class size	S		SJ		
		LR	BiLSTM	LR	BiLSTM	P-BiLSTM
pants-fire	92	0.12	0.11	0.38	0.33	0.39
false	250	0.31	0.31	0.35	0.32	0.35
mostly-false	214	0.25	0.15	0.35	0.27	0.33
half-true	267	0.24	0.26	0.41	0.27	0.34
mostly-true	249	0.23	0.30	0.35	0.35	0.33
true	211	0.25	0.16	0.37	0.36	0.41
total/avg	1283	0.25	0.23	0.37	0.31	0.35

Table 4: F1 Score Per Class on Test Set

Deep Learning Models. We chose to use Bi-Directional Long Short-term Memory (BiLSTM) (Hochreiter and Schmidhuber, 1997) architectures that have been shown to be successful for various related NLP tasks such a textual entailment and argument mining. For the S condition we use just one BiLSTM to model the statement. We use Glove pre-trained word embeddings (Pennington et al., 2014), a 100 dimension embedding layer that is followed by a BiLSTM layer of size 32. The output of the BiLSTM layer is passed to a soft-max layer. In the S^+M condition, a normalized count vector of those features (described above) is concatenated with the output of the BiLSTM layer to form a merge layer before the softmax. We used a categorical cross-entropy loss function and ADAM optimizer (Kingma and Ba, 2014) and trained the model for 10 epochs. For the SJ and S^+MJ conditions we experiment with two architectures: in the first one we just concatenate the justification to the statement and pass it to a single BiLSTM, and in the second one we use a dual/parallel architecture where one BiLSTM reads the statement and another one reads the justification (architecture denoted as P-BiLSTM). The outputs of these BiLSTMs are concatenated and passed to a softmax layer. This latter architecture has been proven to be effective for tasks that model two inputs such as textual entailment (Conneau et al., 2017) or sarcasm detection based on conversation context (Ghosh et al., 2017; Ghosh and Veale, 2017).

4 Results and Error Analysis

Table 2 shows the results both for the binary and the six-way classification tasks under all 4 conditions (S, SJ, S^+M and S^+MJ) for our feature-based machine learning models (LR and SVM) and the deep learning models (BiLSTM and P-BiLSTM). For the binary runs we grouped pants on fire, false and mostly false as FALSE and true, mostly true and half true as TRUE. As reference, Wang (2017 best models (text and metadata) obtained 0.277 F1 on validation set and 0.274 F1 on test set in the six-way classification, showing relatively similar results with our equivalent S^+M condition.

It is clear from the results shown in Table 2 that including the justification (SJ and S^+MJ conditions) improves over the conditions that do not use the justification (S and S^+M, respectively) for all models, both in the binary and the six-way classification tasks. For example, for the six-way classification, we see that the BiLSTM model for the SJ condition obtains 0.35 F1 compared to 0.23 F1 in the S condition. LR model has a similar behaviour with 0.37 F1 for the SJ condition compared to 0.25 F1 in S condition. For the S^+MJ conditions the best model (LR) shows an F1 of 0.38 compared to 0.26 F1 in the S^+M condition (similar results for the deep learning). The dual/parallel BiLSTM architecture provides a small improvement over the single BiLSTM only in the six-way classification.

We also present the per-class results for the six-way classification for the S and SJ conditions. Table 3 shows the results on validation set, while Table 4 on the test set. In the S condition, we

ID	Statement	Justification	label	S	S$^+$M	SJ	S$^+$MJ
1	We have the highest tax rate anywhere in the world.	Trump, while lamenting the condition of the middle class, said the U.S. has "the highest tax rate anywhere in the world." All sets of data we examined for individual and family taxes prove him wrong. Statutory income tax rates in the U.S. fall around the end of the upper quarter of nations. More exhaustive measures - which compute overall tax burden per person and as a percentage of GDP - show the U.S. either is in the middle of the pack or on the lighter end of taxation compared with other advanced industrialized nations.	false	X	✓	✓	✓
2	"Says Rick Scott cut education to pay for even more tax breaks for big, powerful, well-connected corporations."	A TV ad by the Florida Democratic Party says Scott "cut education to pay for even more tax breaks for big, powerful, well-connected corporations." However, the ad exaggerates when it focuses attention on tax breaks for "big, powerful, well-connected corporations." Some such companies benefited, but so did many other types of businesses. And the question of whether the tax cuts and the education cuts had any causal relationship is murkier than the ad lets on.	half-true	X	X	✓	✓
3	Says Donald Trump has given more money to Democratic candidates than Republican candidates.	but public records show that the real estate tycoon has actually contributed around $350,000 more to Republicans at the state and federal level than Democrats. That, however, is a recent development. Fergusons statement contains an element of truth but ignores critical facts.	mostly-false	X	X	✓	✓
4	Says out-of-state abortion clinics have marketed their services to minors in states with parental consent laws.	As Cousins clinic in New York told Yellow Page users in Pennsylvania, "No state consents." This is information the clinics wanted patients or potential patients to have, and paid money to help them have it. Whether it was to help persuade them to come in or not, it provided pertinent facts that could help them in their decision-making. It fit the definition of marketing.	true	X	X	X	✓
5	Obamacare provision will allow forced home inspections by government agents.	But the program they pointed to provides grants for voluntary help to at-risk families from trained staff like nurses and social workers. What bloggers describe would be an egregious abuse of the law not whats allowed by it.	pants-fire	X	X	X	✓
6	In the month of January, Canada created more new jobs than we did.	In November 2010, the U.S. economy created 93,000 jobs, compared to 15,200 for Canada. And in December 2010, the U.S. created 121,000 jobs, compared to 22,000 for Canada. "But on a per capita basis, in recent months U.S. job creation exceeded Canada's only in October." January happened to be a month when U.S. job creation was especially low and Canadian job creation was especially high, but it is the most recent month and it reflects the general pattern when you account for population.	true	X	X	X	X
7	There has been $5 trillion in debt added over the last four years.	number is either slightly high or a little low, depending on the type of measurement used, and thats actually for a period short of a full four years. His implication that Obama and the Democrats are to blame has some merit, but it ignores the role Republicans have had.	mostly-true	X	X	X	X

Table 5: Error analysis of Six-way Classification (Logistic Regression)

see a larger degree of variation in performance among classes, with the worst being the pants-on-fire for all models, and for the deep learning model also the mostly-false and true classes. In the SJ condition, we notice a more uniform performance on all classes for all the models. We notice the biggest improvement for the pants-on-fire class for all models, half-true for LR and mostly-false and true for the deep learning models. When comparing the P-BiLSTM and BiLSTM we noticed that the biggest improvement comes from the half-true class and the pants-on-fire class.

Error Analysis In order to further understand the cause of the errors made by the models, we analyzed several examples by looking at the statement, justification and predictions by the logistic regression model when using the S, S$^+$M, SJ, and S$^+$MJ conditions (Table 5). Logistic regression was selected since it has the best numbers for the six-way classification task.

The first example in Table 5 was wrongly classified in the S condition, but classified correctly in the S$^+$M, SJ and S$^+$MJ conditions. The justification text has a sentence saying "Statutory income tax rates in the U.S. fall around the end of the upper quarter of nations.", which contradicts the statement and thus is classified correctly when modeling the justification.

The second and third examples in Table 5 were correctly predicted only when the justification was modeled (SJ and S$^+$MJ conditions). For statement 2, the justification text has a sentence "However, the ad exaggerates..." indicates that the statement has some false and some true information. Therefore, the model predicts the correct label "half-true" when modeling the justification text. Also, the justification for statement 3 was simple enough for the model to predict the gold label "mostly-false". It has a phrase like "more to Republicans" while the statement had "more to Democratic candidates" which indicates falsehood in the statement as well as discourse markers indicating concessive moves ("but" and "however").

Sometimes justification features alone were not enough to get the correct prediction without using the *enhanced statement* and metadata features. The justification for statement 4 in Table 5 is complex and no direct connection can be made to the statement. Therefore, the model fails when using SJ and S$^+$M conditions and only succeed when using all features (i.e., S$^+$MJ condition). In addition, consider the 5th statement in Table 5 about Obamacare, it seems that metadata features, which have the history of the speaker, might have helped

in predicting its factuality to be "pants on fire",
while it was wrongly classified when modeling
only the statement and the justification.

For around half of the instances in validation
set, all models had wrong predictions. This is
not surprising since the best model had an average
F1 score of less than 0.40. The last two example
in Table 5 are instances where the model makes
mistakes under all 4 conditions. The claim and
justification refer to temporal information which
is harder to model by the rather simple and shal-
low approaches we used. Incorporating temporal
and numeric information when modeling the claim
and justification would be essential for capturing
the correct context of a given statement. Another
source of error for justification-based conditions
was the noise in the extraction of the justification
particularly when the "our ruling" and "summing
up" headers were not included and we resorted to
extract the last 5 sentences from the fact-checking
articles. Improving the extraction methods will be
helpful to improving the justification-based classification results.

5   Conclusion and Future Work

We presented a study that shows that modeling
the human-provided justification form the fact-
checking article associated with a claim is important leading to significant improvements when
compared to modeling just the claim/statement
and metadata for all the machine learning models both in a binary and a six-way classification task. We released LIAR-PLUS, the extended
LIAR dataset that contains the automatically extracted justification. We also provided an error
analysis and discussion of per-class performance.

Our simple method for extracting the justification from the fact-checking article can lead to
slightly noisy text (for example it can contain a
repetition of the claim or it can fail to capture
the entire evidence). We plan to further refine
the justification extraction method so that it contains just the summary evidence. In addition, we
plan to develop methods for evidence extraction
from the web (similar to the goals of the FEVER
shared task (Thorne et al., 2018)) and compare
the results of the automatically extracted evidence
with the human-provided justifications for fact-
checking the claims.

References

Ramy Baly, Mitra Mohtarami, James Glass, Lluís
Màrquez, Alessandro Moschitti, and Preslav Nakov.
2018. Integrating stance detection and fact checking
in a unified corpus. In *Proceedings of the 2018 Conference of the North American Chapter of the Association for Computational Linguistics: Human Language Technologies, Volume 2 (Short Papers)*, pages
21–27.

Alexis Conneau, Douwe Kiela, Holger Schwenk, Loïc
Barrault, and Antoine Bordes. 2017. Supervised
learning of universal sentence representations from
natural language inference data. In *Proceedings of
the 2017 Conference on Empirical Methods in Natural Language Processing*, pages 670–680. Association for Computational Linguistics.

Aniruddha Ghosh and Tony Veale. 2017. Magnets for
sarcasm: Making sarcasm detection timely, contextual and very personal. In *Proceedings of the 2017
Conference on Empirical Methods in Natural Language Processing*, pages 482–491.

Debanjan Ghosh, R. Alexander Fabbri, and Smaranda
Muresan. 2017. The role of conversation context
for sarcasm detection in online interactions. In *Proceedings of the 18th Annual SIGdial Meeting on Discourse and Dialogue*, pages 186–196. Association
for Computational Linguistics.

Sepp Hochreiter and Jürgen Schmidhuber. 1997.
Long short-term memory. *Neural computation*,
9(8):1735–1780.

Diederik P. Kingma and Jimmy Ba. 2014. Adam:
A method for stochastic optimization. *CoRR*,
abs/1412.6980.

Yunfei Long, Qin Lu, Rong Xiang, Minglei Li,
and Chu-Ren Huang. 2017. Fake news detection
through multi-perspective speaker profiles. In *Proceedings of the Eighth International Joint Conference on Natural Language Processing (Volume 2:
Short Papers)*.

Saif M Mohammad and Peter D Turney. 2010. Emotions evoked by common words and phrases: Using mechanical turk to create an emotion lexicon. In
*Proceedings of the NAACL HLT 2010 workshop on
computational approaches to analysis and generation of emotion in text*, pages 26–34. Association for
Computational Linguistics.

James W Pennebaker, Martha E Francis, and Roger J
Booth. 2001. Linguistic inquiry and word count:
Liwc 2001. *Mahway: Lawrence Erlbaum Asso-
ciates*, 71(2001):2001.

Jeffrey Pennington, Richard Socher, and Christopher
Manning. 2014. Glove: Global vectors for word
representation. In *Proceedings of the 2014 conference on empirical methods in natural language processing (EMNLP)*, pages 1532–1543.

Martin Potthast, Johannes Kiesel, Kevin Reinartz, Janek Bevendorff, and Benno Stein. 2018. A stylometric inquiry into hyperpartisan and fake news. In *Proceedings of the 56th Annual Meeting of the Association for Computational Linguistics (Volume 1: Long Papers)*, pages 231–240. Association for Computational Linguistics.

Hannah Rashkin, Eunsol Choi, Jin Yea Jang, Svitlana Volkova, and Yejin Choi. 2017. Truth of varying shades: Analyzing language in fake news and political fact-checking. In *Proceedings of the 2017 Conference on Empirical Methods in Natural Language Processing*, pages 2931–2937.

Ruty Rinott, Lena Dankin, Carlos Alzate Perez, Mitesh M. Khapra, Ehud Aharoni, and Noam Slonim. 2015. Show me your evidence - an automatic method for context dependent evidence detection. In *Proceedings of the 2015 Conference on Empirical Methods in Natural Language Processing*, pages 440–450.

Mike Thelwall, Kevan Buckley, Georgios Paltoglou, Di Cai, and Arvid Kappas. 2010. Sentiment strength detection in short informal text. *Journal of the Association for Information Science and Technology*, 61(12):2544–2558.

J Thorne and A Vlachos. 2018. Automated fact checking: Task formulations, methods and future directions. In *Proceedings of the 27th International Conference on Computational Linguistics (COLING 2018)*.

James Thorne, Andreas Vlachos, Christos Christodoulopoulos, and Arpit Mittal. 2018. FEVER: a large-scale dataset for fact extraction and verification. In *NAACL-HLT*.

Andreas Vlachos and Sebastian Riedel. 2014. Fact checking: Task definition and dataset construction. In *Proceedings of the ACL 2014 Workshop on Language Technologies and Computational Social Science*, pages 18–22.

William Yang Wang. 2017. "liar, liar pants on fire": A new benchmark dataset for fake news detection. In *Proceedings of the 55th Annual Meeting of the Association for Computational Linguistics (ACL 2017)*, Vancouver, BC, Canada. ACL.

Xuezhi Wang, Cong Yu, Simon Baumgartner, and Flip Korn. 2018. Relevant document discovery for fact-checking articles. In *Companion of the The Web Conference 2018 on The Web Conference 2018*, pages 525–533. International World Wide Web Conferences Steering Committee.

Affordance Extraction and Inference
based on Semantic Role Labeling

Daniel Loureiro, Alípio Mário Jorge
LIAAD - INESC TEC
Faculty of Sciences - University of Porto, Portugal
`dloureiro@fc.up.pt, amjorge@fc.up.pt`

Abstract

Common-sense reasoning is becoming increasingly important for the advancement of Natural Language Processing. While word embeddings have been very successful, they cannot explain which aspects of 'coffee' and 'tea' make them similar, or how they could be related to 'shop'. In this paper, we propose an explicit word representation that builds upon the Distributional Hypothesis to represent meaning from semantic roles, and allow inference of relations from their meshing, as supported by the affordance-based Indexical Hypothesis. We find that our model improves the state-of-the-art on unsupervised word similarity tasks while allowing for direct inference of new relations from the same vector space.

1 Introduction

The word representations used more recently in Natural Language Processing (NLP) have been based on the Distributional Hypothesis (DH) (Harris, 1954) — "words that occur in the same contexts tend to have similar meanings". This simple idea has led to the development of powerful word embedding models, starting with Latent Semantic Analysis (LSA) (Landauer and Dumais, 1997) and later, the popular word2vec (Mikolov et al., 2013) and GloVe (Pennington et al., 2014) models. Although, effective at quantifying the similarity between words (and phrases) such as 'tea' and 'coffee', they cannot relate that judgement to the fact that both can be sold, for instance. Furthermore, current representations can't inform us about possible relations between words occurring in mostly distinct contexts, such as using a 'newspaper' to cover a 'face'. While there have been substantial improvements to word embedding models over the years, these shortcomings have endured (Camacho-Collados and Pilehvar, 2018).

Word Pairs	Affordances
(w_1, w_2)	$(w_1$ as ARG0, w_2 as ARG1$)$
shop, tea	sell, import, cure
doctor, patient	diagnose, prescribe, treat
newspaper, face	cover, expose, poke
man, cup	drink, pour, spill

Table 1: Results from affordance meshing (coordination) using automatically labelled semantic roles.

Glenberg et al. (2000) identified these issues soon after LSA was introduced, and cautioned that high-dimensional word representations, such as those based on the DH, lack the necessary grounding to be proper semantic analogues. Instead, Glenberg proposed the Indexical Hypothesis (IH) which supports that meaning is constructed by (a) indexing words and phrases to real objects or perceptual, analog symbols; (b) deriving affordances from the objects and symbols; and (c) meshing the affordances under the guidance of syntax. Following Glenberg et al. (2000), this work considers an object's affordances as its possibilities for action constrained by its context, including actions which may not be directly perceived, which differs slightly from Gibson (1979)'s original definition. Even though the language grounding advocated by the IH is beyond the reach of NLP by itself, we believe that its representation of meaning through affordances can still be captured to a useful extent.

Our contribution[1] is a word-level representation that allows for the affordance correspondence and meshing supported by the IH. These affordances are approximated from occurrences of semantic roles in corpora through an adaptation of models based on the DH. Our work is motivated by two observations: (1) a pressing need to integrate common-sense knowledge in NLP mod-

---

[1]Code, data and demo: https://a2avecs.github.io

91

Proceedings of the First Workshop on Fact Extraction and VERification (FEVER), pages 91–96
Brussels, Belgium, November 1, 2018. ©2018 Association for Computational Linguistics

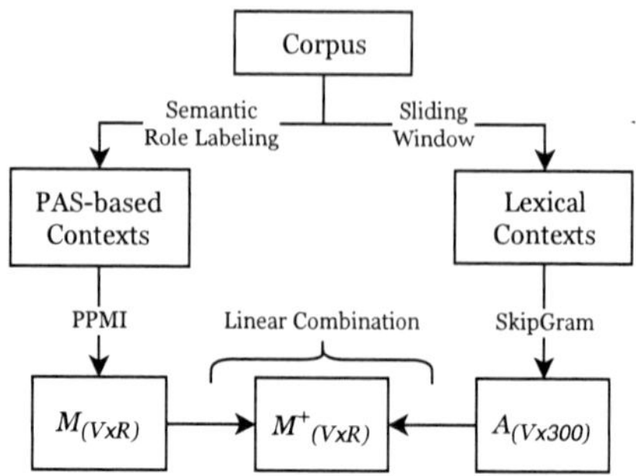

Figure 1: Outline of model pipeline.

els and (2) recent improvements to Semantic Role Labeling (SRL) have made affordance extraction from raw corpora sufficiently reliable. We find that our model (A2Avecs) performs competitively on word similarity tasks while enabling novel 'who-does-what-to-whom' style inferences (Table 1).

2 Related Work

This work is closely related to the research area of selectional preferences, where the goal is to predict the likelihood of a verb taking a certain argument for a particular role (e.g. likelihood of *man* being an *agent* of *drive*). Most notably, Erk et al. (2010) proposed a distributional model of selectional preferences that used SRL annotations as a primary set of verb-role-arguments from which to generalize using word representations based on the DH and several word similarity metrics. Progress in selectional preferences is usually measured through correlations with human thematic fit judgements and, more recently, neural approaches (de Cruys, 2014; Tilk et al., 2016) obtained state-of-the-art results.

While this work shares some of these same elements (i.e. SRL and word embeddings), they are used to predict potential affordances instead of selectional preferences. Consequently, our representations are designed to enable the meshing proposed by the IH, allowing us to infer affordances that would not be likely under a selectional preference learning scheme (e.g. *newspaper-cover-face* from Table 1). Additionally, this work is concerned with showing that information derived from SRL is complementary to information derived from DH methods, and thus focuses its evaluation on tasks related to lexical similarity rather than thematic fit correlations.

3 Method

Our word representations are modelled using Predicate-Argument Structures (PASs). These structures are obtained through SRL of raw corpora, and used to populate a sparse word/context co-occurrence matrix W where roles serve as contexts (features), and argument spans serve as the co-occurrence windows. The roles are predicates specified by argument type (e.g. eat|ARG0) and used in place of affordances. See Table 2 for a comparison of this context definition with the traditional lexical definition.

	Context	Words
Role	drinks|ARG0	John
	drinks|ARG1	red, wine
	drinks|ARGM-MNR	slowly
Adjacency	John	drinks, red
	drinks	John, red, wine
	red	John, drinks, wine, slowly
	wine	drinks, red, slowly
	slowly	red, wine

Table 2: Different context definitions applied to the sentence 'John drinks red wine slowly'. Top: Our proposed definition; Bottom: Lexical adjacency definition (with window size of 2).

After computing our co-occurrence matrix we follow-up with the additional steps employed by traditional bag-of-words models. We use Positive Pointwise Mutual Information (PPMI) to improve co-occurrence statistics, as used successfully by Bullinaria and Levy (2007); Levy and Goldberg (2014b), and maintain explicit high-dimensional representations in order to preserve the context information required for affordance meshing. Previous works, such as Levy and Goldberg (2014a) and Stanovsky et al. (2015), have also produced word representations from syntactic context definitions (dependency parse trees and open information extraction, respectively) but have opted for following-up with the word2vec's SkipGram (SG) model, presumably influenced by a much higher number of contexts in their approaches.

We reduce the sparsity of our explicit PPMI matrix by linear combination and interpolation of semantically related vectors. The semantic relatedness is obtained from the cosine similarity of SG vectors. As evidenced by Baroni et al. (2014), SG seem best suited for estimating relatedness (or association). These steps are further described in remainder of this section (See Fig. 1).

3.1 Extracting PASs

We use the AllenNLP (Gardner et al., 2017) implementation of He et al. (2017) state-of-the art SRL to extract PASs from an English Wikipedia dump from April 2010 (1B words). Since the automatic identification of predicates by an end-to-end SRL may produce erroneous results, we ensure that these predicates are valid by restricting them to the set of verbs tagged on the Brown corpus (Francis and Kucera, 1979). We also use the spaCy parser (Honnibal and Montani, 2017) to reduce each argument phrase to its head noun phrase, reducing the dilution of the more relevant noun and predicate co-occurrence statistics (See Fig. 2). Additionally, we lemmatize the predicates (verbs) to their root form using WordNet's Morphy Lemmatizer (Miller, 1992). Finally, we trim the vocabulary size and the number of roles by discarding those which occur less than 100 times, and consider only core and adjunct argument types. The result is a set C of observed contexts, such as $<$chase|ARG1, (the, cat)$>$, used to populate W.

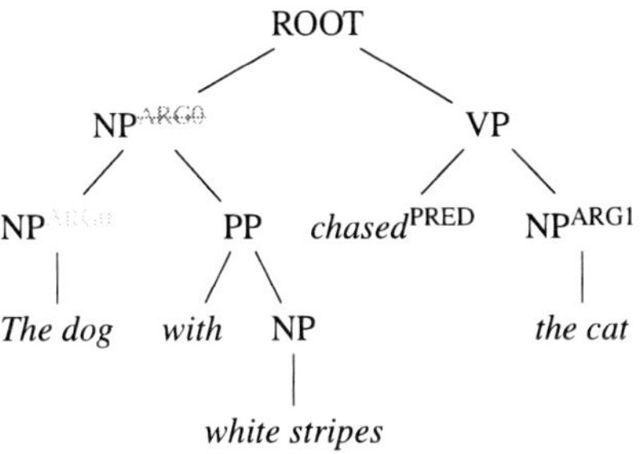

Figure 2: Parse tree for the sentence 'The dog with white stripes chased the cat.'. The label for ARG0 is repositioned to the smaller subtree.

3.2 Argument-specific PPMI

The authors of PropBank (Kingsbury and Palmer, 2002), which provides the annotations used for learning SRL, state that arguments are predicate-specific. Still, they also acknowledge that there are some trends in the argument assignments. For instance, the most consistent trends are that ARG0 is usually the agent, and ARG1 is the direct object or theme of the relation. This realisation leads us to adapting the PPMI measure to better account for the correlations between roles of the same argument types. Thus, we segment C by argument type, and apply PPMI independently considering

PST	PMI	THR	RND	MEN	SP
L				.249 (1)	98.71
L+H				.309 (47)	99.41
L+H	P			.606 (47)	99.58
L+H	A+P			.611 (47)	99.59
L+H	A+P	0.5		N/A^a	< 41.2
L+H	A+P	0.5	HDR	**.687 (0)**	98.21
L+H	A+P	0.6	HDR	.654 (14)	97.98
L+H	A+P	0.4	HDR	.668 (0)	98.77

^{a}Failed after using too much memory.

Table 3: Sensitivity/Impact analysis for some parameters of our approach.
Legend: **PST**: Post-Processing (L: Lemmatization; H: Head noun phrase isolation); **PMI**: PMI Variations (P: PPMI; A: Arg-specific PPMI); **THR**: Similarity threshold (tested values); **RND**: Rounding (HDR: Half down rounding); **MEN**: MEN-3K task (Spearman correlation, #OOV failures); **SP**: Sparsity (percentage of zero values on a 155Kx18K matrix).

each C_{ARG}, such that for each $W_{w,p}$:

$$PPMI(w, r) = max(PMI(w, r), 0)$$

$$PMI(w, r) = log\frac{f(w, r)}{f(w)f(r)} = log\frac{\#(w, r) \cdot |C_{ARG}|}{\#(w) \cdot \#(r)}$$

where w is a word from the vocabulary V, r is a role (context) from the set R of the same argument type as C_{ARG}, and f is the probability function. The resulting matrix $M = PPMI(W)$ maintains the dimensions W and is slightly sparser.

3.3 Leveraging Association

The constraints imposed by SRL yield a very reduced number of PAS-based contexts that can be extracted from a corpus, in comparison to lexical adjacency-based contexts. Moreover, the post-processing steps we perform, while otherwise beneficial (see Table 3), further trim this information. To mitigate this issue, we also compute an embedding matrix A (see Section 3 for parameters), using the state-of-the-art lexical-based SG model of Bojanowski et al. (2017), and use those embeddings to obtain similarity values that can be used to interpolate missing values in M, through weighted linear combination. This way, existing vectors are re-computed as:

$$\vec{v}_w = \frac{\vec{v}_1 * \alpha_1 \, | \, ... + \vec{v}_n * \alpha_n}{\sum_{i=1}^{n} \alpha_i}$$

with α_i defined as:

$$\alpha_i = \begin{cases} \dfrac{A_{\vec{v}_w} \cdot A_{\vec{v}_i}}{\|A_{\vec{v}_w}\|\|A_{\vec{v}_i}\|} = cos_A(\vec{v}_w, \vec{v}_i), \\ \qquad\qquad \text{if } cos_A(\vec{v}_w, \vec{v}_i) > 0.5 \\ 0, \quad \text{otherwise} \end{cases}$$

where cos_A corresponds to the cosine similarity in the SG representations.

The similarity threshold is tested on a few natural choices (0.5 ± 0.1) and validated from results on a single word similarity task (see Table 3). This approach is also used to define representations for words that are out-of-vocabulary (OOV) for M, but can be interpolated from related representations, similarly to Zhao et al. (2015). In conjunction with the interpolation, we apply half down rounding to the vectors, before and after re-computing them, so that our representations remain efficiently sparse while benefitting from improved performance. Finally, we apply a quadratic transformation to enlarge the influence of meaningful co-occurrences, obtaining $M^+ = interpolate(M, A)^2$.

3.4 Inferring Relations

The examples shown in Table 1 are easily obtained with our model through a simple procedure (see Algorithm 1) that matches different arguments of the same predicates. As was the case with Arg-specific PPMI, this procedure is made possible by the fact that a significant portion of argument assignments remain consistent across predicates.

Algorithm 1 Affordance Meshing Algorithm

1: **procedure** INFERENCE(M^+, w_1, w_2, a_1, a_2)
2: $\quad$ $relations \leftarrow []$
3: $\quad$ $\vec{v}_1, \vec{v}_2 \leftarrow get\_vec(w_1, M^+), get\_vec(w_2, M^+)$
4: $\quad$ **for** $f_1 \in features(\vec{v}_1) \wedge arg(f_1) = a_1$ **do**
5: $\quad\quad$ **for** $f_2 \in features(\vec{v}_2) \wedge arg(f_2) = a_2$ **do**
6: $\quad\quad\quad$ **if** $pred(f_1) = pred(f_2)$ **then**
7: $\quad\quad\quad\quad$ $relations.add((f_1 * f_2, pred(f_1)))$
8: $\quad$ **return** $sorted(relations)$

---

4 Evaluation and Experiments

The A2Avecs model introduced in this paper is used to generate 155,183 word vectors of 18,179 affordance dimensions. This section compares our model with lexical-based models (word2vec (Mikolov et al., 2013), GloVe (Pennington et al., 2014) and fastText (Bojanowski et al., 2017)) and other syntactic-based models (Deps (Levy and Goldberg, 2014a) and OpenIE (Stanovsky et al., 2015)). We're using Deps and OpenIE embeddings that the respective authors trained on a Wikipedia corpus and distributed online. Lexical models were trained using the same parameters, wherever applicable: Wikipedia corpus from April 2010 (same as mentioned in section 2.1); minimum word frequency of 100; window size of 2; 300 vector dimensions; 15 negative samples; and ngrams sized from 3 to 6 characters.

We also show that our approach can make use of high-quality pretrained embeddings. We experiment with a fastText model pretrained on 600B tokens, referred to as 'fastText 600B' in contrast with the fastText model trained on Wikipedia.

4.1 Model Introspection

The explicit nature of the representations produced by our model makes them directly interpretable, similarly to other sparse representations such as Faruqui and Dyer (2015b). The examples presented at Table 4 demonstrate the relational capacity of our model, beyond associating meaningful predicates. In this introspection we highlight the top role contexts for a set of words, inspired by (Levy and Goldberg, 2014a) which presented the top syntactic context for the same words, and note that this introspection produces results that should correspond to Erk et al. (2010)'s inverse selectional preferences.

Our online demonstration provides access to additional introspection queries, such as top words for given affordances, or which affordances are most distinguishable between a pair of words (determined by absolute difference).

batman	hogwarts	turing
foil|ARG0	ambush|ARGM-MNR	travel|ARGM-TMP
flirt|ARGM-MNR	rock|ARGM-LOC	pass|ARGM-ADV
apprehend|ARG0	express|ARG0	solve|ARG0
subdue|ARG0	prevent|ARGM-LOC	simulate|ARG1
rescue|ARGM-DIR	expel|ARG2	prove|ARG1
florida	**object-oriented**	**dancing**
base|ARGM-MNR	define|ARG1	dance|ARG0
vacation|ARG1	define|ARG0	dance|ARGM-MNR
reside|ARGM-DIS	use|ARG1	dance|ARGM-LOC
fort|ARG1	implement|ARG1	dance|ARGM-ADV
vacation|ARGM-LOC	express|ARGM-MNR	dance|ARG1

Table 4: Words and their top role contexts. Using the same words from the introspection of (Levy and Goldberg, 2014a) to clarify the difference in the representations of both approaches.

Context	Model	SL-666	SL-999	WS-SIM	WS-ALL	MEN	RG-65
Lexical	word2vec	.426	.414	.762	.672	.721	.793
	GloVe	.333	.325	.637	.535	.636	.601
	fastText (A)	.426	.419	**.779**	**.702**	**.751**	.799
Syntactic	Deps	**.475**	**.446**	.758	.629	.606	.765
	Open IE	.397	.390	.746	.696	.281	.801
	A2Avecs (M^+)	.461	.412	.734	.577	.687	**.802**
	A2Avecs (SVD(M^+))	.436	.386	.672	.509	.599	.789

Lexical SOTA	fastText 600B (A)	.523	.504	.839	**.791**	**.836**	**.859**
Intp. w/SOTA	A2Avecs (M^+)	.513	.468	.780	.619	.744	.814
Intp. & Conc.	A2Avecs ($M^+ \parallel A$)	**.540**	**.521**	**.846**	.771	.829	.857
Deps Conc.	Deps $\parallel A$	.524	.503	.818	.752	.770	.835

Table 5: Spearman correlations for word similarity tasks (see Faruqui and Dyer (2014) for task descriptions). Top section shows results from training on the Wikipedia corpus exclusively. Bottom section shows results where we used SG embeddings (A) trained on a larger corpus for performing interpolation and concatenation on the same set of roles used above. For comparison, we also show results for Deps concatenated with those embeddings.

4.2 Word Similarity

The results presented on Table 5 show that our model can outperform lexical and syntactic models, in spite of maintaining an explicit representation. In fact, applying Singular Value Decomposition (SVD) to obtain dense 300-dimensional embeddings degrades performance. We achieve best results with the concatenation of the fastText 600B vectors with our model interpolated using those same vectors for the vocabulary $V_{M+} \cap V_A$, after normalizing both to unit length (L_2). Interestingly, the same concatenation process with Deps embeddings doesn't seem as beneficial, suggesting that our representations are more complementary.

5 Conclusion

Our results suggest that semantic similarity can be captured in a vector space that also allows for the inference of new relations through affordance-based representations, which opens up exciting possibilities for the field. In the process, we presented more evidence to support that information obtained from SRL is complementary to information obtained from adjacency-based contexts, or even contexts based on syntactical dependencies. We believe this work helps bridge the gap between selectional preferences and semantic plausibility, beyond frequentist generalizations based on the DH. In the near term, we expect that specific tasks such as Entity Disambiguation and Coreference can benefit from these representations. With further developments, semantic plausibility assessments should also be useful for more broad tasks such as Fact Verification and Story Understanding.

References

Marco Baroni, Georgiana Dinu, and Germán Kruszewski. 2014. Don't count, predict! a systematic comparison of context-counting vs. context-predicting semantic vectors. In *ACL*.

Piotr Bojanowski, Edouard Grave, Armand Joulin, and Tomas Mikolov. 2017. Enriching word vectors with subword information. *TACL*, 5:135–146.

John A. Bullinaria and Joseph P. Levy. 2007. Extracting semantic representations from word co-occurrence statistics: a computational study. *Behavior research methods*, 39 3:510–26.

José Camacho-Collados and Mohammad Taher Pilehvar. 2018. From word to sense embeddings: A survey on vector representations of meaning.

Tim Van de Cruys. 2014. A neural network approach to selectional preference acquisition. In *EMNLP*.

Katrin Erk, Sebastian Padó, and Ulrike Padó. 2010. A flexible, corpus-driven model of regular and inverse selectional preferences. *Computational Linguistics*, 36:723–763.

Manaal Faruqui and Chris Dyer. 2014. Community evaluation and exchange of word vectors at wordvectors.org. In *ACL*.

Manaal Faruqui and Chris Dyer. 2015b. Non-distributional word vector representations. In *ACL*.

W. Nelson Francis and Henry Kucera. 1979. The Brown Corpus: A Standard Corpus of Present-Day Edited American English. Brown University Liguistics Department.

Matt Gardner, Joel Grus, Mark Neumann, Oyvind Tafjord, Pradeep Dasigi, Nelson F. Liu, Matthew Peters, Michael Schmitz, and Luke S. Zettlemoyer. 2017. Allennlp: A deep semantic natural language processing platform.

J. J. Gibson. 1979. The ecological approach to visual perception. *Brain and language*.

Arthur M. Glenberg, David A. Robertson, Brianna Benjamin, Jennifer Dolland, Jeanette Hegyi, Katherine V Kortenkamp, Erik Kraft, Nathan Pruitt, Dana Scherr, and Sara Steinberg. 2000. Symbol grounding and meaning: A comparison of high-dimensional and embodied theories of meaning.

Zellig Harris. 1954. Distributional structure. page 10(23):146162.

Luheng He, Kenton Lee, Mike Lewis, and Luke S. Zettlemoyer. 2017. Deep semantic role labeling: What works and what's next. In *ACL*.

Matthew Honnibal and Ines Montani. 2017. spacy 2: Natural language understanding with bloom embeddings, convolutional neural networks and incremental parsing. *To appear*.

Paul Kingsbury and Martha Palmer. 2002. From treebank to propbank. In *LREC*.

Thomas K. Landauer and Susan T. Dumais. 1997. A solution to plato's problem: The latent semantic analysis theory of acquisition, induction, and representation of knowledge.

Omer Levy and Yoav Goldberg. 2014a. Dependency-based word embeddings. In *ACL*.

Omer Levy and Yoav Goldberg. 2014b. Linguistic regularities in sparse and explicit word representations. In *CoNLL*.

Tomas Mikolov, Wen tau Yih, and Geoffrey Zweig. 2013. Linguistic regularities in continuous space word representations. In *HLT-NAACL*.

George A. Miller. 1992. Wordnet: A lexical database for english. *Commun. ACM*, 38:39–41.

Jeffrey Pennington, Richard Socher, and Christopher D. Manning. 2014. Glove: Global vectors for word representation. In *EMNLP*.

Gabriel Stanovsky, Ido Dagan, and Mausam. 2015. Open ie as an intermediate structure for semantic tasks. In *ACL*.

Ottokar Tilk, Vera Demberg, Asad B. Sayeed, Dietrich Klakow, and Stefan Thater. 2016. Event participant modelling with neural networks. In *EMNLP*.

Kai Zhao, Hany Hassan, and Michael Auli. 2015. Learning translation models from monolingual continuous representations. In *HLT-NAACL*.

UCL Machine Reading Group:
Four Factor Framework For Fact Finding (HexaF)

Takuma Yoneda
Computational Intelligence Lab.
Toyota Technological Institute
`sd18438@toyota-ti.ac.jp`

Jeff Mitchell, Johannes Welbl,
Pontus Stenetorp, Sebastian Riedel
Dept. of Computer Science
University College London
`{j.mitchell, j.welbl,`
`p.stenetorp, s.riedel}@cs.ucl.ac.uk`

Abstract

In this paper we describe our 2nd place
FEVER shared-task system that achieved a
FEVER score of 62.52% on the provisional
test set (without additional human evaluation),
and 65.41% on the development set. Our system is a four stage model consisting of document retrieval, sentence retrieval, natural language inference and aggregation. Retrieval
is performed leveraging task-specific features,
and then a natural language inference model
takes each of the retrieved sentences paired
with the claimed fact. The resulting predictions are aggregated across retrieved sentences
with a Multi-Layer Perceptron, and re-ranked
corresponding to the final prediction.

1 Introduction

We often hear the word "Fake News" these days.
Recently, Russian meddling, for example, has
been blamed for the prevalence of inaccurate news
stories on social media,[1] but even the reporting on
this topic often turns out to be fake news (Uberti,
2016). An abundance of incorrect information can
plant wrong beliefs in individual citizens and lead
to a misinformed public, undermining the democratic process. In this context, technology to automate fact-checking and source verification (Vlachos and Riedel, 2014) is of great interest to both
media consumers and publishers.

The Fact Extraction and Verification (FEVER)
shared task provides a benchmark for such tools,
testing the ability to assess textual claims against
a corpus of around 5.4M Wikipedia articles. Each
claim is labeled as SUPPORTS, REFUTES or NOT
ENOUGH INFO, depending on whether relevant
evidence from the corpus can support/refute it.
Systems are evaluated on the proportion of claims
for which both the predicted label is correct *and*

---

[1] https://www.bbc.co.uk/news/world-us-canada-
41821359

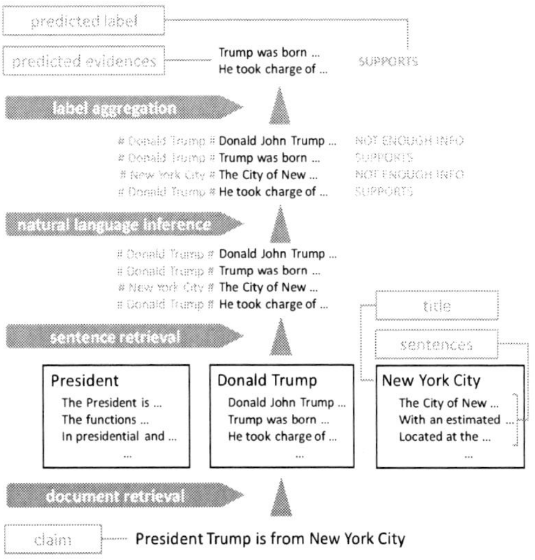

Figure 1: Illustration of the model pipeline for a claim.

a complete set of relevant evidence sentences has
been identified.

The original dataset description paper (Thorne
et al., 2018) evaluates a simple baseline system that achieves a score of ~33% on this metric, using tf-idf based retrieval to find the relevant evidence and a natural language inference (NLI) model to classify the relation between
the returned evidence and the claim. Our system
attempts to improve on this baseline by addressing two major weaknesses. Firstly, the original
retrieval component only finds a full evidence set
for 55% of claims. While tf-idf is an effective
task agnostic approach to information retrieval, we
find that a simple linear model using task-specific
features is able to achieve much stronger performance. Secondly, the NLI component uses an
overly simplistic strategy for aggregating retrieved
evidence, by simply concatenating all the sentences into a single paragraph. Instead, we employ

97

Proceedings of the First Workshop on Fact Extraction and VERification (FEVER), pages 97–102
Brussels, Belgium, November 1, 2018. ©2018 Association for Computational Linguistics

an explicit aggregation step to combine the knowledge gained from each evidence sentence. These improvements allow us to achieve a FEVER score of 65.41% on the development set, and 62.52% on the test set.

2 System Description

Our system is a four stage model consisting of document retrieval, sentence retrieval, NLI and aggregation. Document retrieval attempts to find the name of a Wikipedia article in the claim, and then ranks each article based on capitalisation, sentence position and token match features. A set of sentences are then retrieved from the top ranked articles, based on token matches with the claim and position in the article. The NLI model is subsequently applied to each of the retrieved sentences paired with the claim, giving a prediction for each potential evidence sentence. The respective predictions are aggregated using a Multi-Layer Perceptron (MLP), and the sentences are finally re-ranked so that the evidence which is consistent with the final prediction are placed at the top.

2.1 Document Retrieval

Our method begins by building a dictionary of article titles, based on the observation that the FEVER claims frequently include the title of a Wikipedia article containing the required evidence. These titles are first normalised by lowercasing, converting underscores to spaces and truncating to the first parenthesis if present. An initial list of potential articles is then constructed by detecting any such title in the claim. For each article, the probability of containing the gold evidence is predicted by a logistic regression model, using as features the position and capitalisation within the claim, presence of stop words, and token match counts between the first sentence of the article and the claim. Likewise we include the same counts also for the rest of the article as features, alongside whether the name was truncated, and whether the excised words are mentioned in the claim (e.g., "Watchmen" vs "Watchmen (film)").

The model is trained on a balanced set of positive and negative examples drawn from the training set, and the top-ranked articles are then passed on to the sentence retrieval component.

This process is related to, but goes substantially beyond entity recognition and linking (Mendes et al., 2017). These processes attempt to identify

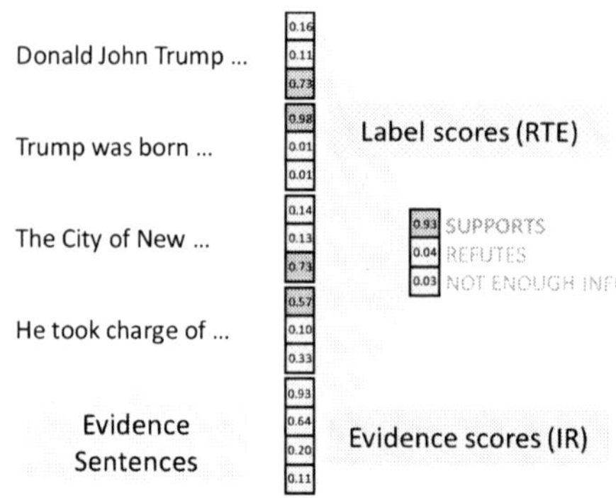

Figure 2: Overview: Aggregation Network

mentions of names from a limited class of entities (e.g. people, places, organisations). In our case, the mentions cover a much wider range of lexical items, including not only names but also common nouns, verbs or adjectives. Nonetheless, both types of model share the objective of finding mentions and linking them to a reference set.

2.2 Sentence Retrieval

We observed that many evidence sentences appear at the beginning of an article, and they often mention the article title. We thus train a logistic regression model, using as features the position of the sentence within the article, its length, whether the article name is present, token matching between the sentence and the claim, and the document retrieval score. The top-ranked sentences from this model are then passed to the subsequent NLI stage.

2.3 Natural Language Inference (NLI)

In this component, an NLI model predicts a label for each pair of claim and retrieved evidence sentence. We adopted the Enhanced Sequential Inference Model (ESIM) (Chen et al., 2017) as NLI model. ESIM employs a bidirectional LSTM (BiLSTM) to encode premise and hypothesis, and also encodes local inference information so that the model can effectively exploit sequential information. We also experimented with the Decomposable Attention Model (DAM) (Parikh et al., 2016) — as used in the baseline model, however ESIM consistently performed better. The Jack the Reader (Weissenborn et al., 2018) framework was used for both DAM and ESIM.

We first pre-trained the ESIM model on the Stanford Natural Language Inference (SNLI) corpus (Bowman et al., 2015), and then fine-tuned on the FEVER dataset. We used 300-dimensional pre-trained GloVe word embeddings (Pennington et al., 2014). As training input, we used gold evidence sentences for SUPPORTS and REFUTES samples, and retrieved evidence sentences for NOT ENOUGH INFO.

It is worth noting that there are two kinds of evidences in this task. The first is a complete set of evidence, which can support/refute a claim, and can consist of multiple sentences. The second is incomplete evidence, which can support or refute the claim only when paired with other evidence.

The baseline model (Thorne et al., 2018) simply concatenates all evidence sentences and feeds them into the NLI model, regardless of their evidence type. In contrast, we generate NLI predictions individually for each predicted evidence, thus processing them in parallel.

Furthermore, we observed that evidence sentences often include a pronoun referring to the subject of the article without explicitly mentioning it. This co-reference is opaque to the NLI model without further information. To resolve this, we prepend the corresponding title of the article to the sentence, along with a separator as described in Figure 1. We also experimented with adding line numbers to represent sentence position within the article, which did not, however, improve the label accuracy.

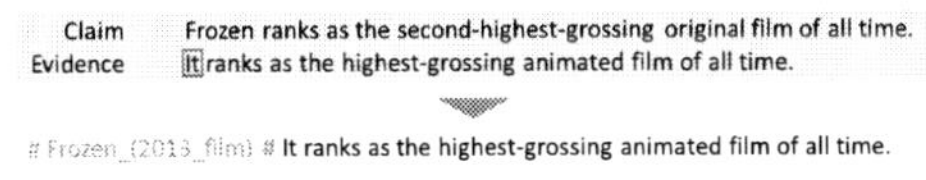

Figure 3: Illustration for the co-reference problem with individual sentences: What 'it' refers to is not obvious for a NLI model.

2.4 Aggregation

In the aggregation stage, the model aggregates the predicted NLI labels for each claim-evidence pair and outputs the final prediction.

The NLI model outputs three prediction scores per pair of sentences, one for each label. In our aggregation model, these scores are all fed into an MLP, alongside the evidence confidence scores for each of the (ranked) evidence sentences. Since the label balance in the training set is significantly biased, we give the samples training weights which are inversely proportional to the size of their respective class. We also experimented with drawing samples according to the size of each class,

but using the full training data with class weights performed better. The final MLP model contains 2 hidden layers with 100 hidden units each and Rectified Linear Unit (ReLU) nonlinearities (Nair and Hinton, 2010). We observed only minor performance differences when modifying the size and number of layers of the MLP.

Aside from this neural aggregation module, we also tested *logical aggregation*, *majority-vote* and *top-1 sentence*. In *logical aggregation*, our module takes the NLI predictions for all evidence sentences, and outputs either SUPPORTS or REFUTES if at least one of them has such a label, and NOT ENOUGH INFO if all predictions have that label. In cases where both SUPPORTS and REFUTES appear among the predictions, we take one from the highest ranked evidence. *Majority-vote* counts the frequency of labels among prediction and outputs the most frequent label. 15 predicted evidence sentences are used in each aggregation method.

3 Results

3.1 Aggregation Results

Table 1 shows the development set results of our model under the different aggregation settings. Note that the Evidence Recall and F1 metrics are calculated based on the top 5 predicted evidences. We observe that the *Majority-vote* aggregation method only reaches 43.94% of FEVER Score and 45.36% of label accuracy, either of which are much lower than other methods. Since there are only a few gold evidence sets for most claims, the majority of NLI predictions tend to be NOT ENOUGH INFO, rendering a majority aggregation method impractical.

Conversely, the *top-1 sentence* aggregation only uses the top-ranked sentence alone to form a label prediction. In this scenario a failure of the retrieval component is critical, nevertheless the system can achieve a FEVER score of 63.36%, leaving a large gap to the baseline model (Thorne et al., 2018). The *logical aggregation* improves slightly over omitting aggregation entirely (*top-1 sentence*). However, the neural aggregation module produces the best overall results, both in terms of FEVER score and label accuracy. This demonstrates the advantage of using a neural aggregation model operating on individual NLI confidence scores, compared to the more rigid use of only the predicted labels in *logical aggregation*.

Aggregation Method	FEVER Score	Label Accuracy	Evidence Recall	Evidence F1
Majority-vote	43.94	45.36	83.91	35.36
Top-1 sentence	63.36	66.30	84.62	35.72
Logical	64.29	68.26	85.03	36.02
MLP	65.41	69.66	84.54	35.84

Table 1: Development set scores for different aggregation methods, all numbers in percent.

Gold \ Prediction	*supports*	*refutes*	*not enough info*	**Total**
supports	5,345	336	985	6,666
refutes	827	4,196	1,643	6,666
not enough info	1,288	989	4,389	6,666
Total	7,460	5,521	7,017	19,998

Table 2: Confusion matrix on the development set.

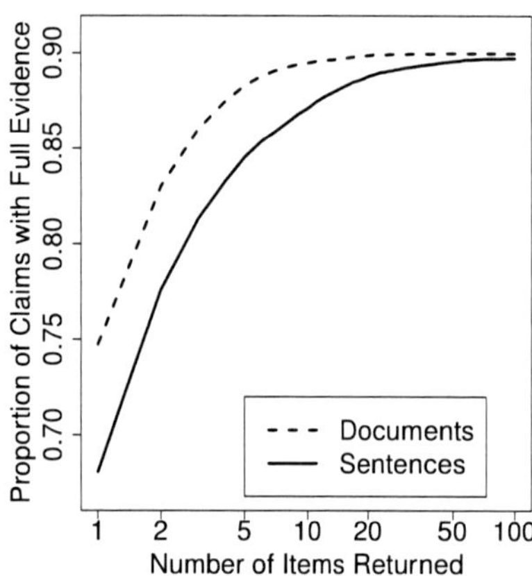

Figure 4: Performance of retrieval models on the development set.

Finally, after obtaining the aggregated label with the MLP, the model re-sorts its evidence predictions in such a way that those evidences with the same predicted label as the final prediction are ranked above those with a different label (see upper part of Figure 1). We observed that this re-ranking increased the evidence recall by 0.18 points (when used with MLP aggregation).

The overall FEVER score is the proportion of claims for which both the correct evidence is returned and a correct label prediction is made. We first describe the performance of the retrieval components, and then discuss the results for NLI.

3.2 Retrieval Results

On the development set, the initial step of identifying Wikipedia article titles within the text of the claim returns on average 62 articles per claim. These articles cover the full evidence set in 90.8% of cases and no relevant evidence is returned for only 2.9% of claims. Ranking these articles, using the model described above, achieves 81.4% HITS@1, and this single top-ranked article contains the full evidence in 74.7% of instances. Taking the text of the 15 best articles and ranking the sentences achieves 73.7% HITS@1, which is equivalent to returning the full evidence for 68% of claims. Figure 4 illustrates the performance of the IR components as the number of returned items increases.

4 Error Analysis

Table 2 shows the confusion matrix for the development set predictions. We observe that the system finds it easiest to classify instances labelled as SUPPORTS, whereas using the NOT ENOUGH INFO label correctly is most difficult.

We next describe some frequent failure cases of our model in the description below.

Limitations of word embeddings. Numerical expressions like years (1980s *vs* 80s) or months (January *vs* October) tend to have similar word embeddings, rendering it is difficult for a NLI model to distinguish them and correctly predict REFUTES cases. This was the most frequent error type encountered in the development set.

Confusing sentence. An NLI model aligns two sentences and predicts their relationship. For example, when two sentences are "Bob is in his house and he cannot sleep" and "Bob is awake", a model can conclude that the second sentence follows from the first one by simply aligning *Bob* with *Bob* and *cannot sleep* with *awake*. However, it sometimes fails to capture a correct alignment, which results in a fail prediction. For example, "Andrea Pirlo is an *American* professional footballer" *vs* "Andrea Pirlo is an *Italian* professional footballer who plays for an *American* club."

Sentence Complexity. In some cases, just taking an alignment is not enough to predict the correct label. In these cases, the model needs to capture the relationship between multiple words. For example, "Virginia keeps all computer chips manufactured within the state for use in Virginian electronics." *vs.* "Virginia's computer chips became the state's leading export by monetary value."

5 Future Work

For the model to read sentences that includes numerical expressions correctly, it could be helpful to explicitly encode the numerical expression and obtain a representation that captures the numerical features (Spithourakis and Riedel, 2018). Leveraging context-dependent pre-trained word embeddings such as ELMo (Peters et al., 2018) could help dealing better with more complex sentences.

6 Conclusion

In this paper, we described our FEVER shared-task system. We employed a four stage framework, composed of document retrieval, sentence retrieval, natural language inference, and aggregation. By applying task specific features for a retrieval model, and connecting an aggregation network on top of the NLI model, our model achieves a score of 65.41% on the development set and 62.52% on the provisional test set.

Acknowledgments

This work has been supported by the European Union H2020 project SUMMA (grant No. 688139), by an Allen Distinguished Investigator Award, and by an Engineering and Physical Sciences Research Council scholarship.

References

Samuel R. Bowman, Gabor Angeli, Christopher Potts, and Christopher D. Manning. 2015. A large annotated corpus for learning natural language inference. In *Proceedings of the 2015 Conference on Empirical Methods in Natural Language Processing*, pages 632–642. Association for Computational Linguistics.

Qian Chen, Xiaodan Zhu, Zhen-Hua Ling, Si Wei, Hui Jiang, and Diana Inkpen. 2017. Enhanced lstm for natural language inference. In *Proceedings of the 55th Annual Meeting of the Association for Computational Linguistics (Volume 1: Long Papers)*, pages 1657–1668. Association for Computational Linguistics.

Afonso Mendes, David Nogueira, Samuel Broscheit, Filipe Aleixo, Pedro Balage, Rui Martins, Sebastiao Miranda, and Mariana S. C. Almeida. 2017. Summa at tac knowledge base population task 2017. In *Proceedings of the Text Analysis Conference (TAC) KBP 2017*, Gaithersburg, Maryland USA. National Institute of Standards and Technology.

Vinod Nair and Geoffrey E. Hinton. 2010. Rectified linear units improve restricted boltzmann machines. In *Proceedings of the 27th International Conference on International Conference on Machine Learning*, ICML'10, pages 807–814, USA. Omnipress.

Ankur P. Parikh, Oscar Täckström, Dipanjan Das, and Jakob Uszkoreit. 2016. A decomposable attention model for natural language inference. *CoRR*, abs/1606.01933.

Jeffrey Pennington, Richard Socher, and Christopher D Manning. 2014. Glove: Global vectors for word representation. In *EMNLP*, volume 14, pages 1532–1543.

Matthew E. Peters, Mark Neumann, Mohit Iyyer, Matt Gardner, Christopher Clark, Kenton Lee, and Luke Zettlemoyer. 2018. Deep contextualized word representations. *CoRR*, abs/1802.05365.

Georgios P. Spithourakis and Sebastian Riedel. 2018. Numeracy for language models: Evaluating and improving their ability to predict numbers. *CoRR*, abs/1805.08154.

James Thorne, Andreas Vlachos, Christos Christodoulopoulos, and Arpit Mittal. 2018. FEVER: a large-scale dataset for fact extraction and verification. In *NAACL-HLT*.

David Uberti. 2016. Washington post fake news story blurs the definition of fake news. *Columbia Journalism Review*.

Andreas Vlachos and Sebastian Riedel. 2014. Fact checking: Task definition and dataset construction. In *Proceedings of the ACL 2014 Workshop on Language Technologies and Computational Social Science*, pages 18–22, Baltimore, MD, USA. Association for Computational Linguistics.

Dirk Weissenborn, Pasquale Minervini, Tim Dettmers, Isabelle Augenstein, Johannes Welbl, Tim Rocktaschel, Matko Bosnjak, Jeff Mitchell, Thomas Demeester, Pontus Stenetorp, and Sebastian Riedel.

2018. Jack the Reader A Machine Reading Framework. In *Proceedings of the 56th Annual Meeting of the Association for Computational Linguistics (ACL) System Demonstrations.*

UKP-Athene: Multi-Sentence Textual Entailment for Claim Verification

Andreas Hanselowski[†*]**, Hao Zhang**[*]**, Zile Li**[*]**, Daniil Sorokin**[†*]**,**
Benjamin Schiller[*]**, Claudia Schulz**[†*]**, Iryna Gurevych**[†*]

[†]Research Training Group AIPHES
Computer Science Department, Technische Universität Darmstadt
`https://www.aiphes.tu-darmstadt.de`

[*]Ubiquitous Knowledge Processing Lab (UKP-TUDA)
Computer Science Department, Technische Universität Darmstadt
`https://www.ukp.tu-darmstadt.de/`

Abstract

The Fact Extraction and VERification (FEVER) shared task was launched to support the development of systems able to verify claims by extracting supporting or refuting facts from raw text. The shared task organizers provide a large-scale dataset for the consecutive steps involved in claim verification, in particular, document retrieval, fact extraction, and claim classification. In this paper, we present our claim verification pipeline approach, which, according to the preliminary results, scored third in the shared task, out of 23 competing systems. For the document retrieval, we implemented a new entity linking approach. In order to be able to rank candidate facts and classify a claim on the basis of several selected facts, we introduce two extensions to the Enhanced LSTM (ESIM).

1 Introduction

In the past years, the amount of false or misleading content on the Internet has significantly increased. As a result, information evaluation in terms of fact-checking has become increasingly important as it allows to verify controversial claims stated on the web. However, due to the large number of fake news and hyperpartisan articles published online every day, manual fact-checking is no longer feasible. Thus, researchers as well as corporations are exploring different techniques to automate the fact-checking process[1].

In order to advance research in this direction, the Fact Extraction and VERification (FEVER) shared task[2] was launched. The organizers of the FEVER shared task constructed a large-scale dataset (Thorne et al., 2018) based on Wikipedia. This dataset contains 185,445 claims, each of which comes with several evidence sets. An evidence set consists of facts, i.e. sentences from Wikipedia articles that jointly support or contradict the claim. On the basis of (any one of) its evidence sets, each claim is labeled as *Supported*, *Refuted*, or *NotEnoughInfo* if no decision about the veracity of the claim can be made. Supported by the structure of the dataset, the FEVER shared task encompasses three sub-tasks that need to be solved.

Document retrieval: Given a claim, find (English) Wikipedia articles containing information about this claim.

Sentence selection: From the retrieved articles, extract facts in the form of sentences that are relevant for the verification of the claim.

Recognizing textual entailment: On the basis of the collected sentences (facts), predict one of three labels for the claim: *Supported*, *Refuted*, or *NotEnoughInfo*. To evaluate the performance of the competing systems, an evaluation metric was devised by the FEVER organizers: a claim is considered as correctly verified if, in addition to predicting the correct label, a correct evidence set was retrieved.

In this paper, we describe the pipeline system that we developed to address the FEVER task. For document retrieval, we implemented an entity linking approach based on constituency parsing and handcrafted rules. For sentence selection, we developed a sentence ranking model based on the *Enhanced Sequential Inference Model* (ESIM) (Chen et al., 2016). We furthermore extended the ESIM for recognizing textual entailment between multiple input sentences and the claim using an attention mechanism.

According to the preliminary results of the

---

[1]`https://fullfact.org/media/uploads/`
`full_fact-the_state_of_automated_`
`factchecking_aug_2016.pdf`
[2]`http://fever.ai/task.html`

103

Proceedings of the First Workshop on Fact Extraction and VERification (FEVER), pages 103–108
Brussels, Belgium, November 1, 2018. ©2018 Association for Computational Linguistics

FEVER shared task, our systems came third out of 23 competing teams.

2   Background

In this section, we present underlying methods that we adopted for the development of our system.

2.1   Entity linking

The document retrieval step requires matching a given claim with the content of a Wikipedia article. A claim frequently features one or multiple *entities* that form the main content of the claim.

Furthermore, Wikipedia can be viewed as a knowledge base, where each article describes a particular *entity*, denoted by the article title. Thus, the document retrieval step can be framed as an entity linking problem (Cucerzan, 2007). That is, identifying entity mentions in the claim and linking them to the Wikipedia articles of this entity. The linked Wikipedia articles can then be used as the set of the retrieved documents for the subsequent steps.

2.2   Enhanced Sequential Inference Model

Originally developed for the SNLI task (Bowman et al., 2015) of determining entailment between two statements, the ESIM (Enhanced Sequential Inference Model) (Chen et al., 2016) creates a rich representation of statement-pairs. Since the FEVER task requires the handling of claim-sentence pairs, we use the ESIM as the basis for both sentence selection and textual entailment. The ESIM solves the entailment problem in three consecutive steps, taking two statements as input.

Input encoding: Using a bidirectional LSTM (BiLSTM) (Graves and Schmidhuber, 2005), representations of the individual tokens of the two input statements are computed.

Local inference modeling: Each token of one statement is used to compute attention weights with respect to each token in the other statement, giving rise to an attention weight matrix. Then, each token representation is multiplied by all of its attention weights and weighted pooling is applied to compute a single representation for each token. This operation gives rise to two new representations of the two statements.

Inference composition: These two statement representations are then fed into two BiLSTMs, which again compute sequences of representations for each statement. Maximum and average pool-

ing is applied to the two sequences to derive two representations, which are then concatenated (last hidden state of the ESIM) and fed into a multilayer perceptron for the classification of the entailment relation.

3   Our system for fact extraction and claim verification

In this section, we describe the models that we developed for the three FEVER sub-tasks.

3.1   Document retrieval

As explained in Section 2.1, we propose an *entity linking* approach to the document retrieval sub-task. That is, we find entities in the claims that match the titles of Wikipedia articles (documents). Following the typical entity linking pipeline, we develop a document retrieval component that has three main steps.

Mention extraction: Named entity recognition tools focus only on the main types of entities (Location, Organization, Person). In order to find entities of different categories, such as movie titles, that are numerous in the shared task data set, we employ the constituency parser from AllenNLP (Gardner et al., 2017). After parsing the claim, we consider every *noun phrase* as a potential entity mention. However, a movie or a song title may be an adjective or any other type of syntactic phrase. To account for such cases, we use a heuristic that adds all words in the claim before the main verb as well as the whole claim itself as potential entity mentions. For example, a claim *"Down With Love is a 2003 comedy film."* contains the noun phrases '*a 2003 comedy film*' and '*Love*'. Neither of the noun phrases constitutes an entity mention, but the tokens before the main verb, '*Down With Love*', form an entity.

Candidate article search: We use the MediaWiki API[3] to search through the titles of all Wikipedia articles for matches with the potential entity mentions found in the claim. The MediaWiki API uses the Wikipedia search engine to find matching articles. The top match is the article whose title has the largest overlap with the query. For each entity mention, we store the seven highest-ranked Wikipedia article matches.

The MediaWiki API uses the online version of Wikipedia and since there are some discrepancies

---

[3] `https://www.mediawiki.org/wiki/API:Main_page`

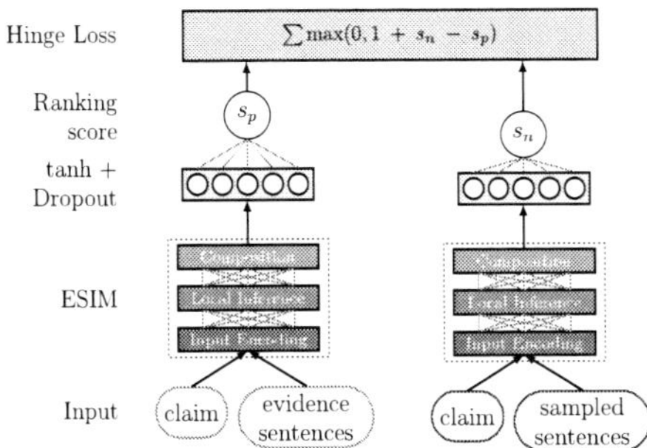

Figure 1: Sentence selection model

between the 2017 dump used in the shared task and the latest version, we also perform an exact search over all Wikipedia article titles in the dump. We add these results to the set of the retrieved articles.

Candidate filtering: The MediaWiki API retrieves articles whose title overlaps with the query. Thus, the results may contain articles with a title longer or shorter than the entity mention used in the query. Similarly to previous work on entity linking (Sorokin and Gurevych, 2018), we remove results that are longer than the entity mention and do not overlap with the rest of the claim. To check this overlap, we first remove the content in parentheses from the Wikipedia article titles and stem the remaining words in the titles and the claim. Then, we discard a Wikipedia article if its stemmed article title is not completely included in the stemmed claim.

We collect all retrieved Wikipedia articles for all identified entity mentions in the claim after filtering and supply them to the next step in the pipeline. The evaluation of the document retrieval system on the development data shows the effectiveness of our ad-hoc entity linking approach (see Section 4).

3.2 Sentence selection

In this step, we select candidate sentences as a potential evidence set for a claim from the Wikipedia articles retrieved in the previous step. This is achieved by extending the ESIM to generate a ranking score on the basis of two input statements, instead of predicting the entailment relation between these two statements.

Architecture: The modified ESIM takes as input a claim and a sentence. To generate the ranking score, the last hidden state of the ESIM (see Section 2.2) is fed into a hidden layer which is con-

nected to a single neuron for the prediction of the ranking score. As a result, we are able to rank all sentences of the retrieved documents according to the computed ranking scores. In order to find a potential evidence set, we select the five highest-ranked sentences.

Training: Our adaptation of the ESIM is illustrated in Fig. 1. In the training mode, the ESIM takes as input a claim and the concatenated sentences of an evidence set. As a loss function, we use a modified hinge loss with negative sampling: $\sum max(0, 1 + s_n - s_p)$, where s_p indicates the positive ranking score and s_n the negative ranking score for a given claim-sentence pair. To get s_p, we feed the network a claim and the concatenated sentences of one of its ground truth evidence sets. To get s_n, we take all Wikipedia articles from which the ground truth evidence sets of the claim originate, randomly sample five sentences (not including the sentences of the ground truth evidence sets for the claim), and feed the concatenation of these sentences into the same ESIM. With our modified hinge loss function, we then try to maximize the margin between positive and negative samples.

Testing: At testing time, we calculate the score between a claim and each sentence in the retrieved documents. For this purpose, we deploy an ensemble of ten models with different random seeds. Then, the mean score of a claim-sentence pair over all ten models of the ensemble is calculated and the scores for all pairs are ranked. Finally, the five sentences of the five highest-ranked pairs are taken as an output of the model.

3.3 Recognizing textual entailment

In order to classify the claim as *Supported*, *Refuted* or *NotEnoughInfo*, we use the five sentences retrieved by our sentence selection model described in the previous section. For the classification, we propose another extension to the ESIM, which can predict the entailment relation between *multiple* input sentences and the claim. Fig. 2 gives an overview of our extended ESIM for the FEVER textual entailment task.

As word representation for both claim and sentences, we concatenate the Glove (Pennington et al., 2014) and FastText (Bojanowski et al., 2016) embeddings for each word. Since both types of embeddings are pretrained on Wikipedia, they are particularly suitable for our problem setting.

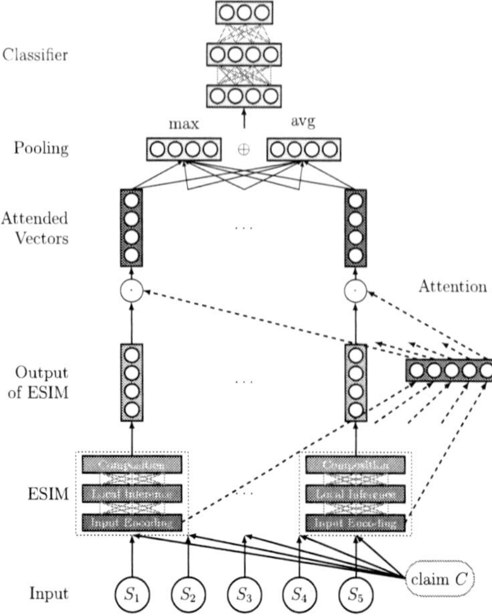

Figure 2: Extended ESIM for recognizing textual entailment

To process the five input sentences using the ESIM, we combine the claim with each sentence and feed the resulting pairs into the ESIM. The last hidden states of the five individual claim-sentence runs of the ESIM are compressed into one vector using attention and pooling operations.

The attention is based on a representation of the claim that is independent of the five sentences. This representation is obtained by summing up the *input encodings* of the claim in the five ESIM runs. In the same way, we derive five sentence representations, one from each of the five runs of the ESIM, which are independent of the claim. For each claim-sentence pair, the single sentence representation and the claim representation are then individually fed through a single layer perceptron. The cosine similarity of these two vectors is then used as an attention weight. The five output vectors of all ESIMs are multiplied with their respective attention weights and we apply average and max pooling on these vectors in order to reduce them to two representations. Finally, the two representations are concatenated and fed through a 3-layer perceptron to predict one of the three classes *Supported*, *Refuted* or *NotEnoughInfo*. The idea behind the described attention mechanism is to allow the model to extract information from the five sentences that is most relevant for the classification of the claim.

4 Results

Table 1 shows the performance of our document retrieval and sentence selection system when retrieving different numbers of the highest-ranked Wikipedia articles. In contrast to the results reported in Table 3, here we consider a single model instead of an ensemble. The results show that both systems benefit from a larger number of retrieved articles.

#search results	doc. accuracy	sent. recall
3	92.60	85.37
5	93.30	86.02
7	**93.55**	**86.24**

Table 1: Performance of the retrieval systems using different numbers of MediaWiki search results

For the subtask of recognizing textual entailment, we also experiment with different numbers of selected sentences. The results in Table 2 demonstrate that our model performs best with all five selected sentences.

#sentence(s)	label accuracy	FEVER score
1	67.94	63.64
2	68.33	64.30
3	67.82	63.72
4	67.61	63.59
5	**68.49**	**64.74**

Table 2: Performance of the textual entailment model using different numbers of sentences

In Table 3, we compare the performance of our three systems as well as the full pipeline to the baseline systems and pipeline implemented by the shared task organizers (Thorne et al., 2018) on the development set. As the results demonstrate, we were able to significantly improve upon the baseline on each sub-task. The performance gains over the whole pipeline add up to an improvement of about 100% with respect to the baseline pipeline.

5 Error analysis

In this section, we present the error analysis for each of the three sub-tasks, which can serve as a basis for further improvements of the system.

5.1 Document retrieval

The typical errors encountered for the document retrieval system can be divided into three classes.

Task (metric)	system	score (%)
Document retrieval	baseline	70.20
(accuracy)	our system	93.55
Sentence selection	baseline	44.22
(recall)	our system	87.10
Textual entailment	baseline	52.09
(label accuracy)	our system	68.49
Full pipeline	baseline	**32.27**
(FEVER score)	our system	**64.74**

Table 3: Performance comparison of our system and the baseline system on the development set

Spelling errors: A word in the claim or in the article title is misspelled. E.g. *"Homer Hickman wrote some historical fiction novels."* vs. *"Homer Hickam"*. In this case, our document retrieval system discards the article during the filtering phase.

Missing entity mentions: The entity mention represented by the title of the article, which needs to be retrieved, is not related to any entity mention in the claim. E.g. Article title: *"Blue Jasmine"* Claim: *"Cate Blanchett ignored the offer to act in Cate Blanchett."*.

Search failures: Some article titles contain a category name in parentheses for the disambiguation of the entity. This makes it difficult to retrieve the exact article title using the MediaWiki API. E.g. the claim *"Alex Jones is apolitical."* requires the article *"Alex Jones (radio host)"*, but it is not contained in the MediaWiki search results.

5.2 Sentence selection

The most frequent case, in which the sentence selection model fails to retrieve a correct evidence set, is that the entity mention in the claim does not occur in the annotated evidence set. E.g. the only evidence set for the claim *"Daggering is nontraditional."* consists of the single sentence *"This dance is not a traditional dance."*. Here, *"this dance"* refers to *"daggering"* and cannot be resolved by our model, since the information that *"daggering"* is a dance is not mentioned in the evidence sentence or in the claim. Some evidence sets contain two sentences one of which is less related to the claim. E.g. the claim *"Herry II of France has three cars."* has an evidence set that contains the two sentences *"Henry II died in 1559."* and *"1886 is regarded as the birth year of the modern car."*. The second sentence is not directly related to the claim, thus, it is ranked very low by our model.

5.3 Recognizing textual entailment

A large number of claims are misclassified due to the model's disability to interpret numerical values. For instance, the claim *"The heart beats at a resting rate close to 22 beats per minute."* is not classified as *refuted* on the basis of the evidence sentence *"The heart beats at a resting rate close to 72 beats per minute."*. The only information refuting the claim is the number, but neither GloVe nor FastText embeddings can embed numbers distinctly enough. Another problem are challenging *NotEnoughInfo* cases. For instance, the claim *"Terry Crews played on the Los Angeles Chargers."* (annotated as *NotEnoughInfo*) is classified as *refuted*, given the sentence *"In football, Crews played ... for the Los Angeles Rams, San Diego Chargers and Washington Redskins, ..."*. The sentence is related to the claim but does not exclude it, which makes this case difficult.

6 Conclusion

In this paper, we presented the system for fact extraction and verification, which we developed in the course of the FEVER shared task. According to the preliminary results, our system scored third out of 23 competing teams. The shared task was divided into three parts: (i) Given a claim, retrieve Wikipedia documents that contain facts about the claim. (ii) Extract these facts from the document. (iii) Verify the claim on the basis of the extracted facts. To address the problem, we developed models for the three sub-tasks. We framed document retrieval as entity linking by identifying entities in the claim and linking them to Wikipedia articles. To extract facts in the articles, we developed a sentence ranking model by extending the ESIM. For claim verification we proposed another extension to the ESIM, whereby we were able to classify the claim on the basis of multiple facts using attention. Each of our three models, as well as the combined pipeline, significantly outperforms the baseline on the development set.

7 Acknowledgements

This work has been supported by the German Research Foundation as part of the Research Training Group Adaptive Preparation of Information from Heterogeneous Sources (AIPHES) at the Technische Universität Darmstadt grant No. GRK 1994/1.

References

Piotr Bojanowski, Edouard Grave, Armand Joulin, and Tomas Mikolov. 2016. Enriching word vectors with subword information. *arXiv preprint arXiv:1607.04606*.

Samuel R Bowman, Gabor Angeli, Christopher Potts, and Christopher D Manning. 2015. A large annotated corpus for learning natural language inference. *arXiv preprint arXiv:1508.05326*.

Qian Chen, Xiaodan Zhu, Zhenhua Ling, Si Wei, Hui Jiang, and Diana Inkpen. 2016. Enhanced LSTM for natural language inference. *arXiv preprint arXiv:1609.06038*.

Silviu Cucerzan. 2007. Large-Scale Named Entity Disambiguation Based on Wikipedia Data. In *Proceedings of the 2007 Joint Conference on Empirical Methods in Natural Language Processing and Computational Natural Language Learning (EMNLP-CoNLL)*, pages 708–716, Prague, Czech Republic.

Matt Gardner, Joel Grus, Mark Neumann, Oyvind Tafjord, Pradeep Dasigi, Nelson F. Liu, Matthew Peters, Michael Schmitz, and Luke S. Zettlemoyer. 2017. AllenNLP: A deep semantic natural language processing platform.

Alex Graves and Jürgen Schmidhuber. 2005. Framewise phoneme classification with bidirectional LSTM and other neural network architectures. *Neural Networks*, 18(5-6):602–610.

Jeffrey Pennington, Richard Socher, and Christopher Manning. 2014. Glove: Global vectors for word representation. In *Proceedings of the 2014 conference on empirical methods in natural language processing (EMNLP)*, pages 1532–1543.

Daniil Sorokin and Iryna Gurevych. 2018. Mixing Context Granularities for Improved Entity Linking on Question Answering Data across Entity Categories. In *Proceedings of the 7th Joint Conference on Lexical and Computational Semantics (*SEM 2018)*, pages 65–75. Association for Computational Linguistics.

James Thorne, Andreas Vlachos, Christos Christodoulopoulos, and Arpit Mittal. 2018. FEVER: A large-scale dataset for fact extraction and verification. In *NAACL-HLT*.

Team Papelo: Transformer Networks at FEVER

Christopher Malon
NEC Laboratories America
malon@nec-labs.com

Abstract

We develop a system for the FEVER fact extraction and verification challenge that uses a high precision entailment classifier based on transformer networks pretrained with language modeling, to classify a broad set of potential evidence. The precision of the entailment classifier allows us to enhance recall by considering every statement from several articles to decide upon each claim. We include not only the articles best matching the claim text by TFIDF score, but read additional articles whose titles match named entities and capitalized expressions occurring in the claim text. The entailment module evaluates potential evidence one statement at a time, together with the title of the page the evidence came from (providing a hint about possible pronoun antecedents). In preliminary evaluation, the system achieves .5736 FEVER score, .6108 label accuracy, and .6485 evidence F1 on the FEVER shared task test set.

1 Introduction

The release of the FEVER fact extraction and verification dataset (Thorne et al., 2018) provides a large-scale challenge that tests a combination of retrieval and textual entailment capabilities. To verify a claim in the dataset as supported, refuted, or undecided, a system must retrieve relevant articles and sentences from Wikipedia. Then it must decide whether each of those sentences, or some combination of them, entails or refutes the claim, which is an entailment problem. Systems are evaluated on the accuracy of the claim predictions, with credit only given when correct evidence is submitted.

As entailment data, premises in FEVER data differ substantially from those in the image caption data used as the basis for the Stanford Natural Language Inference (SNLI) (Bowman et al., 2015)

dataset. Sentences are longer (31 compared to 14 words on average), vocabulary is more abstract, and the prevalence of named entities and out-of-vocabulary terms is higher.

The retrieval aspect of FEVER is not straightforward either. A claim may have small word overlap with the relevant evidence, especially if the claim is refuted by the evidence.

Our approach to FEVER is to fix the most obvious shortcomings of the baseline approaches to retrieval and entailment, and to train a sharp entailment classifier that can be used to filter a broad set of retrieved potential evidence. For the entailment classifier we compare Decomposable Attention (Parikh et al., 2016; Gardner et al., 2017) as implemented in the official baseline, ESIM (Chen et al., 2017), and a transformer network with pre-trained weights (Radford et al., 2018). The transformer network naturally supports out-of-vocabulary words and gives substantially higher performance than the other methods.

2 Transformer network

The core of our system is an entailment module based on a transformer network. Transformer networks (Vaswani et al., 2017) are deep networks applied to sequential input data, with each layer implementing multiple heads of scaled dot product attention. This attention mechanism allows deep features to be compared across positions in the input.

Many entailment networks have two sequence inputs, but the transformer is designed with just one. A separator token divides the premise from the hypothesis.

We use a specific transformer network released by OpenAI (Radford et al., 2018) that has been pre-trained for language modeling. The network consists of twelve blocks. Each block consists of a

Proceedings of the First Workshop on Fact Extraction and VERification (FEVER), pages 109–113
Brussels, Belgium, November 1, 2018. ©2018 Association for Computational Linguistics

multi-head masked self-attention layer, layer normalization (Ba et al., 2016), a feed forward network, and another layer normalization. After the twelfth block, two branches exist. In one branch, matrix multiplication and softmax layers are applied at the terminal sequence position to predict the entailment classification. In the other branch, a hidden state is multiplied by each token embedding and a softmax is taken to predict the next token. The language modeling branch has been pre-trained on the BookCorpus dataset (Zhu et al., 2015). We take the pre-trained model and train both branches on examples from FEVER.

3 Reframing entailment

The baseline FEVER system (Thorne et al., 2018) ran the AllenNLP (Gardner et al., 2017) implementation of Decomposable Attention (Parikh et al., 2016) to classify a group of five premise statements concatenated together against the claim. These five premise statements were fixed by the retrieval module and not considered individually. In our system, premise statements are individually evaluated.

We collect training data as the five sentences with the highest TFIDF score against the claim, taken from the Wikipedia pages selected by the retrieval module. If any ground truth evidence group for a claim requires more than one sentence, the claim is dropped from the training set. Otherwise, each sentence is labeled with the truth value of the claim if it is in the ground truth evidence set, and labeled as neutral if not. The resulting data forms an entailment problem that we call "FEVER One." For comparison, we form "FEVER Five" and "FEVER Five Oracle" by concatenating all five retrieved sentences, as in the baseline. In FEVER Five Oracle, the ground truth is the claim ground truth (if verifiable), but in FEVER Five, ground truth depends on whether the retrieved evidence is in the ground truth evidence set.

Several FEVER claims require multiple statements as evidence in order to be supported or refuted. The number of such claims is relatively small: in the first half of the development set, only 623 of 9999 claims were verifiable and had no singleton evidence groups. Furthermore, we disagreed with many of these annotations and thought that less evidence should have sufficed. Thus we chose not to develop a strategy for multiple evidence statements.

To compare results on FEVER Five to FEVER One, we must aggregate decisions about individual sentences of possible evidence to a decision about the claim. We do this by applying the following rules:

1. If any piece of evidence supports the claim, we classify the claim as supported.

2. If any piece of evidence refutes the claim, but no piece of evidence supports it, we classify the claim as refuted.

3. If no piece of evidence supports or refutes the claim, we classify the claim as not having enough information.

We resolve conflicts between supporting and refuting information in favor of the supporting information, because we observed cases in the development data where information was retrieved for different entities with the same name. For example, Ann Richards appeared both as a governor of Texas and as an Australian actress. Information that would be a contradiction regarding the actress should not stop evidence that would support a claim about the politician.

Even if a sentence is in the evidence set, it might not be possible for the classifier to correctly determine whether it supports the claim, because the sentence could have pronouns with antecedents outside the given sentence. Ideally, a coreference resolution system could add this information to the sentence, but running one could be time consuming and introduce its own errors. As a cheap alternative, we make the classifier aware of the title of the Wikipedia page. We convert any undersores in the page title to spaces, and insert the title between brackets before the rest of each premise sentence. The dataset constructed in this way is called "FEVER Title One."

The FEVER baseline system works by solving FEVER Five Oracle. Using Decomposable Attention, it achieves .505 accuracy on the test half of the development set. Swapping in the Enhanced Sequential Inference Model (ESIM) (Chen et al., 2017) to solve FEVER Five Oracle results in an accuracy of .561. Because ESIM uses a single out-of-vocabulary (OOV) token for all unknown words, we expect it to confuse named entities. Thus we extend the model by allocating 10,000 indices for out-of-vocabulary words with randomly initialized embeddings, and taking a hash of each

Problem	Support		Claim	
	Accuracy	Kappa	Accuracy	Kappa
ESIM on FEVER One	.760	.260	.517	.297
ESIM on FEVER Title One	.846	.394	.639	.433
Transformer on FEVER Title One	.958	.660	.823	.622

Table 1: Effect of adding titles to premises.

Problem	Support		Claim	
	Accuracy	Kappa	Accuracy	Kappa
ESIM on FEVER Title Five Oracle	N/A	N/A	.591	.388
ESIM on FEVER Title Five	N/A	N/A	.573	.110
ESIM on FEVER Title One	.846	.394	.639	.433
Transformer on FEVER Title Five Oracle	N/A	N/A	.673	.511
Transformer on FEVER Title Five	N/A	N/A	.801	.609
Transformer on FEVER Title One	.958	.660	.823	.622

Table 2: Concatenating evidence or not.

System	Retrieval
FEVER Baseline (TFIDF)	66.1%
+ Titles in TFIDF	68.3%
+ Titles + NE	80.8%
+ Titles + NE + Film	81.2%
Entire Articles + NE + Film	90.1%

Table 3: Percentage of evidence retrieved from first half of development set. Single-evidence claims only.

System	Development	Test
FEVER Title Five Oracle	.5289	—
FEVER Title Five	.5553	—
FEVER Title One	.5617	.5539
FEVER Title One (Narrow Evidence)	.5550	—
FEVER Title One (Entire Articles)	.5844	.5736

Table 4: FEVER Score of various systems. All use NE+Film retrieval.

OOV word to select one of these indices. With extended ESIM, the accuracy is .586. Therefore, we run most later comparisons with extended ESIM or transformer networks as the entailment module, rather than Decomposable Attention.

The FEVER One dataset is highly unbalanced in favor of neutral statements, so that the majority class baseline would achieve 93.0% on this data. In fact it makes training ESIM a challenge, as the model only learns the trivial majority class predictor if the natural training distribution is followed. We reweight the examples in FEVER One for ESIM so that each class contributes to the loss equally. Then, we use Cohen's Kappa rather than the accuracy to evaluate a model's quality, so that following the bias with purely random agreement is not rewarded in the evaluation. In Table 1 we compare FEVER One to FEVER Title One, both at the level of classifying individual support statements and of classifying the claim by aggregating these decisions as described above. On a support basis, we find a 52% increase in Kappa by adding the titles.

When ESIM is replaced by the transformer network, class reweighting is not necessary. The network naturally learns to perform in excess of the majority class baseline. Cohen's Kappa is 68% higher than that for ESIM.

The possibility of training on oracle labels for a concatenated set of evidence allows a classifier to simply guess whether the hypothesis is true and supported somewhere, rather than having to consider the relationship between hypothesis and premise. For example, it is possible to classify 67% of SNLI examples correctly without reading the premise (Gururangan et al., 2018). As we show in Table 2, for ESIM, we find that this kind of guessing makes the FEVER Title Five Oracle performance better than FEVER Title Five. The Transformer model is accurate enough that oracle guessing does not help. Both models perform best when classifying each bit of evidence separately and then aggregating.

4   Improving retrieval

Regardless of how strong the entailment classifier is, FEVER score is limited by whether the document and sentence retrieval modules, which produce the input to the entailment classifier, find the right evidence. In Table 3, we examine the percentage of claims for which correct evidence is retrieved, before filtering with the entailment classifier. For this calculation, we skip any claim with an evidence group with multiple statements, and count a claim as succesfully retrieved if it is not verifiable or if the statement in one of the evidence groups is retrieved. The baseline system retrieves the five articles with the highest TFIDF score, and then extracts the five sentences from that collection with the highest TFIDF score against the claim. It achieves 66.1% evidence retrieval.

Our first modification simply adds the title to each premise statement when computing its TFIDF against the claim, so that statements from a relevant article get credit even if the subject is not repeated. This raises evidence retrieval to 68.3%.

A more significant boost comes from retrieving additional Wikipedia pages based on named entity recognition (NER). We start with phrases tagged as named entities by SpaCy (Honnibal and Johnson, 2015), but these tags are not very reliable, so we include various capitalized phrases. We retrieve Wikipedia pages whose title exactly matches one of these phrases.

The named entity retrieval strategy boosts the evidence retrieval rate to 80.8%, while less than doubling the processing time. However, sometimes the named entity page thus retrieved is only a Wikipedia disambiguation page with no useful information. Noticing a lot of questions about films in the development set, we modify the strategy to also retrieve a page titled "X (film)" if it exists, whenever "X" is retrieved. The film retrievals raise evidence retrieval to 81.2%.

Finally, we eliminate the TFIDF sentence ranking to expand sentence retrieval from five sentences to entire articles, up to the first fifty sentences from each. Thus we obtain 2.6 million statements to classify regarding the 19,998 claims in the shared task development set, for an average of 128 premises per claim. The evidence retrieval rate, including all these premises, increases to 90.1%. We continue to apply the entailment module trained with only five premise retrievals. Running the entailment module on this batch using a machine with three NVIDIA GeForce GTX 1080Ti GPU cards takes on the order of six hours.

Retrieving more than five sentences means that we can no longer submit all retrieved evidence as support for the claims. Instead, we follow the aggregation strategy from Section 3 to decide the claim label, and only submit statements whose classification matches. Limiting evidence in this way when only five statements are retrieved ("narrow evidence" in Table 4) pushes FEVER score down very little, to .5550 from .5617 on the development set, so we have confidence that the extra retrieval will make up for the loss. Indeed, when the system reviews the extra evidence, FEVER score goes up to .5844 on the development set.

Table 4 compares the end-to-end performance of systems that evaluate five retrieved statements together, evaluate five retrieved statements separately, and evaluate all statements from entire articles separately. Evaluating the statements separately gives better performance. We submit the systems that retrieve five statements and entire articles for evaluation on the test set, achieving preliminary FEVER scores of .5539 and .5736 respectively (label accuracy of .5754 and .6108, evidence recall of .6245 and .5002, evidence F1 of .2542 and .6485). In preliminary standings, the latter system ranks fourth in FEVER score and first in evidence F1.

5   Discussion

Our approach to FEVER involves a minimum of heuristics and relies mainly on the strength of the Transformer Network based entailment classification. The main performance gains come from adding retrievals that resolve named entities rather than matching the claim text only, filtering fewer of the retrievals, and making the entailment classifier somewhat aware of the topic of what it is reading by including the title. If higher quality and more plentiful multi-evidence claims would be constructed, it would be nice to incorporate dynamic retrievals into the system, allowing the classifier to decide that it needs more information about keywords it encountered during reading.

References

Lei Jimmy Ba, Ryan Kiros, and Geoffrey E. Hinton. 2016. Layer normalization. *CoRR*, abs/1607.06450.

Samuel Bowman, Gabor Angeli, Christopher Potts, and Christopher Manning. 2015. A large annotated corpus for learning natural language inference. In *Proceedings of the Conference on Empirical Methods in Natural Language processing (EMNLP)*.

Qian Chen, Xiaodan Zhu, Zhen-Hua Ling, Si Wei, Hui Jiang, and Diana Inkpen. 2017. Enhanced LSTM for natural language inference. In *Proceedings of the 55th Annual Meeting of the Association for Computational Linguistics (Volume 1: Long Papers)*, pages 1657–1668.

Matt Gardner, Joel Grus, Mark Neumann, Oyvind Tafjord, Pradeep Dasigi, Nelson F. Liu, Matthew Peters, Michael Schmitz, and Luke S. Zettlemoyer. 2017. AllenNLP: A deep semantic natural language processing platform. *CoRR*, abs/1803.07640.

Suchin Gururangan, Swabha Swayamdipta, Omer Levy, Roy Schwartz, Samuel Bowman, and Noah A. Smith. 2018. Annotation artifacts in natural language inference data. In *Proceedings of the Conference of the North American Chapter of the Association for Computational Linguistics: Human Language Technologies (NAACL-HLT), Volume 2*, pages 107–112.

Matthew Honnibal and Mark Johnson. 2015. An improved non-monotonic transition system for dependency parsing. In *Proceedings of the Conference on Empirical Methods in Natural Language Processing (EMNLP)*, pages 1373–1378.

Ankur Parikh, Oscar Täckström, Dipanjan Das, and Jakob Uszkoreit. 2016. A decomposable attention model for natural language inference. In *Proceedings of the Conference on Empirical Methods in Natural Language Processing (EMNLP)*, pages 2249–2255.

Alec Radford, Karthik Narasimhan, Tim Salimans, and Ilya Sutskever. 2018. Improving language understanding by generative pre-training. In *OpenAI Blog*.

James Thorne, Andreas Vlachos, Christos Christodoulopoulos, and Arpit Mittal. 2018. FEVER: a large-scale dataset for fact extraction and verification. In *Proceedings of the Conference of the North American Chapter of the Association for Computational Linguistics: Human Language Technologies (NAACL-HLT), Volume 1*.

Ashish Vaswani, Noam Shazeer, Niki Parmar, Jakob Uszkoreit, Llion Jones, Aidan N Gomez, Ł ukasz Kaiser, and Illia Polosukhin. 2017. Attention is all you need. In *Advances in Neural Information Processing Systems 30*, pages 5998–6008.

Yukun Zhu, Ryan Kiros, Richard S. Zemel, Ruslan Salakhutdinov, Raquel Urtasun, Antonio Torralba, and Sanja Fidler. 2015. Aligning books and movies: Towards story-like visual explanations by watching movies and reading books. In *Proceedings of the IEEE International Conference on Computer Vision (ICCV)*, pages 19–27.

Uni-DUE Student Team: Tackling fact checking through decomposable attention neural network

Jan Kowollik
University of Duisburg-Essen
jan.kowollik@stud.uni-due.de

Ahmet Aker
University of Duisburg-Essen
a.aker@is.inf.uni-due.de

Abstract

In this paper we present our system for the FEVER Challenge. The task of this challenge is to verify claims by extracting information from Wikipedia. Our system has two parts. In the first part it performs a search for candidate sentences by treating the claims as query. In the second part it filters out noise from these candidates and uses the remaining ones to decide whether they support or refute or entail not enough information to verify the claim. We show that this system achieves a FEVER score of 0.3927 on the FEVER shared task development data set which is a 25.5% improvement over the baseline score.

1 Introduction

In this paper we present our system for the FEVER Challenge[1]. The FEVER Challenge is a shared task on fact extraction and claim verification. Initially Thorne et al. (2018) created an annotated corpus of $185,445$ claims and proposed a baseline system to predict the correct labels as well as the pieces of evidence for the claims.

Our system consist of two parts. In the first part we retrieve sentences that are relevant to a claim. The claim is used as query and is submitted to Lucene search API. The sentences found are candidates for pieces of evidence for the claim. Next in the second part we run a modified version of the Decomposable Attention network (Parikh et al., 2016) to predict the textual entailment between a claim and the candidate sentences found through searching but also between claim and all candidate sentences merged into one long text. This step gives us entailment probabilities. We also use a point system to filter out some noise (irrelevant sentences). Based on the remaining candidates we perform label prediction, i.e. whether the claim is

supported, refuted or there is not enough evidence. Our system achieves a FEVER score of 0.3927 on the FEVER shared task development data set which is a 25.5% improvement over the baseline score.

2 Data

The data consists of two parts: the FEVER data set and the Wikipedia dump (Thorne et al., 2018).

The Wikipedia dump contains over five million pages but for each page only the first section was taken. The text on each page was split into sentences and each sentence was assigned an index. The page title is written using underscores between the individual words instead of spaces.

The FEVER data set contains the annotated claims that should be correctly predicted by the developed system. Each claim is annotated with one of the three labels *SUPPORTS* (verifiably true), *REFUTES* (verifiably false) and *NOT ENOUGH INFO* (not verifiable). For claims with the first two labels the pieces of evidence are provided as a combination of Wikipedia page title and sentence index on that page.

The FEVER data set created by Thorne et al. (2018) is split into a training set with $145,449$, a development set with $19,998$ and a test set with $19,998$ annotated claims. The development and test sets are balanced while the training set has an approximately 16:6:7 split on the three labels. Each data set and also the Wikipedia dump is available at the FEVER web page[2].

3 System

We decided to adopt the general two part structure of the baseline for our system with a key difference. The first part takes the claim and finds candidate sentences that ideally have a high chance of

---

[1] http://fever.ai

[2] http://fever.ai/data.html

Proceedings of the First Workshop on Fact Extraction and VERification (FEVER), pages 114–118
Brussels, Belgium, November 1, 2018. ©2018 Association for Computational Linguistics

being evidence for the claim. The second part determines the label and selects evidence sentences.

The baseline system uses the sentences found in the first part directly as evidence. In our system we only find candidate sentences in the first part and select the actual evidence sentences at the end of the second part. This allows us to operate on a larger number of sentences in the second part of the system and achieve higher recall.

3.1 Finding Candidate Sentences

The main idea of the first part of our system is to mimic human behavior when verifying a claim. If we take a claim about a person as an example, a human is likely to just take few keywords such as the person's name and use this to search for the right Wikipedia page to find evidence. We mimic this behavior by first extracting few keywords from the claim and use them to find candidate sentences in the Wikipedia dump.

Extracting Keywords

We use Named Entity Recognition (NER), Constituency Parsing and Dependency Parsing to extract keywords from each claim. For NER we use the neural network model created by Peters et al. (2018). We use all found named entities as keywords. For the Constituency Parsing we use the neural network model created by Stern et al. (2017). We extract all NP tagged phrases from the first two recursion layers as keywords because we found that this finds mostly subjects and objects of a sentence. These two neural networks both use the AllenNLP library (Gardner et al., 2018). For the dependency parsing we use the Standford Dependency Parser (Chen and Manning, 2014). We extract all subject and object phrases as keywords.

The NE recognition is our main source for keywords extraction while the other two systems provide additional keywords that either have not been found by the NER or that are not named entities in the first place. Example of the keywords being extracted from claims shown in Table 2 are shown in Table 1.

Indexing the Wikipedia Dump

After extracting the keywords we use the Lucene search API[3] to find candidate sentences for each claim. Before searching with Lucene the Wikipedia texts need to be indexed. We treat each sentence as a separate document and index it. We

exclude sentences that are empty and also those that are longer than 2000 characters.

For each sentence we also add the Wikipedia page title and make it searchable. For the title we replace all underscores with spaces to improve matching. In each sentence we replace the words *He*, *She*, *It* and *They* with the Wikipedia page title that the sentence was found in. When looking at an entire Wikipedia page it is obvious who or what these words refer to but when searching individual sentences we do not have the necessary context available. We perform this replacement to provide more context.

Searching for the Candidate Sentences

We use three types of queries to search for candidate sentences for a claim:

- **Type 1:** For each keyword we split the keyword phrase into individual words and create a query that searches within the Wikipedia page titles requiring all the individual words to be found.

- **Type 2:** We split all keywords into individual words and combine those into one query searching within the Wikipedia page titles to find sentences on those pages where as many words as possible match the title of the page.

- **Type 3:** We combine all keywords as phrases into one query searching within the sentences to find those sentences where as many keywords as possible match.

We limit the number of results to the two most relevant sentences for the first query type and 20 sentences for the other two queries because the first query type makes one query per keyword while the other two only make one query per claim. An example of the queries being generated is given in Table 3. If the same sentence is found twice we do not add it to the candidate list again. For each of the candidate sentences we add the Wikipedia page title at the beginning of the sentence if it does not already contain it somewhere.

3.2 Making the Prediction

The second part of our system first processes the candidate sentences in three independent steps that can be run in parallel:

- We use a modified version of the Decomposable Attention neural network (Parikh et al.,

---

[3] `https://lucene.apache.org/core/`

#	Named Entity Recognition	Constituency Parser	Dependency Parser
1	Northern Isles, Scotland	The Northern Isles	The Northern Isles
2	-	Artificial intelligence, concern	Artificial intelligence, concern
3	Walk of Life	album, the highest grossing album	-

Table 1: Generated keywords from the three systems (see Table 2 for claims). For the first claim the NE recognition correctly finds the two named entities while the other two systems miss one entity and got an additional *The* into the keyword. The second claim has no named entities and the other systems correctly find the relevant parts. In the third example the named entity found by the NE recognition is disambiguated by the Constituency Parser.

#	Claim
1	The Northern Isles belong to Scotland.
2	Artificial intelligence raises concern.
3	Walk of Life (album) is the highest grossing album.

Table 2: Example claims used in tables 1/3.

2016) to predict the textual entailment between each candidate sentence and its corresponding claim.

- We merge all candidate sentences of a claim into one block of text and predict the textual entailment between this block of text and the claim.

- We assign points to each candidate sentence based on POS-Tags.

Finally our system combines the results in order to decide on the label and to predict the evidence sentences for each claim.

Textual Entailment

We started with the Decomposable Attention network (Parikh et al., 2016) that is also used in the baseline except that we predict the textual entailment for each pair of candidate sentence and claim. We found that for long sentences the network has high attention in different parts of the sentence that semantically belong to different statements. Using the idea that long sentences often contain multiple statements we made the following additions to the Decomposable Attention network.

We include an additional 2-dimensional convolution layer that operates on the attention matrix in case of sufficiently large sentences. Based on our testing we decided on a single convolution layer with a kernel size of 12. The output of this convolution layer contains a different amount of elements depending on the size of the attention matrix. This makes sense as longer sentences can contain multiple statements. We use a *CnnEn-coder*[4] to change the different length output into a same length output. This is necessary in order to use the result of the convolution layer in a later step of the network and can be seen as a selection of the correct statement from the available data. The output of the *CnnEncoder* is concatenated to the input of the aggregate step of the network. If either the claim or the candidate sentence are shorter than 12 then we skip this additional step and concatenate a zero vector instead.

When predicting the textual entailment we do not reduce the probabilities to a final label immediately but keep working with the probabilities in the final prediction (see Section Final Prediction).

Merge Sentences

For each claim we merge all the candidate sentences into one block of text similarly to the baseline. We predict the textual entailment using our modified decomposable attention network. We found that the *REFUTES* label is predicted with very high accuracy. However, this is not the case for the other two labels. By including the results of this step we can improve the predicted labels for the *REFUTES* label as shown in Table 5. Comparing that to the full result given in Table 4 we can see that about 29.3% of correct *REFUTES* predictions are due to this step.

Creating POS-Tags and Assigning Points

We use the Stanford POS-Tagger (Toutanova et al., 2003) to create POS-Tags for all candidate sentences and all claims. We found that the Stanford POS-Tagger only uses a single CPU core on our system so we wrote a script that splits the file containing all claim or candidate sentences into multiple files. Then the script calls multiple POS-Tagger instances in parallel, one for each file. The results are then merged back into a single file.

---

[4] https://allenai.github.io/
allennlp-docs/api/allennlp.modules.
seq2vec_encoders.html

Query type	Query	Occurrence	Limit
Type 1	"Artificial" "intelligence"	must occur	2
Type 1	"concern"	must occur	2
Type 2	"Artificial" "intelligence" "concern"	should occur	20
Type 3	"Artificial intelligence" "concern"	should occur	20

Table 3: Generated queries for claim 2 (see Table 2). Claim 2 has two keywords where one contains two words. For the Type 1 query we create two queries where one query contains two separate words. For the Type 2 query we split all words and use them all in one query. For type 3 we omit the split and use entire keyword phrases as query.

	SUP	REF	NEI
SUP	3291	370	3005
REF	1000	3159	2507
NEI	1710	1142	3814

Table 4: Confusion matrix of the full system prediction. Columns are predictions and rows the true labels.

	SUP	REF	NEI
SUP	-8	+52	-44
REF	-2	+926	-924
NEI	-4	+152	-148

Table 5: Confusion matrix change due to including the merge feature. Columns are predictions and rows the true labels.

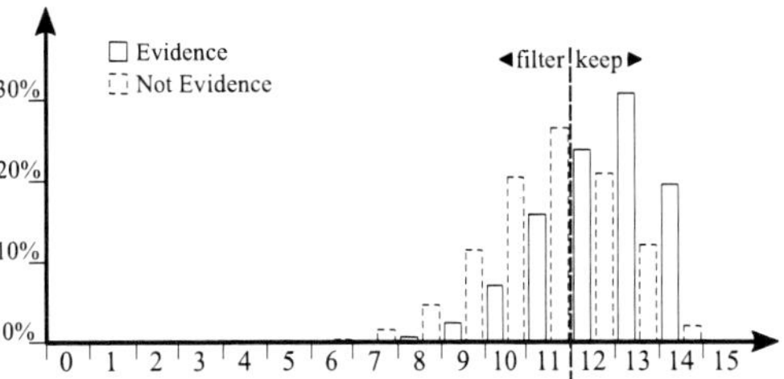

Figure 1: Histogram of how many candidate sentences (y-axis) received how many points (x-axis) for the development set. 65.07% of non-evidence and 26.21% of evidence sentences get filtered with the threshold between 11 and 12.

Using the generated POS-Tags we assign scores to the candidate sentences. First each candidate sentence is assigned 5 different scores, one for each of the following POS-Tag categories: verbs, nouns, adjectives, adverbs and numbers. Each category score starts at 3 and is decreased by 1 for each word of the respective POS-Tag category that is in the claim but not in the candidate sentence. Duplicate words are considered only once. We do not allow the category scores to go negative. At the end the category scores are added together to create the final score which can be a maximum of 15.

Final Prediction

We create a matrix from the per candidate sentence textual entailment probabilities with the three labels as columns and one row per candidate. We reduce all three probabilities of a candidate sentence if it received 11 or less points. The number 11 is empirically determined using the development set. As shown in Figure 1 we are able to filter out most of the non-evidence sentences by looking only at candidate sentences whose point score is more than 11. Reducing the probabilities is done by multiplying them with 0.3. This way they are always reduced below the minimum highest prob-

ability of non-filtered sentences (= 33.33...%).

Finally we predict the label and decide on the evidence sentences. If the *Merge Sentences* prediction predicted *REFUTES* then we use *REFUTES* as final label. Otherwise we find the highest value in the matrix and select the column it appears in as final label. We sort the matrix based on the column of the final label and select the top 5 candidate sentences as evidence.

3.3 Training

For training the modified Decomposable Attention network we are using the SNLI data set and the FEVER training set (Bowman et al., 2015; Thorne et al., 2018). For claims labeled as *NOT ENOUGH INFO* we first search for Wikipedia page titles that contain a word from the claim and then randomly choose one of the sentences on that page. If no Wikipedia page is found this way we randomly select one. We concatenate the generated training data with the SNLI data set to create the final training data containing $849,426$ claims.

4 Results

Our system achieves a FEVER score of 0.3927 on the shared task development set containing $19,998$

	Label	Recall	Score
All	0.5132	0.3581	0.3927
Unmodified DA	0.5170	0.3880	0.3909
Without Points	0.4545	0.1169	0.3665
Without Merge	0.4747	0.3294	0.3815

Table 6: Contribution of each feature. *Label* refers to the label accuracy, while *Recall* refers to the evidence recall.

claims. This is a 25.5% improvement over the baseline score of 0.3127 on the development set. The confusion matrix for the predicted labels is given in Table 4. It shows that the highest incorrect predictions are for the *NOT ENOUGH INFO* label while the *REFUTES* label is predicted with the least amount of errors.

For the test set our system generated $773,862$ pairs of candidate sentences and claim sentences. Only for a single claim out of all $19,998$ claims no candidate sentences were found.

For the development set the candidate sentences found in the first part of our system include the actual evidence of 77.83% of the claims. In comparison the baseline (Thorne et al., 2018) only finds 44.22% of the evidence. Our system finds 38.7 sentences per claim on average, while the baseline is limited to 5 sentences per claim.

When looking at how much each feature improves the final score in Table 6, we can see that the point system using POS-Tags results in the biggest improvement.

5 Conclusion

In this paper we have presented our system for the FEVER Challenge. While keeping the two-part structure of the baseline we replaced the first part completely and heavily modified the second part to achieve a 25.5% FEVER score improvement over the baseline. In our immediate future work we will investigate alternative ways of obtaining higher recall in the first part but also improve the textual entailment to further reduce noise.

References

Samuel R. Bowman, Gabor Angeli, Christopher Potts, and Christopher D. Manning. 2015. A large annotated corpus for learning natural language inference. *CoRR*, abs/1508.05326.

Danqi Chen and Christopher Manning. 2014. A fast and accurate dependency parser using neural networks. In *Proceedings of the 2014 Conference on Empirical Methods in Natural Language Processing (EMNLP)*, pages 740–750. Association for Computational Linguistics.

Matt Gardner, Joel Grus, Mark Neumann, Oyvind Tafjord, Pradeep Dasigi, Nelson F. Liu, Matthew E. Peters, Michael Schmitz, and Luke Zettlemoyer. 2018. Allennlp: A deep semantic natural language processing platform. *CoRR*, abs/1803.07640.

Ankur P Parikh, Oscar Täckström, Dipanjan Das, and Jakob Uszkoreit. 2016. A decomposable attention model for natural language inference. *arXiv preprint arXiv:1606.01933*.

Matthew E. Peters, Mark Neumann, Mohit Iyyer, Matt Gardner, Christopher Clark, Kenton Lee, and Luke Zettlemoyer. 2018. Deep contextualized word representations. *ArXiv e-prints*, 1802.05365.

Mitchell Stern, Jacob Andreas, and Dan Klein. 2017. A minimal span-based neural constituency parser. *CoRR*, abs/1705.03919.

James Thorne, Andreas Vlachos, Christos Christodoulopoulos, and Arpit Mittal. 2018. FEVER: a large-scale dataset for fact extraction and verification. *CoRR*, abs/1803.05355.

Kristina Toutanova, Dan Klein, Christopher D. Manning, and Yoram Singer. 2003. Feature-rich part-of-speech tagging with a cyclic dependency network. In *Proceedings of the 2003 Human Language Technology Conference of the North American Chapter of the Association for Computational Linguistics*.

SIRIUS-LTG: An Entity Linking Approach to Fact Extraction and Verification

Farhad Nooralahzadeh and Lilja Øvrelid
Department of Informatics
University of Oslo, Norway
{farhadno,liljao}@ifi.uio.no

Abstract

This article presents the SIRIUS-LTG system for the Fact Extraction and VERification (FEVER) Shared Task. It consists of three components: 1) *Wikipedia Page Retrieval*: First we extract the entities in the claim, then we find potential Wikipedia URI candidates for each of the entities using a SPARQL query over DBpedia 2) *Sentence selection*: We investigate various techniques i.e. Smooth Inverse Frequency (SIF), Word Mover's Distance (WMD), Soft-Cosine Similarity, Cosine similarity with unigram Term Frequency Inverse Document Frequency (TF-IDF) to rank sentences by their similarity to the claim. 3) *Textual Entailment*: We compare three models for the task of claim classification. We apply a Decomposable Attention (DA) model (Parikh et al., 2016), a Decomposed Graph Entailment (DGE) model (Khot et al., 2018) and a Gradient-Boosted Decision Trees (TalosTree) model (Sean et al., 2017) for this task. The experiments show that the pipeline with simple Cosine Similarity using TFIDF in sentence selection along with DA model as labelling model achieves the best results on the development set (F1 evidence: 32.17, label accuracy: 59.61 and FEVER score: 0.3778). Furthermore, it obtains 30.19, 48.87 and 36.55 in terms of F1 evidence, label accuracy and FEVER score, respectively, on the test set. Our system ranks 15th among 23 participants in the shared task prior to any human-evaluation of the evidence.

1 Introduction

The Web contains vast amounts of data from many heterogeneous sources, and the harvesting of information from these sources can be extremely valuable for several domains and applications such as, for instance, business intelligence. The volume and variety of data on the Web are increasing at a very rapid pace, making their use and processing increasingly difficult. A large volume of information on the Web consists of unstructured text which contains facts about named entities (NE) such as people, places and organizations. At the same time, the recent evolution of publishing and connecting data over the Web dubbed "Linked Data" provides a machine-readable and enriched representation of many of the world's entities, together with their semantic characteristics. These structured data sources are a result of the creation of large knowledge bases (KB) by different communities, which are often interlinked, as is the case of DBpedia (Lehmann et al., 2015) [1], Yago [2] (Suchanek et al., 2007) and FreeBase [3] (Bollacker et al., 2008). This characteristic of the Web of data empowers both humans and computer agents to discover more concepts by easily navigating among the datasets, and can profitably be exploited in complex tasks such as information retrieval, question answering, knowledge extraction and reasoning.

Fact extraction from unstructured text is a task central to knowledge base construction. While this process is vital for many NLP applications, misinformation (false information) or disinformation (deliberately false information) from unreliable sources, can provide false output and mislead the readers. Such risks could be properly managed by applying NLP techniques aimed at solving the task of *fact verification*, i.e., to detect and discriminate misinformation and prevent its propagation. The Fact Extraction and VERification (FEVER) shared task [4] (Thorne et al., 2018) addresses both problems. In this work, we introduce a pipeline system for each phase of the FEVER shared task. In our pipeline, we first identify entities in a given claim, then we extract candidate Wikipedia pages for each of the entities and the most similar sen-

---

[1] dbpedia.org
[2] www.mpi-inf.mpg.de/yago/
[3] www.freebase.com
[4] www.fever.ai

Proceedings of the First Workshop on Fact Extraction and VERification (FEVER), pages 119–123
Brussels, Belgium, November 1, 2018. ©2018 Association for Computational Linguistics

tences are obtained using a textual similarity measure. Finally, we label the claim with regard to evidence sentences using a textual entailment technique.

2 System description

In this section, we describe our system which consists of three components which solve the three following tasks: Wikipedia page retrieval, sentence selection and textual entailment.

2.1 Wiki-page Retrieval

Each claim in the FEVER dataset contains a single piece of information about an entity that its original Wikipedia page describes. Therefore we first extract entities using the Stanford Named Entity Recognition (StanfordNER) (Finkel et al., 2005). We observe that StanfordNER is sometimes unable to extract entity names in the claim due to limited contextual information like in example 1 below:

Example 1 *A View to a Kill is an action movie.*
NER: *[ ]*
Noun-Phrases: *[A View to a Kill, an action movie]*

To tackle this problem, we also extract noun phrases using the parse tree of Stanford CoreNLP (Manning et al., 2014) and the longest multi-word expression that contains words with the first letter in upper case. This enables us to provide a wide range of potential entities for the retrieval process. We then retrieve a set of Wikipedia page candidates for an entity in the claim using a SPARQL (Prud'hommeaux and Seaborne, 2008) query over DBpedia, i.e. the structured version of Wikipedia.

The SPARQL query aids the retrieval process by providing a list of candidates to the subsequent system components, particularly when the claim is about *film, song, music album, bands and etc.* Listing 1 shows the query employed for the entity *Meteora* in Example 2 below, which outputs the resulting Wikipedia pages (Pages):

Example 2 *Meteora is not a rock album.*
Entity: *[Meteora]*
Pages: *['Meteora', 'Meteora (album)', 'Meteora Monastary', 'Meteora (Greek monasteries)', 'Meteora (film)']*

The query retrieves all the Wikipedia pages which contains the entity mention in their title.

```
prefix rdfs:<http://www.w3.org/2000/01/rdf-schema#>
prefix fn:<http://www.w3.org/2005/xpath-functions/#>

SELECT DISTINCT ?resource
    WHERE {?resource rdfs:label ?s.
    ?s <bif:contains> '"Meteora"'.

    FILTER (lang(?s) ="en")
    FILTER ( fn:string-length
    (fn:substring-after(?resource,
    "http://dbpedia.org/resource/"))>1)
    FILTER (regex(str(?resource),
    "http://dbpedia.org/resource")
    && !regex(str(?resource),
    "http://dbpedia.org/resource/File:")
    && !regex(str(?resource),
    "http://dbpedia.org/resource/Category:")
    && !regex(str(?resource),
    "http://dbpedia.org/resource/Template:")
    && !regex(str(?resource),
    "http://dbpedia.org/resource/List")
    && !regex(str(?resource), "(disambiguation)")
        )
    }
```

Listing 1: SPARQL query to extract Wikipedia page candidates for entity mention (e.g. *Meteora*)

2.2 Sentence Selection

Given a set of Wikipedia page candidates, the similarity between the claim and the individual text lines on the page is obtained. We here experiment with several methods for computing this similarity:

Cosine Similarity using TFIDF: Sentences are ranked by unigram TF-IDF similarity to the claim. We modified the fever-baseline code to consider the candidate list from the Wiki-page retrieval components.

Soft-Cosine Similarity: Following the work of Charlet and Damnati (2017), we measure the similarity between the candidate sentences and the claim. This textual similarity measure relies on the introduction of a relation matrix in the classical cosine similarity between bag-of-words. The relation matrix is calculated using the *word2vec* representations of words.

Word Mover's Distance(WMD): The WMD distance "measures the dissimilarity between two text documents as the minimum amount of distance that the embedded words of one document need to 'travel' to reach the embedded words of another document" (Kusner et al., 2015). The *word2vec* embeddings is used to calculate semantic distances of words in the embedding space.

Smooth Inverse Frequency (SIF): We also create sentence embeddings using the SIF weighting scheme (Arora et al., 2017) for a claim and candidate sentences. Then we calculate the cosine similarity measure between these embedding vectors.

2.3 Entailment

The previous component provides the most similar sentences as an evidence set for each claim. In this component, the aim is to find out whether the selected sentences enable us to classify a claim as being either *SUPPORTED*, *REFUTED* or *NOT ENOUGH INFO*. In cases where multiple sentences are selected as evidence, their strings are concatenated prior to classification. If the set of selected sentences is empty for a specific claim, due to the failure in finding related Wiki-page, we simply assign *NOT ENOUGH INFO* as an entailment label. In order to solve the entailment task we experiment with the use of several existing textual entailment systems with somewhat different requirements and properties. We follow the instruction from the Git-Hub repositories of the three following models and investigate their performances in the FEVER textual entailment subtask:

Decomposable Attention (DA) model (Parikh et al., 2016): We used the publicly available DA model [5] which is trained on the FEVER shared task dataset. We asked the model to predict an inference label for each claim based on the evidence set which is provided by the *sentence selection* component.

Decomposed Graph Entailment (DGE) model: Khot et al. (2018) propose a decomposed graph entailment model that uses structure from the claim to calculate entailment probabilities for each node and edge in the graph structure and aggregates them for the final entailment computation. The original DGE model [6] uses Open IE (Khot et al., 2017) tuples as a graph representation for the claim. However, it is mentioned that the model can use any graph with labeled edges. Therefore, we provide a syntactic dependency parse tree using the Stanford dependency parser (Manning et al., 2014) which outputs the Enhanced Universal Dependencies representation (Schuster and Manning, 2016) as a graph representation for the claim.

Gradient-Boosted Decision Trees model: We also experiment with the *TalosTree* model [7] (Sean et al.,

	Evidence		
Similarity	Precision	Recall	F1
Cosine Similarity using TFIDF	**21.14**	**67.24**	**32.17**
Soft-Cosine Similarity	19.50	65.53	30.05
Word Movers Distance (WMD)	18.24	59.29	27.90
Smooth Inverse Frequency (SIF)	15.19	50.33	23.33
FEVER Baseline	-	-	17.18

Table 1: Evidence extraction results on development set

2017) which was the winning system in the Fake News Challenge (Pomerleau and Ra, 2017). The *TalosTree* model utilizes text-based features derived from the claim and evidences, which are then fed into Gradient Boosted Trees to predict the relation between the claim and the evidences. The features that are used in the prediction model are word count, TF-IDF, sentiment and a singular-value decomposition feature in combination with word2vec embeddings.

3 Experiments

3.1 Dataset

The shared-task (Thorne et al., 2018) provides an annotated dataset of 185,445 claims along with their evidence sets. The shared-task dataset is divided into 145,459 , 19,998 and 19,998 train, development and test instances, respectively. The claims are generated from information extracted from Wikipedia. The Wikipedia dump (version June 2017) was processed with Stanford CoreNLP, and the claims sampled from the introductory sections of approximately 50,000 popular pages.

3.2 Evaluation

In this section we evaluate our system in the two main subtasks of the shared task: I) *evidence extraction* (wiki-page retrieval and sentence selection) and II) *Entailment*. Since, the scoring formula in the shared-task considers only the first 5 predicted sentence evidences, we choose 5-most similar sentences in the sentence selection phase (Section 2.2).

3.2.1 Evidence Extraction

Initially, the impact of different similarity measures in sentence selection is evaluated. Table 1 shows the results of the various similarity measures described in section 2 for the evidence extraction subtask on the development set. The re-

---

[5] https://github.com/sheffieldnlp/fever-baselines
[6] https://github.com/allenai/scitail
[7] https://github.com/Cisco-Talos/fnc-1

| Model | Label | F1 | | | Label Accuracy | FEVER Score |
		Precision	Recall	F1		
DA	NOT ENOUGH INFO	46.00	10.00	17.00	**50.61**	**37.78**
	REFUTES	61.00	60.00	60.00		
	SUPPORTS	46.00	82.00	59.00		
DGE	NOT ENOUGH INFO	41.00	5.00	8.00	42.24	30.31
	REFUTES	62.00	30.00	41.00		
	SUPPORTS	38.00	92.00	54.00		
TalosTree	NOT ENOUGH INFO	28.00	1.00	3.00	44.93	31.54
	REFUTES	66.00	42.00	51.00		
	SUPPORTS	40.00	92.00	55.00		
FEVER baseline*					51.37	31.27

Table 2: Pipeline performance on the dev set with the sentence selection module. (*) In the FEVER baseline the label accuracy uses the annotated evidence instead of evidence from the evidence extraction module.

sults suggest that the simple cosine similarity using TF-IDF is the best performing method for the sentence selection component when compared to the other similarity techniques. With an F1-score of 32.17 it clearly outperforms the Soft-Cosine Similarity (F1 30.05), WMD (F1 27.90) and SIF (F1 23.22) measures. This component clearly also outperforms the FEVER baseline for this subtask (F1 17.18).

3.2.2 Entailment

This component is trained on pairs of annotated claims and evidence sets from the FEVER shared-task training dataset. We here train two different models i.e. *DGE* and *TalosTree* and we utilize the pre-trained *DA* model. We evaluate classification accuracy on the development set, assuming that the evidence sentences are extracted in the evidence extraction phase with the best performing setup. The results are presented in Table 2 and show that the *NOT ENOUGH INFO* class is difficult to detect for all three models. Furthermore, the *DA* model achieves the best accuracy and FEVER score compared to the others. We also observe that the label accuracy has a significant impact on the total FEVER score.

3.2.3 Final System

The final system pipeline is established with the *SPARQL query* and *cosine similarity using TFIDF* in the evidence extraction module, and using the decomposable attention model for the entailment subtask. Table 3 depicts the final submission results over the test set using our system.

| Similarity | Evidence | | | | FEVER |
	P	R	F1	Acc.	Score
Our System	19.19	70.72	30.19	48.87	36.55
FEVER Baseline	-	-	18.26	48.84	27.45

Table 3: Final system pipeline results over test set.

4 Conclusion

We present our system for the FEVER shared task to extract evidence from Wikipedia and verify each claim w.r.t. the obtained evidence. We examine various configurations for each component of the system. The experiments demonstrate the effectiveness of the TF-IDF cosine similarity measure and decomposable attention on both the development and test datasets.

Our future work includes: 1) to implement a semi-supervised machine learning method for evidence extraction , and 2) to investigate different neural architectures for the verification task.

References

Sanjeev Arora, Yingyu Liang, and Tengyu Ma. 2017. A simple but tough-to-beat baseline for sentence embeddings.

Kurt Bollacker, Colin Evans, Praveen Paritosh, Tim Sturge, and Jamie Taylor. 2008. Freebase: A collaboratively created graph database for structuring human knowledge. In *Proceedings of the 2008 ACM SIGMOD International Conference on Management of Data*, SIGMOD '08, pages 1247–1250, New York, NY, USA. ACM.

Delphine Charlet and Geraldine Damnati. 2017. Simbow at semeval-2017 task 3: Soft-cosine semantic similarity between questions for community question answering. In *Proceedings of the 11th International Workshop on Semantic Evaluation (SemEval-2017)*, pages 315–319. Association for Computational Linguistics.

Jenny Rose Finkel, Trond Grenager, and Christopher Manning. 2005. Incorporating non-local information into information extraction systems by gibbs sampling. In *Proceedings of the 43rd Annual Meeting on Association for Computational Linguistics*, ACL '05, pages 363–370, Stroudsburg, PA, USA. Association for Computational Linguistics.

Tushar Khot, Ashish Sabharwal, and Peter Clark. 2017. Answering complex questions using open information extraction. In *Proceedings of the 55th Annual Meeting of the Association for Computational Linguistics (Volume 2: Short Papers)*, pages 311–316. Association for Computational Linguistics.

Tushar Khot, Ashish Sabharwal, and Peter Clark. 2018. SciTail: A textual entailment dataset from science question answering. In *AAAI*.

Matt J. Kusner, Yu Sun, Nicholas I. Kolkin, and Kilian Q. Weinberger. 2015. From word embeddings to document distances. In *Proceedings of the 32Nd International Conference on International Conference on Machine Learning - Volume 37*, ICML'15, pages 957–966. JMLR.org.

Jens Lehmann, Robert Isele, Max Jakob, Anja Jentzsch, Dimitris Kontokostas, Pablo N. Mendes, Sebastian Hellmann, Mohamed Morsey, Patrick van Kleef, Sören Auer, and Christian Bizer. 2015. DBpedia - a large-scale, multilingual knowledge base extracted from wikipedia. *Semantic Web Journal*, 6(2):167–195.

Christopher D. Manning, Mihai Surdeanu, John Bauer, Jenny Finkel, Steven J. Bethard, and David McClosky. 2014. The Stanford CoreNLP natural language processing toolkit. In *Association for Computational Linguistics (ACL) System Demonstrations*, pages 55–60.

Ankur Parikh, Oscar Täckström, Dipanjan Das, and Jakob Uszkoreit. 2016. A decomposable attention model for natural language inference. In *Proceedings of the 2016 Conference on Empirical Methods in Natural Language Processing*, pages 2249–2255. Association for Computational Linguistics.

Dean Pomerleau and Delip Ra. 2017. Fake news challenge. http://fakenewschallenge.org/,.

Eric Prud'hommeaux and Andy Seaborne. 2008. SPARQL Query Language for RDF. W3C Recommendation. http://www.w3.org/TR/rdf-sparql-query/.

Sebastian Schuster and Christopher D. Manning. 2016. Enhanced english universal dependencies: An improved representation for natural language understanding tasks. In *LREC*.

Baird Sean, Sibley Doug, and Pan Yuxi. 2017. Talos targets disinformation with fake news challenge victory. http://blog.talosintelligence.com/2017/06/talos-fake-news-challenge, Accessed: 2018-07-01.

Fabian M. Suchanek, Gjergji Kasneci, and Gerhard Weikum. 2007. Yago: a core of semantic knowledge. In *Proceedings of the 16th international conference on World Wide Web*, WWW '07, pages 697–706, New York, NY, USA. ACM.

James Thorne, Andreas Vlachos, Christos Christodoulopoulos, and Arpit Mittal. 2018. FEVER: a large-scale dataset for fact extraction and verification. In *NAACL-HLT*.

Integrating Entity Linking and Evidence Ranking for Fact Extraction and Verification

Motoki Taniguchi *

motoki.taniguchi@fujixerox.co.jp

Tomoki Taniguchi *

taniguchi.tomoki@fujixerox.co.jp

Takumi Takahashi

takahashi.takumi@fujixerox.co.jp

Yasuhide Miura

yasuhide.miura@fujixerox.co.jp

Tomoko Ohkuma

ohkuma.tomoko@fujixerox.co.jp

Fuji Xerox Co., Ltd.

Abstract

We describe here our system and results on the
FEVER shared task. We prepared a pipeline
system which composes of a document selection, a sentence retrieval, and a recognizing
textual entailment (RTE) components. A simple entity linking approach with text match
is used as the document selection component,
this component identifies relevant documents
for a given claim by using mentioned entities as clues. The sentence retrieval component selects relevant sentences as candidate evidence from the documents based on TF-IDF.
Finally, the RTE component selects evidence
sentences by ranking the sentences and classifies the claim simultaneously. The experimental results show that our system achieved the
FEVER score of 0.4016 and outperformed the
official baseline system.

1 Introduction

The increasing amounts of textual information
on the Web have brought demands to develop techniques to extract and verify a fact.
The Fact Extraction and VERification (FEVER)
task (Thorne et al., 2018) focuses on verification of textual claims against evidence. In the
FEVER shared task, a given claim is classified
as SUPPORTED, REFUTED, or NOTENOUGHINFO
(NEI). Evidence to justify a given claim is required
for SUPPORTED or REFUTED claims. The evidence
is not given and must be retrieved from Wikipedia.

This paper describes our participating system in
the FEVER shared task. The architecture of our
system is designed by following the official baseline system (Thorne et al., 2018). There are two

---

*Authors contributed equally

main differences between our system and the baseline system. The first one is identifying documents
that contain evidence by using text match between
mentioned entities in a given claim and Wikipedia
page title. The details are described in Section 2.1.
The next one is a neural network based model,
details of which are described in Section 2.3, for
selecting evidence sentences as ranking task and
classifying a claim simultaneously.

2 System

We propose a pipeline system which composes of
a document selection, a sentence retrieval, and a
recognizing textual entailment (RTE) components.
A simple entity linking approach with text match
is used as the document selection component.
This component identifies relevant documents for
a given claim by using mentioned entities as clues.
The sentence retrieval component selects relevant
sentences as candidate evidence from the documents based on Term Frequency-Inverse Document Frequency (TF-IDF). Finally, the RTE component selects evidence sentences by ranking the
candidate sentences and classifies the claim as
SUPPORTED, REFUTED, or NOTENOUGHINFO simultaneously. Details of the components are described in the following Section.

2.1 Document selection

Wikipedia pages of entities mentioned in a claim
can be good candidate documents containing the
SUPPORTED/REFUTED evidence. Therefore, we
use a simple but efficient entity linking approach
as a document selection component. In our entity linking approach, relevant documents are retrieved by using exact match between page titles
of Wikipedia and words in a claim. We expect

Proceedings of the First Workshop on Fact Extraction and VERification (FEVER), pages 124–126
Brussels, Belgium, November 1, 2018. ©2018 Association for Computational Linguistics

this component to select only surely correct documents. In other words, we decided to prefer precision of evidence rather than recall. In fact, our preliminary experiment indicates that 68% of claims excluding NEI in a development set can be fully supported or refuted by the retrieved documents with our approach. This corresponds roughly to the accuracy of 10 nearest documents retrieved by the DrQA (Chen et al., 2017) based retrieval approach used in the baseline system. The average number of selected documents in our approach is 3.7, and thus our approach is more efficient than the baseline system.

2.2 Sentence retrieval

Following the baseline system, we use a sentence retrieval component which returns K nearest sentences for a claim using cosine similarity between unigram and bigram TF-IDF vectors. The K nearest sentences are retrieved from the documents selected by the document selection component. We selected optimal K using grid search over $\{5, 10, 15, 20, 50\}$ in terms of the performance of the full pipeline system on a development set. The optimal values was $K = 15$.

2.3 Recognizing textual entailment

As RTE component, we adopt DEISTE (Deep Explorations of Inter-Sentence interactions for Textual Entailment) model that is the state-of-the-art in RTE tasks (Yin et al., 2018). RTE component is trained on labeled claims paired with sentence-level evidence. To build the model, we utilize the NEARESTP dataset described in Thorne et al. (2018). In a case where multiple sentences are required as evidence, the texts of the sentences are concatenated. We use Adam (Kingma and Ba, 2014) as an optimizer and utilize 300 dimensional GloVe vector which is adapted by the baseline system. The other model parameters are the same as the parameters described in Yin et al. (2018).

Claims labelled as NEI are easier to predict correctly than SUPPORTED and REFUTED because unlike SUPPORTED and REFUTED, NEI dose not need evidence. Therefore, our RTE component are designed to predict the claims as NEI if the model can not predict claims as SUPPORTED or REFUTED with high confidence. RTE prediction process is composed of three steps. Firstly, we calculate the probability score of each label for pairs of a claim and candidate sentence using DEISTE model. Secondly, we decide a prediction label using the following equations.

$$
\begin{aligned}
SR &= \underset{s \in S, a \in A}{\arg\max}\, P_{s,a} \\
P_{max} &= \max_{s \in S, a \in A} P_{s,a}
\end{aligned}
$$

$$
Label_{pred} = \begin{cases} SR & (P_{max} > \mathrm{P_t}) \\ NEI & (\text{otherwise}) \end{cases}
$$

where S is a set of pairs of a claim and candidate sentence; $A = \{SUPPORTED, REFUTED\}$; $P_{s,a}$ is a probability score of a pair for label a; $\mathrm{P_t}$ is a threshold value; $Label_{pred}$ is prediction label for a claim. Finally, we sort candidate sentences in descending order of scores and select at most 5 evidence sentences with the same label as predicted label. We also apply grid search to find the best threshold P_t and set it to 0.93.

3 Evaluation

3.1 Dataset

We used official training dataset for training RTE component. For parameter tuning and performance evaluation, we used a development and test datasets used in (Thorne et al., 2018). Table 1 shows statistics of each dataset.

	SUPPORTED	REFUTED	NEI
Training	80,035	29,775	35,639
Development	3,333	3,333	3,333
Test	3,333	3,333	3,333

Table 1: The number of claims in each datasets.

3.2 In-house Experiment

We evaluated our system and baseline system on the test dataset with FEVER score, label accuracy, evidence precision, evidence recall and evidence F1. FEVER score is classification accuracy of claims if the correct evidence is selected. Label accuracy is classification accuracy of claims if the requirement for correct evidence is ignored. Table 2 shows the evaluation results on the test dataset. Our system achieved FEVER score of 0.4016 and outperformed the baseline system. As expected, our system produced a significant improvement of 59 points in evidence precision against the baseline system. Though evidence recall decreased, evidence F1 increased by 17 points compared to the baseline system.

Table 3 shows the confusion matrix on the development dataset. Even though our model

	FEVER Score	Label Accuracy	Evidence Precision	Evidence Recall	Evidence F1
Baseline	0.2807	0.5060	0.1084	0.4599	0.1755
Ours	0.4016	0.4851	0.6986	0.2265	0.3421

Table 2: Evaluation results on the test dataset.

Actual class \ Predicted class	SUPPORTED	REFUTED	NEI	Total
SUPPORTED	929	181	2223	3333
REFUTED	104	1331	1898	3333
NEI	363	300	2670	3333
Total	1396	1812	6791	9999

Table 3: Confusion matrix on the development dataset.

	FEVER Score	Label Accuracy	Evidence F1
Ours	0.3881	0.4713	0.1649

Table 4: Final results of our submissions.

tends to predict claims as NEI, the precisions of SUPPORTED (929/1396 = 0.67) and REFUTED (1331/1812 = 0.73) are higher than the precision of NEI (2670/6791 = 0.39).

3.3 Submission run

Table 4 presents the evaluation results of our submissions. The models showed similar behavior as in the in-house experiment excepting evidence F1. Our submission were ranked in 9th place.

4 Conclusion

We developed a pipeline system which composes of a document selection, a sentence retrieval, and an RTE components for the FEVER shared task. Evaluation results of in-house experiment show that our system achieved improvement of 12% in FEVER score against the baseline system.

Even though document selection component of our system has contributed to find more correct evidence document, the component was too strict, and thus degraded evidence recall. Therefore, as a future work, we plan to explore more sophisticated entity linking approach.

References

Danqi Chen, Adam Fisch, Jason Weston, and Antoine Bordes. 2017. Reading wikipedia to answer open-domain questions. In *Proceedings of the 55th Annual Meeting of the Association for Computational Linguistics (Volume 1: Long Papers)*, pages 1870–1879. Association for Computational Linguistics.

Diederik P Kingma and Jimmy Ba. 2014. Adam: A method for stochastic optimization. *arXiv preprint arXiv:1412.6980*.

James Thorne, Andreas Vlachos, Christos Christodoulopoulos, and Arpit Mittal. 2018. Fever: a large-scale dataset for fact extraction and verification. In *Proceedings of the 2018 Conference of the North American Chapter of the Association for Computational Linguistics: Human Language Technologies, Volume 1 (Long Papers)*, pages 809–819. Association for Computational Linguistics.

Wenpeng Yin, Dan Roth, and Hinrich Schütze. 2018. End-task oriented textual entailment via deep explorations of inter-sentence interactions. In *Proceedings of the 56th Annual Meeting of the Association for Computational Linguistics (Volume 2: Short Papers)*, pages 540–545. Association for Computational Linguistics.

Robust Document Retrieval and Individual Evidence Modeling for Fact Extraction and Verification.

Tuhin Chakrabarty and **Tariq Alhindi**
Department of Computer Science
Columbia University
tc2896@columbia.edu
tariq@cs.columbia.edu

Smaranda Muresan
Department of Computer Science
Data Science Institute
Columbia University
smara@columbia.edu

Abstract

This paper presents the ColumbiaNLP submission for the FEVER Workshop Shared Task. Our system is an end-to-end pipeline that extracts factual evidence from Wikipedia and infers a decision about the truthfulness of the claim based on the extracted evidence. Our pipeline achieves significant improvement over the baseline for all the components (Document Retrieval, Sentence Selection and Textual Entailment) both on the development set and the test set. Our team finished 6th out of 24 teams on the leader-board based on the preliminary results with a FEVER score of 49.06 on the blind test set compared to 27.45 of the baseline system.

1 Introduction and Background

Fact checking is a type of investigative journalism where experts examine the claims published by others for their veracity. The claims can range from statements made by public figures to stories reported by other publishers. The end goal of a fact checking system is to provide a verdict on whether the claim is true, false, or mixed. Several organizations such as `FactCheck.org` and `PolitiFact` are devoted to such activities.

The FEVER Shared task aims to evaluate the ability of a system to verify information using evidence from Wikipedia. Given a claim involving one or more entities (mapping to Wikipedia pages), the system must extract textual evidence (sets of sentences from Wikipedia pages) that supports or refutes the claim and then using this evidence, it must label the claim as Supported, Refuted or NotEnoughInfo. The dataset for the shared task was introduced by Thorne et al. (2018) and consists of 185,445 claims. Table 1 shows three instances from the data set with the claim, the evidence and the verdict.

Claim : Fox 2000 Pictures released the film Soul Food. **[wiki/Soul_Food_(film)]** **Evidence**: Soul Food is a 1997 American comedy-drama film produced by Kenneth "Babyface" Edmonds , Tracey Edmonds and Robert Teitel and released by Fox 2000 Pictures . **Verdict**: SUPPORTS
Claim : Murda Beatz's real name is Marshall Mathers. **[wiki/Murda_Beatz]** **Evidence**: Shane Lee Lindstrom (born February 11, 1994), known professionally as Murda Beatz, is a Canadian hip hop record producer and songwriter from Fort Erie, Ontario. **Verdict**: REFUTES
Claim : L.A. Reid has served as the CEO of Arista Records for four years. **[wiki/L.A._Reid]** **Evidence**: He has served as the chairman and CEO of Epic Records, a division of Sony Music Entertainment, the president and CEO of Arista Records, and the chairman and CEO of the Island Def Jam Music Group. **Verdict**: NOT ENOUGH INFO

Table 1: Examples of claims, the extracted evidence from Wikipedia and the verdicts from the shared task dataset (Thorne et al., 2018)

The baseline system described by Thorne et al. (2018) uses 3 major components:

- **Document Retrieval**: Given a claim, identify relevant documents from Wikipedia which contain the evidence to verify the claim. Thorne et al. (2018) used the document retrieval component from the DrQA system (Chen et al., 2017), which returns the k nearest documents for a query using cosine similarity between binned unigram and bigram TF-IDF vectors.

- **Sentence Selection**: Given the set of retrieved document, identify the candidate evidence sentences. Thorne et al. (2018) used a modified document retrieval component of

Proceedings of the First Workshop on Fact Extraction and VERification (FEVER), pages 127–131
Brussels, Belgium, November 1, 2018. ©2018 Association for Computational Linguistics

DrQA (Chen et al., 2017) to select the top most similar sentences w.r.t the claim, using bigram TF-IDF with binning.

- **Textual Entailment**: For the entailment task, training is done using labeled claims paired with evidence (labels are SUPPORTS, REFUTES, NOT ENOUGH INFO). Thorne et al. (2018) used the decomposable attention model (Parikh et al., 2016) for this task. For the case where multiple sentences are required as evidence, the strings were concatenated.

Our system implements changes in all three modules (Section 2), which leads to significant improvements both on the development and test sets. On the shared task development set our document retrieval approach covers 94.4% of the claims requiring evidence, compared to 55.30% in the baseline. Further, on the dev set our evidence recall is improved by 33 points over the baseline. For entailment, our model improves the baseline by 7.5 points on dev set. Overall, our end-to-end system shows an improvement of 19.56 in FEVER score compared to the baseline (50.83 vs. 31.27) on the dev set . On the blind test set we achieve an evidence recall of 75.89 and an entailment accuracy of 57.45 (9 points above baseline) resulting in a FEVER score of 49.06 (Section 3). Together with the results we discuss some lessons learned based on our error analysis and release our code [1].

2 Methods

2.1 Document Retrieval

Document Retrieval is a crucial step when building an end-to-end system for fact extraction and verification. Missing a relevant document could lead to missed evidence, while non-relevant documents would add noise for the subsequent tasks of sentence selection and textual entailment. We propose a multi-step approach for retrieving documents relevant to the claims.

- **Google Custom Search API**: Wang et al. (2018) looked at retrieving relevant documents for fact-checking articles, looking at generating candidates via search. Inspired by this, we first use the Custom Search API of Google to retrieve documents having information about the claim. We add the token

`wikipedia` to the claim and issue a query and collect the top 2 results.

- **Named Entity Recognition**: Second, we use the AllenNLP (Gardner et al., 2017) pretrained bidirectional language model (Peters et al., 2017) for named entity recognition [2]. After finding the named entities in the claim, we use Wikipedia python API [3] to collect the top wikipedia document returned by the API for each named entity.

- **Dependency Parse**: Third, to increase the chance of detecting relevant entities in the claim, we find the first lower case verb phrase (VP) in the dependency parse tree and query the Wikipedia API with all the tokens before the VP. The reason for emphasizing lower case verb phrase is to avoid missing entities in claims such as "Finding Dory was directed by X", where the relevant entity is "Finding Dory".

To deal with entity ambiguity, we also add the token `film` in our query where the claim contains keywords such as `film`, `stars`, `premiered` and `directed by`. For example in "Marnie was directed by Whoopi Goldberg.", Marnie can refer to both wikipedia pages `Marnie (film)` and `Marnie`. Our point of interest here is `Marnie (film)`. We only experimented with `film` to capture the performance gains. One of our future goals is to build better computational models to handle entity ambiguity or entity linking.

- **Combined**: We use the union of the documents returned by the three approaches as the final set of relevant documents to be used by the Sentence Selection module.

Method	Avg k	Coverage
Google API	2	79.5%
NER	2	77.1%
Dependency Parse	1	80.0%
Combined	3	**94.4%**
(Thorne et al., 2018)	5	55.3%

Table 2: Coverage of claims that can be fully supported or refuted by the retrieved documents (dev set)

Table 2 shows the percentage of claims that can be fully supported or refuted by the retrieved docu-

---

[1] https://github.com/tuhinjubcse/FEVER-EMNLP

[2] http://demo.allennlp.org/named-entity-recognition
[3] https://pypi.org/project/wikipedia/

ments before sentence selection on the dev set. We see that our best approach (combined) achieved a high coverage 94.4% compared to the baseline (Thorne et al., 2018) of 55.3%. Because we do not have the gold evidences for the blind test set we cannot report the claim coverage using our pipeline .

2.2 Sentence Selection

For sentence selection, we used the modified document retrieval component of DrQA (Chen et al., 2017) to select sentences using bigram TF-IDF with binning as proposed by (Thorne et al., 2018). We extract the top 5 most similar sentences from the k-most relevant documents using the TF-IDF vector similarity. Our evidence recall is 78.4 as compared to 45.05 in the development set of FEVER (Thorne et al., 2018), which demonstrates the importance of document retrieval in fact extraction and verification. On the blind test set our sentence selection approach achieves an evidence recall of 75.89.

However, even though TF-IDF proves to be a strong baseline for sentence selection we noticed on the dev set that using all 5 evidences together introduced additional noise to the entailment model. To solve this, we further filtered the top 3 evidences from the selected 5 evidences using distributed semantic representations. Peters et al. (2018) show how deep contextualized word representations model both complex characteristics of word use (e.g., syntax and semantics), and usage across various linguistic contexts. Thus, we used the ELMo embeddings to convert the claim and evidence to vectors. We then calculated cosine similarity between claim and evidence vectors and extracted the top 3 sentences based on the score. Because there was no penalty involved for poor evidence precision, we returned all five selected sentences as our predicted evidence but used only the top three sentences for the entailment model.

2.3 Textual Entailment

The final stage of our pipeline is recognizing textual entailment. Unlike Thorne et al. (2018), we did not concatenate evidences, but trained our model for each claim-evidence pair. For recognizing textual entailment we used the model introduced by Conneau et al. (2017) in their work on supervised learning of universal sentence representations.

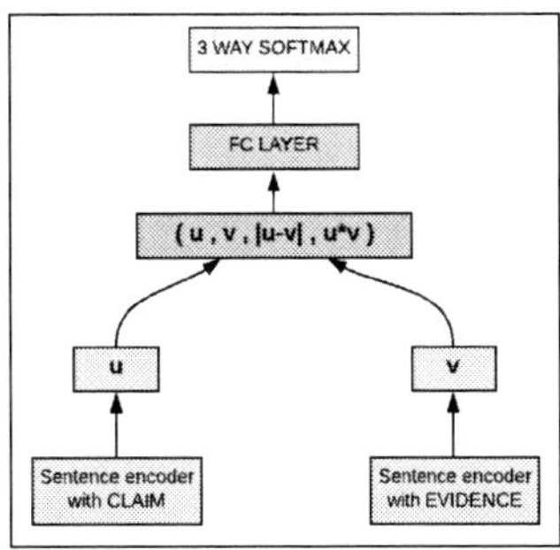

Figure 1: The architecture for recognizing textual entailment (adapted from (Conneau et al., 2017))

The architecture is presented in Figure 1. We use bidirectional LSTMs (Hochreiter and Schmidhuber, 1997) with max-pooling to encode the claim and the evidence. The text encoder provides dense feature representation of an input claim or evidence. Formally, for a sequence of T words $w_{t=1,..,T}$, the BiLSTM layer generates a sequence of h_t vectors, where h_t is the concatenation of a forward and a backward LSTM output. The hidden vectors h_t are then converted into a single vector using max-pooling, which chooses the maximum value over each dimension of the hidden units. Overall, the text encoder can be treated as an operator Text $\rightarrow R^d$ that provides d dimensional encoding for a given text.

Out of vocabulary issues in pre-trained word embeddings are a major bottleneck for sentence representations. To solve this we use fastText embeddings (Bojanowski et al., 2017) which rely on subword information. Also, these embeddings were trained on Wikipedia corpus making them an ideal choice for this task.

As shown in Figure 1, the shared sentence encoder outputs a representation for the claim u and the evidence v. Once the sentence vectors are generated, the following three methods are applied to extract relations between the claim and the evidence: (i) concatenation of the two representations (u, v); (ii) element-wise product u*v and (iii) absolute element-wise difference $|u - v|$. The resulting vector, which captures information from both the claim and the evidence, is fed into a 3-class classifier consisting of fully connected layers culminating in a softmax layer.

For the final class label, we experimented first by taking the majority prediction of the three

129

(claim, evidence) pairs as our entailment label but this led to lower accuracy on the dev set. So our final predictions are based on the rule outlined in the Algorithm 1, where SUPPORTS = S, REFUTES = R, NOT ENOUGH INFO = N and C is a count function. Because the selected evidences were inherently noisy and our pipeline did not concatenate evidences together we chose this rule over majority prediction to mitigate the dominance of prediction of NOT ENOUGH INFO class.

Algorithm 1 Prediction Rule

---

if $C(S) = 1$ & $C(N) = 2$ **then**
   $label = S$
else if $C(R) = 1$ & $C(N) = 2$ **then**
   $label = R$
else
   $label = \arg\max(C(S), C(R), C(N))$

We also experimented by training a classifier which takes confidence scores of all the three claim evidence pairs along with their position in the document and trained a boosted tree classifier but the accuracy did not improve. Empirically the rule gave us the best results on the dev set and thus used it to obtain the final label.

Table 3 shows the 3 way classification accuracy using the textual entailment model described above.

DataSet	Accuracy
Shared Task Dev	58.77
Blind Test Set	57.45

Table 3: 3 way classification results

Our entailment accuracy on the shared task dev and test set is 7 and 9 points better than the baseline respectively.

Implementation Details. The batch size is kept as 64. The model is trained for 15 epochs using Adam optimizer with a learning rate of 0.001. The size of the LSTM hidden units is set to 512 and for the classifier, we use a MLP with 1 hidden-layer of 512 hidden units. The embedding dimension of the words is set to 300.

3 End to End Results and Error Analysis

Table 4 shows the overall FEVER score obtained by our pipeline on the dev and test sets. In the provisional ranking our system ranked 6th.

On closer investigation we find that neither TF-IDF nor sentence embedding based approaches are

Data	Pipeline	FEVER
DEV	(Thorne et al., 2018)	31.27
	Ours	**50.83**
TEST	(Thorne et al., 2018)	27.45
	Ours	**49.06**

Table 4: FEVER scores on shared task dev and test set

perfect when it comes to sentence selection, although TF-IDF works better.

Fox 2000 Pictures released the film Soul Food	0.29
Soul Food is a 1997 American comedy-drama film produced by Kenneth "Babyface" Edmonds,Tracey Edmonds and Robert Teitel and released by Fox 2000 Pictures	

Table 5: Cosine similarity between claim and supporting evidence

Table 5 goes on to prove that we cannot rely on models that entirely depend on semantics. In spite of the two sentences being similar, the cosine similarity between them is poor mostly because the evidence contains a lot of extra information which might not be relevant to the claim and difficult for the model to understand.

At seventeen or eighteen years of age, he joined Plato's Academy in Athens and remained there until the age of thirty-seven (c. 347 BC)
Shortly after Plato died , Aristotle left Athens and at the request of Philip II of Macedon ,tutored Alexander the Great beginning in 343 BC

Table 6: The top evidence is selected by Annotators and the bottom evidence by our pipeline

We also found instances where the predicted evidence is correct but it does not match the gold evidence. For the claim "Aristotle spent time in Athens", both evidences given in Table 6 support it, but still our system gets penalized on not being able to match the gold evidence.

We found quite a few annotations to be incorrect and hence the FEVER scores are lower than expected. Table 7 show two instances where the gold labels for the claims was NOT ENOUGH INFO, while in fact they should have been SUPPORTS and REFUTES, respectively.

Table 8 reflects the fact that NOT ENOUGH INFO is often hard to predict and that is where our model needs to improve more.

The lines between SUPPORTS and NOT ENOUGH INFO are often blurred as shown in

Claim: Natural Born Killers was directed by Oliver Stone
Evidence: Natural Born Killers is a 1994 American satirical crime film directed by Oliver Stone and starring Woody Harrelson , Juliette Lewis , Robert Downey Jr. , Tom Sizemore , and Tommy Lee Jones .
Claim:Anne Rice was born in New Jersey
Evidence: Born in New Orleans, Rice spent much of her early life there before moving to Texas, and later to San Francisco

Table 7: Wrong gold label (NOT ENOUGH INFO)

	S	N	R
S	**4635**	1345	686
N	2211	**3269**	1186
R	1348	1470	**3848**

Table 8: Confusion matrix of entailment predictions on shared task dev set

Table 8. Our models need better understanding of semantics to be able to identify these. Table 9 shows one such example where the `gospel` keyword becomes the discriminative factor.

Claim: Happiness in Slavery is a gospel song by Nine Inch Nails
Evidence: Happiness in Slavery,is a song by American industrial rock band Nine Inch Nails from their debut extended play (EP), Broken(1992)

Table 9: Example where our model predicts SUPPORTS for a claim labeled as NOT ENOUGH INFO

4 Conclusion

The FEVER shared task is challenging primarily because the annotation requires substantial manual effort. We presented an end-to-end pipeline to automate the human effort and showed empirically that our model outperforms the baseline by a large margin. We also provided a thorough error analysis which highlights some of the shortcomings of our models and potentially of the gold annotations.

References

Piotr Bojanowski, Edouard Grave, Armand Joulin, and Tomas Mikolov. 2017. Enriching word vectors with subword information. *Transactions of the Association for Computational Linguistics*, 5:135–146.

Danqi Chen, Adam Fisch, Jason Weston, and Antoine Bordes. 2017. Reading wikipedia to answer open-domain questions. pages 1870–1879. In Proceedings of the 55th Annual Meeting of the Association for Computational Linguistics (Volume 1: Long Papers).

Alexis Conneau, Douwe Kiela, Holger Schwenk, Loïc Barrault, and Antoine Bordes. 2017. Supervised learning of universal sentence representations from natural language inference data. In *Proceedings of the 2017 Conference on Empirical Methods in Natural Language Processing*, pages 670–680, Copenhagen, Denmark. Association for Computational Linguistics.

Matt Gardner, Joel Grus, Oyvind Tafjord Mark Neumann, Pradeep Dasigi, Nelson Liu, Matthew Peters, Michael Schmitz, and Luke Zettlemoyer. 2017. Allennlp: A deep semantic natural language processing platform.

Sepp Hochreiter and Jurgen Schmidhuber. 1997. Long short-term memory. In *Neural computation, 791*, pages 1735–1780.

Ankur Parikh, Dipanjan Das Oscar Tackstr om, and Jakob Uszkoreit. 2016. A decomposable attention model for natural language inference. pages 2249–2255. In Proceedings of the 2016 Conference on Empirical Methods in Natural Language Processing. Association for Computational Linguistics, Austin, Texas.

Matthew E. Peters, Waleed Ammar, Chandra Bhagavatula, and Russell Power. 2017. Semi-supervised sequence tagging with bidirectional language models. In *ACL*.

Matthew E. Peters, Mark Neumann, Mohit Iyyer, Matt Gardner, Christopher Clark, Kenton Lee, and Luke Zettlemoyer. 2018. Deep contextualized word representations. In *Proc. of NAACL*.

James Thorne, Andreas Vlachos, Christos Christodoulopoulos, and Arpit Mittal. 2018. Fever: a large-scale dataset for fact extraction and verification. pages 809–819. Proceedings of NAACL-HLT 2018.

Xuezhi Wang, Cong Yu, Simon Baumgartner, and Flip Korn. 2018. Relevant document discovery for fact-checking articles. pages 525–533. WWW '18 Companion Proceedings of the The Web Conference 2018.

DeFactoNLP: Fact Verification using Entity Recognition, TFIDF Vector Comparison and Decomposable Attention

Aniketh Janardhan Reddy[*]
Machine Learning Department
Carnegie Mellon University
Pittsburgh, USA
`ajreddy@cs.cmu.edu`

Gil Rocha
LIACC/DEI
Faculdade de Engenharia
Universidade do Porto, Portugal
`gil.rocha@fe.up.pt`

Diego Esteves
SDA Research
University of Bonn
Bonn, Germany
`esteves@cs.uni-bonn.de`

Abstract

In this paper, we describe DeFactoNLP[1], the system we designed for the FEVER 2018 Shared Task. The aim of this task was to conceive a system that can not only automatically assess the veracity of a claim but also retrieve evidence supporting this assessment from Wikipedia. In our approach, the Wikipedia documents whose Term Frequency-Inverse Document Frequency (TFIDF) vectors are most similar to the vector of the claim and those documents whose names are similar to those of the named entities (NEs) mentioned in the claim are identified as the documents which might contain evidence. The sentences in these documents are then supplied to a textual entailment recognition module. This module calculates the probability of each sentence supporting the claim, contradicting the claim or not providing any relevant information to assess the veracity of the claim. Various features computed using these probabilities are finally used by a Random Forest classifier to determine the overall truthfulness of the claim. The sentences which support this classification are returned as evidence. Our approach achieved[2] a 0.4277 evidence F1-score, a 0.5136 label accuracy and a 0.3833 FEVER score[3].

1 Introduction

Given the current trend of massive fake news propagation on social media, the world is desperately in need of automated fact checking systems. Automatically determining the authenticity of a fact is a challenging task that requires the collection and assimilation of a large amount of information. To perform the task, a system is required to find relevant documents, detect and label evidences, and finally output a score which represents the truthfulness of the given claim. The numerous design challenges associated with such systems are discussed by Thorne and Vlachos (2018) and Esteves et al. (2018).

The Fact Extraction and Verification (FEVER) dataset (Thorne et al., 2018) is the first publicly available large-scale dataset designed to facilitate the training and testing of automated fact verification systems. The FEVER 2018 Shared Task required us to design such systems using this dataset. The organizers had provided us a preprocessed version of the June 2017 Wikipedia dump in which the pages only contained the introductory sections of the respective Wikipedia pages. Given a claim, we were asked to build systems which could determine if there were sentences supporting the claim (labelled as "SUPPORTS") or sentences refuting it (labelled as "REFUTES"). If conclusive evidence either supporting or refuting the claim could not be found in the dump, the system should report the same (labelled "NOT ENOUGH INFO"). However, if conclusive evidence was found, it should also retrieve the sentences which either support or refute the claim.

2 System Architecture

Our approach has four main steps: Relevant Document Retrieval, Relevant Sentence Retrieval, Textual Entailment Recognition and Final Scoring

---

[*]Work was completed while the author was a student at the Birla Institute of Technology and Science, India and was interning at SDA Research.

[1]`https://github.com/DeFacto/DeFactoNLP`

[2]The scores and ranks reported in this paper are provisional and were determined prior to any human evaluation of those evidences that were retrieved by the proposed systems but were not identified in the previous rounds of annotation. The organizers of the task plan to update these results after an additional round of annotation.

[3]FEVER score measures the fraction of claims for which at least one complete set of evidences have been retrieved by the fact verification system.

Proceedings of the First Workshop on Fact Extraction and VERification (FEVER), pages 132–137
Brussels, Belgium, November 1, 2018. ©2018 Association for Computational Linguistics

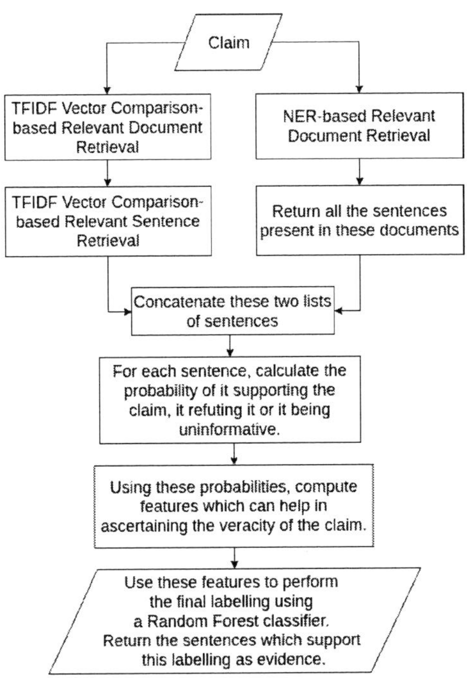

Figure 1: The main steps of our approach

and Classification. Given a claim, Named Entity Recognition (NER) and TFIDF vector comparision are first used to retrieve the relevant documents and sentences as delineated in Section 2.1. The relevant sentences are then supplied to the textual entailment recognition module (Section 2.2) that returns a set of probabilities. Finally, a Random Forest classifier (Breiman, 2001) is employed to assign a label to the claim using certain features derived from the probabilities returned by the entailment model as detailed in Section 2.3. The proposed architecture is depicted in Figure 1.

2.1 Retrieval of Relevant Documents and Sentences

We used two methods to identify which Wikipedia documents may contain relevant evidences. Information about the NEs mentioned in a claim can be helpful in determining the claim's veracity. In order to get the Wikipedia documents which describe them, the first method initially uses the Conditional Random Fields-based Stanford NER software (Finkel et al., 2005) to recognize the NEs mentioned in the claim. Then, for every NE which is recognized, it finds the document whose name has the least Levenshtein distance (Levenshtein, 1966) to that of the NE. Hence, we obtain a set

of documents which contain information about the NEs mentioned in a claim. Since all of the sentences in such documents might aid the verification, they are all returned as possible evidences.

The second method used to retrieve candidate evidences is identical to that used in the baseline system (Thorne et al., 2018) and is based on the rationale that sentences which contain terms similar to those present in the claim are likely to help the verification process. Directly evaluating all of the sentences in the dump is computationally expensive. Hence, the system first retrieves the five most similar documents based on the cosine similarity between binned unigram and bigram TFIDF vectors of the documents and the claim using the DrQA system (Chen et al., 2017). Of all the sentences present in these documents, the five most similar sentences based on the cosine similarity between the binned bigram TFIDF vectors of the sentences and the claim are finally chosen as possible sources of evidence. The number of documents and sentences chosen is based on the analysis presented in the aforementioned work by Thorne et al. (2018).

The sets of sentences returned by the two methods are combined and fed to the textual entailment recognition module described in Section 2.2.

2.2 Textual Entailment Recognition Module

Recognizing Textual Entailment (RTE) is the process of determining whether a text fragment (Hypothesis H) can be inferred from another fragment (Text T) (Sammons et al., 2012). The RTE module receives the claim and the set of possible evidential sentences from the previous step. Let there be n possible sources of evidence for verifying a claim. For the ith possible evidence, let s_i denote the probability of it entailing the claim, let r_i denote the probability of it contradicting the claim, and let u_i be the probability of it being uninformative. The RTE module calculates each of these probabilities.

The SNLI corpus (Bowman et al., 2015) is used for training the RTE model. This corpus is composed of sentence pairs $\langle T, H \rangle$, where T corresponds to the literal description of an image and H is a manually created sentence. If H can be inferred from T, the "Entailment" label is assigned to the pair. If H contradicts the information in T, the pair is labelled as "Contradiction". Otherwise, the label "Neutral" is assigned.

We chose to employ the state-of-the-art RTE model proposed by Peters et al. (2018) which is a re-implementation of the widely used decomposable attention model developed by Parikh et al. (2016). The model achieves an accuracy of 86.4% on the SNLI test set. We selected it because at the time of development of this work, it was one of the best performing systems on the task with publicly available code. Additionally, the usage of preprocessing parsing tools is not required and the model is faster to train when compared to the other approaches we tried.

Although the model achieved good scores on the SNLI dataset, we noticed that it does not generalize well when employed to predict the relationships between the candidate claim-evidence pairs present in the FEVER data. In order to improve the generalization capabilities of the RTE model, we decided to fine-tune it using a newly synthesized FEVER SNLI-style dataset (Pratt and Jennings, 1996). This was accomplished in two steps: the RTE model was initially trained using the SNLI dataset and then re-trained using the FEVER SNLI-style dataset.

The FEVER SNLI-style dataset was created using the information present in the FEVER dataset while retaining the format of the SNLI dataset. Let us consider each learning instance in the FEVER dataset of the form $\langle c, l, E \rangle$, where c is the claim, $l \in \{$SUPPORTS, REFUTES, NOT ENOUGH INFO$\}$ is the label and E is the set of evidences. While constructing the FEVER SNLI-style dataset, we only considered the learning instances labeled as "SUPPORTS" or "REFUTES" because these were the instances that provided us with evidences. Given such an instance, we proceeded as follows: for each evidence $e \in E$, we created an SNLI-style example $\langle c, e \rangle$ labeled as "Entailment" if $l =$ "SUPPORTS" or "Contradiction" if $l =$ "REFUTES". If e contained more than one sentence, we made a simplifying assumption and only considered the first sentence of e. For each "Entailment" or "Contradiction" which was added to this dataset, a "Neutral" learning instance of the form $\langle c, n \rangle$ was also created. n is a randomly selected sentence present the same document from which e was retrieved. We also ensured that n was not included in any of the other evidences in E. Following this procedure, we obtain examples that are similar (retrieved from the same document) but should be labeled differently.

Split	Entail.	Contradiction	Neutral
Training	122,892	48,825	147,588
Dev	4,685	4,921	8,184
Test	4,694	4,930	8,432

Table 1: FEVER SNLI-style Dataset split sizes for ENTAILMENT, CONTRADICTION and NEUTRAL classes

Model	Macro	Entail.	Contra.	Neutral
Vanilla	0.45	0.54	0.44	0.37
Fine-tuned	0.70	0.70	0.64	0.77

Table 2: Macro and class-specific F1 scores achieved on the FEVER SNLI-style test set

Thus, we obtained a dataset with the characteristics depicted in Table 1. To correct the unbalanced nature of the dataset, we performed random under-sampling (He and Garcia, 2009). The fine-tuning had a huge positive impact on the generalization capabilities of the model as shown in Table 2. Using the fine-tuned model, the aforementioned set of probabilities are finally computed.

2.3 Final Classification

Twelve features were derived using the probabilities computed by the RTE module. We define the following variables for notational convenience:

$$cs_i = \begin{cases} 1 & \text{if } s_i \geq r_i \text{ and } s_i \geq u_i \\ 0 & \text{otherwise} \end{cases}$$

$$cr_i = \begin{cases} 1 & \text{if } r_i \geq s_i \text{ and } r_i \geq u_i \\ 0 & \text{otherwise} \end{cases}$$

$$cu_i = \begin{cases} 1 & \text{if } u_i \geq s_i \text{ and } u_i \geq r_i \\ 0 & \text{otherwise} \end{cases}$$

The twelve features which were computed are:

$$f_1 = \sum_{i=1}^{n} cs_i \qquad f_8 = max(r_i) \, \forall i$$

$$f_2 = \sum_{i=1}^{n} cr_i \qquad f_9 = max(u_i) \, \forall i$$

$$f_3 = \sum_{i=1}^{n} cu_i \qquad f_{10} = \begin{cases} \frac{f_4}{f_1} & \text{if } f_1 \neq 0 \\ 0 & \text{otherwise} \end{cases}$$

$$f_4 = \sum_{i=1}^{n} (s_i \times cs_i)$$

$$f_5 = \sum_{i=1}^{n} (r_i \times cr_i) \quad f_{11} = \begin{cases} \frac{f_5}{f_2} & \text{if } f_2 \neq 0 \\ 0 & \text{otherwise} \end{cases}$$

$$f_6 = \sum_{i=1}^{n} (u_i \times cu_i)$$

$$f_7 = max(s_i) \, \forall i \qquad f_{12} = \begin{cases} \frac{f_6}{f_3} & \text{if } f_3 \neq 0 \\ 0 & \text{otherwise} \end{cases}$$

Each of the possible evidential sentences supports a certain label more than the other labels (this can be determined by looking at the computed probabilities). The variables cs_i, cr_i and cu_i are used to capture this fact. The most obvious way to label a claim would be to assign the label with the highest support to the claim. Hence, we chose to use the features f_1, f_2 and f_3 which represent the number of possible evidential sentences which support each label. The amount of support lent to a certain label by supporting sentences could also be useful in performing the labelling. This motivated us to use the features f_4, f_5 and f_6 which quantify the amount of support for each label. If a certain sentence can strongly support a label, it might be prudent to assign that label to the claim. Hence, we use the features f_7, f_8 and f_9 which capture how strongly a single sentence can support the claim. Finally, we used the features f_{10}, f_{11} and f_{12} because the average strength of the support lent by supporting sentences to a given label could also help the classifier.

These features were used by a Random Forest classifier (Breiman, 2001) to determine the label to be assigned to the claim. The classifier was composed of 50 decision trees and the maximum depth of each tree was limited to 3. Information gain was used to measure the quality of a split. 3000 claims labelled as "SUPPORTS", 3000 claims labelled as "REFUTES" and 4000 claims labelled as "NOT ENOUGH INFO" were randomly sampled from the training set. Relevant sentences were then retrieved as detailed in Section 2.1 and supplied to the RTE module (Section 2.2). The probabilities calculated by this module were used to generate the aforementioned features. The classifier was then trained using these features and the actual labels of the claims.

We used the trained classifier to label the claims in the test set. If the "SUPPORTS" label was assigned to the claim, the five documents with the highest ($s_i \times cs_i$) products were returned as evidences. However, if $cs_i = 0\ \forall i$, then the label was changed to "NOT ENOUGH INFO" and a null set was returned as evidence. A similar process was employed when the "REFUTES" label was assigned to a claim. If the "NOT ENOUGH INFO" label was assigned, a null set was returned as evidence.

3 Results and Discussion

Our system was evaluated using a blind test set which contained 19,998 claims. Table 3 compares

Metric	*DeFactoNLP*	*Baseline*	*Best*
Label Accuracy	0.5136	0.4884	0.6821
Evidence F1	0.4277	0.1826	0.6485
FEVER Score	0.3833	0.2745	0.6421

Table 3: System Performance

the performance of our system with that of the baseline system. It also lists the best performance for each metric. The evidence precision of our system was 0.5191 and its evidence recall was 0.3636. All of these results were obtained upon submitting our predictions to an online evaluator. DeFactoNLP had the 5th best evidence F1 score, the 11th best label accuracy and the 12th best FEVER score out of the 24 participating systems.

The results show that the evidence F1 score of our system is much better than that of the baseline system. However, the label accuracy of our system is only marginally better than that of the baseline, suggesting that our final classifier is not very reliable. The low label accuracy may have negatively affected the other scores. Our system's low evidence recall can be attributed to the primitive methods employed to retrieve the candidate documents and sentences. Additionally, the RTE module can only detect entailment between two pairs of sentences. Hence, claims which require more than one sentence to verify them cannot be easily labelled by our system. This is another reason behind our low evidence recall, FEVER score and label accuracy. We aim to study more sophisticated ways to combine the information obtained from the RTE module in the near future.

To better assess the performance of the system, we performed a manual analysis of the predictions made by the system. We observed that for some simple claims (*ex.*"Tilda Swinton is a vegan") which were labeled as "NOT ENOUGH INFO" in the gold-standard, the sentence retrieval module found many sentences related to the NEs in the claim but none of them had any useful information regarding the claim object (*ex.*"vegan"). In some of these cases, the RTE module would label certain sentences as either supporting or refuting the claim, even if they were not relevant to the claim. In the future, we aim to address this shortcoming by exploring triple extraction-based methods to weed out certain sentences (Gerber et al., 2015).

We also noticed that the usage of coreference in

the Wikipedia articles was responsible for the system missing some evidences as the RTE module could not accurately assess the sentences which used coreference. Employing a coreference resolution system at the article level is a promising direction to address this problem.

The incorporation of named entity disambiguation into the sentence and document retrieval modules could also boost performance. This is because we noticed that in some cases, the system used information from unrelated Wikipedia pages whose names were similar to those of the NEs mentioned in a claim to incorrectly label it (*ex.* a claim was related to the movie "Soul Food" but some of the retrieved evidences were from the Wikipedia page related to the soundtrack "Soul Food").

4 Conclusion

In this work, we described our fact verification system, DeFactoNLP, which was designed for the FEVER 2018 Shared Task. When supplied a claim, it makes use of NER and TFIDF vector comparison to retrieve candidate Wikipedia sentences which might help in the verification process. An RTE module and a Random Forest classifier are then used to determine the veracity of the claim based on the information present in these sentences. The proposed system achieved a 0.4277 evidence F1-score, a 0.5136 label accuracy and a 0.3833 FEVER score. After analyzing our results, we have identified many ways of improving the system in the future. For instance, triple extraction-based methods can be used to improve the sentence retrieval component as well as to improve the identification of evidential sentences. We also wish to explore more sophisticated methods to combine the information obtained from the RTE module and employ entity linking methods to perform named entity disambiguation.

Acknowledgments

This research was partially supported by an EU H2020 grant provided for the WDAqua project (GA no. 642795) and by the DAAD under the "International promovieren in Deutschland fr alle" (IPID4all) project.

References

Samuel R. Bowman, Gabor Angeli, Christopher Potts, and Christopher D. Manning. 2015. A large annotated corpus for learning natural language inference. In *EMNLP*, pages 632–642. The Association for Computational Linguistics.

Leo Breiman. 2001. Random forests. *Mach. Learn.*, 45(1):5–32.

Danqi Chen, Adam Fisch, Jason Weston, and Antoine Bordes. 2017. Reading Wikipedia to answer open-domain questions. In *Association for Computational Linguistics (ACL)*.

Diego Esteves, Anisa Rula, Aniketh Janardhan Reddy, and Jens Lehmann. 2018. Toward veracity assessment in rdf knowledge bases: An exploratory analysis. *Journal of Data and Information Quality (JDIQ)*, 9(3):16.

Jenny Rose Finkel, Trond Grenager, and Christopher Manning. 2005. Incorporating non-local information into information extraction systems by gibbs sampling. In *Proceedings of the 43rd Annual Meeting on Association for Computational Linguistics*, ACL '05, pages 363–370, Stroudsburg, PA, USA. Association for Computational Linguistics.

Daniel Gerber, Diego Esteves, Jens Lehmann, Lorenz Bühmann, Ricardo Usbeck, Axel-Cyrille Ngonga Ngomo, and René Speck. 2015. Defacto - temporal and multilingual deep fact validation. *Web Semantics: Science, Services and Agents on the World Wide Web*.

Haibo He and Edwardo A. Garcia. 2009. Learning from imbalanced data. *IEEE Trans. on Knowl. and Data Eng.*, 21(9):1263–1284.

V. I. Levenshtein. 1966. Binary Codes Capable of Correcting Deletions, Insertions and Reversals. *Soviet Physics Doklady*, 10:707.

Ankur Parikh, Oscar Täckström, Dipanjan Das, and Jakob Uszkoreit. 2016. A decomposable attention model for natural language inference. In *Proceedings of the 2016 Conference on Empirical Methods in Natural Language Processing*, pages 2249–2255. Association for Computational Linguistics.

Matthew Peters, Mark Neumann, Mohit Iyyer, Matt Gardner, Christopher Clark, Kenton Lee, and Luke Zettlemoyer. 2018. Deep contextualized word representations. In *Proceedings of the 2018 Conference of NAACL: Human Language Technologies, Volume 1 (Long Papers)*, pages 2227–2237. Association for Computational Linguistics.

Lorien Pratt and Barbara Jennings. 1996. A survey of transfer between connectionist networks. *Connection Science*, 8(2):163–184.

Mark Sammons, V.G.Vinod Vydiswaran, and Dan Roth. 2012. Recognizing textual entailment. In Daniel M. Bikel and Imed Zitouni, editors, *Multilingual Natural Language Applications: From Theory to Practice*, pages 209–258. Prentice Hall.

James Thorne and Andreas Vlachos. 2018. Automated fact checking: Task formulations, methods and future directions. *CoRR*, abs/1806.07687.

James Thorne, Andreas Vlachos, Christos Christodoulopoulos, and Arpit Mittal. 2018. FEVER: a large-scale dataset for fact extraction and verification. In *NAACL-HLT*.

An End-to-End Multi-task Learning Model for Fact Checking

Sizhen Li and **Shuai Zhao** and **Bo Cheng**
State Key Laboratory of networking and switching technology,
Beijing university of posts and telecommunications

Hao Yang
2012 Labs, Huawei Technologies CO., LTD

Abstract

With huge amount of information generated every day on the web, fact checking is an important and challenging task which can help people identify the authenticity of most claims as well as providing evidences selected from knowledge source like Wikipedia. Here we decompose this problem into two parts: an entity linking task (retrieving relative Wikipedia pages) and recognizing textual entailment between the claim and selected pages. In this paper, we present an end-to-end multi-task learning with bi-direction attention (EMBA) model to classify the claim as "supports", "refutes" or "not enough info" with respect to the pages retrieved and detect sentences as evidence at the same time. We conduct experiments on the FEVER (Fact Extraction and VERification) paper test dataset and shared task test dataset, a new public dataset for verification against textual sources. Experimental results show that our method achieves comparable performance compared with the baseline system.

1 Introduction

When we got news from newspapers and TVs which was thoroughly investigated and written by professional journalists, most of these messages are well-found and trustworthy. However, with the popularity of the internet, there are 2.5 quintillion bytes of data created each day at our current pace[1]. Everyone online is a producer as well as a recipient of these emerging information, and some of them are incorrect, fabricated or even with some evil purposes. Most time it is difficult for us to figure out the truth of those emerging news without professional background and enough investigation. Fact checking, which firstly has been produced and received a lot of attention in the industry of journalism, mainly verifying the speeches of public figures, is also important for other domains, e.g. wrong common-sense correction, rumor detection, content review etc.

With the increasing demand for automatic claim verification, several datasets for fact checking have been produced in recent years. Vlachos and Riedel (2014) are the first to release a public fake news detection and fact-checking dataset from two fact checking websites, the fact checking blog of Channel 4[2] and the True-O-Meter from PolitiFact[3]. This dataset only includes 221 statements. Similarly, from PolitiFact via its API, Wang (2017) collected LIAR dataset with 12.8K manually labeled short statements, which permits machine learning based methods used on this dataset. Both dataset don't include the original justification and evidence as it was not machine-readable. However, just verifying the claim based on the claim itself and without referring to any evidence sources is not reasonable and convincing.

In 2015, Silverman launched the Emergent Project[4], a real-time rumor tracker, part of a research project with the Tow Center for Digital Journalism[5] at Columbia University. Ferreira and Vlachos (2016) firstly proposed to use the data from Emergent Project as Emergent dataset for rumor debunking, which contains 300 rumored claims and 2,595 associated news articles. In 2017, the Fake news challenge (Pomerleau and Rao, 2017) consisted of 50K labeled claim-article pairs similarly derived from the Emergent Project. These two dataset stemmed from Emergent Project alleviate the fact checking task by detecting the relationship between claim-article pairs. However, in more common situation, we

---

[1]https://www.forbes.com/sites/bernardmarr/2018/05/21/how-much-data-do-we-create-every-day-the-mind-blowing-stats-everyone-should-read/#62a15bba60ba

[2]http://blogs.channel4.com/factcheck/
[3]http://www.politifact.com/truth-o-meter/statements/
[4]http://www.emergent.info/
[5]https://towcenter.org/

Proceedings of the First Workshop on Fact Extraction and VERification (FEVER), pages 138–144
Brussels, Belgium, November 1, 2018. ©2018 Association for Computational Linguistics

are dealing with plenty of claims themselves online without associated articles which can help to verify the claims.

Fact Extraction and VERification (FEVER) dataset (Thorne et al., 2018) consists of 185,445 claims manually verified against the introductory sections of Wikipedia pages and classified as SUPPORTED, REFUTED or NOTENOUGH-INFO. For the first two classes, the dataset provides combination of sentences forming the necessary evidences supporting or refuting the claim. Obviously, this dataset is more difficult than existing fact-checking datasets. In order to achieve higher FEVER score, a fact-checking system is required to classify the claim correctly as well as retrieving sentences among more than 5 million Wikipedia pages jointed as correct evidence supporting the judgement.

The baseline method of this task comprises of three components: document retrieval, sentence-level evidence selection and textual entailment. For the first two retrieval components, the baseline method uses document retrieval component of DrQA (Chen et al., 2017) which only relies on the unigram and bigram TF-IDF with vector similarity and don't understand semantics of the claim and pages. So, we find that it extracts lots of Wikipedia pages which are unrelated to the entities described in claims. Besides, similarity-based method prefer extracting supporting evidences than refuting evidences. For the recognizing textual entailment (RTE) module, on one hand, the previous retrieval results limit the performance of the RTE model. On the other hand, the selected sentences concatenated as evidences may also confuse the RTE model due to some contradictory information.

In this paper, we introduce an end-to-end multi-task learning with bi-direction attention (EMBA) model for FEVER task. We utilize the multi-task framework to jointly extract evidences and verify the claim because these two sub-tasks can be accomplished at the same time. For example, after selecting relative pages, we carefully scan these pages to find supporting or refuting evidences. If we find some, the claim can be labeled as SUPPORTS or REFUTES immediately. If not, the claim will be classified as NOTENOUGHINFO after we read pages completely. Our model is trained on claim-pages pairs by using attention mechanism in both directions, claim-to-pages and pages-to-claim, which provides complimentary information to each other. We obtain claim-aware sentence representation to predict the correct evidence position and the pages-aware claim representation to detect the relationship between the claim and the pages.

2 Related Work

Natural Language Inference (NLI) or Recognizing textual entailment (RTE) detects the relationship between the premise-hypothesis pairs as "entailment", "contradiction" and "not related". With the renaissance of neural network (Krizhevsky et al., 2012; Mikolov et al., 2010; Graves, 2012) and attention mechanism (Xu et al., 2015; Luong et al., 2015; Bahdanau et al., 2014), the popular framework for the RTE is "matching-aggregation" (Parikh et al., 2016; Wang et al., 2017). Under this framework, words of two sentences are firstly aligned, and then the aligning results with original vectors are aggregated into a new representation vector to make the final decision. The attention mechanism can empower this framework to capture more interactive features between two sentences. Compared to Fever task, RTE provides the sentence to verify against instead of having to retrieve it from knowledge source.

Another relative task is question answering (QA) and machine reading comprehension (MRC), for which approaches have recently been extended to handle large-scale resources such as Wikipedia (Chen et al., 2017). Similar to MRC task which needs to identify the answer span in a passage, FEVER task requires to detect the evidence sentences in Wikipedia pages. However, MRC model tends to identify the answer span based on the similarity and reasoning between the question and passage, while similarity-based method is more likely to ignore refuting evidence in pages. For example, a claim stating "Manchester by the Sea is distributed globally" can be refuted by retrieving "It began a limited release on November 18, 2016" as evidence.

3 Model

The FEVER dataset is derived from the Wikipedia pages. So, we assume each claim contains at least one entity in Wikipedia and the evidence can be retrieved from these relative pages. Thus, we decompose FEVER task into two components: (1) entity linking which detects Wikipedia entities in claim. We use the pages of identified entities

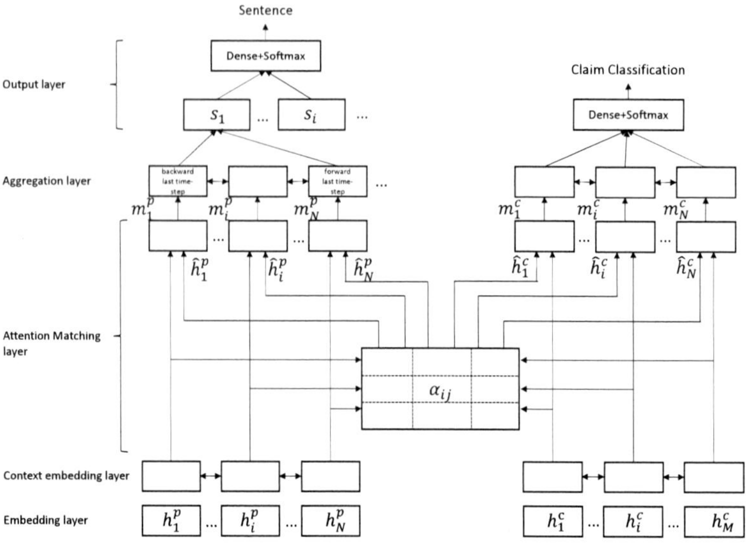

Figure 1: An End-to-End Multi-task Learning Model for Fact Checking

as relative pages. And (2) an end-to-end multi-task learning with bi-direction attention (EMBA) model (in Figure 1) which classify the claim as "supports", "refutes" or "not enough info" with respect to the pages retrieved and select sentences as evidence at the same time.

3.1 Entity Liking

S-MART is a Wikipedia entity linking tool for short and noisy text. For each claim, we use S-MART to retrieve the top 5 entities from Wikipedia. These entity pages are jointed together as the source pages then passed to select correct sentences. For a given claim, S-MART first retrieves all possible entities of Wikipedia by surface matching, and then ranks them using a statistical model, which is trained on the frequency counts with which the surface form occurs with the entity.

3.2 Sentence Extraction and Claim Verification

We now proceed to identify the correct sentences as evidence from relative pages and try to classify the claim as "supports", "refutes" or "not enough info" with respect to the pages retrieved at the same time. Inspired by the recent success of attention mechanism in NLI (Wang et al., 2017) and MRC (Seo et al., 2016; Tan et al., 2017), we propose an end-to-end multi-task learning with bi-pose an end-to-end multi-task learning with bi-direction attention (EMBA) model, which exploits both pages-to-claim attention to verify the claim and claim-to-pages attention to predict the evidence sentence position respectively. Our model consists of:

Embedding layer: This layer represents each word in a fixed-size vector with two components: a word embedding and a character-level embedding. For word embedding, pre-trained word vectors, Glove (Pennington et al., 2014), provides the fixed-size embedding of each word. For character embedding, following Kim (Kim, 2014), characters of each words are embedded into fixed-size embedding, then fed into a Convolutional Neural Network (CNN). The character and word embedding vectors are concatenated together and passed to a Highway Network (Srivastava et al., 2015). The output of this layer are two sequences of word vectors of claim and pages.

Context embedding layer: The purpose of this layer is to incorporate contextual information into the presentation of each word of claim and passage. We utilize a bi-directional LSTM (BiLSTM) on the top of the embedding provided by the previous layers to encode contextual embedding for each word.

Attention matching layer: In this layer, we compute attention in two directions: from pages to claim as well as from claim to pages. To obtain these attention mechanisms, we first calculate a shared similarity matrix between the contextual embedding of each word of the claim $\mathbf{h}_i^c$ and each word of the pages $\mathbf{h}_j^p$:

$$\alpha_{ij} = \mathbf{w}[\mathbf{h}_i^c; \mathbf{h}_j^p; \mathbf{h}_i^c \circ \mathbf{h}_j^p] \quad (1)$$

where α_{ij} represents the attention weights on the i-th claim word by j-th pages word, w is a trainable weight vector, $\circ$ is elementwise multiplication, [;] is vector concatenation across row, and implicit multiplication is matrix multiplication.

Claim-to-pages attention Claim-to-pages attention represents which claim words are most relevant to each word of pages. To obtain attended pages vector, we take α_{ij} as the weight of $\mathbf{h}_j^p$ and weighted sum all the contextual embedding of pages:

$$\tilde{\mathbf{h}}_j = \sum_{i=1}^{N} \alpha_{ij}\mathbf{h}_i / \sum_{i=1}^{N} \alpha_{ij} \quad (2)$$

Finally, we match each contextual embedding with its corresponding attention vector to obtain the claim-aware representation of each word of pages:

$$\mathbf{m}_j = \mathbf{W}[\mathbf{h}_j; \tilde{\mathbf{h}}_j; \mathbf{h}_j \circ \tilde{\mathbf{h}}_j] \quad (3)$$

Pages-to-claim attention Pages-to-claim attention represents which pages words are most relevant to each claim word. Similar to claim-to-pages attention, the attended claim vector and the pages-aware representation of each pages word are calculated by:

$$\tilde{\mathbf{h}}_i = \sum_{j=1}^{N} \alpha_{ij}\mathbf{h}_j / \sum_{j=1}^{N} \alpha_{ij} \quad (4)$$

$$\mathbf{m}_i = \mathbf{W}[\mathbf{h}_i; \tilde{\mathbf{h}}_i; \mathbf{h}_i \circ \tilde{\mathbf{h}}_i] \quad (5)$$

Aggregation layer: The input to the aggregation layer is two sequences of matching vectors, the claim-aware pages word representation and pages-aware claim word representation. The goal of the modeling layer is to capture the interaction among the pages words conditioned on the claim as well as the claim words conditioned on the passage words. This is different from the contextual embedding layer, which captures the interaction among context information independent of matching information.

Sentence selection layer: The FEVER task requires the model to retrieve sentences of the passage as evidence to verify the claim. The sentence representation $\mathbf{s}_t$ is obtained by concatenating vectors from the last time-step of the previous layer

BiLSTM models output sequences. We calculate the probability distribution of the evidence position over the whole pages by:

$$p_t = softmax(\mathbf{w}\mathbf{s}_t) \quad (6)$$

For this sub-task, the objective function is to minimize the negative log probabilities of true evidence index:

$$L_s = -\sum_{t=1}^{N}[y_t \log p_t + (1 - y_t)\log(1 - p_t)] \quad (7)$$

where $y_t \in 0, 1$ denotes a label, $y_t = 1$ means the t-th sentence is a correct evidence, other $y_t = 0$.

Claim verification layer: The input of this layer is pages-aware claim representation produced from the matching layer and the output is a 3-way classification, predicting whether the claim is SUPPORTED, REFUTED or NOTENOUGH-INFO by the pages. We utilize multiple convolution layers, with the output of 3 for classification. We optimize the objective function:

$$L_c = -\sum_{i=1}^{k} y_i \log \hat{g}_i \quad (8)$$

Where k is the number of claims. $y_t \in 0, 1, 2$ denotes a label, meaning the i-th claim is SUPPORTED, REFUTED, and NOTENOUGHINFO by the pages respectively.

Training: The model is trained by minimizing joint objective function:

$$L = L_s + \alpha * L_c \quad (9)$$

where α is the hyper-parameter for weights of two loss functions.

4 Experiments

In this section, we evaluate our model on FEVER paper test dataset and shared task test dataset.

4.1 Model Details

The model architecture used for this task is depicted in Figure 1. The nonlinearity function $f =$ tanh is employed. We use 100 1D filters for CNN char embedding, each with a width of 5. The hidden state size (d) of the model is 100. We use the Adam (Kingma and Ba, 2014) optimizer, with a minibatch size of 32 and an initial learning rate of 0.001. A dropout rate of 0.2 is used for the

	EMBA (paper test)	Baseline (paper dev)
Evidence Score	30.34	32.57
Label Accuracy	45.06	-
Evidence Precision	46.12	-
Evidence Recall	42.84	-
Evidence F1	44.42	-

Table 1: our EMBA model results on the FEVER paper test dataset, Baseline method results on the paper dev dataset.

Evidence F1	Label Accuracy	FEVER Score
39.73	45.38	29.22

Table 2: Model results on the FEVER shared task test dataset.

	NEI	REFUTES	SUPPORTS	recall
NEI	1285	1432	390	41%
REFUTES	992	1937	155	62.8%
SUPPORTS	942	860	1284	41.6%
precision	39.9%	45.8%	70.2%	

Table 3: confusion matrix for claim classification. (NEI = "not enough info")

	Evidence precision	Evidence recall	Evidence F1
SUPPORTS	22.07%	40.08%	28.47%
REFUTES	23.8%	45.18%	31.18%

Table 4: sentences retrieval performance.

CNN, all LSTM layers, and the linear transformation. The parameters are initialized by the techniques described in (Glorot, 2010). The max value used for max-norm regularization is 5. The L_c loss weight is set to $\alpha = 0.5$.

4.2 Experimental Results

We use the official evaluation script[6] to compute the evidence F1 score, label accuracy and FEVER score. As shown in Table 1, our method achieves comparable performance on FEVER paper test dataset comparing with the baseline method on FEVER paper dev dataset. The result shows that jointly verifying a claim and retrieving evidences at same time can be as good as pipelined model. Our method results on the FEVER paper shared task test dataset is showed in Table 2. Besides, We calculate and present the confusion matrix of claim classification results on the FEVER paper test dataset in Table 3. Our model isn't good at identifying the unrelated relationship between claim and pages retrieved. Our model sentence selection performance is recorded in Table 4. We can see that our model doesn't perform well for retrieving evidence. Though with low evidence precision, our model average accuracy without requirement to provide correct evidence (51.97%) is similar to 52.09% accuracy of baseline method, which means that claim verification module and the sentence extraction module are relatively independent in our model.

[6]https://github.com/sheffieldnlp/fever-baselines

4.3 Error Analysis

We investigate the predicted results on the paper test dataset and show several error causes as followings.

Document retrieval We use entity linking tool to retrieve relative Wikipedia pages. Some entity mentions in claims are linked incorrectly, hence we cannot obtain the desired pages containing the correct evidence sentences. The S-MART tool returned correct entities for 70% claims of paper test dataset. A better entity retrieval method should be researched for the FEVER task.

Pages length After document retrieval, the relative pages are concatenated and passed through EMBA model. However, in order to train and predict effectively, the length of the pages is limited to 800 tokens. So, if there are many relative pages and the position of the evidence sentence is near the end of the page, these correct sentences would be cut off.

Evidence composition Some claims require composition of evidences from multiple pages. Furthermore, the selection of second page relies on the correct retrieval of the first page and sentence. For example, claim "Deepika Padukone has been in at least one Indian films" can be supported by combination of "She starred roles in Yeh Jawaani Hai Deewani" and "Yeh Jawaani Hai Deewani is an Indian film" from "Deepika Padukone" and "Yeh Jawaani Hai Deewani" Wikipedia pages respectively. The second page couldn't be found correctly if we don't select the first sentence exactly. 18% claims in train dataset belong to this situation.

5 Conclusion

We propose a novel end-to-end multi-task learning with bi-direction attention (EMBA) model to detect sentences as evidence and classify the claim as "supports", "refutes" or "not enough info" with respect to the pages retrieved at the same time. EMBA uses attention mechanism in both directions to capture interactive features between claim and pages retrieved. Model obtains claim-aware sentence representation to predict the correct evidence position and the pages-aware claim representation to detect the relationship between the claim and the pages. Experimental results on the FEVER paper test dataset show that our approach achieve comparable performance comparing with the baseline method. There are several promising directions that worth researching in the future. For instance, in sentence selection layer, the model just predicts whether a sentence is an evidence. Further, we can try to instantly predict whether a sentence is "supporting", "refuting" or "not related with" the claim. What's more, the hyperparameter α for joint loss function is fixed. A good value for this parameter can achieve one plus one is greater than two. We can try to learn this parameter value during training the model.

6 acknowledgement

This work is supported by National Natural Science Foundation of China (Grant No. 61501048), Beijing Natural Science Foundation (Grant No. 4182042), Fundamental Research Funds for the Central Universities (No. 2017RC12), and National Natural Science Foundation of China (U1536111, U1536112).

References

Dzmitry Bahdanau, Kyunghyun Cho, and Yoshua Bengio. 2014. Neural machine translation by jointly learning to align and translate. *Computer Science*.

Danqi Chen, Adam Fisch, Jason Weston, and Antoine Bordes. 2017. Reading wikipedia to answer open-domain questions. *arXiv preprint arXiv:1704.00051*.

William Ferreira and Andreas Vlachos. 2016. Emergent: a novel data-set for stance classification. In *Proceedings of the 2016 conference of the North American chapter of the association for computational linguistics: Human language technologies*, pages 1163–1168.

Yoshua Bengio Glorot, Xavier. 2010. Understanding the difficulty of training deep feedforward neural networks. In *international conference on artificial intelligence and statistics*, pages 249–256.

Alex Graves. 2012. *Long Short-Term Memory*. Springer Berlin Heidelberg.

Yoon Kim. 2014. Convolutional neural networks for sentence classification. *arXiv preprint arXiv:1408.5882*.

Diederik P. Kingma and Jimmy Ba. 2014. Adam: A method for stochastic optimization. *Computer Science*.

Alex Krizhevsky, Ilya Sutskever, and Geoffrey E. Hinton. 2012. Imagenet classification with deep convolutional neural networks. In *International Conference on Neural Information Processing Systems*, pages 1097–1105.

Minh Thang Luong, Hieu Pham, and Christopher D Manning. 2015. Effective approaches to attention-based neural machine translation. *Computer Science*.

Tomas Mikolov, Martin Karafiát, Lukas Burget, Jan Cernocký, and Sanjeev Khudanpur. 2010. Recurrent neural network based language model. In *INTERSPEECH 2010, Conference of the International Speech Communication Association, Makuhari, Chiba, Japan, September*, pages 1045–1048.

Ankur P Parikh, Oscar Täckström, Dipanjan Das, and Jakob Uszkoreit. 2016. A decomposable attention model for natural language inference. *arXiv preprint arXiv:1606.01933*.

Jeffrey Pennington, Richard Socher, and Christopher Manning. 2014. Glove: Global vectors for word representation. In *Proceedings of the 2014 conference on empirical methods in natural language processing (EMNLP)*, pages 1532–1543.

Dean Pomerleau and Delip Rao. 2017. *Fake News Challenge http://fakenewschallenge.org*.

Minjoon Seo, Aniruddha Kembhavi, Ali Farhadi, and Hannaneh Hajishirzi. 2016. Bidirectional attention flow for machine comprehension. *arXiv preprint arXiv:1611.01603*.

Rupesh Kumar Srivastava, Klaus Greff, and Jürgen Schmidhuber. 2015. Highway networks. *arXiv preprint arXiv:1505.00387*.

Chuanqi Tan, Furu Wei, Nan Yang, Bowen Du, Weifeng Lv, and Ming Zhou. 2017. S-net: From answer extraction to answer generation for machine reading comprehension. *arXiv preprint arXiv:1706.04815*.

James Thorne, Andreas Vlachos, Christos Christodoulopoulos, and Arpit Mittal. 2018. Fever: a large-scale dataset for fact extraction and verification. *arXiv preprint arXiv:1803.05355*.

Andreas Vlachos and Sebastian Riedel. 2014. Fact checking: Task definition and dataset construction. In *Proceedings of the ACL 2014 Workshop on Language Technologies and Computational Social Science*, pages 18–22.

William Yang Wang. 2017. "liar, liar pants on fire": A new benchmark dataset for fake news detection. pages 422–426.

Zhiguo Wang, Wael Hamza, and Radu Florian. 2017. Bilateral multi-perspective matching for natural language sentences.

Kelvin Xu, Jimmy Ba, Ryan Kiros, Kyunghyun Cho, Aaron Courville, Ruslan Salakhutdinov, Richard Zemel, and Yoshua Bengio. 2015. Show, attend and tell: Neural image caption generation with visual attention. *Computer Science*, pages 2048–2057.

Team GESIS Cologne: An all in all sentence-based approach for FEVER

Wolfgang Otto
GESIS – Leibniz-Institute for the Social Sciences in Cologne
Unter Sachsenhausen 6-8
50667 Cologne
wolfgang.otto@gesis.org

Abstract

In this system description of our pipeline to participate at the Fever Shared Task, we describe our sentence-based approach. Throughout all steps of our pipeline, we regarded single sentences as our processing unit. In our IR-Component, we searched in the set of all possible Wikipedia introduction sentences without limiting sentences to a fixed number of relevant documents. In the entailment module, we judged every sentence separately and combined the result of the classifier for the top 5 sentences with the help of an ensemble classifier to make a judgment whether the truth of a statement can be derived from the given claim.

1 Introduction

Our approach is strongly related to the baseline approach. It is using a sentence retrieval method without more in-depth analysis of semantic properties of Wikipedia sentences as a first component. For the IR task no external resources beside the given Wikipedia sentences have been taken into account. The second component is the entailment model which is the same Decomposable Attention Model as the one used to generate the best baseline results in (Thorne et al., 2018). But in both components, there are some differences. In the IR component, there is no document retriever as a first step. Given a claim, we search directly on all Wikipedia sentences of the reference corpus for possible candidate sentences. In the entailment component, the difference lies not at all in the model, but in the data used during training and inference time. We trained the model sentence-wise and not claim-wise. I.e. we split the result set for each claim into combinations of claim and each sentence separately. To be able to handle more than one sentence evidence we introduce new classes. One class to identify evidence sentences which are part of supporting evidence with multiple sentences, and a second one to identify evidence sentences which are part of refuting evidence with more than one sentence.

2 Sentence Retriever

The basic idea of our evidence retrieval engine is the intuition that a preselection of specific Wikipedia articles for a given claim will exclude sentences, which are highly related to the claim-based on a word or even entity overlap, but will be excluded because the Wikipedia article has another topic.

Our approach tries to find sentence candidates from all sentences of the given shared task Wikipedia introduction sentences corpus. To keep the system simple and rely on a well-tested environment we indexed all sentences with a SOLR search engine[1] with the default configuration. Our idea to find relevant candidate sentences, which support or refute the given claim, is to identify those which are connected to the same entities or noun chunks. So we extracted those information from the claim and create a SOLR query to get a ranked sentence list from the search engine.

2.1 Preprocessing

Wikipedia Article Introductions: The problem of only working with single sentences is, that sentences of a Wikipedia article introduction loose the connection to the article title in many cases. To create good retrieval results we need a preprocessing step for coreference resolution to match sentences like "He is the biggest planet in our solar system." from the article about Jupiter to the claim "Jupiter is larger than any other planet in the solar system." We decided on the most straightforward solution and concatenated a cleaned version of the title to the Wikipedia sentences before indexing. For cleaning the title we cut of all parts beginning with a round bracket.

---

[1] http://lucene.apache.org/solr/.

Proceedings of the First Workshop on Fact Extraction and VERification (FEVER), pages 145–149
Brussels, Belgium, November 1, 2018. ©2018 Association for Computational Linguistics

Also underscores will be replaced with spaces. So *"Beethoven_-LRB-TV_series-RRB-"*[2] will be transformed to *"Beethoven"* for example.

Query claim: For the generation of a query for a given claim we extracted all noun chunks and named entities with the natural language processing tool SpaCy[3] (Honnibal and Johnson, 2015) with the provided *en_core_web_sm* language model[4]. Then we filter all resulting individual words and phrases. Given this set of all words and multi-word units, we create a SOLR-query which is giving an advantage to adjacent words of the multi-word units which occur with a maximum word distance of two. Additionally, we query each word of each item in the set separately with a should query. The named entity *Serena Williams* for example is searched with a query where "Serena", "Williams" and "Serena Williams"~2 should all be matched. The swung dash in the last part of this query indicates that search results, where "Serena" and "Williams" occur with a maximum distance of two, will be pushed. The distance of two is chosen because it helps in cases like "Arnold Alois Schwarzenegger" to push the match of the search query "Arnold Schwarzenegger"~2. Here a more complete example:

> *Claim:*
> Serena Williams likes to eat out in a small restaurant in Las Vegas.
> *Named Entities:*
> Serena Williams, Las Vegas.
> *Noun Chunks:*
> Serena Williams, a small restaurant, Las Vegas
> *Unigram searchterms:*
> Serena, Williams, a, small, restaurant, Las, Vegas
> *Pushed bigram searchterms:*
> Serena Williams, a small, small restaurant, Las Vegas

The result of the sentence retriever is a list of sentences and their corresponding Wikipedia titles which matches best in concern of named entities

and noun chunks based on the described extraction and querying.

3 Recognizing Textual Entailment

3.1 Preprocessing

During preprocessing of train and test data, we consider three steps. For the first step of tokenizing claim and Wikipedia sentence, we treat both of them differently. The Wikipedia sentences are already tokenized. The claims are tokenized with the standard SpaCy's rule-based tokenizer. For textual entailment, the same problem of coreference resolution described for the IR component pops up again. Because of this, we decided to add the title information to the Wikipedia sentences as additional information as well. Adding this information can help the entailment model identify the entity explained in the sentence. A working example:

> *Claim:*
> Stars vs. the Forces of Evil is a series.
> *Wikipedia title:*
> Star_vs._the_Forces_of_Evil
> *Wikipedia Sentence (Sentence No. 6):*
> On February 12 , 2015 , Disney renewed the series for a second season prior to its premiere on Disney XD .

Of course, it is a heuristic. There are sentences where the added information doubles the info of the entity. But then again there are sentences where the content does not match the entity described in the title. In practice, we join the tokens of the title to the sentence while excluding the additional information for disambiguation. I. e. for *"Hulk_(Film)"* we only add *"Hulk"* to the corresponding sentence string. For vectorization of the sequence token, we use GloVe word embeddings with a dimension of 300 produced with the method from (Pennington et al., 2014). To maximize the overlap to the words used in our Wikipedia-based dataset we used the ones trained on *Wikipedia 2014 + Gigaword 5* by the Stanford NLP group.[5]

3.2 Prediction Classes

The data set provides the special case where one single sentence is not enough to support or refute a claim. In this case, multiple sentence support

---

[2]Where *"-LRB-"* stands for *"Left Round Bracket"* and *"-RRB-"* for *"Right Round Bracket"* as it can be found in the already tokenized Wikipedia resources which were made available from the organizers of the competition.

[3]`https://spacy.io/`.

[4]`https://spacy.io/models/en#en_core_web_sm`.

[5]`https://nlp.stanford.edu/projects/glove/`.

is delivered. In 9.0% of the validation set claims where supporting or refuting evidence exists, a minimum of two Wikipedia sentences is needed. In 14.7% of the supporting/refuting claims, there is at least one possible multiple sentence evidence. Around 25% of the supporting or refuting sentences are part of multiple sentence evidence in the validation set. Multiple sentence evidence poses a problem for our approach of sentence-by-sentence entailment assessment. On the one hand, the class of a given claim and one sentence of multiple sentence support/refute cannot be classified as supporting or refuting. On the other hand, more information is delivered than in a regular *NOT_ENOUGH_INFO* claim sentence pair. We decided to deal with this by using not three, but five classes. For sentence-wise prediction we have extended the given classes *SUPPORTS*, *REFUTES* and *NOT_ENOUGH_INFO* with the two new classes *PART_OF_SUPPORTS* and *PART_OF_REFUTES*.

3.3 Generating NOT_ENOUGH_INFO sentences

In Thorne et al. (2018) the authors introduced two ways of selecting sentences for claims which are annotated as *NOT_ENOUGH_INFO*. They compared classifiers trained on randomly chosen sentences for this class with classifiers trained on data where the top 5 results of the sentence retriever are used as text input for them. The results show that on the textual entailment validation set both classifiers trained on random sentences show better results than the ones trained on top 5 results. But for the whole pipeline, the resulting accuracy drops around 1% for the Decomposable Attention Model (41.6% vs. 40.6% pipeline accuracy in Thorne et al. (2018)). As we used the same model, we decided to use the approach of selecting the top retrieved sentences for the *NOT_ENOUGH_INFO* annotated claims. To keep the number of sentences per class not too unequal, we chose to use the top 3 results of our sentence retriever for the test and validation set of the Decomposable Attention Model. It should be noted, however, that our sentence retriever is working in a slightly different way than the one used in the baseline approach.

For the occurrence of each label in the sentence-wise validation set for the entailment prediction task see table 1.

label	frequence
NOT ENOUGH INFO	19348
SUPPORTS	7012
REFUTES	7652
PART OF SUPPORTS	2741
PART OF REFUTES	2452

Table 1: Frequences of label in sentence-wise validation set.

3.4 Decomposable Attention Model

For the task of recognizing textual entailment we take a Decomposable Attention Model as described in (Parikh et al., 2016) and is one of the classifiers used in the baseline approach (Thorne et al., 2018). We selected the vanilla version of this network without self-attention on input sequences. This model compares each word vector representation of the input sequences with the representation of phrases of the other input sequence. The process of selecting words from the other sequence for comparison is called attention. After this, the representations for this comparisons are aggregated and in a final step used to predict, if one sequence supports or refutes the other or has not enough information for a decision.

The model is formulated with the aim of learning during training time which words are to be compared, how to compare them and in which entailment relation both sequences are to each other.

Basic Parameters: For training we used the given training and evaluation set for the shared task prepared and preprocessed as described above in a sentence-wise manner. We used batches of size 32 with equal number of words during training and a dropout rate of 0.2 for all three feed forward layers F, G and H of the neural network model. F, G and H are used here analogous to the terminology in (Parikh et al., 2016). We trained the model for 300 epochs on all batches of the training set and choose the best performing model measured on the validation set for the prediction of the test set. Tokens without word embedding representation in the *GloVe Wikipedia 2014 + Gigaword 5* (out of vocabulary words) are treated with the same approach as in (Parikh et al., 2016). The words are hashed to one of 100 random embeddings.

3.5 Ensemble Learner

The result of the entailment classifier is the judgment for each pair of claim and sentence of a Wikipedia introduction if the claim can be entailed from the sentence based on the five introduced classes. For taking part in the FEVER Shared Task, it is needed to decide on each claim one of the labels *SUPPORTS*, *REFUTES* or *NOT ENOUGH INFO*. The second part is to find the right sentence which underpins the judgment. The result of the sentence-based entailment classifier is a list of judgments which might be contradictory. As a result, we need a classifier which aggregates the results for the sentences to one final claim judgment. For this, we combine the entailment judgments from the classifier by using a random forest classifier (Breiman, 1999). As input, we take the probability of the judgments for all five classes of the top 5 results of the sentence retriever. In this way, the number of features can be summed up to 25. We kept the order of the sentences based on the sentence retriever results. We trained this aggregating classifier to predict one of the three classes awaited from the FEVER scorer for the evaluation of the shared task.[6] Together with the top 5 sentences of the sentence retriever, this result represents the output of the whole pipeline. To generate pipeline results for the validation set we trained the classifier on half of the validation set and predict the other half. For the FEVER Shared Task test set prediction we trained the classifier on all samples from the validation set.

4 Evaluation Results and Discussion

4.1 Sentence Retriever

To be able to measure the results returned from the retrieval component we take the FEVER scorer into account, too. To keep a different view on the outcomes, we measured the recall values for different allowed sizes of result sets. For additional analysis, we measured for each result set size separated recall values for only refuting and only supporting values. Figure 1 shows that recall values for the refuting sentences are lower than those for the supporting ones. This seems to reflect the intuition that in refuting sentences the word overlap to the claims are smaller than in supporting sentences. The fact that even with an allowed result set size of 100 the recall with our approach is

[6]https://github.com/sheffieldnlp/
fever-scorer.

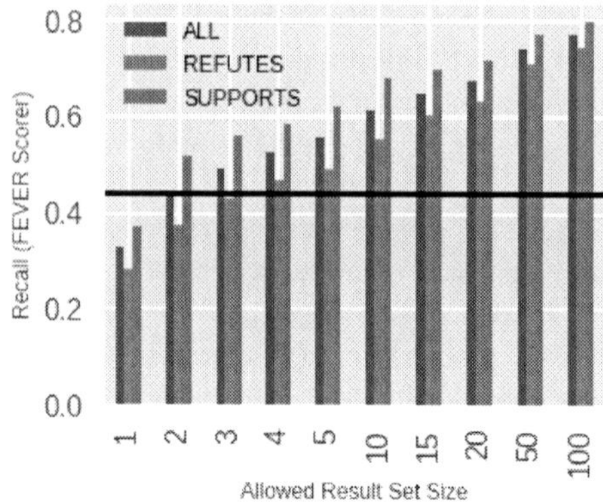

Figure 1: The recall values for sentence retrieval based on different allowed result set sizes. The black line shows the baseline recall for an allowed result set size of five[8]

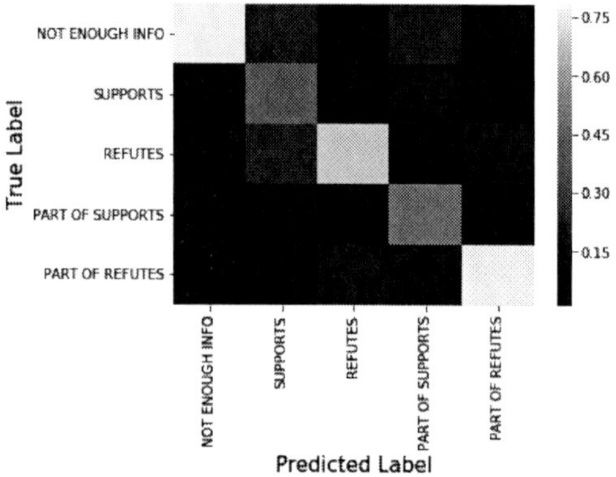

Figure 2: Heatmap of the precision of each class.

77.3% shows that a simple method which is dependent on word overlap between claim and sentences gets to its limits. In comparison to the baseline where 44.22% of the claims in the validation set were fully supported after the document and the sentence selection components, in our approach, 53.6% of them have full support, even though we do not use a document retrieval component at all. This would lead to an oracle accuracy of 69.1% (Baseline: 62.8%).

4.2 Entailment Classifier and full pipeline

The entailment classifier has an accuracy of 64.7% for the sentence-by-sentence prediction of the five classes. This is not comparable with the results of the baseline because of the sentence-wise comparison and the five label classification scheme. A

look at the class-wise precision of the classifier
and the number of sentences per class draws attention to the fact that this value is strongly dependent
on the number of sentences which are generated
for the *NOT ENOUGH INFO* label. It is because
for this class the model achieved the best precision
values and the label is over-represented in the validation set.

As expected the classifier has problems to differentiate between refuting sentences and the ones,
which are part of a multiple sentence refute. The
same applies to the supporting sentences as you
can be seen in Figure 2. For the all in all pipeline
evaluation, we get a FEVER score of 46.7% on
half of the validation set. The other half was used
to train the aggregating ensemble learner. On the
shared task test set, we achieved a FEVER score
of 40.77 (8th place).

The next steps to evolve our system should be to
focus on recall of sentence retrieving for refuting
sentence and split up the strategies for both types
of sentences.

References

Leo Breiman. 1999. Random forests - random features.
Technical Report 567.

Matthew Honnibal and Mark Johnson. 2015. An improved non-monotonic transition system for dependency parsing. In *Proceedings of the 2015 Conference on Empirical Methods in Natural Language
Processing*, pages 1373–1378.

Ankur P Parikh, Oscar Täckström, Dipanjan Das, and
Jakob Uszkoreit. 2016. A decomposable attention
model for natural language inference. *Proceedings
of the 2016 Conference on Empirical Methods in
Natural Language Processing*, pages 2249–2255.

Jeffrey Pennington, Richard Socher, and Christopher D. Manning. 2014. Glove: Global vectors for
word representation. In *Empirical Methods in Natural Language Processing (EMNLP)*, pages 1532–
1543.

James Thorne, Andreas Vlachos, Christos
Christodoulopoulos, and Arpit Mittal. 2018.
FEVER: a large-scale dataset for fact extraction and
verification. In *NAACL-HLT*.

Team SWEEPer: Joint Sentence Extraction and Fact Checking with Pointer Networks

Christopher Hidey[*]
Department of Computer Science
Columbia University
New York, NY 10027
chidey@cs.columbia.edu

Mona Diab
Amazon AI Lab
diabmona@amazon.com

Abstract

Many tasks such as question answering and reading comprehension rely on information extracted from unreliable sources. These systems would thus benefit from knowing whether a statement from an unreliable source is correct. We present experiments on the FEVER (Fact Extraction and VERification) task, a shared task that involves selecting sentences from Wikipedia and predicting whether a claim is supported by those sentences, refuted, or there is not enough information. Fact checking is a task that benefits from not only asserting or disputing the veracity of a claim but also finding evidence for that position. As these tasks are dependent on each other, an ideal model would consider the veracity of the claim when finding evidence and also find only the evidence that is relevant. We thus jointly model sentence extraction and verification on the FEVER shared task. Among all participants, we ranked 5th on the blind test set (prior to any additional human evaluation of the evidence).

1 Introduction

Verifying claims using textual sources is a difficult problem, requiring natural language inference as well as information retrieval if the sources are not provided. The FEVER task (Thorne et al., 2018) provides a large annotated resource for extraction of sentences from Wikipedia and verification of the extracted evidence against a claim. A system that extracts and verifies statements in this framework must consist of three components: 1) Retrieving Wikipedia articles. 2) Identifying the sentences from Wikipedia that support or refute the claim. 3) Predicting supporting, refuting, or not enough info.

We combine these components into two stages: 1) identifying relevant documents (Wikipedia ar-

ticles) for a claim and 2) jointly extracting sentences from the top-ranked articles and predicting a relation for whether the claim is supported, refuted, or if there is not enough information in Wikipedia. We first identify relevant documents by ranking Wikipedia articles according to a model using lexical and syntactic features. Then, we derive contextual sentence representations for the claim paired with each evidence sentence in the extracted documents. We use the ESIM module (Chen et al., 2017b) to create embeddings for each claim/evidence pair and use a pointer network (Vinyals et al., 2015) to recurrently extract only relevant evidence sentences while predicting the relation using the entire set of evidence sentences. Finally, given these components, which are pre-trained using multi-task learning (Le et al., 2016), we tune the parameters of the entailment component given the extracted sentences.

Our experiments reveal that jointly training the model provides a significant boost in performance, suggesting that the contextual representations learn information about which sentences are most important for relation prediction as well as information about the type of relationship the evidence has to the claim.

2 Document Retrieval

For the baseline system, the document retrieval component from DrQA (Chen et al., 2017a) for $k = 5$ documents only finds the supporting evidence 55% of the time. This drops to 44% using the same model for sentence retrieval at $l = 5$ sentences. In comparison, in the original work of Chen et al. (2017a), they find a recall of 70-86% for all tasks with $k = 5$. This is partly due to the misleading information present in the false claims, whereas for question answering, the question is not designed adversarially to contain con-

---

[*]Work completed while at Amazon AI Lab

Proceedings of the First Workshop on Fact Extraction and VERification (FEVER), pages 150–155
Brussels, Belgium, November 1, 2018. ©2018 Association for Computational Linguistics

tradicting information. Examining the supporting
and refuting claims in isolation, we find that document retrieval at $k = 5$ is 59% and 49% respectively and sentence selection at $l = 5$ is 49% and
39%. For example, the false claim "Murda Beatz
was born on February 21, 1994." (his birth date is
February 11) also retrieves documents for people
born on February 21. In the question answering
scenario, an example question might be "Which
rap artist was born on February 11, 1994 in Fort
Erie, Ontario?" which allows an IR system to return documents using the disambiguating n-grams
about his location and place of birth.

This motivates the decision to focus on noun
phrases. Many of the claims contain the correct
topic of the Wikipedia article in the subject position of both the claim and either the first or second sentence. When the topic is not in the first
sentence, it is often because the title is ambiguous
and the first sentence is a redirect. For example,
for the article "Savages (2012 film)" the first two
sentences are "For the 2007 film, see The Savages.
Savages is a 2012 American crime thriller film directed by Oliver Stone."

We thus parse Wikipedia and all the claims using CoreNLP (Manning et al., 2014) and train a
classifier with the following lexical and syntactic
features from the claim and the first two sentences
in the Wikipedia article:

- TF/IDF from DrQA for full article

- Overlap between the subject/object/modifier
  in the claim with the subject/object/modifier
  in the first and second sentence of Wikipedia.
  The topic of the article is often the subject of
  the sentence in Wikipedia, but it is occasion
  ally a disambiguating modifier such as "also
  known as". The topic of the claim is often
  in the subject position as well. We also add
  overlap between named entities (in case the
  parsing fails) and upper case words (in case
  the parsing and NER fails). For each of sub-
  ject/object/modifier/upper/entity, for both upper and lower case, we consider the coverage
  of the claim from the first two Wikipedia sentences, for $25 * 2 * 2 = 100$ features.

- Average/max/minimum of GloVe (Pennington et al., 2014) embeddings in the claim and
  the first and second sentence of Wikipedia.
  This feature captures the type of sentence. If
  it is a person, it may have words like 'born',

Model	Recall at $k = 5$	
	Dev	Test
Baseline (DrQA)	55.3	54.2
MLP without title features	82.7	79.7
MLP with title features	90.7	90.5

Figure 1: Document Retrieval Results

'known as', etc. and if it is a disambiguation
sentence it should have words like 'refers' or
'see' or 'confused'. It also allows for the handling of cases where the sentence tokeniza-
tion splits the first sentence.

- Features based on the title: whether the title
  is completely contained in the claim and the
  overlap between the claim and the title (with
  and without metadata information in parentheses), for both upper and lower case.

2.1 Experiments

We train a Multi-Layer Perceptron (MLP) using
Pytorch (Paszke et al., 2017) on the top 1000 documents extracted using DrQA, which obtains a recall of 95.3%, with early stopping on the paper
development set. We used the Adam optimizer
(Kingma and Ba, 2015) with a learning rate of
0.001 and hyper-parameters of $\beta_1 = 0.9$, $\beta_2 = 0.999$, and $\epsilon = 10^{-8}$. We used pre-trained 300-
dimensional GloVe embeddings. We clip gradi-
ents at 2 and use a batch size of 32.

2.2 Results

Document recall at $k = 5$ articles is presented in
Figure 1. We present results on the paper development and test sets as the evidence for the shared
task blind test set was unavailable as of this writing. The model with lexical and syntactic features
obtains around 25 points absolute improvement
over the DrQA baseline and the title features when
added provide an additional 8 points improvement
on the development set and 10.8 points on test.

3 Joint Sentence Extraction and Relation Prediction

Recurrent neural networks have been shown to be
effective for extractive summarization (Nallapati
et al., 2017; Chen and Bansal, 2018). However,
in this context we want to extract sentences that
also help predict whether the claim is supported or
refuted so we jointly model extraction and relation
prediction and train in a multi-task setting.

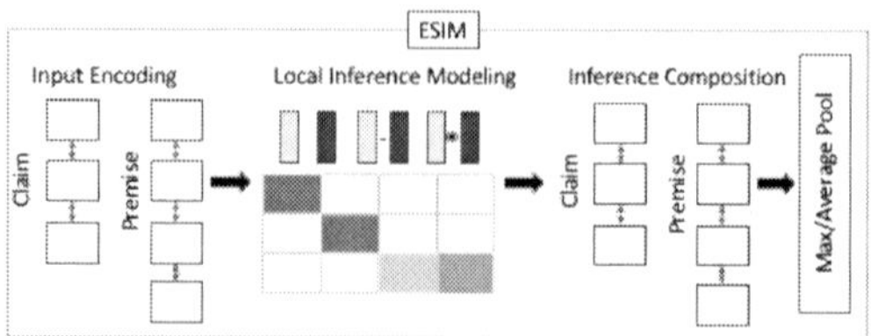

Figure 2: The contextual claim and evidence sentence representations obtained with ESIM.

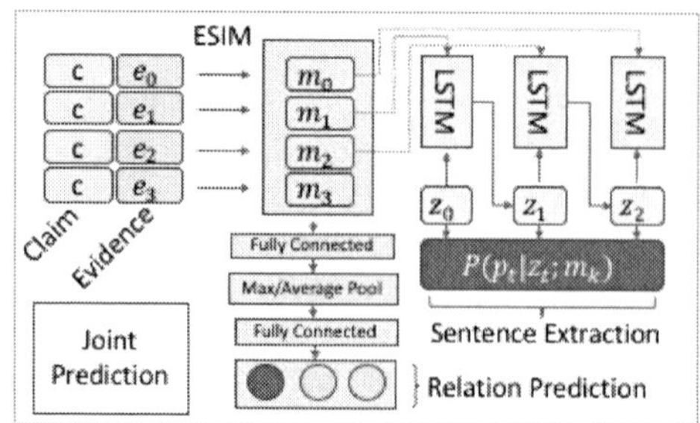

Figure 3: Our multi-task learning architecture with contextual ESIM representations used for evidence sentence extraction via a pointer network and relation prediction with max/average pooling and dense layers.

First, given the top k extracted documents from our retrieval component, we select the top l sentences using a weighted combination of Jaccard similarity and cosine similarity of average word embeddings. Hyper-parameters were tuned so that the model would have minimal difference in recall from the document retrieval stage but still fit in memory on a Tesla V100 with 16GB of memory. We selected $k = 5$ and $l = 50$, with Jaccard similarity weighted at 0.3 and GloVe embeddings weighted at 0.7. We found that recall on the development set was 90.3.

We then store contextual representations of the claim and each evidence sentence in a memory network and use a pointer network to extract the top 5 sentences sequentially. Simultaneously, we use the entire memory of up to l sentences to predict the relation: supports, refutes, or not enough info.

3.1 Sentence Representation

For each sentence in the evidence, we create contextual representations using the ESIM module (Chen et al., 2017b), which first encodes the claim and the evidence sentence using an LSTM, attends to the claim and evidence, composes them using an additional LSTM layer, and finally applies max and average pooling over time (sentence length) to obtain a paired sentence representation for the claim and evidence. This representation is depicted in Figure 2. For more details, please refer to (Chen et al., 2017b).

The representation for a claim c and extracted evidence sentence e_p for c is then:

$$m_p = ESIM(c, e_p) \qquad (1)$$

3.2 Sentence Extraction

Next, to select the top 5 evidence sentences, we use a pointer network (Vinyals et al., 2015; Chen and Bansal, 2018) over the evidence for claim c to

extract sentences recurrently. The extraction probability[1] for sentence e_p at time $t < 5$ is then:

$$u_p^t = \begin{cases} v_e^T \tanh(W[m_p; h^{t,q}]), & \text{if} p_t \neq p_s \forall s < t. \\ -\inf, & \text{otherwise.} \end{cases} \qquad (2)$$

$$P(p_t|p_0 \cdots p_{t-1}) = \text{softmax}(u^t) \qquad (3)$$

with $h^{t,q}$ computed using the output of q hops over the evidence (Vinyals et al., 2016; Sukhbaatar et al., 2015):

$$\alpha^{t,o} = \text{softmax}(v_h^T \tanh(W_{g1}m_p + W_{g2}h^{t,o-1})) \qquad (4)$$

$$h^{t,o} = \sum_j \alpha^{t,o} W_{g1}m_j \qquad (5)$$

At each timestep t, we update the hidden state z_t of the pointer network LSTM. Initially, $h^{t,0}$ is set to z_t. We train and validate the pointer network using the extracted top l sentences. For all training examples, we randomly replace evidence sentences with gold evidence if no gold evidence is found.

3.3 Relation Prediction

In order to predict the support, refute, or not enough info relation, we use a single-layer MLP to obtain an abstract representation of the sentence representation used for extraction, then apply average and max pooling over the contextual representations of the claim and evidence sentences to obtain a single representation m for the entire memory. Finally, we use a 2-layer MLP to predict this relation given m. The entire joint architecture is presented in Figure 3.

---

[1] Set to $-inf$ only while testing

3.4 Optimization

We train the model to minimize the negative log likelihood of the extracted evidence sequence[2] and the cross-entropy loss ($\mathcal{L}(\theta_{rel})$) of the relation prediction. The pointer network is trained as in a sequence-to-sequence model:

$$\mathcal{L}(\theta_{ptr}) = -1/T \sum_{t=0..T} \log P_{\theta_{ptr}}(p_t|p_{0:t-1}) \quad (6)$$

and the overall loss is then:

$$\mathcal{L}(\theta) = \lambda\mathcal{L}(\theta_{ptr}) + \mathcal{L}(\theta_{rel}) \quad (7)$$

Since the evidence selection and relation prediction are scored independently for the FEVER task, we select the parameters using early stopping such that one set of parameters performs the best in terms of evidence recall on the validation set and another performs the best for accuracy.

Although the models are trained jointly to select evidence sentences that help predict the relation to the claim, we may obtain additional improvement by tuning the parameters given the output of the sentence extraction step. In order to do so, we first select the top 5 sentences from the sentence extractor and predict the relation using only those sentences rather than the entire memory as before. In this scenario, we pre-train the model using multi-task learning and tune the parameters for relation prediction while keeping the sentence extraction parameters fixed (and using separate representations for ESIM). We also experimented with a reinforcement learning approach to tune the sentence extractor as in (Chen and Bansal, 2018) but found no additional improvement.

3.5 Experiments

We use Pytorch for our experiments. For the multi-task learning and tuning, we use the Adagrad optimizer with learning rates of 0.01 and 0.001 and gradients clipped to 5 and 2, respectively. For both experiments, we used a batch size of 16. We used the paper development set for early stopping. We initialized the word embeddings with 300-dimensional GloVe vectors and fixed them during training, using a 200-dimensional projection. Out-of-vocabulary words were initialized randomly during both training and evaluation.

	Dev			Test		
	LA	ER	F	LA	ER	F
Base	52.1	44.2	32.6	50.9	45.9	31.9
Gold	68.5	96.0	66.2	65.4	95.2	62.8
MLP	60.4	76.6	51.1	58.7	74.0	49.1
Sep.	56.8	74.9	45.3	53.8	72.7	42.3
MTL	64.0	79.6	55.3	60.5	77.7	52.1
Tune	64.5	79.6	55.8	61.9	77.7	53.2

Figure 4: Paper Development and Test Results (**LA**: Label Accuracy, **ER**: Evidence Recall, **F**: FEVER Score)

The second dimension of all other parameter matrices was 200. For the pointer network, we used a beam size of 5 and $q = 3$ hops. λ was set to 1.

4 Results

In Figure 4, we present the sentence extraction, relation prediction, and overall FEVER score for the paper development and test sets. We compare to the baseline (**Base**) from the work of Thorne et al. (2018). For comparison, we also provide the results when using gold document retrieval with a perfect oracle to illustrate the upper bound for our model (**Gold**). First, we illustrate the difference in performance when we train a feedforward network to score the sentences individually (**MLP**) instead of recurrently with a pointer network. In this setting, the sentence extraction in Figure 3 is replaced by a 2-layer feedforward network that is individually applied to every sentence in the memory. The output of the network is a score which is then used to rank the top $l = 5$ sentences. The model is still trained using multi-task learning but with a binary cross-entropy loss in Equation 7 instead of θ_{ptr}. Furthermore, we show the results of the sentence extraction and relation prediction components when trained separately (**Sep.**). We finally present the best results - when trained with multi-task learning (**MTL**) and then tuned (**Tune**).

Our results demonstrate that jointly training a pointer network and relation prediction classifier improves over training separately. We also note that the pointer network, which extracts sentences recurrently by considering the previous sentence, improves over selecting sentences independently using an MLP. Although we obtained improvement by tuning, the improvement is slight, which suggests that the parameter space discovered by multi-task learning is already learning most of the

---

[2]The evidence as given has no meaningful order but we use the support/refute sequence as provided in the dataset as it may contain annotator bias in terms of importance.

	LA	EF1	F
Paper	62.2	31.6	53.5
Blind	59.7	29.7	49.9
Best	68.2	52.9	64.2

Figure 5: Blind Test Results (**LA**: Label Accuracy, **EF1**: Evidence F1, **F**: FEVER Score)

Num.	LA	ER	DR
0	50	N/A	N/A
1	74	86	93
2	65	17	26
3+	73	3	14

Figure 6: Paper Development Results by Number of Evidence Sentences Required (**Num.**: Sentences Required, **LA**: Label Accuracy, **ER**: Evidence Recall, **DR**: Document Recall)

examples where the model can both identify the correct sentences and label. Finally, we notice that improvements to document retrieval would also improve our model. The gap between **Gold** and **Tune** is around 20 points for evidence recall. When using gold Wikipedia articles (1-2 documents), the number of sentences available (around 20 on average) is less than those selected for our model ($l = 50$), which makes evidence retrieval easier as the memory is smaller. As our models for document retrieval are fairly simple, it is likely that a more complex model could obtain better performance with fewer documents.

Results on the shared task blind test set (prior to any additional human evaluation of the evidence) are presented in Figure 5. For comparison, we show the results on the paper development and test sets (**Paper**) when submitted for the shared task as well as the results of the top system on the leaderboard (**Best**). On the blind test set (**Blind**), overall performance drops by 2-3 points for every metric compared to the paper set. As our analysis in Section 4.1 shows, the performance drops significantly when 2 or more evidence sentences are required. Thus, the performance decrease on the blind test set may be caused by an increase in the number of examples that require additional evidence, although as of this writing the evidence for the test set has not yet been released.

4.1 Analysis

We present an analysis of the performance of the best model (**Tune**) when the model requires multiple pieces of evidence. We present results in Figure 6 for no evidence (for the "not enough info" case) and 1, 2, and 3 or more sentences for label accuracy, evidence recall, and document recall at $k = 5$. When no evidence is required the model only obtains 50% accuracy. We found that this increases to 54% accuracy for the **MTL** model but the accuracy on the other 2 classes decreases. This suggests that using a larger memory improves performance when there is not enough information

to make a prediction. Intuitively, reading all relevant Wikipedia articles in their entirety would be necessary for a human to determine this as well. When only 1 sentence is required the model performs well. However, the performance drops significantly on recall when 2 or more sentences are required. This is largely due to the performance of the document retrieval component, which seems to perform poorly when the evidence retrieval requires 2 different Wikipedia articles. When exactly 2 sentences are required, the pointer network retrieves around 60% of the evidence if the retrieved documents are correct. When 3 or more sentences are required, both components perform poorly, suggesting there is significant room for improvement in this case (although there are very few examples requiring this amount of evidence).

5 Conclusion

We presented the results of our system for the FEVER shared task. We described our document retrieval system using lexical and syntactic features. We also described our joint sentence extraction and relation prediction system with multitask learning. The results of our model suggest that the largest gains in performance are likely to come from improvements to detection of the "not enough info" class and retrieval of Wikipedia articles (especially when more than one is required).

For future work, we plan to improve document retrieval and experiment with different sentence representations. Using title features improved document retrieval but for non-Wikipedia data titles would not be available. Furthermore, in other datasets, the titles may not exactly match the text of a claim very often and named entity disambiguation is sometimes needed. One avenue to explore is neural topic modeling trained using article titles (Bhatia et al., 2016).

References

Shraey Bhatia, Jey Han Lau, and Timothy Baldwin. 2016. Automatic labelling of topics with neural embeddings. In *Proceedings of COLING 2016, the 26th International Conference on Computational Linguistics: Technical Papers*, pages 953–963. The COLING 2016 Organizing Committee.

Danqi Chen, Adam Fisch, Jason Weston, and Antoine Bordes. 2017a. Reading wikipedia to answer open-domain questions. In *Proceedings of the 55th Annual Meeting of the Association for Computational Linguistics (Volume 1: Long Papers)*, pages 1870–1879. Association for Computational Linguistics.

Qian Chen, Xiaodan Zhu, Zhen-Hua Ling, Si Wei, Hui Jiang, and Diana Inkpen. 2017b. Enhanced lstm for natural language inference. In *Proceedings of the 55th Annual Meeting of the Association for Computational Linguistics (Volume 1: Long Papers)*, pages 1657–1668. Association for Computational Linguistics.

Yen-Chun Chen and Mohit Bansal. 2018. Fast abstractive summarization with reinforce-selected sentence rewriting. In *Proceedings of the 56th Annual Meeting of the Association for Computational Linguistics (Volume 1: Long Papers)*, pages 675–686. Association for Computational Linguistics.

Diederik Kingma and Jimmy Ba. 2015. Adam: A method for stochastic optimization. In *International Conference on Learning Represen- tations (ICLR)*.

Quoc Le, Ilya Sutskever, Oriol Vinyals, and Lukasz Kaise. 2016. Multi-task sequence to sequence learning. In *International Conference on Learning Represen- tations (ICLR)*.

Christopher D. Manning, Mihai Surdeanu, John Bauer, Jenny Finkel, Steven J. Bethard, and David Mc-Closky. 2014. The Stanford CoreNLP natural language processing toolkit. In *Association for Computational Linguistics (ACL) System Demonstrations*, pages 55–60.

Ramesh Nallapati, Feifei Zhai, and Bowen Zhou. 2017. Summarunner: A recurrent neural network based sequence model for extractive summarization of documents. In *Proceedings of the Thirty-First AAAI Conference on Artificial Intelligence, February 4-9, 2017, San Francisco, California, USA.*, pages 3075–3081.

Adam Paszke, Sam Gross, Soumith Chintala, Gregory Chanan, Edward Yang, Zachary DeVito, Zeming Lin, Alban Desmaison, Luca Antiga, and Adam Lerer. 2017. Automatic differentiation in pytorch.

Jeffrey Pennington, Richard Socher, and Christopher D. Manning. 2014. Glove: Global vectors for word representation. In *Empirical Methods in Natural Language Processing (EMNLP)*, pages 1532–1543.

Sainbayar Sukhbaatar, Arthur Szlam, Jason Weston, and Rob Fergus. 2015. End-to-end memory networks. In C. Cortes, N. D. Lawrence, D. D. Lee, M. Sugiyama, and R. Garnett, editors, *Advances in Neural Information Processing Systems 28*, pages 2440–2448. Curran Associates, Inc.

James Thorne, Andreas Vlachos, Christos Christodoulopoulos, and Arpit Mittal. 2018. Fever: a large-scale dataset for fact extraction and verification. In *Proceedings of the 2018 Conference of the North American Chapter of the Association for Computational Linguistics: Human Language Technologies, Volume 1 (Long Papers)*, pages 809–819. Association for Computational Linguistics.

Oriol Vinyals, Samy Bengio, and Manjunath Kudlur. 2016. Order matters: Sequence to sequence for sets. In *International Conference on Learning Representations (ICLR)*.

Oriol Vinyals, Meire Fortunato, and Navdeep Jaitly. 2015. Pointer networks. In C. Cortes, N. D. Lawrence, D. D. Lee, M. Sugiyama, and R. Garnett, editors, *Advances in Neural Information Processing Systems 28*, pages 2692–2700. Curran Associates, Inc.

QED: A Fact Verification System for the FEVER Shared Task

Jackson Luken
Department of Computer Science
The Ohio State University
luken.25@osu.edu

Nanjiang Jiang, Marie-Catherine de Marneffe
Department of Linguistics
The Ohio State University
jiang.1879,demarneffe.1@osu.edu

Abstract

This paper describes our system submission to the 2018 Fact Extraction and VERification (FEVER) shared task. The system uses a heuristics-based approach for evidence extraction and a modified version of the inference model by Parikh et al. (2016) for classification. Our process is broken down into three modules: potentially relevant documents are gathered based on key phrases in the claim, then any possible evidence sentences inside those documents are extracted, and finally our classifier discards any evidence deemed irrelevant and uses the remaining to classify the claim's veracity. Our system beats the shared task baseline by 12% and is successful at finding correct evidence (evidence retrieval F1 of 62.5% on the development set).

1 Introduction

The FEVER shared task (Thorne et al., 2018) sets out with the goal of creating a system which can take a factual claim and either verify or refute it based on a database of Wikipedia articles. The system is evaluated on the correct labeling of the claims as "Supports," "Refutes," or "Not Enough Info" (NEI) as well as on valid evidence to support the label (except in the case of "NEI"). Each claim can have multiple evidence sets, but only one set needs to be found so long as the correct label is applied. Figure 1 gives an example of a claim along with the evidence sets that support it, as well as a claim and the evidence that refutes it.

We split the task into three distinct modules, with each module building on the data of the previous one. The first module is a document finder finding key terms in the claim which correspond to the titles of the Wikipedia articles, and returning those articles. The second module takes each document found and finds all sentences which are close enough to the claim to be considered evi-

"Supports" Claim: Ann Richards was professionally involved in politics.
Evidence set 1: Dorothy Ann Willis Richards (September 1, 1933 September 13, 2006) was an American politician and 45th Governor of Texas.
Evidence set 2: A Democrat, she first came to national attention as the Texas State Treasurer, when she delivered the keynote address at the 1988 Democratic National Convention.

"Refutes" Claim: Andrew Kevin Walker is only Chinese.
Evidence set: Andrew Kevin Walker (born August 14, 1964) is an American BAFTA-nominated screenwriter.

Figure 1: Claim/evidence examples from the FEVER data.

dence. Finally, all sentences retrieved for a given claim are classified using an inference system as supporting or refuting the claim, or as "NEI". In the following sections, we detail each module, providing results on the FEVER development set which consists of 19,998 claims (6,666 in each class). Our system focuses on finding evidence sets composed of only one sentence. Of the 13,332 verifiable ("Supports" or "Refutes") claims in the development set, only 9% cannot be satisfied with an evidence set consisting of only one sentence. The code for our system is available at `https://github.com/jluken/FEVER`.

2 Document Finder

To verify or refute a claim, we start by finding Wikipedia articles that correspond to the claim. Key phrases within the claim are extracted and checked against Wikipedia article titles. If the key phrase matches an article title, the corresponding document is returned as potentially containing rel-

Proceedings of the First Workshop on Fact Extraction and VERification (FEVER), pages 156–160
Brussels, Belgium, November 1, 2018. ©2018 Association for Computational Linguistics

evant evidence to assess the claim's veracity.

2.1 Wiki Database Preprocessing

We created three maps of the Wikipedia article titles to deal with unpredictable capitalization and pages with a supplemental descriptor in the title via parenthesis (e.g., "Tool (band)" for the music group vs. the physical item.) The first map is simply a case-sensitive map of the document text mapped to its title. The second is titles mapped to lowercase. The third is a list of every title with a parenthesis description mapped to its root title without parenthesis. These are used as "backup" documents to be searched if no evidence is found in documents returned with the two other maps.

2.2 Key Phrase Identification

The key phrases aim at capturing the "topic" of the claim. We used capitalization, named entity, phrasal and part-of-speech tags, and dependency from the CoreNLP system (Manning et al., 2014) to identify key phrases. Subject, direct object, and their modifier/complement dependencies are marked as "topics". Noun phrases containing those topic words are considered key phrases. Consecutive capitalized terms, allowing for lowercase words not capitalized in titles such as prepositions and determiners, are also considered key phrases. For instance, the key phrases for the claims in Figure 1 are: *Ann Richards*, *politics*; *Andrew Kevin Walker*.

Once all possible key phrases in a claim are found, each key phrase is checked against the maps of Wikipedia titles: if there is a full match between a key phrase and a title, the corresponding article is returned. If the article found is a disambiguation page, each article listed on the page is returned. If the disambiguation page is empty, the results from the parenthesis map are returned.

2.3 Results and Analysis

On the development set, when only considering documents found using the case-(in)sensitive maps, we achieve 19.1% precision and 84.8% recall where at least one of the correct documents are found. However when the backup documents are also taken into consideration, recall raises to 94.2% while precision drops to 7.5%. The drop in precision is largely due to disambiguation pages, for which every document listed on the page gets returned. At this stage, we focus on recall, extracting as many relevant documents as possible (7.64 on average per claim), which will be filtered out in later stages.

Most of the 5.8% claims for which the system does not find any correct document involve noun phrases which CoreNLP fails to recognize (such as the song title *In the End*) as well as number mismatch between the claim and the Wikipedia article title (e.g., the system does not retrieve the page "calcaneal_spur" for the claim "Calcaneal spurs are unable to be detected in any situation.") Working on lemma could alleviate the latter issue.

3 Sentence Finder

Once all potential documents are collected by the Document Finder, each sentence within each document is compared against the claim to see if it is similar enough to be considered relevant evidence.

3.1 Claim Processing

The claim is processed to find information to check each document sentence against. We use the root of the claim and a list of all nouns and named entities in the claim. However, nouns and named entities included in the document's title are discarded from the list. This is done under the assumption that every sentence in a document pertains to the topic of that document (e.g., the second evidence in the "Supports" claim of Figure 1 from the document "Ann_Richards" refers to the subject without explicitly stating so.)

3.2 Extracting Evidence from Documents

A sentence is deemed potential evidence if it contains the root of the claim when the root is a verb other than forms of *be* and *have*.

We also retrieve sentences whose words sufficiently match the claim's list of nouns and named entities:

- If two or more are missing, the sentence is discarded.
- If all items in the noun and named entity list can be found in the document sentence, the sentence is added as evidence.
- If there is only one missing noun item, the sentence is added if there are at least two other matching items in the sentence, both the claim and document sentence are of the form "X is Y", or the document sentence contains a synonym of the noun, according to the MIT Java WordNet interface (Finlayson, 2014).

- If there is only one missing named entity, it can be swapped out with a named entity of the same label type. This allows to capture evidence for refuting a claim, such as mismatch in nationality (e.g., swapping out "American" for "Chinese" in the Andrew Walker example in Figure 1.) However, if a claim is centered around an action, determined by its root being a verb, an entity can be swapped only if the document sentence contains that same verb (or a synonym of the verb).

When the claim contains reference to either a birth or a death, the document sentence needs only to have a date encompassed within a set of parenthesis to be considered a valid piece of evidence.

3.3 Results and Analysis

Given a hypothetical perfect Document Finder (PDF), the Sentence Finder achieves a 51.9% precision and 50.3% recall on the development set. When using our existing Document Finder, precision drops to 24.0% and recall to 46.6%. However, we found that a number of sentences we retrieve are not part of the gold standard when they are in fact valid evidence for the claim. One such example is the sentence "As Somalia's capital city, many important national institutions are based in Mogadishu" to support the claim "There is a capital called Mogadishu." It is unclear how many examples of this there are.

If we evaluate the Sentence Finder on retrieving at least one accurate evidence for the verifiable claims, it achieves an accuracy of 66.2% with PDF, and 61.2% with ours. The Sentence Finder performs better on "Support" claims (70.73% with PDF) than on "Refutes" claims (61.58%).

On average using PDF, 1.14 sentences are returned for every claim for which evidence is found (51.9% of these being in the gold standard.) For 24.5% of the verifiable claims, the system fails to return any evidence (20.4% of "Supports" claims, 28.5% of "Refutes" claims.) Two of the most common causes of failure to retrieve evidence are mis-classification of named entity labels or part-of-speech tags by the CoreNLP pipeline, as well as an unseen correlation of key phrases between the claim and evidence based on context. For instance, our system fails to retrieve any of the evidence for the claim in Figure 1, missing the contextual connection between *politics* and *Governor* or *Democrat*.

4 Inference

Once evidence sentences are retrieved, we used one of the state-of-the-art inference systems to assess whether the sentences verify the claim or not. We chose the decomposable attention model of (Parikh et al., 2016) because it is one of the highest-scored systems on the Stanford Natural Language Inference (SNLI) corpus (Bowman et al., 2015) that has a lightweight architecture with relatively few parameters.

4.1 Preprocessing

Most of the evidence sentences are often in the middle of a paragraph in the document, and the entity the document is about is referred to with a pronoun or a definite description. For instance, *The Southwest Golf Classic*, in its Wikipedia article, is referred to with the pronoun *it* or the noun phrase *the event*. We thus made the simplifying assumption that each pronoun is used to refer to the entity the page is about, and perform a deterministic coreference resolution by replacing the first pronoun in the sentence with the name of the page.

We ran a named entity recognizer trained on OntoNotes (Hovy et al., 2006) on claim and evidence sentences to extracted all the named entities and their types. The named entities concatenated with the sentence are fed into the word embedding layers whereas the named entity types are fed into the entity embedding layers, as described below.

4.2 Embedding

We used GloVe word embeddings (Pennington et al., 2014) with 300 dimensions pre-trained using CommonCrawl to get a vector representation of the evidence sentence. We also experimented training GloVe word embeddings using the provided Wikipedia data, but found that they did not perform as well as the pre-trained vectors. The word embeddings were normalized to 200 dimensions as described in (Parikh et al., 2016). For entity types, we trained an entity type embedding of 200 dimensions. The word embeddings and entity embeddings are concatenated together and used as the input to the network.

4.3 Training

All pairs of evidence/claim from the FEVER training data are fed into the network for training.

	Development set					Test set	
	Baseline	**Our system**				**Baseline**	**Our system**
	All	All	Supports	Refutes	NEI	All	All
FEVER score	31.3	43.9	54.9	24.7	52.0	27.5	43.4
Label Accuracy	51.4	44.7	68.6	31.3	52.0	48.8	50.1
Evidence Precision	N/A	77.5	77.0	78.1	–	N/A	N/A
Evidence Recall	N/A	52.3	56.3	47.8	–	N/A	N/A
Evidence F1	17.2	62.5	65.0	59.3	–	18.3	58.5

Table 1: Scores on the FEVER development and test sets. Baseline is the system from (Thorne et al., 2018). The results are prior to human evaluation of the evidence.

Since the "NEI" class does not have evidence associated with it, we used the evidence found by our Sentence Finder for training the "NEI" class. If our Sentence Finder did not return any evidence for a "NEI" claim, we randomly sampled five sentences from the sentences in the Wiki database and use them as evidence.[1]

The network is trained using the Adam optimizer with a learning rate 0.002 with a batch size of 140 and dropout ratio of 0.2. The network weights are repeatedly saved and we used the model performing best on the FEVER development set.

4.4 Assigning Class Labels

The network outputs a probability distribution for whether the evidence/claim pair has label "Supports", "Refutes", or "NEI". For a given claim, we examine the labels assigned for all evidence sentences returned for that claim. First, we discard the evidence labeled as "NEI". If there are no evidence left, we mark the claim as "NEI". Otherwise, we add together the remaining prediction distribution and use the highest scored label as label for the claim. We return the five highest-scored evidences, including those marked "NEI".

4.5 Results and Analysis

The resulting scores on the development and test sets are in Table 1 (prior to human evaluation of the evidence retrieved by the system.) The FEVER score is the percentage of claims such that a complete set of evidence is found and is classified with the correct label. Precision, Recall, and F1 are the metrics for evaluating evidence retrieval (evidence

Gold \ Labeled as	Supports	Refutes	NEI
Supports	68.59	2.87	28.55
Refutes	31.13	31.26	37.61
NEI	42.29	5.75	51.97

Table 2: Contingency matrix (percentage) in the development set.

retrieval is not evaluated for the "NEI" class.)

Table 2 shows the percentage of claims being labeled as each class in the development set. We see that both "Refutes" and "NEI" are often mislabeled as "Supports", whereas the "Supports" are often mislabeled as "NEI".

Upon closer look at the classification errors, we see that some fine-grained lexical semantics and world knowledge are required to predict the correct label, which the model was not able to capture. For example, the claim "Gin is a drink" is supported by the sentence "Gin is a spirit which derives its predominant flavour from juniper berries (Juniperus communis)", but our system classified the pair as "Refutes".

The network also seemed to pick up on some lexical features present in the annotations. The claim "The Wallace mentions people that never existed" has gold label "NEI", but is labeled as "Refutes" with high probability using three different evidence sentences we retrieved, even though some of the sentences are not relevant at all. This is probably because the word "never" is highly indicative of the "Refutes" class, as we shall see in the next section.

5 Discussion

Our system beats the shared task baseline on evidence retrieval F1 (62.5% vs. 17.2%) and FEVER

---

[1] We could try the NEARESTP sampling method described in (Thorne et al., 2018), which achieves better performance with a decomposable attention model for inference than random sampling.

score (43.9% vs. 31.3%) for the development set. On the test set, prior to human evaluation of the evidence, our system ranked 7th out of 23 teams with a FEVER score of 43.4%. For evidence retrieval F1, we ranked 2nd with a score of 58.5%.

Gururangan et al. (2018) pointed out that natural language inference datasets often contain annotation artifacts. They found that many lexical/syntactic features are highly predictive of entailment classes in most natural language inference datasets. We performed the same analysis on the FEVER training set to see whether a similar pattern holds. We calculated the probability distribution of the length of the claims by tokens for each class. Contrary to Gururangan et al's results, all classes have similar mean and standard deviation sentence length. We also calculated the pointwise mutual information (PMI) between each word and class. We found that negation words such as *not*, *never*, *neither*, and *nor*, have higher PMI value for the "Refutes" class than for the other classes. This is similar to Gururangan et al.'s observation that negation words are strong indicators of contradiction in the SNLI dataset. The "Refutes" claims in the FEVER training data indeed show a high percentage of negation words[2] (13.9% vs. 0.1% for "Supports" and 1.3% for "NEI").

Another source of bias comes from the way evidence annotation in the gold standard has been created with humans manually verifying the claims in Wikipedia. As pointed out in Section 3.3, evidence automatically retrieved can be correct even though not present in the gold standard. The way a human fact-checks might be different from what a computer can achieve. It would be interesting to analyze the evidence correctly retrieved by the systems participating in the shared task but not present in the gold standard, to see whether some patterns emerge.

References

Samuel R. Bowman, Gabor Angeli, Christopher Potts, and Christopher D. Manning. 2015. A large annotated corpus for learning natural language inference. In *Proceedings of the 2015 Conference on Empirical Methods in Natural Language Processing*, pages 632–642.

Mark Alan Finlayson. 2014. Java libraries for accessing the princeton wordNet: Comparison and evaluation. In *Proceedings of the 7th International Global WordNet Conference*, pages 78–85. H. Orav, C. Fellbaum, & P. Vossen (Eds.).

Suchin Gururangan, Swabha Swayamdipta, Omer Levy, Roy Schwartz, Samuel R. Bowman, and Noah A. Smith. 2018. Annotation artifacts in natural language inference data. In *Proceedings of NAACL-HLT 2018*, pages 107–112.

Eduard Hovy, Mitchell Marcus, Martha Palmer, Lance Ramshaw, and Ralph Weischedel. 2006. OntoNotes: The 90% solution. In *Proceedings of the Human Language Technology Conference of the NAACL*, pages 57–60.

Christopher D. Manning, Mihai Surdeanu, John Bauer, Jenny Finkel, Steven J. Bethard, and David McClosky. 2014. The Stanford CoreNLP natural language processing toolkit. In *Association for Computational Linguistics (ACL) System Demonstrations*, pages 55–60.

Ankur P. Parikh, Oscar Täckström, Dipanjan Das, and Jakob Uszkoreit. 2016. A decomposable attention model for natural language inference. In *Proceedings of the 2016 Conference on Empirical Methods in Natural Language Processing*, pages 2249–2255.

Jeffrey Pennington, Richard Socher, and Christopher D. Manning. 2014. GloVe: Global vectors for word representation. In *Empirical Methods in Natural Language Processing (EMNLP)*, pages 1532–1543.

James Thorne, Andreas Vlachos, Christos Christodoulopoulos, and Arpit Mittal. 2018. FEVER: A large-scale dataset for Fact Extraction and VERification. In *Proceedings of NAACL-HLT 2018*, pages 809–819.

---

[2]We used the neg dependency tag as the criterion for a negation word.

Team UMBC-FEVER : Claim verification using Semantic Lexical Resources

Ankur Padia, Francis Ferraro and Tim Finin
Computer Science and Electrical Engineering
University of Maryland, Baltimore County
Baltimore, MD 20150 USA
{pankur1,ferraro,finin}@umbc.edu

Abstract

We describe our system used in the 2018 FEVER shared task. The system employed a frame-based information retrieval approach to select Wikipedia sentences providing evidence and used a two-layer multilayer perceptron to classify a claim as correct or not. Our submission achieved a score of 0.3966 on the Evidence F1 metric with accuracy of 44.79%, and FEVER score of 0.2628 F1 points.

1 Introduction

We describe our system and its use in the FEVER shared task (Thorne et al., 2018). We focused on two parts of the problem: (i) *information retrieval* and (ii) *classification*. For the first we opted for a linguistically-inspired approach: we automatically annotated claim sentences and Wikipedia page sentences with syntactic features and semantic frames from FrameNet (Baker et al., 1998a) and used the result to retrieve sentences relevant to the claims that provide evidence of their veracity. For classification, we used a simple two-layer perceptron and experimented with several configurations to determine the optimal settings.

Though the overall classification of our best version was lower than the best approach from Thorne et al. (2018), which used a more sophisticated classification approach, we scored 10th out of 24 for the information retrieval task (measured by F_1). The improvement in our system worked well on the IR task, obtaining a relative improvement of 131% on retrieving evidence over the baseline F1 measure Thorne et al. (2018).

2 Approach

The FEVER task requires systems to assess a sentence making one of more factual claims (e.g., "Rocky Mountain High is an Australian song") as true or false by finding sentences in Wikipedia that

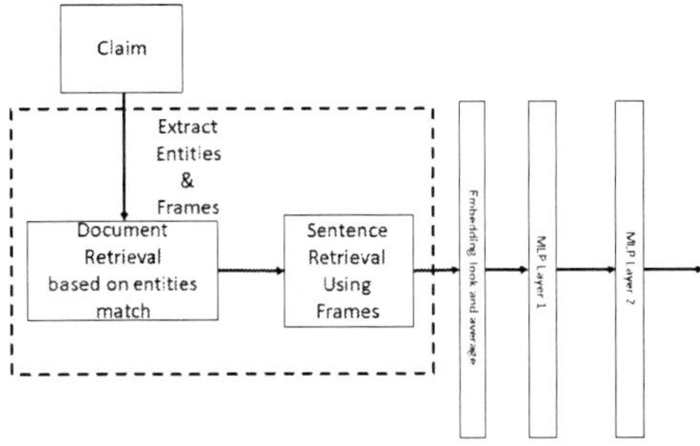

Figure 1: Our system used a semantic frame approach to support both retrieval of claim evidence and classification of claims.

provide evidence to support or refute the claim(s). This naturally leads to two sub-tasks, an *information retrieval* task that returns a set of Wikipedia sentences that are relevant to the assessment and a *classification* task that analyzes the evidence and labels the claim as Supported, Refuted or NotEnoughInfo. Figure 1 shows the overall flow of our system, which uses semantic frames to analyze and match a claim sentence to potential evidence sentences and a multilayer perceptron for claim classification.

2.1 Finding Relevant Evidence Sentences

Our approach used semantic frames from FrameNet (Baker et al., 1998b) as part of the analysis in matching a claim with sentences that might provide evidence for its veracity. A frame is a semantic schema that describes a situation, event or relation and its participants. The FrameNet collection has more than 1,200 frames and 13,000 lexical units which are lemmas that evoke or trigger a frame; see Fig. 2 for an example of this schema. Complex concepts and situations can be described by multiple frames. As an example, the sentence 'John bought a new

Proceedings of the First Workshop on Fact Extraction and VERification (FEVER), pages 161–165
Brussels, Belgium, November 1, 2018. ©2018 Association for Computational Linguistics

Who	Classifier	Training type	Classification		Predicting evidence		
			FEVER Score	ACC	Precision	Recall	F1
UMBC$_1$	MLP	**NFC**	0.2572	0.4398	0.4868	0.3346	0.3966
UMBC$_2$	MLP	**NFUC**	0.2628	0.4479	**0.4868**	**0.3346**	**0.3966**
UMBC$_3$	MLP	**NFIC**	0.2599	0.4069	0.4868	0.3346	0.3966
Baseline$_1$	MLP	(Thorne et al., 2018, Tab. 4)	0.1942	40.64	–	–	–
Baseline$_2$	DA	CodaLab results	**0.3127**	**0.5137**	–	–	0.1718

Table 1: Performance on development dataset of the system on different settings. We achieve comparable classification performance with simple classifier model thanks to better evidence retrieval.

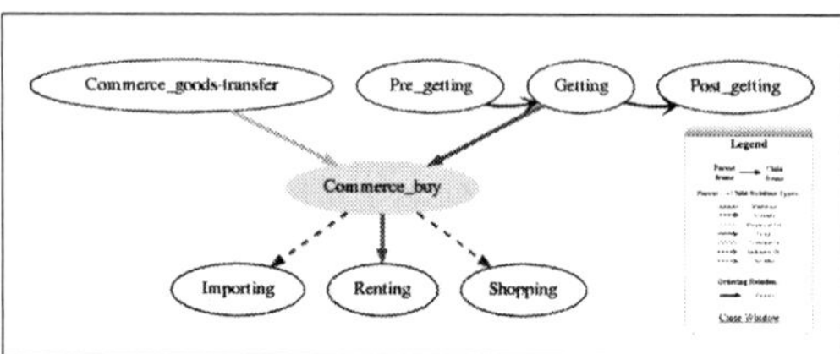

Figure 2: The FrameNet Commerce_buy frame and its immediate neighbors

bike' can trigger two frames: 'Claim_ownership'[1] and 'Commerce_buy'.[2]

Our annotation processing differed slightly for claims and potential evidence. We processed the claims in the dataset with the annotation pipeline described in Ferraro et al. (2014). Each claim was annotated using a named entity recognizer, dependency parser and POS tagger from CoreNLP (Manning et al., 2014) and also by a frame annotator (Das et al., 2010). For the evidence sentences, we used the pre-existing semantically annotated version of Wikipedia (Ferraro et al., 2014) that contained the same types of annotations for all of Wikipedia pages from a 2016 Wikipedia dump, serialized as Thrift objects using the *concrete* schema (HLTCOE, 2018).

Depending on the dataset, we performed document and sentence retrieval. We did only sentence retrieval for the training data and for development and testing data we did document and sentence retrieval. Our motivation was to understand the effect of frame-based retrieval, assuming the named entity recognizer correctly identified the entity.

For the training dataset, we used the dataset's document titles to retrieve Wikipedia documents directly and choose its sentences that triggered some frame as candidate evidence sentences. We applied exact frame matching, in which a sentence is predicted as evidence if it triggers a frame that is also triggered by the claim. All sentences that had an exact match to one of the claim's frames were added to the final evidence set.

The extraction of the documents and the sentences was different in the case of the development and testing datasets as no gold standard document identifiers were available. We used a two-layer multilayer perceptron to label the claim given the evidence as either SUPPORTS, REFUTES or NotEnoughInfo.

One complication was that the evidence was extracted from a different Wikipedia dump (2017) than our frame-annotated Wikipedia corpus (2016). While the page title's aligned well between the two Wikipedia dumps, their sentences exhibited more variations. This is the result of Wikipedia editors making changes to the page, including rearrangements, updates, adding material or stylistic modifications. In order to find the correct sentence index in the page, we used the Hungarian algorithm (Kuhn, 1955) to find the matching sentences. We cast this problem as a dissimilarity minimization problem, where the dissimilarity between a pair of sentences was 1 minus a Jacard similarity metric over the set of sentence tokens.

2.2 Classifying Claims Given the Evidence

To produce features, we converted each claim word to a 400 dimension embedding (Mikolov et al., 2013) representation and took the average over the length of the claim, using a zero vector for out-of-vocabulary words. We trained a two-layer MLP to label the claim using stochastic gradient descent with L2 and dropout to avoid overfitting. We chose the final parameter values for the claim classifier that gave best result on development dataset, which are shown in Table 2.

---

[1]The *Claimant* asserts rights or privileges, typically ownership, over some *Property*. The *Claimant* may be acting on the behalf of a *Beneficiary*.

[2]The *Buyer* wants the *Goods* and offers *Money* to a *Seller* in exchange for them.

Parameter	Value
learning rate	0.01
number of layers	2
optimizer	SGD
hidden layer size	50
L2 regularize	1e-06
epoch	2
batch_size	64
dropout	0.5

Table 2: MLP classifier parameter values

3 Ablation Study

We explored our approach by evaluating performance with settings corresponding to three different information retrieval strategies.

- **NFC**: NER document retrieval + Frame sentence retrieval + Classification
- **NFUC**: NER document retrieval + Frame sentence retrieval + (Union) introduction section of the Wikipedia page (Thorne et al., 2018) + Classification
- **NFIC**: NER document retrieval + Frame sentence retrieval + (intersection) introduction section of Wikipedia page + Classification

3.1 Results

Table 1 shows confusion matrices of our system when trained with the three different settings. The performance to predict the score is the same as we are retrieving the frame based sentences from the documents and adding FEVER processed Wikipedia sentences on the fly at the training time. The addition of FEVER-processed Wikipedia sentences slightly increases the performance of the system.

Since the frame annotator is not perfect, it sometimes fails to trigger appropriate frames. This means that while the vast majority of claims could be matched with potential evidence, there are claims that cannot be matched with evidence. This was neither uncommon nor rare: in the development set, 21.43% of the claims could not be matched with evidence sentences (the testing and training datasets had miss rates of 17.43% and 25.78%, respectively).

As evident from the classification performance, additional data improves performance, with NFUC performing better than other two settings. Compared to the results in the test dataset, we scored nearly twice as well as the baseline in

		Predicted		
		Support	**Refute**	**Neither**
Actual	**Support**	4646	171	1849
	Refute	3050	1198	1618
	Neither	4123	391	2152

(a) Dev confusion matrix for frame-based sentence retrieval only (NFC).

		Predicted		
		Support	**Refute**	**Neither**
Actual	**Support**	4499	173	1994
	Refute	2777	2125	1764
	Neither	3968	365	2333

(b) Dev confusion matrix for the union of frame-based and introduction-based sentence retrieval (NFUC).

		Predicted		
		Support	**Refute**	**Neither**
Actual	**Support**	4370	87	2209
	Refute	3122	1474	2070
	Neither	4159	214	2293

(c) Dev confusion matrix for the intersection of frame-based and introduction-based sentence retrieval (NFIC).

Table 3: Classification-without-provenance accuracy confusion matrices on the development dataset for the three classes under.

terms of information retrieval with simple frame matching. This is evidence for the effectiveness of using semantic frames in determining the credibility of the claim, despite the recall issues discussed above.

3.2 Discussion

The three settings had similar performance measures because the set of sentences found by our system was a superset of those found by the human assessors. Our frame-based retrieval found 516,670 evidence sentences when matching frames across the entire document mentioning entities and not just the introduction section. The set found by assessors included 34,797 evidence sentences, all of which were included the frame-based retrieval set.

Fig. 3 shows a correct and incorrect example. A manual examination revealed that the predicting evidence was correct nearly every time when an appropriate frame was in the document. When a frame is in the claim and not in the document,

Claim: **Last Man Standing does not star Tim Allen**
Predicted evidence (Correct):
1. Timothy Allen Dick (born June 13, 1953), known professionally as Tim Allen, is an American actor, comedian and author
2. He is known for his role as Tim "The Toolman" Taylor in the ABC television show Home Improvement (1991) as well as for his starring roles in several films, including the role of Buzz Lightyear in the Toy Story franchise
3. From 2011 to 2017, he starred as Mike Baxter in the TV series Last Man Standing
Predicted Label: **REFUTES (due to evidence (3))**
Actual Label: **REFUTES**

(a) Relevant evidence is correctly retrieved and is classified correctly as refuting the claim.

Claim: **Rocky Mountain High is an Australian song**
Predicted evidence (Correct):
1. "Rocky Mountain High" is a folk rock song written by John Denver and Mike Taylor about Colorado, and is one of the two official state songs of Colorado
2. The song also made #3 on the Easy Listening chart, and was played by some country music stations
3. Denver told concert audiences in the mid-1970s that the song took him an unusually long nine months to write
4. Members of the Western Writers of America chose it as one of the Top 100 Western songs of all time
Predicted Label: **SUPPORTS**
Actual Label: **REFUTES**

(b) Relevant evidence is correctly retrieved, but was misclassified by the classifier as supporting the claim.

Figure 3: Error analysis examples of predicting evidence and classification. As evident from the examples, the frame based retrieval extracts high quality evidence sentences when available in the document. However, the performance of the system is reduced depending on the classifier predictions, and perfection of the automatic frame annotator.

the retrieval component gives empty results and, depending on the gold standard, the performance suffers. The mismatch happens due to differences with the Wikipedia version dumps. The FEVER dataset used a 2017 dump and we used one from 2016. A second error source was annotation/misclassification by our frame annotation system. However, whenever there is a match, the quality of the evidence is high, as shown by the first and second example claims. Table 3 shows the confusion matrices for the three classes (Support, Refute, Not enough information) for each of the three settings.

4 Discussion and Conclusion

Our submission was an initial attempt to explore the idea of using semantic frames to match claims with sentences providing evidence that might support or refute them. The approach has the advantage of being able to exploit relations between frames such as entailments, temporal ordering, causality and generalization that can capture common sense knowledge. While the classification scores were lower than we hoped, the evidence retrieval scores represent impressive and promising improvements.

We plan to continue developing the approach and add it as a component of a larger system for cleaning noisy knowledge graphs (Padia, 2017; Padia et al., 2018).

We expect that the performance measures will improve when the datasets are all extracted from the identical Wikipedia versions. Possible enhancements include using the Kelvin (Finin et al., 2015) information extraction system to add entity coreference and better entity linking to a knowledge graph of background knowledge, such as Freebase, DBpedia or Wikidata. This will support linking nominal and pronominal mentions to a canonical named mention and provide access to more common aliases for entities. Such features have been shown to improve entity-based information retrieval (Van Durme et al., 2017).

We also hope to exploit Kelvin's ability to reason about entities and relations. Its knowledge graph knows, for example, that while one can only be born in single geo-political location, such places are organized in a *part-of* hierarchy. An event that happens in one a place can be said to also take place at its enclosing locations. The system's background knowledge includes that *Honolulu* is part of *Hawaii* which in turn is part of the *United States*. Moreover, it knows that if you were born in a country, it is very likely that you are a citizen of that country. This will allow it to recognize "Obama was born in Honolulu" as evidence that supports the claim that "Obama is a citizen of the U.S.".

Acknowledgments

This research was partially supported by gifts from the IBM AI Horizons Network and Northrop Grumman and by support from the U.S. National Science Foundation for UMBC's high performance computing environment.

References

Collin F. Baker, Charles J. Fillmore, and John B. Lowe. 1998a. The berkeley framenet project. In *Proceedings of the 17th International Conference on Computational Linguistics - Volume 1*, COLING '98, pages 86–90. Association for Computational Linguistics.

Collin F Baker, Charles J Fillmore, and John B Lowe. 1998b. The berkeley framenet project. In *Proceedings of the 17th international conference on Computational linguistics-Volume 1*, pages 86–90. Association for Computational Linguistics.

Dipanjan Das, Nathan Schneider, Desai Chen, and Noah A Smith. 2010. Probabilistic frame-semantic parsing. In *Human language technologies: The 2010 annual conference of the North American chapter of the association for computational linguistics*, pages 948–956. Association for Computational Linguistics.

Francis Ferraro, Max Thomas, Matthew R Gormley, Travis Wolfe, Craig Harman, and Benjamin Van Durme. 2014. Concretely annotated corpora. In *AKBC Workshop at NIPS*.

Tim Finin, Dawn Lawrie, Paul McNamee, James Mayfield, Douglas Oard, Nanyun Peng, Ning Gao, Yiu-Chang Lin, Josh MacLin, and Tim Dowd. 2015. HLTCOE participation in TAC KBP 2015: Cold start and TEDL. In *Text Analytics Conference (TAC)*.

HLTCOE. 2018. Concrete. http://hltcoe.github.io-/concrete/.

Harold W. Kuhn. 1955. The Hungarian Method for the assignment problem. *Naval Research Logistics Quarterly*, page 8397.

Christopher Manning, Mihai Surdeanu, John Bauer, Jenny Finkel, Steven Bethard, and David McClosky. 2014. The Stanford CoreNLP natural language processing toolkit. In *Proceedings of 52nd annual meeting of the association for computational linguistics: system demonstrations*, pages 55–60.

Tomas Mikolov, Ilya Sutskever, Kai Chen, Greg S Corrado, and Jeff Dean. 2013. Distributed representations of words and phrases and their compositionality. In *Advances in neural information processing systems*, pages 3111–3119.

Ankur Padia. 2017. Cleaning Noisy Knowledge Graphs. In *Proceedings of the Doctoral Consortium at the 16th International Semantic Web Conference*, volume 1962. CEUR Workshop Proceedings.

Ankur Padia, Frank Ferraro, and Tim Finin. 2018. KG-Cleaner: Identifying and correcting errors produced by information extraction systems. *arXiv preprint arXiv:1808.04816*.

James Thorne, Andreas Vlachos, Christos Christodoulopoulos, and Arpit Mittal. 2018. FEVER: a large-scale dataset for fact extraction and verification. *CoRR*, abs/1803.05355.

Benjamin Van Durme, Tom Lippincott, Kevin Duh, , Deana Burchfield, Adam Poliak, Cash Costello, Tim Finin, Scott Miller, James Mayfield, Philipp Koehn, Craig Harmon, Dawn Lawrie, Chandler May, Max Thomas, Annabelle Carrell, and Julianne Chaloux. 2017. CADET: Computer Assisted Discovery Extraction and Translation. In *8th International Joint Conference on Natural Language Processing (System Demonstrations)*, pages 5–8.

A Mostly Unlexicalized Model For Recognizing Textual Entailment

Mithun Paul, Rebecca Sharp, Mihai Surdeanu
University of Arizona, Tucson, AZ, USA
{mithunpaul,bsharp,msurdeanu}@email.arizona.edu

Abstract

Many approaches to automatically recognizing entailment relations have employed classifiers over hand engineered lexicalized features, or deep learning models that implicitly capture lexicalization through word embeddings. This reliance on lexicalization may complicate the adaptation of these tools between domains. For example, such a system trained in the news domain may learn that a sentence like "Palestinians recognize Texas as part of Mexico" tends to be unsupported, but this fact (and its corresponding lexicalized cues) have no value in, say, a scientific domain. To mitigate this dependence on lexicalized information, in this paper we propose a model that reads two sentences, from any given domain, to determine entailment without using lexicalized features. Instead our model relies on features that are either unlexicalized or are domain independent such as proportion of negated verbs, antonyms, or noun overlap. In its current implementation, this model does not perform well on the FEVER dataset, due to two reasons. First, for the information retrieval portion of the task we used the baseline system provided, since this was not the aim of our project. Second, this is work in progress and we still are in the process of identifying more features and gradually increasing the accuracy of our model. In the end, we hope to build a generic end-to-end classifier, which can be used in a domain outside the one in which it was trained, with no or minimal re-training.

1 Introduction

The rampant spread of fake data recently (be it in news or scientific facts) and its impact in our day to day life has renewed interest in the topic of disambiguating between fake, or unsupported, information and real, or supported, information (Wang, 2017).

Last year, the fake news challenge (Pomerleau and Rao, 2017) was organized as a valuable first step towards creating systems to detect inaccurate claims. This year the fact verification challenge (FEVER) (Thorne et al., 2018) was organized to further this. Specifically it was organized to foster the development of systems that combine information retrieval (IR) and textual entailment recognition (RTE) together to address the fake claim problem. However, developing a system that is trained to tackle the issue only in one area (in this case for fake news detection) does not solve the problem in other domains. For example, models developed to specifically detect fake news might not work well to detect fake science articles.

An alternative will be to create systems that can be trained in broader domains and can then be used to test on specific domains with minimal modification and/or parameter tuning. Such a system should also be able to capture the underlying idiosyncratic characteristics of the human author who originally created such fake data. For example some common techniques used by writers of such fake articles include using hedging words (e.g., *possibly*), circumventing facts, avoiding mentioning direct evidence, hyperbole etc. To this end, we propose a largely *unlexicalized* approach that, when coupled with an information retrieval (IR) system that assembles relevant articles for a given claim, would serve as a cross-domain fake-data detection tool which could either stand-alone or potentially supplement other domain-specific lexicalized systems.

The goal of this paper is to present a description of such a preliminary system developed for the FEVER challenge, its performance, and our intended future work.

Proceedings of the First Workshop on Fact Extraction and VERification (FEVER), pages 166–171
Brussels, Belgium, November 1, 2018. ©2018 Association for Computational Linguistics

2 Approach

We approach the task of distinguishing between fake and real claims in a series of steps. Specifically, given a claim, we:

1. **Information retrieval (IR):** We use an IR component to gather claim-relevant texts from a large corpus of evidence (i.e., Wikipedia articles). For retrieving the Wikipedia articles which contain sentences relevant to the given claim, we reused the competition-provided information retrieval system (Thorne et al., 2018) since we are focusing here on the RTE portion of the task. To be specific, we used the DrQA (Chen et al., 2017) for document retrieval. For sentence selection the modified DrQA with binning with comparison to unigram TF-IDF implementation using NLTK (Bird and Loper, 2004) was used. The k and l parameters values, for document retrieval and sentence selection, respectively, was also left as is to be 5. Any claim which had the label of NOT ENOUGH INFO was removed from the Oracle setting.

2. **Evidence aggregation:** As part of the competition-provided IR system we next aggregate the top 10 documents and combine the evidence sentences into a single document.

3. **Classification:** Finally, we compare the claim to the evidence document to classify it as either SUPPORTS or REFUTES. For our learning framework, we employ a support vector machine (SVM) (Hearst et al., 1998) with a linear kernel.

2.1 Features

In this section we describe the various groups of features that were used for the classification task in the last component of the approach introduced above. To create these features, the claim and evidence were tokenized and parsed using CoreNLP (Manning et al., 2014). The majority of the features are either proportions or counts so as to maintain the unlexicalized aspect. Specific lexical content was used only when the semantics were domain independent (i.e., as with certain discourse markers such as *however, possible, not,* etc).

- **Word overlap:** This set of features was based on the proportion of words that overlap between the claim and the evidence. Specifically, given a claim and a body of evidence, c and e, we compute the proportion of words in $c \cup e$ that overlap: $\frac{|c \cap e|}{|c \cup e|}$. We made similar features for verb and noun overlap as well, where we also include two sub features for the proportion of words in c and also the proportion of words in e: $\frac{|c \cap e|}{|c|}$ and $\frac{|c \cap e|}{|e|}$. For all these features, we used the lemma form of the words and first removed stop words (see Appendix A for the list of stop words that were removed). In all, there were 5 features in this feature set, two each for noun and verb overlap as defined above and one for word overlap.

- **Hedging words:** Hedging is the process of using cautious or vague language to vary the strengths of the argument in a given sentence. When present, it can indicate that the author is trying to circumvent facts. To capture this, we have a set of indicator features that mark the presence of any word from a given list of hedging words (see Appendix A for the list of hedging words used) in either the claim or evidence sentences This feature set has a total of 60 hedging features. While these features are lexicalized, their semantics are domain-independent and therefore in scope of our approach.

- **Refuting words and negations:** When present, refuting words can indicate that the author is unequivocally disputing a claim. To capture this, as with the hedging words above, we include a set of indicator features for refuting words (see Appendix A for the complete list of refuting words used) that are present in either the claim or evidence sentences. Also as with the hedging features, the semantics of these words are expected to be consistent across domains. This feature is a one hot vector denoting the existence (or absence) of any of the aforementioned 19 refuting words, creating a feature vector of length 19.

Another signal of disagreement between two texts is the presence of a verb in one text which is negated in the other text, largely regardless of the identity of the verb (e.g.,

Barack Obama was *not born* in the United States). To capture this, features were created to indicate whether a verb in the claim sentence was negated in the evidence and vice versa. This polarity indicator, created through dependency parsing, thus contained 4 features, each indicating tuples (positive claim-negative evidence, negative claim-positive evidence, etc.)

- **Antonyms:** Presence of antonyms in evidence sentences may indicate contradictions with the claim (e.g.: The movie was *impressive* vs the movie was *dreadful*). This feature captures the number of nouns or adjectives in the evidence sentence that were antonyms of any noun or adjective in the claim sentence (and vice versa). Similar to the word overlap feature mentioned above, every such antonym feature has two sub features, each denoting the proportion over antonyms in claim and evidence, respectively. Thus, there are a total of 4 antonym features. The list of antonyms used were extracted from Word Net (Miller, 1995).

- **Numerical overlap:** Human authors of fake articles often exaggerate facts (e.g., claiming *Around 100 people were killed as part of the riots*, when the evidence shows a lower number). To approximately measure this, we find the intersection and difference of numerical values between claim and the evidence, making it 2 features.

- **Measures of lexical similarity:** While the use of specific lexical items or their corresponding word embeddings goes against the *unlexicalized*, domain-independent aim of this work, here we use relative distributional similarities between the texts as features. Particularly, the relative position of the words in an embedding space carries significant information for recognizing entailment (Parikh et al., 2016). To make use of this, we find the maximum, minimum, and average pairwise cosine similarities between each of the words in the claim and the evidence. We additionally include the overall similarity between the two texts, using a bag-of-words average to get a single representation for each text. We used the Glove (Pennington et al., 2014) embeddings for these features.

Model	Evidence F1	Label Accuracy	FEVER score
Baseline	0.1826	0.4884	0.2745
Our model	0.1826	0.3694	0.1900

Table 1: Performance of our submitted model on the test data.

Model	Label Accuracy
Baseline (Thorne et al., 2018)	65.13
Our model at submission	55.60
Our model post submission	56.88

Table 2: Oracle classification on claims in the development set using gold sentences as evidence

3 Experiments

3.1 Data and Tuning

We used the data from the FEVER challenge (Thorne et al., 2018), training on the 145,449 claims provided in the training set and tuning on the provided development set (19,998 claims). Since we were focusing only on the textual entailment part, we removed the claims which had the label NOT ENOUGH INFO during training. As a result, we trained on the remaining 109,810 claims in the training set and tuned on the remaining 13,332 in the development set.

3.2 Baseline

We compare against the provided FEVER baseline. The IR component of the baseline is identical to ours as we reuse their component, but for the textual entailment they use the fully lexicalized state of the art decomposable attention model of (Parikh et al., 2016).

4 Results

The performance of our submitted domain-independent model on the test data (using the baseline IR system) can be found in Table 1, along with the performance of the fully lexicalized baseline. The current performance of our model is below that of the baseline, presumably due to the lack of domain-specific lexicalized features.

Since here we focus on the RTE component only, we also provide the model's performance in an oracle setting on the development set, where we use the gold sentences as evidence in Table 2. Included in the table are the results both at the time of submission and post-submission. At the time of submission, the model included only the word overlap, negated and refuting words, hedg-

Feature group removed	Accuracy
With all features	56.89 %
− Word overlap	50.89 %
− Hedging words	50.96 %
− Antonyms	52.17 %
− Measures of lexical similarity	55.60 %
− Refuting words and negations	55.82 %

Table 3: Ablation results: performance of our model on development after removing each feature group, one at a time. Performance is given in the oracle setting, using the gold sentences as evidence.

ing words and antonym features. Post-submission, we added the lexical similarity features.

Making use of the relative interpretability of our feature-based approach, we performed an ablation test on the development data (again, in the oracle setting using gold sentences as evidence) to test the contribution of each feature group. The results are shown in Table 3 . The word-overlap and hedging features had the largest contribution. The relatively small contribution of the refuting words and negation features, on the other hand, could be due to the limited word set or the lack of explicit refuting in the evidence documents.

5   Analysis

To find the importance of each of the features as assigned by the classifier we printed the weights for the top five features for each class, shown in Table 4. As can be seen in this table, the feature that was given the highest weight for the class REFUTES is the polarity feature that indicates a conflict in the polarity of the claim and evidence (as determined by finding a verb which occurs in both, but is negated in the claim and not negated in the evidence). The feature with the second highest weight for the REFUTES class is the proportion of nouns that were common between claim and evidence. Another feature that the classifier has given a high importance for belonging to this class, is the count of numbers that were present in the claim but not in evidence (numbers are defined as tokens having *CD* as their part of speech tag).

Similarly, the feature which had the highest weights for the class SUPPORTS is that of the word overlap (which denotes the proportion of unique words that appear both in claim and evidence). Notably, the existence of some of the hedging words were found to be indicative of the REFUTES class (e.g., *question* and *predict*) while others were indicative of the SUPPORTS class (*argue*, *hint*, *prediction* and *suggest*).

While most of the weights as generated by the classifier are intuitive, these features are clearly insufficient, as demonstrated by the low accuracy of the classifier. To address this we manually analyzed 30 data points from the development data set that were wrongly classified by our model. A particular focus was to try to understand and trace back which features contributed (or did not contribute) to the SUPPORTS and REFUTES classes.

Several of the data points demonstrated ways in which straightforward extensions of the approach (i.e., additional features) could help. For example consider this data point below, which belongs to the class REFUTES but was classified to be in the class SUPPORTS by our model:

Claim: *Vedam was written and directed by Christopher Nolan .*
Evidence: *Vedam is a 2010 Telugu language Indian drama film written and directed by Radhakrishna Jagarlamudi....*

We conjecture that this error occurred due to the lack of syntactic information in our system. For example, a simple extension to our approach that could address this example would look for similar (and dissimilar) syntactic dependencies between the claim and evidence.

On the other hand, a few of the data points contained more complex phenomenon that would be difficult to capture in the current approach. Consider the following example which belongs to the class REFUTES but was wrongly classified as SUPPORTS by our model:

Claim: *Sean Penn is only ever a stage actor.*
Evidence: *Following his film debut in the drama Taps and a diverse range of film roles in the 1980s, ... Penn garnered critical attention for his roles in the crime dramas At Close Range, State of Grace, and Carlito's Way .*

This example shows the difficulty involved in capturing the underlying complexities of words that indirectly capture negation such as *only*, which our features do not capture presently.

Lastly, we found that certain aspects of our approach, even with minimal dependence on lexicalization, are still not as domain-independent as desired. Consider the example below, whose gold label is SUPPORTS, but was classified as REFUTES by our model.

Weight	Feature Name	Description
1.30	polarity_neg_claim_pos_ev	Presence of verb negated in the claim but not in the evidence
0.537	noun_overlap	Proportion of nouns in claim and evidence that overlap
0.518	hedging_evidence_question	Presence of the hedging word *question* in the evidence
0.455	num_overlap_diff	Count of numbers present in claim but not in the evidence
0.385	hedging_claim_predict	Presence of the hedging word *predict* in the claim
-0.454	hedging_evidence_suggest	Presence of the hedging word *suggest* in the evidence
-0.477	hedging_evidence_prediction	Presence of the hedging word *prediction* in the evidence
-0.584	hedging_claim_hint	Presence of the hedging word *hint* in the claim
-0.585	hedging_claim_argue	Presence of the hedging word *argue* in the claim
-1.59	word_overlap	Proportion of words in the claim and evidence that overlap

Table 4: Top five features with the highest weight in each class, where the positive class is REFUTES and the negative class is SUPPORTS.

Claim: The Gettysburg Address is a speech.
Evidence: Despite the speech's prominent place in the history and popular culture of the United States, the exact wording and location of the speech are disputed.

We believe this error occurred because we have more argumentative features (for example, in this case the presence of the word *despite*), and fewer features to capture the type of *neutral* sentences common in data sources like Wikipedia pages, which have more informative, objective content. On the other hand, fake news articles contain more subjective language, for which argumentative features are well-suited.

Keeping all these errors in mind our future goal is to enhance the performance of the system by adding more potent unlexicalized/domain independent features, including features that take advantage of dependency syntax and discourse information. Also another possibility we would like to explore is replacing the current classifier with other non-linear classifiers including a simple feed-forward neural network. Through these steps, we hope to improve the accuracy of the classifier predictions, pushing the performance closer to that of a fully lexicalized systems, and yet able to transfer between domains.

6 Conclusion

Despite our current low performance in the FEVER challenge, we would like to propose this system as a precursor to an effort towards building a cross-domain fake data detection model, especially considering its basic implementation. The added benefit for our simple system, when compared to other complicated neural network/deep learning architectures (which are harder to interpret), is that this also provides an opportunity to peek into the what features contribute (or do not contribute) to the development of such a cross-domain system.

Acknowledgements

We would like to thank Ajay Nagesh and Marco A. Valenzuela-Escárcega for their timely help.

References

Steven Bird, Ewan Klein, and Edward Loper. 2009. *Natural language processing with Python: analyzing text with the natural language toolkit.* " O'Reilly Media, Inc.".

Steven Bird and Edward Loper. 2004. Nltk: the natural language toolkit. In *Proceedings of the ACL 2004 on Interactive poster and demonstration sessions*, page 31. Association for Computational Linguistics.

Danqi Chen, Adam Fisch, Jason Weston, and Antoine Bordes. 2017. Reading wikipedia to answer open-domain questions. *arXiv preprint arXiv:1704.00051.*

Marti A. Hearst, Susan T Dumais, Edgar Osuna, John Platt, and Bernhard Scholkopf. 1998. Support vector machines. *IEEE Intelligent Systems and their applications*, 13(4):18–28.

Christopher Manning, Mihai Surdeanu, John Bauer, Jenny Finkel, Steven Bethard, and David McClosky. 2014. The stanford corenlp natural language processing toolkit. In *Proceedings of 52nd annual meeting of the association for computational linguistics: system demonstrations*, pages 55–60.

George A Miller. 1995. Wordnet: a lexical database for english. *Communications of the ACM*, 38(11):39–41.

Ankur P Parikh, Oscar Täckström, Dipanjan Das, and Jakob Uszkoreit. 2016. A decomposable attention model for natural language inference. *arXiv preprint arXiv:1606.01933*.

Jeffrey Pennington, Richard Socher, and Christopher Manning. 2014. Glove: Global vectors for word representation. In *Proceedings of the 2014 conference on empirical methods in natural language processing (EMNLP)*, pages 1532–1543.

Dean Pomerleau and Delip Rao. 2017. Fake news challenge.

James Thorne, Andreas Vlachos, Christos Christodoulopoulos, and Arpit Mittal. 2018. Fever: a large-scale dataset for fact extraction and verification. *arXiv preprint arXiv:1803.05355*.

William Yang Wang. 2017. " liar, liar pants on fire": A new benchmark dataset for fake news detection. *arXiv preprint arXiv:1705.00648*.

A Supplemental Material

A.1 Hedging words

allegedly, argument, belief, believe, conjecture, consider, hint, hypotheses, hypothesis, hypothesize, implication, imply, indicate, predict, prediction, previous, previously, proposal, propose, question, reportedly, speculate, speculation, suggest, suspect, theorize, theory, think, whether

A.2 Stop words

We used a subset of the stop words (and partial words) that come from the python Natural Language Toolkit (NLTK) (Bird et al., 2009):

a, about, ain, all, am, an, and, any, are, aren, aren't, as, at, be, been, being, by, can, couldn, couldn't, did, did n't, didn, do, does, doesn, doesn't, doing, don't, few, for, from, further, had, hadn, hadn't, has, hasn, hasn't, have, haven, haven't, having, he, her, here, hers, herself, him, himself, his, how, i, if, in, into, is, isn, isn't, it, it's, its, itself, just, ll, me, mightn, mightn't, more, most, mustn, mustn't, my, myself, needn, needn't, nor, of, on, or, our, ours, ourselves, own, shan, shan't, she, she's, should, should've, shouldn, shouldn't, so, some, such, than, that, that'll, the, their, theirs, them, themselves, then, there, these, they, this, those, through, to, too, until, ve, very, was, wasn, wasn't, we, were, weren, weren't, what, when, where, which, while, who, whom, why, will, with, won't, wouldn, wouldn't, y, you, you'd, you'll, you're, you've, your, yours, yourself, yourselves

A.3 Refuting words

bogus, debunk, denies, deny, despite, doubt, doubts, fake, false, fraud, hoax, neither, no, nope, nor, not, pranks, refute, retract

Author Index

Association for Computational Linguistics
209 N. Eighth Street
Stroudsburg, Pennsylvania 18360

ISBN 978-1-5108-7422-0